# THE SACRED AND THE FEMININE

# THE SACRED AND THE FEMININE

## Imagination and Sexual Difference

EDITED BY

GRISELDA POLLOCK AND VICTORIA TURVEY SAURON

Published in 2007 by I.B.Tauris & Co Ltd
6 Salem Road, London W2 4BU
175 Fifth Avenue, New York NY 10010
www.ibtauris.com

In the United States of America and Canada distributed by Palgrave Macmillan
a division of St. Martin's Press, 175 Fifth Avenue, New York NY 10010

ISBN (HB): 978 1 84511 520 3
ISBN (PB): 978 1 84511 521 0

A full CIP record for this book is available from the British Library
A full CIP record is available from the Library of Congress

Library of Congress Catalog Card Number: available

Printed and bound in the Czech Republic by FINIDR, s.r.o.
From camera-ready copy edited and supplied by the author

# CONTENTS

# LIST OF ILLUSTRATIONS

# ACKNOWLEDGEMENTS

The research for this book was supported by the Arts and Humanities Research Council and the University of Leeds, and the editors gratefully acknowledge that support. The book would not have appeared without the patient editorial and gifted design work of Anna Johnson. We would also like to acknowledge the work of Josine Opmeer, CentreCATH's former administrator, and the enthusiasm and courage of our editor at I.B.Tauris, Susan Lawson.

This volume uses Common Era (CE) and Before Common Era (BCE) in lieu of AD and BC for all dates.

# SERIES PREFACE

# NEW ENCOUNTERS
## Arts, Cultures, Concepts
### *Griselda Pollock*

*How do we think about visual art these days? What is happening to art history? Is visual culture taking its place? What is the status of cultural studies, in itself or in relation to its possible neighbours art, art history and visual studies? What is going on? What are the new directions? To what should we remain loyal?*

*New Encounters: Arts, Cultures, Concepts* proposes some possible ways of thinking through these questions. Firstly, the series introduces and works with the concept of a transdisciplinary initiative. This is not a synonym for the interdisciplinary combination that has become de rigueur. It is related to a second concept: research as *encounter*. Together transdisciplinary and encounter mark the interaction between ways of thinking, doing and making in the arts and humanities that retain distinctive features associated with disciplinary practices and objects: art, history, culture, practice, and the new knowledge that is produced when these different ways of doing and thinking encounter one another across, and this is the third intervention, *concepts*, circulating between different intellectual or aesthetic cultures, inflecting them, finding common questions in distinctively articulated practices. The aim is to place these different practices in productive relation to one another mediated by the circulation of concepts.

We stand at several cross-roads at the moment in relation to the visual arts and cultures, historical, and contemporary, and to theories and methods of analysis. *Cultural Analysis, Theory and History* (CATH) is offered as one experiment in thinking about how to maintain the momentum of the momentous intellectual, cultural revolution in the arts and humanities that characterized the last quarter of the twentieth century while adjusting to the different field of analysis created by it.

In the 1970s–1990s, the necessity, or the intrusion, according to your position, was Theory: a mythic concept with a capital T that homogenized vastly different intellectual undertakings. Over those decades, research in the arts and humanities was undoubtedly reconfigured by the engagement with structuralist and poststructuralist theories of the sign, sociality, the text, the letter, the image, the subject, the post-colonial, and above all, difference. Old disciplines were deeply challenged and new interdisciplines—called studies—emerged to contest the academic field of knowledge production and include hitherto academically ignored constituencies. These changes were wrought through specific engagements with Marxist, feminist, deconstructionist, psychoanalytical, discourse and minority theory. Texts and authors were branded according to their theoretical engagements. Such mapping produced divisions between the proliferating theoretical models. (Could one be Marxist, and feminist, and use psychoanalysis?) A deeper split, however, emerged between those who, in general, were theoretically oriented, and those who apparently did without theory: a position easily critiqued by the theoretically minded because being atheoretical is, of course, a theoretical position, just one that did not carry a novel identity associated with the intellectual shifts of the post-1968 university.

The impact of 'the theoretical turn' has been creative; it has radically reshaped work in the arts and humanities in terms of what is studied (content, topics, groups, questions) and also how it is studied (theories and methods). Yet some scholars currently argue that work done under such overt theoretical rubrics now appears tired; theory constrains the creativity of the new generation of scholars familiar, perhaps too familiar, with the legacies of the preceding intellectual revolution that can too easily be reduced to Theory 101 slogans (the author is dead, the gaze is male, the subject is split, there is nothing but text, etc.). The enormity of the initial struggles—the paradigm shifting—to be able to speak of sexual difference, subjectivity, the image, representation, sexuality, power, the gaze, postcoloniality, textuality, difference, fades before a new phase of normalization in which every student seems to bandy around terms that were once, and in fact, still are, challengingly difficult and provocative.

Theory, of course, just means thinking about things, puzzling closely over what is going on, reflecting intently on the process of that puzzling and thinking. A reactive turn away from active engagement with theoretical developments in the arts and humanities is increasingly evident in our area of academe. It is, however, dangerous and misleading to talk of a post-theory moment, as if we can relax after so much intellectual gymnastics and once again become academic couch-potatoes. The job of thinking critically is even more urgent as the issues we confront become even more complex, and we now have extended means of analysis that make us appreciate ever more the complexity of language, subjectivity, symbolic practices, affects and aesthetics. So how to continue the creative and critical enterprise fostered by the theoretical turn of the late twentieth century beyond the initial engagement determined by specific theoretical paradigms? How does it translate into *a practice of analysis that can be consistently productive*?

This series argues, following Mieke Bal's proposals for both cultural analysis and travelling concepts, that we can go forward, with and beyond, *by transdisciplinary encounters with and through concepts*. Concepts themselves arise inside specific theoretical projects. They now move out of—*travel from*—their own originating site to become tools for thinking within the larger domain of cultural analysis, a domain that seeks to create a space of encounter between the many practices that constitute the arts and humanities: the fields of thought that puzzle over what we are and what it is that we do, think, feel, say, understand and live.

Centre for Cultural Analysis, Theory and History
University of Leeds, 2007

# EDITORS' INTRODUCTION

*Griselda Pollock and Victoria Turvey Sauron*

The initiating editor for this collection, Victoria Turvey Sauron, is an art historian working on the visual representation of the ecstatic woman in Western art and culture as an undecidable figure of the challenge to art and culture posed by female sexuality and subjectivity. Famously, Bernini's sculptural installation of Teresa of Avila in her vision (13.1) has challenged interpreters to deal with the ambivalence of the image: hovering between a spiritual and an erotic experience. Tracing the genealogy of the iconography and visuality of the enraptured female body through to contemporary representations that appear more overtly sexual, Victoria Turvey Sauron identifies the problematic of a visual representation of embodied feminine subjectivity and sexuality that refuses monistic interpretations and instead brings into view shifting borderlines between interior and exterior.

This book further arose out of one of CentreCATH's strategic research themes: the Politics and Ethics of Indexicality and Virtuality—a challenging exploration of both the imaginary and the semiotic in relation to embodiment, materiality, sociality and history itself. Virtuality and virtual realities appear to be the territory of new media and technologies that are capable of unforeseen fabrications and hence destabilizations of our notions of the real, possible, and actual or artificed. Yet philosophers claim that thought is virtual, language is virtual, the psyche is virtual in a different sense of holding open potentiality and change. We must distinguish between debates about virtualities and materialities and virtualities and indexicalities: the indexical drawn from the semiotics of C. S. Peirce retains its status as a form of meaning-making, a signifying process, in which the relation between signifier and signified has some kind of existential or experiential connection.

At this intersection, the concepts travelling in this collection are the sacred and the feminine. These open out onto a politics of meanings and subjectivities inscribed in a range of practices of thought, representation, analysis, visualization and even political action. The sacred is not synonymous with the divine, even if the ways in which religions conceptualize the divine render it sacred. Nor is the feminine synonymous with women or social constructions of gender. Grasped theoretically and analytically, the feminine points to ways of thinking and principles of social organization around the eternal challenge of human responses to living and dying, and the making sense of the times, generations, sexualities and bodies involved in these defining processes. This book is not situated within theology or religious studies, although many papers may cross over with those disciplines, and writers speak from specific religious, cultural and geo-political positions. The book addresses feminist questions of creativity and the imaginary that stand firmly on anthropological, philosophical and psychoanalytical ground.

The collection is both an art-historical engagement with and theoretical response to the published correspondence between Julia Kristeva and Catherine Clément titled *The Feminine and the Sacred* that appeared in 1998 and was translated into English in 2001.[1] In a new, almost superseded tradition of women's epistolary literature, a Marxist-Jewish anthropologist and essayist travelling between Senegal and India corresponds with a self-declared Marxist psychoanalyst atheist deeply steeped in both the passionate Christianity of her father and in avant-garde textuality. In a series of embattled letters, radically different conceptions of the relation between women and the sacred are explored. Linked with Victoria Turvey Sauron's research, Clément opens with the suggestion that 'the sacred among women may express an instantaneous revolt that passes through the body and cries out.' Kristeva resists such hystericization and considers 'life as the intimate visage of the sacred'. As their arguments unfold through proposition and counter-proposition, revealing deep rifts between their underpinning cultural imaginaries, they seek to disentangle the sacred from issues of belief and religion in order to explore the sacred as a facet of human subjectivity: 'an unconscious perception the human being has of its untenable eroticism: always on the borderline between nature and culture, the animalistic and the verbal, the sensible and the nameable? What if the sacred were … the jouissance of that *cleavage*?'[2]

Kristeva's position is to place the sacred, therefore, between life and meaning, to which she believes women have a particular and overdetermined relation through both the psychic freight of becoming mothers and the disposition of the feminine in terms of a phallocentric symbolic within which the feminine subject is a figure, not of exclusion, but of disillusion and hence less prey to unquestioned belief. For Clément the sacred does not lend itself to such privileging. Rather it blows the roof off sexual difference, playing figuratively through forms of ambivalence: bisexuality or hybridity playing between purity and defilement.

Moving on through sacred cows, the Marian cult of the Virgin, pollution and sacrifice, their correspondence ends in late 1997 after the funeral of Princess Diana and the extraordinary public expression of grief associated with it. What happened in that moment around the tragic and sudden death of this young woman? Each has some thoughts on massacre and healing, on the necessary privacy of the sacred and public totalization, of the intersection between body and thought, biology and memory.

In a culture in which popular texts such as Dan Brown's *Da Vinci Code* (2003) or Kevin Smith's film *Dogma* (1999) are recirculating a certain kind of religious mystery associated with a reclaiming of sacredness for either the Mary of Magdala or Mary of Nazareth's descendants—that both build their challenge to orthodox religious Christianity on linking the Christ figure with a woman in sexual and procreative love, sensible and nameable—we must surely resist this degradation of the problematic relation of the sacred in human culture and sexual difference to a comforting recreation of a sacred feminine: a mythically divine woman. Instead this book has drawn upon the work of theoretically engaged international cultural thinkers from several disciplines and many traditions to meet the challenge of thinking critically the imaginary space, borderline, cleavage, alterity, that is the meaning of the sacred. Derived from the Latin word *sacer*, it means that which is set apart. *Sacer* gives rise to sacrifice: to be made set apart. The Hebrew word *kadosh* has the same resonance. Thus it marks a border, the fundamental mark of division and difference that is the condition of meaning and in the Hegelian tradition of becoming. Yet it also retains the relation it thus creates between its own becoming-other and that which is set up in the same instance as the profane, the ordinary, the unproblematic and unchallenging, the knowable, the masterable, utilitarian and productive.

In *Moses and Monotheism*, Sigmund Freud provided a psychoanalytical interpretation of the sacred.[3] Defined fundamentally by a prohibition that sets something apart from use, Freud sees the incest taboo and exogamy that follows it as prime exemplars of the sacred. Far from deriving from any remarkable features, the sacred inscribes into culture the 'will of the primal father', a figure of terrifying omnipotence and selfishness. Whether Freud's conception of human prehistory remains valid or not—it was after all a retrospective projection based on evidence regularly thrown up by patients and cultures in the present of analysis—the legacy of his analysis is to remind us of the sources of the emotional or affective dimensions of experiences or ideas to which we give the epithet sacred as a way of marking a specialness, an awe, an intensity. These sources are in the complex movement of the human subject from the conditions of pre-human birth into full sociality in the matrix of relations to powerful others, powerful needs, and powerful rules.

This second book in the *New Encounters* series is a small contribution to the creation of a theoretical and analytical space in which to consider the relations within this imaginary territory: the sacred and sexual difference. This is considered from an actively international feminist perspective that has run through and transformed the many disciplines for which this conjunction holds intellectual interest: art, literature, art history, theology, philosophy, critical theory, anthropology—in a word: thought.

Our title has reversed the terms of the Kristeva/Clément study: drawing on the mis-given title of a painting by Venetian artist Titian, known as *Sacred and Profane Love*. By placing the *feminine* in the position of the profane in the oppositional pairing, sacred and profane, we wish also to open a space to question the claim made by Julia Kristeva that there is a special intimacy between the feminine and the sacred, while accepting that the sacred is a fascinating area of research for transdisciplinary feminist studies that wish both to examine the genealogies of the feminine and the sacred and critically to explore new relations between body and language, the sensible and the verbal, based not on being set apart, but on being the active and embodied, hence psychically differenced makers of meaning.

The essays in the first part of the book have an ecumenical look which is, in fact, an international perspective on the more formalized traditions of thinking the sacred associated with both classical pagan, classical Hindu and the varieties of monotheistic traditions. Starting with a framing essay on sacred cows that journeys from Lascaux and the Hebrew Bible to contemporary feminist psychoanalytical theory, the first group of essays passes through analyses of the sacred and the feminine in Christian, post-Christian, Hindu, Muslim, Greek and Jewish thought to confront a challenging question of life and death in the contemporary imaginary world of that most challenging of recent phenomena: the suicide-bomber, analysed daringly here in the context of Kristevan thought on the psycho-economy of violence. Feminist cultural analysis provides the space for encounters outside of and across confined disciplinary spaces so that the problematic of thinking life and death, self and the other—the core of both the sacred and the feminine—can emerge from traditions that are formally perceived as patriarchal or phallocentric.

The second part of the book takes the challenge of thinking the sacred and the feminine through aesthetic practices, music, film, image, form, movement. The focus falls much more on cultural analysis. Here it is the productions themselves, whether art, poetry, or film, which form the lens through which the concepts of the sacred and the feminine are seen.

Upon reading these eight papers together, a common discourse emerges. The past, whether in the form of visual or literary culture, myth or personal history or trauma, interacts with the present in the formation of a space both deeply personal to the creative artist, writer or academic but also able to negotiate much wider questions.

Nina Danino's presentation and contextualization of her film *Stabat Mater* is the first paper in this second part. Beginning with a powerful portrayal of the voice of the mother, which also haunts her film, Danino ponders the specificity of the visuality, materiality and temporality of film and its relation to language, sound and voice. Positioned as the fulcrum of this book, Danino's presentation of her creative work functions as a compelling proposal for a description of the space of the sacred and the feminine.

The representation, in the text of an academic article, of the visual, auditory and temporal experience of watching a film, while acting as an exemplar of the textual capture of this elusory medium also acts as an introduction to the second part of the book, where a combination of experienced and emerging researchers present cultural articulations of the encounter between the two concepts which form the heart of this book.

Ranjana Thapalyal's invitation to rethink the depiction of the space of the sacred with reference to the powerful Hindu feminine interacts productively with Céline Boyer's evocation of myth in her work on the expression of the sacred in poetry. Boyer shows how concepts from ancient cultures, such as the myth of Isis, are part of a monomyth of rebirth which the poetess Kathleen Raine inscribes in the feminine, in a poetry sited in corporeality, maternity, sacrifice—these metaphors enabling the poet to take on the role of the shaman, the conduit for the inexpressible sacred emerging from within the secret of her own consciousness.

The creative act, sited in the feminine, is also the subject of the five following papers. Themes of motherhood and the body return in Maria Aline Seabra Ferreira's work on Paula Rego. Ferreira argues that Rego's representation of the Virgin Mary in labour recovers the Virgin's physicality and bodilyness. Tracing representations of the pregnant Virgin throughout the history of art, Ferreira reads Rego's portrayal of the Virgin Mary as well as her representations of angels through the writings of Luce Irigaray. She emphasizes the power of the image of the Virgin, after Rego, as a paradoxical potential feminist icon of fatherless motherhood.

Anne Creissels' work also engages with a contemporary female artist, Ana Mendieta, in a critique of that artist's ambiguous position as regards the female body in culture and the roles of artist, performer and spectator. Where Ferreira sees Rego's Virgins as inscribing a missing discourse of maternity, Creissels cannot characterize Mendieta's role so clearly. In artworks dealing with concepts ranging from rape and sacrifice to nature and virginity, the artist is seen to enact both the liberation and objectification of the body. Framed by references to the myths of Leda and Daphne, Creissels presents a compelling debate about what affirmation is possible for the female artist.

Victoria Turvey Sauron's continues in many ways several of the concerns raised in Creissels' work. In a discussion of the traditional structure of viewing the female body within art history, resulting in the opposition between beautiful surface and horrific interior, she proposes examples of works of art which seem to uphold this discourse, and then examples which transgress it. Drawing together and setting up encounters between disparate texts, from Bernini to Anish Kapoor, from Cindy Sherman to Georges Bataille, and finishing with certain sculptural works by Louise Bourgeois, Turvey Sauron traces the discourse of a fetishistic visual mentality before conjecturing about a form of art, and a form of art history, which does not think in terms of inside or outside, and which escapes from the visual model of the feminine imposed on women by fetishism.

Notions of the relationship between the body and the materiality of the artwork are also theorized by Leila McKellar in her invocation of Helen Chadwick's response to the cultural associations surrounding the Virgin Mary. She demonstrates how this artist has reconfigured and rewritten one of the most iconic representations of maternity in the Western world. McKellar's engagement with Chadwick's art discusses how the mother-daughter relationship is the backdrop for debate about the apparent dichotomy between Word and flesh, so spectacularly *mise-en-scène* within Western Christian discourse.

To bring the book to a close, a final encounter with a female artist again presents a debate about issues surrounding the female body and subjectivity. Vanessa Corby's analysis of Tracey Emin's artwork sites Emin as the initiator of a discourse on abortion, occulted from cultural representation due to the hyper-politicization of the debate, and the persistence of a maternalistic anti-abortion culture which, despite decades of feminist work continues to be reinforced, for example by three-dimensional ultrasound images which negate the mother while upholding an impression of personhood for the foetus. Corby argues that Emin's work is a process of mourning, which, unlike traditional Freudian models, functions through the body, acting as a 'corporeal mnemonic reservoir' which prolongs the psychic existence of the lost object while repeating the trauma. Emin's art, returning again and again to the experience of abortion, therefore provides 'something to show' for an experience which leaves no other signifier.

All these papers attempt to find a place for something they name 'the feminine'—whether negotiated through the figure of the mother, the body, the voice, the image, or sited at the point of interaction between all these concepts. They also engage in a profound sense with the agenda of a new generation of cultural analysis, which is finding itself renegotiating approaches to gender and creativity. Within these debates, the notion of the sacred, which haunts each paper, is gradually developed through and across these concepts of the feminine, as well as these disparate contexts, which nevertheless give a sense of a unity of purpose and of mindset. Perhaps Boyer's association of *sacred* and *secret* is particularly relevant here—both are forms of interiority which it is the specificity of the poet to be able to unveil. The intensely personal engagement of the writers with their subject matter is a crucial element of a type of analysis which is concerned with the tension between interior spaces and the nature of their interactions within culture.

# 1

# SACRED COWS
## Wandering in Feminism, Psychoanalysis and Anthropology
### *Griselda Pollock*

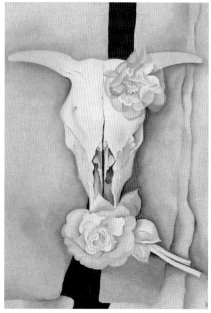

1.1   Georgia O'Keeffe, *Cow's Skull with Calico Roses*, 1932, oil on canvas, 92.2 × 61.3 cm, The Art Institute of Chicago (Gift of Georgia O'Keeffe, 1947.712).

This paper eavesdrops on an epistolary conversation between two women. When it was published, the correspondence was framed by a painting by Georgia O'Keeffe (1.1). Why was an image of a cow chosen?

A legacy of British colonialism in India, the phrase, *sacred cows*, refers to any thing or opinion considered beyond question, too holy to mess with, not up for discussion. Originating in Hinduism's respect for the cow as a principle of the sacred maternal, the visual and verbal relay between cows and holiness is an inscription of the deep resonances between the sacred and the feminine which I shall track through psychoanalysis and anthropology to feminism: each field respectively figuring histories of the social bond and of subjectivity nestling inside religious and pre-religious systems of thought and fantasy.

In the preface to the publication of her correspondence with Catherine Clément, Julia Kristeva writes about the letter-writers' shared topic:

> For myself, 'that' could only be what had always preoccupied us, visible in our trajectories as intellectuals and novelists, on the edge of the unconscious and of the social tie, which the imminent end of the second millennium charged with burning relevance: the sacred. Not religion or its opposite, atheistic negation, but the experience that beliefs both shelter and exploit, at the crossroads of sexuality and thought, body and meaning, which women feel intensely but without being preoccupied by it and about which there remains much for them—for us—to say. Does a specifically feminine sacred exist?[1]

Reflecting on the grandeur of another sentence in Kristeva's preface: 'the awakening of women in the coming millennium', anthropologist Catherine Clément writes:

> As a matter of fact, in eleven years of living abroad, I have seen women everywhere more advanced than they are in France. And everywhere, I have seen them use the sacred with more intelligence than we do: in India, Africa, and even in Austria, the beginning of the East.[2]

Kristeva continues her theme:

> That is another dimension of the sacred: self-assurance here and now, which comes from the assurance that one has time. Not the fear of castration, in which man dresses up his fear of death, to the point of making the latter the sleepless lookout and ultimate support of the sacred; not the catastrophe of mourning, which women know in the flesh and which makes them eternal hired mourners, with or without dead bodies … No. That attitude so serene that one hesitates to link it with the sacred … is rooted in a certainty about life. There is life and women can give it; *we* can give it … No, I will cling to life as the ultimate visage of the sacred.[3]

Kristeva is both talking about mere biological life: *zoë*, in Greek, and *bios*, life as a meaningful socio-historical existence, shaped by affect and signification. For Kristeva, life is the junction of giving life and giving meaning, giving meaning to the act of giving life, that, in exceeding our modes of understanding, forms the sacred: 'the impossible, nevertheless, sustained connection between life and meaning'.[4] Wondering about the impact of technology on all of lived life (*zoë* and *bios*), and indeed through contraception and other managements of fertility and child-making, Kristeva wonders if we are not on the edge of a 'new era of the sacred', shaped by the disappearance of the 'ancestral division between those who give life (women) and those who give meaning (men)':

> After two thousand years of world history dominated by the sacredness of Baby Jesus, might women be in a position to give a different coloration to the ultimate sacred, the miracle of human life: not life for itself, but life bearing meaning, for the formulation of which women are called upon to offer their desire and their words?[5]

Countering already evident Christianocentrism and Eurocentrism admitted by Kristeva when she recognizes her reference point as 'the European tribe', Clément's letters are more inclusive, dealing with trances, a rite of exorcism from Senegal, and wondering about vapours, smells, a kind of olfactory dissemination that links to sex (is sex sacred? she ponders), and reminding us of the sacred cows of India:[6]

> Like the Goddess Hathor in Egypt, the sacred cow in India is the envelope of the universe, since it is within the sewn skin of a cow that the first man was born. Male, that goes without saying. The cow is thus maternal and enveloping, granted. The Hindus draw the consequence. Everything that falls from the cow is not only sacred but useful ... The Hindus, however, are perfectly logical, since, in the mother, everything is good. As you can see, the maternal component cannot exempt itself from secretions, however fetid they may be.[7]

Yet in all their fascinating arguments, and they do hot up, neither Clément nor Kristeva talks about a related sacred cow that will bring both Egypt and Israel into the field that appears in the Bible, Numbers 19, to which I will return.

I was initially surprised to discover that 'the sacred', that most elusive and yet seemingly still potent of terms in twentieth century thought—we always think immediately of Georges Bataille—was claimed by both Clément and Kristeva as a central, yet quietly pursued rather than overtly declared, thread of their lives' works as anthropologist, literary critic, novelist, and psychoanalyst. To pose the question of the sacred and sexual difference, or rather, to ask if there is a specificity of the feminine in relation to this crossroad between human consciousness and imagination on the one hand, and the mysteries of life and death on the other, between thought and body, corporeality and meaning, takes us deep into the feminist project. Whether writing about the literary avant-garde, abjection, love, maternity, melancholy or nationalism, it is clear that Kristeva has been researching at this frontier for many decades, illuminated for us by post-structuralist studies of language, subjectivity and sexual difference and facilitated by the encounter of psychoanalysis with semiotics: 'semanalyse'.[8]

Hunting down the deeper structures of cultural myths and narratives, Clément is known for both her dialogue with Hélène Cixous on the hysteric and her work on operatic killing off of women, the culturally aestheticized sacrifice of women to the creation of drama, music and its apogee in modern opera.[9] Approaching the sacred through clearly defined feminist, Marxist, Freudian and post-structuralist theories of sign, meaning, and the psyche, ensures that we are not in the space of theology or spirituality. We are speaking *otherwise* what was once spoken through ritual, myth and very much later, institutionalized religious practice and belief.

As art historian and cultural analyst, I, too, had been working at that crossroads but within the expanded field of art's and culture's histories, of psychoanalysis and aesthetics, generously covered by the neologism cultural analysis. In my case, this was linked back to Aby Warburg's 'nameless science': *Kulturwissenschaft*, that sought a visual psychology of the persistence of paganism through the image (what Warburg called the *pathos formula*: the image as unconscious memory-bearer of the charged emotions out of which the gesture, dance or ritual first emerged). Warburg stands in opposition to the teleological, developmental model of an autonomous stylistic art history. Seeking to formulate means to catch the relations of art to its generating social structures *and* to its remembered emotional, psychological intensities, cultural analysis is, therefore, *transdisciplinary:* attending to the several disciplines through which these questions are posed and explored, excavated and discussed, opening the theoretical passageways for respectful dialogue rather than confusing confection.

## II Analysing the history of religion: from cult to writing

Challenged at a conference in Leeds in 1996 about her 'Catholic proclivity', Julia Kristeva declared:

> to continue with the thread of memory: we do not have a choice but to put into practice a history of religion as a demystification. We have to rid ourselves of the history of religion. *We have to say what it spoke of, otherwise* … We must not allow ourselves to remain

ignorant of this heritage. Instead, as before we have to question it ... [10]

In an earlier text of 1973 that forged her initial meeting of Marxism and semiotics, of signification and the mode of production, Kristeva had charted a complex convergence of family, state and church in modern bourgeois society against whose unholy union she posed transgressive avant-garde textuality. She defined religion as working on behalf of the social ensemble to manage that which is excessive, but also necessary, to it, constrained in permitted forms of semiotic transgressivity and mystery.

> The unity, of state and family, is achieved at the price of a murder and a sacrifice—that of the *soma*, the drive and the process. This is recognised by religion, which thus arrogates to itself the privilege of representing and of speaking of the infinite element the ensemble oppresses and yet demands to be spoken. Religion is here that discourse that knows, as far as possible, what is at stake in the relation between socio-symbolic homogeneity and the heterogeneity of the drives at work within and upon homogeneity. Complicity with the state and the family to the extent that it restores its other to them, this religious discourse appears not only as the speculative (and often specular) forms of what is unrepresentable in orgasmic pleasure (*jouissance*) and of what is uncapitalizable in the expenditure of productive forces.[11]

Kristeva also identified, in the Hebrew and Christian scriptures as texts of historical cultures, two issues that had consistently and theoretically preoccupied her as both literary and psycho-analyst. The trajectory of Kristeva's work from linguistic semiotics to psychoanalysis, and the trajectory that she proposes in perhaps her most pertinent book (for this topic), *Powers of Horror*, traces a movement in a specific tradition of human cultural thought and practice in dealing with alterity and narcissism.[12]

The architecture of Kristeva's brilliant and much abused 'essay on abjection' maps out three, successive 'moments' that are interwoven strata in histories of both religion and subjectivity and the supersession of the former by the emergence of the latter. Kristeva begins her study of the sacred with what is accepted as its foundational era: the archaic era of sacrificial cults which deal with defilement by creating systems of taboo, exclusion, transgression and hence sacralization. A major literary codex of this moment is revealed and articulated in the Mosaic book of Leviticus. There taboo, transgression and sacrifice form the language of negotiation of the thresholds between life and death, community and otherness. *Sacer*, the Latin for making separate, like the Hebrew *Kadosh*, meaning set apart, catches this active work of division, exclusion and boundary-making as well as the rituals for dealing with transgression of the boundaries through act, illness or the unforeseen contact with death by killing or dying. A different moment or economy is that of the polemical displacement of Judaic sacrificial negotiation of defilement (otherness)—what Nietzsche called 'the eternal defilement of mankind'—by the Helleno-Christian mystery religion which internalized a concept of (original) sin, interiorizing rather than sacrificially purging abjection. One of the effects of Helleno-Christianity, working through oralization to speech led, through prayer and confession, to a fostering of a new kind of increasingly individuated, guilt-sensitized interiority: subjectivity.

With a modernist waning of the exclusively theological view of the universe, the Helleno-Christian legacy in the West both fosters and is displaced onto *writing*—literature—in a moment in which psychoanalysis will later emerge to be the *otherwise* speaking of 'the crossroads of sexuality and thought, body and meaning' that will enable us, in reading modern literature at its extremes, to see 'what lies hidden by God'.[13] At that point, powerful, communally dispersed anxieties around life and death, the body, its drives and limits, its anxious perplexity before inside/outside, self and other, that, in the history of social, economic and cultural processes found other compelling but individuating forms through the institutions of religions such as Christianity (that themselves 'produced' their own subject, and subjectivity as the internalized site of anxiety and its violence, desire and its turmoil), produce both the subject of psychoanalysis and a psychoanalysis of the subject. In *Powers of Horror*, Kristeva's reading of the fascist, excremental, ecstatic texts of anti-Semite, homophobe writer Céline, poses the question of that transition from communal 'acting out' through the psychologization of sin to the process (process meaning also trial) of writing. In writing, the crossroads communally experienced via the 'sacred' now struggles, *subjectively*, with 'abjection', that lining of the trajectory to speaking subjectivity with its disintegrating, border-crossing intimation of the formless condition from which subjectivity is forged, and 'written' so that it becomes alienated in and enunciated by language.

Kristeva's arc of analysis runs a thread from the space of the ancient sacrificial Judaic sacred, to the formalities of a specific mystery religion and on to its modernist beyond: with all its potential dangers, horrors and transformations occurring and repeating and being worked through on the plane of language. Language is not a system alone. It is revolutionized by the pressure of subjectivity, by the semiotic of drive-ridden corporeality. Far from dismissing, therefore, what religious thought and practice holds before us through atheistic negation, which remains tied to that which it negates as the mirroring of the same, semiotic-psycho-analytical cultural analysis tracks the intensities secreted within, and veiled by, the late accretions of formalized religion. The aim is not to discuss whether there is a deity or not. Instead, we want to know what fuels the imaginaries and the registers of our distinctively human attempts to understand self-other relations which include those of sociality itself, of affection and desire as well as our position vis-à-vis that against which human identity construes itself—the world, and the radical alterity of the non-human, animal, plant, planetary and meteorological forces. Long before the recasting of these relations through the abstract figuration or (im)personation of the divine, comes the sacred: the site of these constitutively human negotiations of life, death, sex and difference.

The religious imaginary, as a veiling and very erudite, late development in human culture, is shaped around love for, bonding with, and exile from, powerful figures of otherness, or the Other as figures of power encountered in both human infancy and in the foundational moments of cultural human becoming.[14] Religious representation so often bears the trace of the historical, social (hierarchical) and familial forms of human life. Gods are mothers and fathers, and kings and sovereigns. In seeking insight into human cultures by studying contemporary societies less disrupted by formal religion or Modernity, Claude Lévi-Strauss proposed what he called 'wild thinking'—wild as in the forms of flora and fauna that are not more 'primitive' than their cultivated relatives, but are less prescribed and thus exhibit something more of the inception and structure shared by both the wild and the cultivated.[15] Classical scholar, Jane Harrison, of whom more anon, writes in the opening paragraph of *Themis* in 1912:

> In the *Prolegomena* I was chiefly concerned to show that the religion of Homer was no more primitive than his language. The Olympian gods—that is the anthropomorphic gods of Homer and Pheidias and the mythographers—seemed to me like a bouquet of cut-flowers whose bloom is brief, because they have been severed from their roots. To find these roots, we must burrow deep into a lower stratum of thought, of those chthonic cults which underlay their life and from which sprang all their brilliant blossoming.[16]

The cultivated cannot be as rich or valuable a source for our self-analysis and cultural investigation as that which retains, more vividly, the traces of founding urgencies. Increasing degrees of social and cultural mediation mask but never fully erase the driving emotional forces, just as growing up from infancy into childhood, puberty and adulthood are not developmental phases in psychoanalytical terms. They represent determining levels, variously reacting to, and transforming, the ever-determining emotions and anxieties of the archaic structuration of subjectivity, its worlds and relations.

The meta-psychoanalytical study of religious thought, practice and its imaginaries, therefore, sees its foundations and psychical resources in the crucible of human subjective formation in living, *social* experience: in those radicalizing processes that turn speechless animals (*infans*) into sexed, speaking, and *jouissant* social-human subjects experiencing themselves within a cultural or social group. These processes are relational, forming a series of situational complexes, whose powerful intensities imprint and unconsciously determine the very creativity and capacities that define human possibility. Hence what we believe, whether projectively or on the basis of our absolute convictions, matters a great deal as this mirrors back, to the collectivity of human subjects that form communities, certain persistent and effective *self* and *other* understandings, freighted with the emotional and conceptual forces of intense necessity and 'drama.' Between Freud and Durkheim, this is nothing new.

If we review the moment at which this kind of thinking about human society, culture, religion and subjectivity acquired a density that forms the foundations of modern sociology, anthropology, psychology and art history around the turn of the nineteenth century, we immediately recognize that this kind of historical-self-consciousness is already a mark and product of Modernity. Itself a cultural phenomenon, it is an exploration of the modern self/culture through an encounter with its own otherness often projected out on to other peoples in disfiguring ways. Equally, these researches formed a kind of mass cultural-psychoanalysis that, I suggest, registers an anxiety about an unspecifiable loss: the loss of the sacred itself that could only be found in a second-hand re-creation of ancient worlds through archaeology or in a tourist re-connection through anthropology. As a historian, I am sure that I, too, share this delusion of wanting to speak with ghosts from ages that seem imaginatively richer than my own.

### III The waning of the sacred: Modernity
Thus we have heard many times about the waning of the sacred under the smashing pressures of Modernity. Industrial time, disciplined, proletarianized labour, urban migration, shattered community, social alienation, capitalist colonization of the pores of everyday life with

commodification of everything and everyone, are but the latest in many stages of socio-economically forged estrangement from the powerful experience of the sacred that was represented as so vivid and lived, through the emerging disciplines of retrospect (history, archaeology and anthropology) and introspection (sociology and psychology).

At the same time, we have also seen that traces of the sacred constantly burst forth, registering its strange heritage of intensities of violence, *jouissance* or undecidability in a variety of places: the voice, and music, visual representation, poetry, politics, and above all in drama with its foundations in ritual.

In his cross-cultural reflections on the rituals performed with snakes by indigenous Pueblo peoples such as the Hopi living in towns in the desert regions of Arizona and New Mexico in the United States, which he visited in the 1890s, the German-Jewish art historian, Aby Warburg concluded his book with a photograph of a contemporary white American man walking on the streets of San Francisco, whom he called 'Uncle Sam' (1.2).

Warburg witnessed the conceptual universe and the ritual practices such a conception gave rise to amongst the Pueblo peoples in relation to the most vital force in their universe: rain, which they invoked through the serpent, itself a richly freighted sign of the earth in which it silently moves and darkly lives. The snake is also a signifier of lightning whose forked current sometimes dramatically connected the two decisive conditions of life: the rain-bearing sky and the food-giving earth. Beyond that link between the serpent, the earth or chthonic creature *par excellence* and the jagged streak of powerful light that bridged from the upper spheres bringing fertilizing rain, the snake also holds the signification of persistence, recycling and rebirth as a signifier that can be tracked through many cultures from the Cretans to the Egyptians, the indigenous peoples of the North American continent to the Greeks and Romans. Drawing on the work of Jane Harrison, Warburg cites ancient societies such as Egypt, Greece, and Judea, tracking the image of the serpent into Renaissance Catholic Italy where the serpent ap-

1.2 'Uncle Sam', photograph reproduced by Aby Warburg in his lecture 'Images from the region of the Pueblo Indians of North America', 21 April 1923. Reproduced courtesy of the Warburg Institute, London.

pears in the Sistine Chapel with Michelangelo's pictorial rendering of the Biblical narrative of Moses and the brazen serpent which he links with the pagan mysteries of Apollo and Python which were the subject of elaborate court masques in Italian court culture in the fifteenth and sixteenth centuries. Confronting, however, modern man walking down a San Francisco street beneath the wires that invisibly carried industrially generated, reliable and constant electricity to the house and office, where a mere flick of a switch brought instant illumination or power, Warburg wrote:

> The conqueror of the serpent cult and the fear of lightning, the inheritor of indigenous peoples and the gold seeker who ousted them is captured in this photograph ... above his top hat runs an electric wire. In this copper of Edison's, he has wrested lightning from nature ...
>
> The modern Prometheus and the modern Icarus, Franklin and the Wright Brothers, who invented the dirigible airplane, are precisely those ominous destroyers of a sense of distance, who threaten to lead the planet back into chaos. Telegram and telephone destroy the cosmos. Mythical and symbolic thinking strive to form spiritual bonds between humanity and the surrounding worlds, shaping distance into the space required for devotion and reflection [*Denkraum*]: the distance undone by the instantaneous electric connection.[17]

In the form of technological mastery over the natural resources on which human survival persists, Modernity radically transforms the conditions of artistic and cultural reflexes, destroying the distance that shapes what Warburg called *Denkraum*: the 'space for devotion and reflection'. Warburg's tragic vision echoes what Karl Marx wrote more analytically in 1857, in the *Grundrisse* where he discusses the disparity between the exquisite achievements of Greek art and epic literature and the relatively low level of economic development of that society, attributing to the charm of Greek art its role as metaphorical childhood of humanity. Relating, as a materialist would, cultural forms and even its underlying imaginary to the stages of development of the social relations of production, Marx points to the unevenness of that relation in the case of the Greeks, whose glories of the epic are no longer possible in an age of industrial mastery of energy and communication:

> It is well known that Greek mythology is not only the arsenal of Greek art but its foundation. Is the view of nature and of social relations on which the Greek imagination and hence Greek

[mythology] is based possible with the self-acting mule spindles and railways and locomotives and electrical telegraphs? What chance has Vulcan against Roberts & Co., Jupiter against the lightning rod, and Hermes against the *Crédit Mobilier*? All mythology overcomes and dominates and shapes the forces of nature in the imagination and by the imagination; it therefore vanishes with the advent of real mastery over them. What becomes of Fama beside Printing House Square [the original home of *The Times* newspaper]?[18]

What mystery is there is the production of communication and the message once these are technologically instantaneous? Perhaps Marx could not yet imagine the deification of technology itself in the information age. This is an issue for further discussion; the media is massively mythic but more in a Barthesian sense of bourgeois ideology's constant refiguring of the historical in terms of a mythifying naturalism. Warburg's lament, like Walter Benjamin's diagnosis of the end of the auratic in the age of mechanical reproduction, finds its counterpart in modernism's forced and reflexive understanding of the mythic universe of the sacred in which it no longer lives, but which remains the legacy of human thought.[19] In Warburg's terms, it is perhaps a necessary condition for any art at all which arises in that space for devotion and reflection, that sense of human/other relations, dependency and mystery, that has taken so many forms over the millennia of conscious, socialized human existence.

I keep stressing this awkward intimacy between social and the human to counter one aspect of bourgeois and specifically Christian illusion: that the singular discrete self comes first and confronts the social as its secondary Other. Drawing my inspiration from both Jane Harrison and Julia Kristeva, it is clear that whatever is human consciousness of itself as human arises firstly in a collective, communal but *not*, therefore, *impersonal* way. The abolition of the personalized individual (collectivist socialism) or the excessively isolated elevation of the individual (liberal capitalism) are two sides of Modernity: the fascists, by contrast, stole the sacred and realized that success would lie precisely in reanimating that exultant finding and losing of the exacerbated self in the group projected onto the Hero that had its flowering in the ancient, constitutive cults of history to which the fascists' bad racist anthropology led them in the search for re-enchantment.

In her *A Room of One's Own*, 1928, Virginia Woolf's reflections on a proposed lecture on women and fiction opens with a vividly imagined scene deeply relevant to this topic. The author is in Cambridge, epitomizing the privileged classical university education from which, as a woman of her moment and class, Woolf felt excluded. As a 'daughter of educated men', deprived of the intellectual sustenance her father and brothers automatically acquired by gender, class and nation in the university, her own thought would have to forge less formal means for its elaboration, seeking resources that would challenge the patriarchal establishment at every level.[20] Her trip to Cambridge exposed Virginia Woolf to a hurtful experience of exclusion as she 'trespassed' on a College Fellows' lawn only to be shooed off by an officious Beadle, not merely as not belonging to the College, but completely out of place as a woman in a masculine enclave. Instead of dining in style at one of the rich men's colleges, Virginia Woolf takes her homely and plain dinner of gravy soup, tough beef followed by prunes and custard, at one of the poorer, women's colleges. Here, however, as she approaches the dining hall across the lawns, the author looks up and sees a ghost that can offer some compensation in her intellectual exile:

> Somebody was in a hammock, some-body, but in this light they were phantoms only, half guessed, half seen, raced across the grass—would no one stop her?—and then on the terrace, as if popping out to breathe the air, to glance at the garden, came a bent figure, formidable yet humble, with her great forehead and her shabby dress—could it be the famous scholar, could it be J—— H—— herself? All was dim, yet intense too, as if the scarf which the dusk had flung over the garden were torn asunder by a star or sword—the *flash of some terrible reality leaping, as its way is, out of the heart of the spring.*[21]

We know this fascinating passage to be a curiously guarded invocation of the ideas as well as an image of the renowned and pioneering classical scholar, Jane Harrison (1.3). Harrison is thus significantly embedded in the modernist Woolf's arch-feminist text as both a revered image of learning 'in the feminine' that counters the exclusive masculinity of the university, and as the icon of a feminist interpretation of ancient pre-classical culture. Harrison's work validated a feminine principle at the very foundations of religion signalled by a *bounding* movement: the running of the band that accompanied the *daimon* of the Spring, at rebirth festivals. Harrison's distinctive interpretations of the spring rituals of the *daimon* that only later become personified by Dionysus, the Son, are invoked by Woolf's poetic condensation of Harrison's key work *Themis* in the phrases 'a flash of some terrible reality leaping' … 'out of the heart of the spring'.[22]

As a major scholar within not only the university but in its privileged discipline, Classics, Jane Harrison's symbolic importance is surely con-

1.3 Augustus John, *Jane Ellen Harrison* (1850–1928), 1909, oil on canvas, 62 × 75 cm, Newnham College, Cambridge.

nected to her intellectual intervention in that domain of cultural memory and Eurocentric ideology. Through her courageous, *feminist* reworking of Nietzsche, Bergson, Freud and Durkheim, Harrison challenged the patriarchal, rationalist and idealistically Apollonian interpretation of Classical culture that was serving as the mirror of modern nationalistic and patriarchal cultures, her own included. Harrison's insistently *social* theory of the origins of religion in rituals or cults relating to food and structured around the Mother/Son rather than the Father paradigm, typical of patriarchal thought, supplied modernist women writers such as Virginia Woolf with the resource for another vision of the feminine and of the aesthetic that would sustain the ambition of Woolf's own modernist literature as a radically different form and psychic economy.

Feminist scholars, identifying the profound influence of Jane Harrison's work on modernist writers such as James Joyce and T. S. Eliot, as well as Woolf, reveal the ways in which the novels of the latter can be read for their literary internalization and creative transformation/domestication of Harrison's feminist identification of matrilinear and collectively oriented mythic structures, notably in the novel *To the Lighthouse* (1927). Jane Harrison's work installed a place for the feminine in the classical and pre-classical cultures that 'leapt' across historical time to infuse Virginia Woolf's modernism with its mytho-poetical resources at the juncture of modernism's attempt to think differently, beyond religion, while not losing the imaginary and archaic intensities religions had for so long managed on behalf of the symbolic contract. Harrison's differencing readings of the origins of ancient art in ritual—the title of another of her books—countered the menace of Victorian ideals of feminine vacuity and passivity.[23] Harrison challenged the heavily patriarchal, narcissistically masculine privilege of an exclusive access to a Classical hence universal knowledge. Precisely in hypothesizing a feminine counter-principle within the archaic seed-bed of the cultural archive and hence at the foundations of western art itself, notably through her book *Themis*, (1912 and 1927), Harrison thus transformed a phallic lack into a feminist legacy.

### IV Women's Time

Jane Harrison belonged to a group of transdisciplinary classical scholars at the turn of the nineteenth century known as the Cambridge Ritualists.[24] They punched through the back wall of the history of Classical and hence white Euro-Christian West's self-representation to discover the much more ancient, chthonic origins of religion and indeed of art itself in ritual. Like Warburg, her contemporary, drawing on the work of anthropologists Tylor and Frazer, as well as on Nietzsche, Bergson and Durkheim, Harrison proposed a theory of the *social* origins of Greek religion and hence art in rituals handling the immediate needs of any social group, that is, survival by basic sustenance: food. Once discovered to be seasonally available, the need for food led to a cycle of seasonal rituals particularly focused on spring and on the theme of death and rebirth. These themes the rituals re-enact and prophylactically anticipate through enactment: *dromenon*, action, whose residual, veiled memory persists into the pathos-formulae (to borrow Warburg's terms) of *drama*. Harrison argued that the initiating experience of this need and the actions undertaken as response to it and in order to secure food was a group experience not the less emotionally intense for that collectivity. The initial ground of what we must understand as religious thought and practice was, according to Harrison, matrilinear, but this focus is *figured* by the young man, *Kouros*, who later takes a specific form as the son-figure, Dionysus. Harrison, therefore, draws a significant distinction between the Dionysian and his Asiatic affine Orpheus, and the later, formalized and anthropomorphic Olympian gods ruled over by Big Daddy Zeus whom she considers fundamentally 'non-religious'. 'Primitive religion … was a web of practices emphasizing particular parts of life, issuing necessarily in representations and ultimately dying out into abstract conceptions.' She adds:

> … I had come to see the real distinction between the mystery-god Dionysus and the Olympians … I saw why Dionysus, the mystery-god, who is the expression and representation of *durée* [Bergson], is, alone among the Greek divinities, constantly attended by a *thiasos*, which is a cardinal matter for understanding of his nature.[25] The mystery-god arises out of those instincts, emotions and desires which attend and express life; but these emotions, desires, instincts, in so far as they are religious, are at the outset rather of a group than of individual consciousness. The whole history of epistemology is the history of an evolution of clear, rational thought, out of the haze of collective and sometimes contradictory representations. It is a necessary and most important corollary to this doctrine, that the form taken by divinity reflects the social

structure of the group to which the divinity belongs. Dionysus is the Son of his Mother because he issues from a matrilinear group.[26]

Harrison is not positing a utopian matriarchal era. She is identifying the historical and textual evidence for a socio-symbolic and imaginary order that pre-dates the patriarchal—itself epitomized by the squabbling family of the Olympians with the stern Father, the unhappy but powerful Mother and the stay-at-home daughters making jealous mischief. The older order is of that of the Mother (not of women) as bearer of the *Kouros*, the young man, the son, who is sown like seeds to bring forth the new life needed each year. This order signifies imaginatively thought about giving life and about a kind of monumental and cyclical experience of duration: of time as changing sequences of dying and re-birth around which this meaning system is elaborated and figured.

### V The loss of the sacred

We can follow this thread to a second Modernist text, the film *Medea*, made by Italian director Pier Paolo Pasolini in 1970. Lamenting the loss of the sacred in Modernity, Pasolini uses Euripides's Greek tragedy, *Medea*, as his cinematic vehicle for philosophizing about the lost imaginative worlds held in strange and perplexing beauty before our modern, rationalist, uncomprehending minds by the literary remnants of the struggle between archaic and classical Greece: between *dromenon* and *drama* perhaps. In a stunningly visual realization, Pasolini's film uses landscape, sound and architecture as its semantic figures. It opens with the childhood of Jason, hidden with a satyr (a Dionysus figure) among the marshy lakes when his father is murdered by his uncle Peleas who usurps his brother's kingdom. Raised in simplicity, Jason is taught the ancient wisdom by the satyr who subsequently turns into a human form as Jason's conscience and cultural memory. He is the poet.[27] Just before Jason comes of age and begins the destined quest to reclaim his heritage, the satyr declares:

All is sacred. All is sacred. All is sacred.
There is nothing natural about nature.
When nature seems natural to you, all will be finished and something else will begin.
Farewell sky. Farewell sea.
What a beautiful sky, so close, so benign.
Is there a fragment of that sky unnatural, not possessed by a god?
And the sea, what do you see? Something natural?

All you see behind you is an apparition;
Wherever you glance, a god is present.
If he is absent, the signs of his sacred presence will be there:
Silence, smell of grass, cool water.
Yes, all is sacred, but holiness is also a curse.
The gods that can love, can also hate.

Perhaps I am too much of a liar for you, too much the poet.
In the ancient world myths and ritual are a living reality, part of
man's everyday existence.
Reality is such a perfect entity that the emotion he experiences before a tranquil sky equals the most profound personal emotion of
modern man.

Moving to an interior and thus human architecture shielding man
against the nature in which the satyr was so lyrically immersed, the satyr-
turned-man talks now of how once agriculture was found, humans saw
seeds and grass and in them they saw resurrection. Now we know seed
and understand grass and the old mystery of resurrection is a discarded
memory. He foresees that Jason will be sent on a quest to a distant
place in search of the golden fleece (a remnant sign of a totemic cult
where human sacrifice is ritually practised). The satyr-poet tells him
that there, in a strange other place, men reason differently. We the viewers are switched with Jason to this other world, recreated by Pasolini in
a striking landscape in Eastern Turkey where he imagines cinematically
a pagan world that lives the unity of life and death and performs its
ritual sacrifice of the young man crowned symbolically with wheat
sheaves on head and groin to fertilize its crops with his living blood.
Controversially, enacting a literal as opposed to symbolic human sacrifice, Pasolini makes clear the necessarily collective nature of these rituals, and the function of the priesthood to be set apart as the 'sacred
executioners' who are both elevated and reviled for undertaking or
overseeing the necessary transgression of the sanctity of life in order
to secure the life of the community through rituals that hope to ensure
the fertility of the land.[28] The Mother/son figuration is presented
through the sister/brother shared priesthood. Medea, the sister/priest-
ess, falling in love with the stranger, Jason, lured by the otherness of
Jason, betrays this whole world and steals the talisman: the golden
fleece, sacrificing her brother/husband to this new, foreign love. Soon,
however, she experiences the full force of her exile from the unified
world over which she once presided. When Jason and his Argonauts
(the young man is always with a band of *Kouretes*) settle back in the
marshes in which he grew up and set up tents and begin to cook the

food they have scavenged, Medea is outraged. For the first time in the 30 minutes of the film that has elapsed, she speaks. Rather she shrieks: a cry rushes forth, Clément-like, from her body:

> This place will sink because it has no foundation.
> You do not call God's blessing on your tents.
> You do not speak to God.
> You do not seek a centre.
> You do not mark a centre.
> Look for a tree, a post, a stone.

Exhibiting increasing distress and bewilderment at this irreligious approach to the ordinary processes of shelter and food, Medea rushes away from the encampment into a landscape that becomes increasingly desiccated and desert-like where she wanders about in abandoned distress.

> Speak to me earth; let me hear your voice.
> I have forgotten your voice.
> Speak to me sun; let me hear your voice.
> I have forgotten your voice.
> Are you losing your way never to return again?
> Grass, speak to me! Stone speak to me! …
> Earth, where is your meaning?
> Where can I find you again?
> Where is the bond that linked you to the sun?
> My feet touch the earth;
> I do not recognise it.
> My eyes see the sun;
> I do not recognise it.

This is a moment of dreadful pathos where Medea, the once beautiful 'pole' or centre of a ritually unified social and natural space, functioning through its system of transgressive sacrifice and rebirth, is now the isolated, abandoned and 'wild' woman, hysterical in her alienation from those forces through which she lived unity, connectivity and a relation to life and death. A new kind of death is now initiated by the men in their rapacious appetites for goods, power, gold, and women. Not a sacred death, but mundane: war. Medea will be taken to the court of Peleas where again she kills on behalf of Jason, bewitching the king's daughters to kill the usurping uncle only to find that this action causes Jason's criminal exile from his long awaited kingdom. They move to Corinth, to another Greek city state signified above all by its harsh geometric architecture. Its calculated geometry is the other of Medea's homeland, where homes and sanctuaries were hewn, cave-like out of, or rather into, the natural rock formations offering strange shelter and intricate, labyrinthine interiors, levels and secret places. The unyielding architectural symbolization of the new law, this other, patriarchal reason, the modern knowledge of the Greek *polis* which confines her to the socially segregated *oiko*s, the home, appears, like the architecture of Thebes, in the background of Ingres' perplexing painting of the moment Oedipus confronted the Sphinx in her cave, with the remnants of a sacrificed man at her animalistic feet (1808, Louvre, Paris).

The Sphinx is another version of the Medea figure that Pasolini so generously and sympathetically represents and Maria Callas iconically enacts. What drives Medea to the second murder/execution/sacrifice we see her commit and the third in which she participates—that of the sons she bore with Jason—is the cruel violence of this new patriarchal order. It can dispense with the Mother of sons precisely because it has lost its relation to the sacred, its contact with the earth and the sun. These once living relations are, in the patriarchal succession, the discarded memories, remnants of which become abstract and frivolous personifications of the Olympians. Medea's incantation, her negative hymns to a lost connectedness, stand for the mode of that moment: it is replaced by Jason's political calculus in which the Mother, like the earth, is obliterated for his political ambition. His proposed marriage to Glauce, the daughter of King Creon of Corinth, produces woman as sign and woman as exchange that will bond the men in a political allegiance and legal succession. Nature that was once an order of knowing and a mode of being is reduced to *nature* and is placed outside the polis, outside the city walls, rewritten as the violent, irrational cannibalistic and bestial, breasted Sphinx whose question about *durée,* about life as passage, is reduced to a riddle, a non-sense.

It is not maternalist politics that feminism resumed when in the title of Laura Mulvey and Peter Wollen's film of 1976 we pondered once again *The Riddles of the Sphinx.* It was a question, asked otherwise via psychoanalysis and cinema, and displaced deep in the historical legacy of patriarchy's obliteration of the matrilineal imaginary, about that relation of the feminine and the sacred, about the threshold of body and meaning that can only logically, imaginatively, rhetorically and psychically be posed through the Mother, understood in the ancient sacral life-giving and not the modern bourgeois, bio-political sense. It is the question that modern daughters, living like hysterical Medeas, exiled in a patriarchal desert, have also ask if they are to begin to think about the feminine as an ethical principle of life.

In 1996, Julia Kristeva was questioned after a formal lecture about the relation between the concept of maternity as she elaborates and values it, and the choices of women to decide whether or not to have a child, whether or not to accommodate to heterosexuality. Kristeva replied:

> I want to fill in a void in feminist theory around maternity … Since the moment of Simone de Beauvoir and her circle, there has been an insistence on the necessity for women to claim their sexual freedom, which often involved a rejection of motherhood … This trend, however, suspended many critical issues. For instance, we were unable to rethink the working norms of civilisation and culture around motherhood, for it seemed as if the pleasures and desires as well as the social regulations figured by the concept of the mother in the home—*la mère au foyer*—were null and without future significance. For this reason the vast majority of women were unmoved by the feminist movement … This revealed to me that although we have a dominant discourse on rights, we have no discourse on the necessity for the human race to guarantee its transmission, its reproduction. Thus we have a discourse on rights, but no discourse on history.[29]

Already revealing her increasingly open engagement with the work of Hannah Arendt, Kristeva returns through Arendt to the question who gives life in order to define maternity or the maternal body as a profoundly social figure of enormous significance:

> The maternal body is in a position to transform the violence of eroticism—which in the process of sexual liberation women now know for themselves—into tenderness. The maternal body is the frontier for that translation that permits a human being to live, to not become psychotic, to not die of solitude, but to live. This gives women an enormous role, namely the destiny of humanity is in the hands of women.[30]

'The violence of eroticism is transmuted into sensitivity and language,' she declares, but this role is not biological; it is a social function and can be enacted in varied forms, such as friendship or teaching.

> Thus alongside the paternal function, there is also a maternal function of transmutation. Every woman will not be able to do this, or desire to enter into this maternal function for herself. But there are

so many social roles in which this attitude towards the other may be enacted on the edge, where the sado-masochism that characterises the competitiveness of the technocratic society is muted by generosity, by the favour of the self extended towards the other, as in the mother's experience of the child. This position as mediator is possible for the 'professor'—the university teacher.[31]

Inevitably, Kristeva will also see this function of translation and transposition in writing, in literature, citing another modernist homosexual intellectual—Pasolini is my first—Proust as the textual practice embodying this and thus necessarily putting the lie to dull gender identity politics without losing in any way the fundamental feminism of the argument. As Spivak taught us, there is a double movement. We work *against* sexism and *for* feminism, and 'as women' is not a sufficient ground for such critical intellectual politics.[32]

### VI The sacred cow

From these metaphorical 'sacred cows' in the world of contemporary theory and politics, it is time to encounter a real sacred cow. The Lascaux caves, discovered, of course, only on 12 September 1940, were first introduced to art history in 1955 by Skira, the leading French art publishing house, through a text by surrealist and sociologist of the sacred: Georges Bataille. This perfectly confirmed my hunch: that our knowledge of the deep past was, in fact, embedded in *modernist* consciousness, time and space. Here, while American painters in New York like Lee Krasner read Jane Harrison and wondered about the Navajo sand painters of the American plains, Bataille postulated a theory of the sacred at the origins of art or art as the origin of the sacred. Anyone studying these still imperfectly understood paintings and carvings deep underground in a pre-electric age of oil lamps dating from 30,000–15,000 years ago, will wonder about the meaning of the animals who are specific in their genus, disposition and sex. There are indeed bulls in the caves—the totem image of the young male. But there are also cows, black and red cows (1.4).

1.4   *Red Cow*, 15–13,000 BCE, Lascaux Dordogne, France. French Ministry of Communication and Culture.

The word in English now bears the inverse of its sacred meaning: to call a woman a 'cow' is to de-

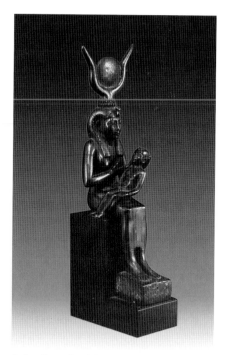

1.5　*Isis Suckling the Infant Horus*,
Egyptian, Late Period, 664–525
BCE, Bronze, height 21.5 cm,
Freud Museum, London.

grade and disdain her for unkind-
ness or ugliness. We know, of
course, that the cow is sacred to
the Hindus and cannot be consumed. In the ancient imaginary in
which the human pictured itself in
relation to its other, the animal was
a powerful signifier for what the
human was learning to think itself
through this language of the
Other. Traces of the richness of
this vocabulary remain for us to
decipher in the Egyptian world of
animal headed or animal-attributed
deities (the very things that
monotheistic, patriarchal Mosaic
prohibitions most exclude: graven
images of anything that is the
heaven above [Sun and Moon], the
earth below [animals and birds], or
below the earth [serpents], or in
the sea [fish and sea mammals]).

Central to the mythic world of
the Egyptians is the Isis-Osiris-
Horus structure, too full and rich
to be elaborated here. But let me
introduce a statuette of Isis, wife of Osiris who was torn to pieces and
scattered, not before he had sown a future, a son Horus, who sits on
his mother's knee. The group of Mother and Son also form an icono-
graphic precedent for the later Christianized recovery of this powerful
imagery of futurity and life, death and resurrection in the Madonna
and Child and the Pietà. But note that the distinguishing mark of Isis
is her horned headdress: she, the mother and the persistent gatherer
of her husband's scattered fertile seed inherits an association with the
cow goddess, Hathor. The persistence, the link, the afterlife of the sacred cow goes further into Christianity. Firstly, I must identify this statuette. It belonged in the extensive collection of pagan deities that filled
the consulting room and study of Sigmund Freud (1.5).

Many scholars have noted with perplexity the deeply archaeological
Freud's cursory attention to any evidence from the ancient worlds he
collected of non- and pre-patriarchal cults and their imaginary foundations. A fragment of a head by Demeter and a strange sculpture of
Demeter's maid, Baubo, exposing her vagina to comfort her bereaved

mistress by making her laugh, there is this tiny Isis and Horus, and that is all in the collection.[33] Passing references in his Lecture on Femininity (1932) to the Evans' discoveries on Crete of Minoan civilization that he uses to grant some different psychic reality to the pre-Oedipal phase for the girl-child and that is it in the Freudian literature. Freud's modern German redactor, analyst Ilse Grubrich-Simitis has argued that a silence so complete itself becomes a symptom, not merely of Freud himself, but of Freud as exemplar of the masculine—and Olympian—man who repudiates utterly the trauma of his helpless dependency on woman rather than transforming it into an economy of interdependence, relationality and generosity.[34] The way in which the maternal-feminine thus appears even in psychoanalysis is marked by the patriarchal, familial economy, and the social structure of modern (i.e. postclassical) European men's worlds. Degradingly animalized, deprived of all rights over the very body that makes life, forced into domestic servitude, sexually policed and repressed, denied the very dignities of her human status, intellectually, materially and emotionally impoverished, often physically brutalized and even mutilated in the service of patrilinearity, the maternal-feminine is made cruelly into the other, thing, meaningless. Worse, women are made to despise their femininity too, even erecting massive theoretical defences under the rubric of anti-essentialist theory. The quickest shortcut to intellectual suicide in even feminist circles is to talk to young women about the maternal-feminine. If Kristeva's hunch has any value that what we are dealing with is life, and that life is linked to the feminine, we need to sort this out as a matter of political and social urgency. But how do we get beyond the binary terms in which the patriarchal economy and patrilinear thought imprisons us?

### VI The red cow: an ancient trace in Judaic sacrificial thought

Let me follow the Jewish-atheist Clément down her line to Judaic writings and the strangest and most sacralizing cow: the 'Red Cow' in the Hebrew Bible. In the weekly portion, *Chukat,* Numbers 19, we have the description of a ritual that has mystified Jewish scholars down the ages. It is a ritual for dealing with corpse-impurity within a complex system of 'ritual purity' that structured the ancient Judaic concepts of order, morality and justice. It describes a ritual that has several strange elements. The sacrifice in this ritual atypically involves a *female* animal— which is unique since among such large animals, a bull or a bullock is usual. The female animal must furthermore be 'without blemish', thus never having been put to work or to a bull. She is a kind of 'virgin' or *parthenos* with all the difficulty of understanding that term as being not chaste but still singularly and totally herself, not part of any production or reproduction system. She is feminine for herself. The chosen cow must also be red. She must be entirely burnt up, including all entrails, dung and specially all her blood; normally blood is shed and splattered on the altar while the bled meat of larger animals feeds the priests. Her ashes must be taken *outside* the Temple and the city where they are combined with cedar, hyssop and scarlet wool and made into a red 'water' that is then used to free people from the most extreme impurity: contact with a corpse. In structuralist analysis, this would be explained thus: when a living person touches someone who has moved into another state, its opposite, death, the living person must be purified—brought back into the world of the living after this contact with difference through the opening of the boundary between two states. Only this complexly and ritually created red 'water' is efficacious against such a rent in the fabric of communal and individual life.

It is this system or code of Israelite ritual purity, without discussing this ritual at all, that Julia Kristeva situated as the first phase in her Christianocentric teleology from sacrificial cult to avant-garde textuality in *Powers of Horror*. Kristeva drew on anthropologist Mary Douglas's *Purity and Danger* (1969) which used structuralist methods to explain the logic of the imaginative universe in which such systems of purity and taboo are created to negotiate the destabilizing crossing of frontiers of ordered life and social emplacement.[35] Events such as birth, death, illness, puberty—that is, transitions of any kind—open the symbolic frontiers between settled and changing states of being. These attract taboos and rituals for managing the dangerous effects of change. Childbirth and menstruation will be central features of any purity system since the mystery of human life, like the mystery of life itself, will attract the maximum sense of awe, anxiety and respect for its inexplicable potencies.

The use of terms such as clean and unclean have been much misunderstood once they wander out of the imaginative universe and symbolic systems of the worlds in which they were such potent organizers of experience and meaning. According to Hyam Maccoby, ritual purity and impurity reflect on the ways such societies attempted to understand and deal with 'human conditions that occur despite human volition'.[36] Reading the Judaic system semiotically, Julia Kristeva sees the Biblical laws regulating purity and impurity as the register of a deeper power struggle which, in its socially activated practice, can be associated with certain cultic stages of human thought. These remain, however, embedded subjectively in the construction of the subject (a dimension that will become clearer to us only as the interiorization, psychologization and privatization of human subjectivity is itself produced with socio-economic complexity typical of Modernity. The degree of subjectivity is not changed.) She writes, and I want to quote at length:

> As I see it, biblical impurity is permeated with a tradition of defilement; in that sense, it *points to* but does not *signify* an autonomous force that *can* be threatening for the divine agency.[37]

Here she is commenting on two theories about biblical impurity. One argues that 'it is dependent on divine will' and the other that it represents a 'demonic force alien and threatening to divinity'.

> I shall suggest that such a force is rooted, historically (in the history of religions) and subjectively (in the structuration of the subject's identity), in the cathexis of maternal function—mother, women, reproduction. But the biblical test—and therein lies its extraordinary specificity—performs the tremendous forcing that consists in subordinating maternal power (whether historical or phantasmatic, natural or reproductive) to symbolic order as pure logical order regulating social performance, as divine Law attended to in the Temple. To the extent that the Temple *is* the Law, one is biblically pure or impure only with respect to social order, that is, with respect to the Law or the cult. If, on the other hand, one tries to go back further into the archaeology of that impurity, one indeed encounters fear in the face of a power (maternal? natural?— at any rate insubordinate and not liable to being subordinated by the Law) that might become an autonomous evil but is not, so long as the hold of the subjective and social order endures. Biblical impurity is thus always already a logicizing of *what departs from the symbolic*, and for that very reason it prevents it from being actualized as demonic evil.[38]

Kristeva will explore, therefore, the logic and the semiotic system of 'distribution' that has an internal dynamic and is not just an explanation of beliefs. The drama she plots is that impurity is what cannot be allowed within the Temple, the Temple being not just Judaic Law but a figure of Law, of an ordering imposed on materials and experiences that, by the effect of the 'rule', become meaningful through the work of distinctions. In this case, what is inside is orderly and what is outside (whatever potential it has for meaning in any other system) becomes the threat to order, without orderability. It is thus to be subdued or excluded. Behind this formulation lies Kristeva's semanalytical hypothesis drawn from, but transforming, the psychoanalytical tradition. Psychoanalysis proposes that to become a subject, we must confront an *symbolic* Otherness (language and the Name of the Father) and effect separation from an archaic, chaotic confusion with an unarticulated Otherness that Bracha Ettinger will track in Lacan as 'Woman-Other-Thing'. Each subject is required to individuate (know a boundary of its own inside/outside, self/other) from a confusion with, and extreme dependency, on the archaic m/Other(ness)—inexplicable because as the infant confronts its world and others, it has no means of deciphering what these Others project, and 'insert' into 'it'. The infant's encounter with the world of Otherness is, therefore, necessarily traumatic, in this logic, registering real effects in the becoming subject excessive to its own not-yet-formed psychic apparatus for dealing with such 'input'.[39]

In psychoanalytical logic, but constantly suppressed by its founding architect, that initiating and initial traumatic encounter is with m/Otherness: the maternal-feminine. This, according to Kristeva, needs to take its place in our understanding of the histories of religion and the histories of subjectivity—the two so significantly entwined for the former to be a research archive for the latter and vice versa. So while key theorists of the sacred—for this is the lynchpin between the two—have focused on the paternal Other, Freud will posit the pre-religious murder of the primal father in his *Totem and Taboo* as establishing 'in one stroke, the sacred, exogamy and society'.[40] Bataille will also see murder, taking life, as the foundational taboo and sacrifice its ritualized negotiation.[41] Kristeva, by contrast, sees how another highly significant element haunts even Freud's writing—the incest taboo—and thus she concludes:

> Could the sacred be, whatever its variants, a two-sided formation? One aspect founded by murder and the social bond made up of murder's guilt-ridden atonement, with all the projective mechanisms and obsessive rituals that accompany it; and another aspect, like a lining, more secret still and invisible, non-representable, oriented towards those uncertain spaces of unstable identity, toward the fragility—both threatening and fusional—of the archaic dyad, toward the non-separation of subject, object, on which language has no hold but one woven of fright and repulsion?[42]

This second aspect is, therefore, the 'confrontation with the feminine'. Does it, however, have to be 'woven of fright and repulsion'? According to Freud, all primally repressed foundations of subjectivity acquire anxiety when they, the repressed, uncannily return to haunt us. But that does not mean, as Ettinger has so eloquently argued, that all of our archaic experiences were, *in themselves* frightening and full of anxiety.[43]

Death and incest (and I stress this concerns the prohibition *of* the mother) form the dominant issues not at the level of imagining sex with the mother, but as a rule to ensure the proper distance and separation between Mother/Son. Please recall here as counterpoint Harrison's argument above that another social/psychic structure exists in which the Mother/Son is the foundational pair; not a sexual, relational pair, but a pairing of symbolic entities of the creative Mother and the blossoming, new rod or branch of resurrected annual fertility; the Son's son-ness is the sign of his youth and seed-bearing. That is, a young man becomes a signifier of, or is, the figuration of the concept, Spring, to the Mother as *durée*, time and continuity, the seasonal cycle and the cycle of life and death.

Two different systems become visible. One is based on Father-right whose transgressive origin is the primal crime of the sons' collective patricide: its symbolic focus is death and the guilt of the sons which gives rise to totemism when the father is imagined as an ancestral animal and is ritually consumed on an annual festival that bonds the community defined collectively as the sons. The other order is based on Mother (to which the daughter succeeds)/Son pair whose once orderly systems focused on life and cyclical resurrection. Once this encounters the patriarchal system, it is inverted by incorporation: hence the mother-son incest taboo that destroys the feminine as the Mother always conceived in relation to a creative partnership and reduces the maternal-feminine to the harping wife. (I have the Zeus and Hera myth in mind.)

Julia Kristeva restores to this whole field of enquiry into the sacred the repressed, overlaid, or foreclosed dimension of feminine Otherness and its constitutive place in both the formation of the social bond and the subjective braid. In her formulations, however, she, nonetheless, retains only the sense of the struggle to separate, the risks of failing, and the sense of the maternal-feminine, however constitutive, as full of fright and danger. So beyond any thought about thinking women dirty or unclean, we can now reapproach the rituals associated with purity and impurity as a semiotic system, the production of rules and the rituals associated for dealing with the inevitable life-processes that, disturbing them, cause them to come into existence. Impurity thus refers to an experience of encounter with the most heavily freighted zones of experience at the indelibly entwined social/subjective threshold: life and death and the way in which this gives rise to a concept of the feminine. Nothing in the ancient world is derived; it is always constitutive within a meaning system, so there is no danger of essentialism or biological determinism.

## VII A structural reading of the 'Red Cow'

There are many complexities in the ritual of the Red Cow, notably that the whole process of preparing the sacrifice, doing it, collecting the ashes, adding the water and sprinkling the water on the affected person,

(a)                                    (b)

1.6  (a) Master of Flémalle, *The Nativity*, 1420, oil on wood, 87 × 70 cm, Musée des Beaux-Arts, Dijon. Detail. (b) Sandro Botticelli, *Mystic Nativity*, 1500, oil on canvas, 108.6 × 74.9 cm, NG 1034, National Gallery, London. Detail.

*makes the agent himself impure*. So the rite for the maximum purification itself defiles. It is this ambiguity that draws Hyam Maccoby to his reinterpretation of a ritual that has left Rabbinic and later commentators, all men, stumped. The crucial clue to the ritual's meaning is there in language, particularly in the phrase used for the *water* resulting from the infusion of the ashes of the wholly *burnt* Red Cow: *mei niddah*. *Niddah* is usually translated as separation and its most common use in the Biblical text refers to *menstruation* and the rules for sexual relations between men and women around this significant monthly process. Thus *mei niddah* is usually translated as 'waters of … *lustration, purification*'. Puzzling? Anything to avoid the perplexing, and for some scholars, obviously horrifying presence of the idea that purification from contact with death might come through contact with a symbolic form of *menstrual water, i.e. symbolic menstrual blood*, hence requiring and recreating through ritual the feminine in its corporeal, creative force. The red animal, burnt (purified by red fire) made red by scarlet threads and dyes incarnates and transmutes into menstrual blood itself.

Hyam Maccoby is not made anxious by this. Firstly, approaching the ritual through a comparative religio-anthropological framework, reminiscent of Catherine Clément cited above, he writes:

Both the redness and the cowness of the Red Cow are striking features that should turn our minds in the direction of comparative religion, rather than Israelite priestly technicalities. The cow goddess in Egypt and India, and her precursor in prehistoric times are relevant …

The surprising appearance of the expression *mei niddah*, water of menstruation, puts the Red Cow outside the confines of the priestly system of purity. It suggests we are dealing here, not just with a sacrificial animal, but with an incarnation of the Goddess, powerful for both good and evil. The goddess Isis-Hathor in Egypt was a cow-goddess, often portrayed with a cow's head. Her appearance with her child Horus in a cow-byre was the inspiration for the Gospel story of Jesus' birth in a manger [(1.6)]. In India, the cow [is] a holy animal who embodied the feminine principle, immune from normal slaughter for food, yet the most potent of sacrifices, whose death had cosmic significance.[44]

By way of support for his identification of *mei niddah* as menstrual blood, Hyam Maccoby reminds us that there is plenty of evidence for the awe and reverence for menstrual blood in ancient literature and contemporary anthropological studies. Many peoples believed that foetuses are formed from menstrual blood which later becomes the milk that nourished the born baby. If the menstrual blood is discarded from the body, unused, its enormous life-creating power, now out of place, crossing the frontier from inside to outside, acquires potential for danger and hence defilement. This links with the issue of the Red Cow's status as a 'virgin'. Maccoby glosses this as not being about a state of childless purity—the Christian misreading of the biblical Hebrew word for a young woman. He argues it means: 'female fecundity owing nothing to the male'.

In varieties of religion where the female was supreme, the male being overwhelmed and overawed by the female mysteries of procreation, sexual intercourse was not regarded (or deliberately ignored) as necessary for childbirth. Just as the female was subject to periodic mysterious bleeding owing nothing to the male and everything to the phases of the divine Moon, so she periodically went into paroxysms of childbirth. These processes were conducted away from male eyes in the female compound, which only later took on an aspect of servitude, isolation and impurity. The word *niddah* undoubtedly means 'separation', but separation is a double-edged concept, as can be seen in the word qodesh ('holiness') which can have negative as well as positive connotations (compare also the ambivalence of the word *badad* 'alone').[45]

Maccoby, therefore, proposes that the ritual of the Red Cow involves a relation between the person who has been made impure by contact with the dead undergoing a kind of ritual re-birth through symbolic re-immersion in the menstrual blood of life. With all our cult of spilt blood, murder, we forget the fertile, life-giving blood specific to the female body. The ritual of the Red Cow produces, therefore, 'living water'—'the active moisture of the Earth itself'. Maccoby reminds us that in Greek religion, too, the worship of the older earth goddesses such as Demeter would also take place outside the Temple—including of course, cow sacrifices known as *Chthonia*. Thus Maccoby discerns, deep inside the texts of Israel's cult of the Sky-God, vestiges of the far more ancient and tenacious cults of the Earth-Goddess:

> The Red Cow is the last vestige in the religion of the Israelite Sky-God of the Earth-Goddess. She is retained to cope with the impurity of death which the Sky-God himself disdains to handle or approach. In the person of the Red Cow, the Goddess gives herself to death, and overcomes it by being transmuted into a substance, *mei niddah*, that is sovereign against death-impurity. There is a kind of resurrection. The Red Cow … is the only sacrifice in the Israelite religion which survives its death, and is preserved, though in a changed form.[46]

Thus the priestly ritual purity code created in the seventh–fifth centuries BCE by urbanized intellectuals elaborating the sophisticated philosophical and theological cult of Judaism's monotheistic version of the Olympians—the One immortal Sky-God—retained, out of loyalty or custom, a deep trace of the preceding cults of the earth-deities whose rituals enact the cycle of birth and death, particularly creating the principle of resurrection from the blood-body-earth. Julia Kristeva, too, sees the maternal-feminine buried inside the priestly system as the dangerous other from which separation must be enforced for the sake of the clarity of the Father's unique Law.

Both models, productive as they are, leave us with that implicit sense of a subsequent progression. In Kristeva's brilliant balancing of anthropological researches in the archaeology of human thought encoded in its cults and rituals, theologies and symbolic systems, with her psychoanalytical archaeology of the strata of subjectivity with its repressed, unconscious but inscribed histories of becoming, we still find that the potential of the maternal-feminine to be a principle of life and hospitality, generosity and transformation is ambivalently qualified by acceptance of the maternal as having to be abjected, mourned and lost. But we can bring it further back into our lives by means of that psychoanalytical insight that as human subjects we are always carrying the potential of all these systems and encounters that were once externalized through the cults and rituals of communal life.

## VIII A matrixial reading of the Red Cow Effect

In 'The Red Cow Effect: The Metramorphosis of Hallowing the Hollow and Hollowing the Hallow' (Hallow being an ancient English word for Holy, as in Hallowe'en, meaning sacred), Bracha Ettinger takes the ambivalence inherent in the textual description of the ritual of the Red Cow as a figure through which to propose a way to think the feminine *beside* the phallic rather than *before,* something necessarily superseded in the patriarchal history of religion (culture) or of the phallicized history of the subject.[47] What Ettinger defines as 'the phallic paradigm' is the logic of the Father-God system: a binary logic of clearly demarcated separations and divisions—on/off, inside/outside, absence/presence—that cannot tolerate passage or ambiguity, sharing or connection, hybridity or plurality. The ambivalence of passage between life and death, between one stage and another, or the perverse 'contagion' of contact across a boundary, such as the living with the dead are the stuff of phallically re-ordering rituals. Yet, as Maccoby revealed, the potency of the Red Cow lay precisely in its ambiguity; the purifying renders impure and purification comes from contact with what in another context is impure-making. The Sky-God logic does not deal with death, and hence cannot deal with life, with process, intermingling, hybridization or confusion of boundaries. Yet the older Earth-Goddess cult was a representation of a mode of thinking and feeling, modes of temporality and cycle, that lived through and dared to encounter intermediate and transformative states. Can we think this psychoanalytically, going beyond its theoretical pairing of castration (division and logic setting) and abjection (the repudiation of incest as the contamination of the maternal body's porous boundaries)? Can this be a feminist move? It could be, but only if we learn to think even more radically beyond this kind of opposition: closed/open, clean/porous, fixed/shifting, pure/impure. Under phallic logic, any oppositional move only reconfirms the logic, even in inversion. So we do not need opposition but a supplementary way of thinking that co-exists with phallic ordering, so useful for thinking logically, but shifts it, allowing transformation, allowing co-affections, and co-emergences and creative borderspace.

Bracha Ettinger is increasingly recognized for proposing such a 'shift inside the phallic paradigm' of both psychoanalysis and the patriarchal symbolic.[48] Recall if you will Julia Kristeva's argument that the study of the history of religions was linked with psychoanalysis and modern cultural theory through engagement with two issues: narcissism and alterity. To these Ettinger makes a specifically feminist contribution by exposing the *masculine* narcissism that has expunged from thought any meaning for the feminine except as its negated other, used, emptied, feared, degraded. If the human forges meaning through the encounter with otherness and the forming of a sense of self, what we are dealing with are two paradigms (at least). One is the *castration* paradigm based on the necessity of separations culminating in that performed by the Symbolic which 'castrates' all subjects, obliging a *sacrifice,* a giving up of something precious of oneself in order to be accessioned to the signifying, familial and social order defined by the Law of the Father. In this model, the initial dyad of Other and Child, Mother and Child in which the Mother includes all Others and carers, yields under the Father's Law. His name (*nom*)/prohibition (*non*) denies the Mother to the Child: the incest taboo. To escape the Father's wrath, the child (neutral at this point but not for long) sacrifices corpo-reality in exchange for a relation (having or being) to the patriarchal Father's signifier: the Phallus. This incorporates into its symbolic function as signifier the sacrificed real of the penis (standing for the *jouissance* of the infantile sexual corporeality shaped by the pulsations and topographies of the drives). This account makes some sense of the accession of the masculine subject. It makes some sense for feminine subjects too, who must also sacrifice the corpo-real to enter the Symbolic and become speaking subjects. But the terms of the deal remain problematic: what does the girl-child sacrifice if she never had a penis fantasmatically to mortgage to the symbolic Phallus? This problem has generated some very fruitful excavations of the mother-daughter bond and continuing effects of the pre-Oedipal phase in feminine subjectivity, each of which has much to offer us: but still they all leave vital areas for further research.

More radically than anyone else to date, Ettinger proposes that, *beside* and *behind* rather than *before* the phallic-castration model, we can discern another model for dealing with the issue of the Other and the formation of a sense of self: subjectivity. She names this supplementary stratum the *matrixial.* As symbol, the Matrix is not an alternative to the Phallus, not a Mother-centred as opposed to Father-centred model, not an Earth versus Sky alternative. It is a different model because it is non-phallic; it is not based on the logic of on/off, present/absent, pure/impure. In one sense, it is a theorization of the sacred in the feminine as passage and frontier understood as borderspace and borderlinking. Ettinger draws into symbolic and imaginative effect what she identifies as borderspace, the potential of the shared threshold, the creative partnership of encounter, the joint transmission and its different registration in each sharing element, hence the shared without fusion, the different without opposition.

The Matrix and its figure, *metramorphosis,* can be approached through a close reading and reworking of Lacanian concepts such as *objet a*— his formulation of the psychic remnant of archaic modes of experience, from the corpo-real, sensory and perceptive zones that are inscribed as the invisible scars of the cutting out of the subject from the cloth of undifferentiated experience of pre-verbal intensities and pre-objective elements.[49] For Lacan, the mother's voice, touch, gaze, and breast leave only the trace of their *absence* in this invisible underside of the emerging subject.[50] The *objet a* can also be tracked through the ambiguities of the ritual of the Red Cow—defined in the Hebrew language with its sexed imagination and grammar as a she-law: Ettinger takes real notice of the formula *Chuka*, a femininized rendering of the normal, masculine word *Chok*: a rule. She-laws do not obey the same logic: they are not just the subordinated feminine of the phallic logic. They open onto other ways we might think subjectivity/sociality and its dilemmas. Challenging those theorists for whom any transgression of the castrative, phallic 'universal' principle of order risks perversion Ettinger argues:

> Where indeed such a transgression in the phallic paradigm does stand for a collapse of the difference between desire, phantasm and event while castration establishes the difference between event and representation, my argument is that in the matrixial paradigm, differentiation-in-transgression stands for a creative principle which does not correspond to the phallic Law and Order and *does not replace* them either. For the Matrix, creation is before-as-beside the univocal line of birth/Creation-as-castration; it is in the impure zone of *neither* day *nor* night, of *both* light *and* darkness. From the prism that I have called *matrixial*, a *feminine espacement hollows* channels of meaning and sketches an area of difference, with sublimatory outlets and ethical values, indeed paradoxical for the phallic paradigm.[51]

Ettinger retranslates *niddah* as 'wandering' rather than separation. Thus the Red Cow becomes an image that refuses the clear-cut of division: on/off. It becomes creative/poetic as the route of transmission and translation that goes beyond the Lacanian binary masculine law: castration = meaning/feminine body: *jouissance* = non-meaning.

> Matrixial aspects are articulated in/for/from art, *neither* via male castration and paternal prohibition *nor* via female body-jouissance-without-sacrifice. The Red Cow effect is a metramorphosis of *impurity as a wandering between* pure and defiled; it negotiates *both* purity *and* impurity/defilement with no collapsing of each into the other yet no separation intended to repress or exclude the darker side, while producing a third stance of im-purity. This metramorphosis vacillates its borderlinks as a re-questioning in *deference* [meaning

both awe/reverence and transport/transmission] of both poles, to be re-negotiated with each new encounter, with no refuge in the Phallus, no pre-arranged resolution.[52]

Ettinger defines metramorphosis—which is to the matrixial what metaphor and metonymy are to the phallic—as a 'creative potentiality that exchanges and transmits traces, phantasies, affects and information within a joint space, where in each exchange an addition is inscribed and which turns reciprocity into a lack of equivalence'.[53]

Most controversially, and subject both to rational misunderstanding and unconscious anxiety-led resistance, Ettinger dares to pose her post-Lacanian model on a passage in Freud's essay on the uncanny where, in discussing the aesthetic effect, Freud mentions two sources of anxiety repressed in infantile complexes. One is castration; the other arises from womb phantasies—*Muttersleibphantasien*—also translated, with Freud's approval, as intra-uterine fantasies.[54] The psychic residue of fantasy material associated with the becoming of human being in the intimacy—the pre-birth incest—of the feminine sexual body is, however, repressed. It is repressed by the subject as is all the primary material, including castration. But it is also subject to another kind of repression by a subject being formed in a phallocentric culture. The relevance, or potential for fantasy and thought, of the sexual specificity of the feminine, the maternal-feminine in Kristeva above, is simply refused by the boys, little ones as well as grown-up psychoanalysts. This is on narcissistic grounds, which Freud fully acknowledged: masculinity has to deny the 'womb' because of what is at stake for its own narcissism. Hence the infantile belief that babies are born from the gender-neutral anus. Freud writes: 'It was only logical that the child should refuse to grant to women the painful prerogative of giving birth' since to do so would be to admit that 'the child' whose neutrality we must explode and say the boy-child cannot admit without damage to his narcissism that he does not possess all the valuable organs. But we do not want to get stuck here with a childish competition about who's got the best or the biggest. The matrixial is not about organs at all. It theorizes subjectivizing principles/processes through which subjectivity is formed, and through which we make meanings based on that deep ambiguity of human subjectivity operating across the thresholds of body and meaning, of corpo-reality and symbolization.

### IX Life and meaning 'in, of, from the feminine'
For thousands of years human societies and their thought systems have struggled to think life, to think *human* becoming and ending. This is where the sacred is not about theology or spirituality but is the domain

of sociology, anthropology, psychoanalysis and aesthetics. Feminism has emerged to articulate its profound discontent with the phallocentric-patriarchal in all its myriad forms, with the exclusive occupation of our symbolic and imaginary universes by the Sky-God, the Father, the One. There is no going back, however, to the nostalgically religious revivalism in some feminisms of a Goddess as a solution. That would allow feminism to fall fatally into religion. There is everything to be gained by understanding in what forms of ancient and contemporary culture the principle, that is figured by such an abstraction, has struggled for articulation in response to our need for understanding of, and perplexity before, the question of our becoming and our passing. In the world beyond enchantment in Modernity, people long for the poetic intensity of ritual and attempt to recover or re-invent it in all sorts of spiritual tourisms and manufactured archaicisms. I think the question is what to do now that we have created knowledge of the human conditions of their origin in our material and emotional needs and the social relations and symbolic-aesthetic systems in which humans struggled to meet them. We are products of history. The growing up enjoined upon us since the Enlightenment by Kant and then Freud involves the painful self-realism and disenchantment of adulthood, and hence the move into cultural theory: the space of critical knowledge combined with psychoanalysis as a method of learning about the layers and strata of our own formations that charge our adult worlds with their archaic intensities, anxieties and fantasies.

Ettinger's work is thus about 'thinking' with a set of models arising out of psychoanalysis at its intersection with feminism and art: the same territory on which Julia Kristeva poses her practice. What I have wanted to explore is how this modern legacy/moment is the 'speaking otherwise' of what was culturally embedded in cult, ritual and, much later, in religion. So I want to conclude by two last returns to the Red Cow. One concerns sacrifice: making sacred from the Latin *sacer facere*. The other concerns the immigrant/stranger. Ettinger writes:

> The Red Cow effect is a metramorphosis in the *register of sacrifice*, where, I suggest, the *im-pure* is exposed as a specific category for *hybridised incompatible composites*, to be differentiated from the phallic opposition of impure/defiled *versus* pure.[55]

Any subject must sacrifice some of his *jouissance* to have access to the Symbolic. Lacan defined what is sacrificed as *objet a*. For Lacan and the phallic system, woman is the *objet a* of the masculine subject and the infant in the womb is woman's *objet a*. There is always a price to pay for us to become sexed speaking human subjects. Woman is sacrificed to become unsignifiable Other-Thing for the phallic law. But through metramorphosis and the hypothesis of the matrixial supplementary stratum, available to *both men and women subjects*, irrespective of gender or sexual orientation, we can suggest that there is another kind of sacrifice of which the Red Cow is her emblem:

> No pure presence, no pure absence, no pure [schism], and their price to pay, but transmissions and transgressions, im-purity and hybridisation, fragmentation, partialisation and pluralisation, and their special price to pay.[56]

These all refer to Ettinger's definition of the matrixial stratum of subjectivity as *subjectivity as encounter*, a severalized capacity for trans-subjectivity bequeathed by its conditions of becoming in the pre-birth incest of feminine sexual specificity as always at least *several*, sharing between partial and unknown grains of subjects-to-be mutually transformed by their un-cognized encounter. Thus this feminine event in the real is the basis for a principle or a dimension of human subjectivity *creatively severalized at a shared borderspace*. The price to pay for this borderlinking and sharing between *unknown* elements of irreducible otherness that are nonetheless co-affecting and co-emerging is the impossibility of not, once fragilized, sharing the trauma of the unknown other, *non-I*, of not processing something of the *non-I* while the other may be processing parts of *me*.

Thus we come to ethics—the relations to the other, alterity, which is what lies behind and finds form in the rituals and symbolic systems remote from us, but in which we participate in just becoming human through the complex formations of our psyches as speaking subjectivities. Ettinger writes:

> The *objet a* is designated as a holy, forbidden, and lost 'sacrifice' proffered as a self-offering to God or to the grand Other, which marks out sublimational processes, indexes aesthetic objects and arouses the experience of the *uncanny*—as phallic … The location of femininity in psychoanalysis by means of the *objet a* as a foreign body involves us fatally with the question of the place of the migrant and exile as psychic reality, as social distress, as aesthetic experience and as ethical problem.[57]

Here follows a lengthy but necessary quotation which I want to work through section by section.

> In the phallic paradigm which opens from the *One* and the *All* and moves between *either* being *or* lack, each imaginary other that the *I* relates to, is a parasitic foreign body destined for annihilation by way of assimilation or banishment: 'it's either me or him' … In the matrixial borderspace, the foreigner *can not* be articulated as a parasite. Here, the exiled is not clipped-out from the system. Here, along the metramorphic borderlinks, the *other* and *I* share connections that when *fading* by ways of transformation are leaving traces in both.[58]

This demonstrates that the phallic and the matrixial paradigms are not symmetrical or opposites. The matrixial introduces a differencing economy for encountering alterity. In the phallic paradigm otherness is either something I can assimilate to identity, identification, incorporation or it is to be repudiated, threat and anxiety policing the borders between self and other. I can either recognize as like me or fear what is different. In the matrixial, *without effacing difference and distinction*, borderspaces that can become thresholds are posited which allow transmissions that register *differently* in each partner through their radical, irreducible unknown-ness that, none the less, exists simultaneously with connectivity and co-affecting. This is because, unlike the phallic paradigm, where the self is cut out from the cloth of the archaic Other and becomes a subject under threat of castration—separation—legislated by the Symbolic Other (language/culture), the Matrix traces through registers of fantasy and thought (imaginary and symbolic) alliance, covenant, and connectivity always-already containing difference and the co-emergence of the several: *subjectivity as encounter* (rather than the phallic model of fusion versus separation). Ettinger continues:

> In the matrixial model which opens from *severality* and *contingency*, the *I* and the unrecognised *non-I* are partners in a temporary, unpredictable and unique covenant, in which each participant—subjects and objects—is partial and relative in a composite, joint space. The *non-I* is *not* Other, but, like the *I,* is a *becoming-in-ter-with* and therefore, a clear cut between the living and the dead, the pure and impure, so basic in the Phallus is beyond the matrixial scope; a voyage [*niddah*] between them, so paradoxical in the Phallus becomes meaningful in the Matrix.[59]

This takes us back to the Red Cow effect which she can now interpret as a figure of such travelling dispersion:

The ashes of the Red Cow are dispersed, diffracted, aspired, and sprayed according to a becoming-feminine-Other-desire. The Red Cow sacrificial borderlink which quivers and glints from *beyond appearance* is not *the* Holy—as Other or God—nor it is *the* Impure—as yet another Other or Dead; but it is the *transversion* of the holy with the impure and their co-emergence in im-purity without blending and without annihilation with-in a process of a *becoming-woman-between, inter-with the Other*.

Thus 'woman' is not an ontology, or a condition of an anatomically sexed body. The feminine is available to all subjects as an originary psychic-symbolic positioning and potentiality for relatedness and connectivity. For those of us who become feminine subjects or who have certain potentialities to give life in a particular relation of sexuality and generation of a child, the Matrix repeats. It repeats, in fantasy since we *know* nothing of the body's processes in this except as we, already subjects, imagine and think their *meaning* and *affects,* the archaic but ever-acting matrixial severality of our own human becoming. Feminine subjects who bear a child thus have additionally charged but never exclusive access or susceptibility to the matrixial dimension. The phrasing 'becoming-woman-between, inter-with the Other' forces phallic language to allow in the differencing matrixial level.

The *Red Cow effect* expresses a metramorphosis that does not perish in a split but diminishes to a small or large extent as a consequence of dispersion and stretching among the several. Wandering, scattered and sprayed, it is impossible to re-gather the Red Cow's ashes-traces; one can only find some of them in other and additional matrixes, and follow their footsteps to a labyrinth not envisioned in advance, woven in the course of creating its route through strolling along it.

A feature of the matrixial covenant is that it is contingent and unpredictable: it is not a law of being generating its neuroses in the play of unity and process, law and perversion. It is entirely dependent on the potentiality of the partners-in-difference. Hence it is par excellence *poetic,* that is to say, creative, and *aesthetic,* transforming the subject's inner world through the affect registered there by an other that is non-I, and *ethical* since it is contingent on susceptibility and hospitality or fragilization towards an unknown other whose alterity yet shapes me intimately. The Matrix is, therefore, neither about historical time, the time of se-

quence, narrative, development and nation nor monumental and cyclical, the *durée* of which Kristeva writes in 'Women's Time'.[60] It opens
passageways to the past, the lost histories and histories of loss which
are caught in the no-time of the traumatic. It opens to the future
through the processing by others which Ettinger thinks through recent
work on the notion of the wit(h)ness—belatedly enabling the movement from frozen traumatization to co-processed memory.

> My matrixial *objet a* initiates yours to join in; you proffer in it the
> relation that you lost together with others, you are the witness of
> your offering and you offer your witnessing on to further assem-
> blages so that not in total perishing a matrixial sacrifice is inscribed
> in culture.[61]

It will be by these means that the intense issues that confront us
today—*us* being in need of narrowed, geo-cultural specification to the
world I am thinking in now: Europe, industrial, globalizing, capitalist
countered by thinking feminist dissidence—the issues of other as exile,
migrant, refugee, the postcolonial struggle against racism, the violent
and militant forms of xenophobia at the heart of fundamentalism that
we will see that feminism is far from over and spent. It is literally vital
to any future. It is in feminist thought at this level that we will find, not
the nostalgic route back to Neolithic, pre-industrial, agricultural cultic
solutions to necessity and alterity, but a means of transformation, a poetic principle that is committed, as was that ancient world, to life.

I hear in Julia Kristeva's attempt to make feminists think about maternity without enacting the phallic mother-phobia, a call for an Arendt-
ian ethics of life that she firmly places in the feminine. I hear an ethics
of life-oriented shared-alterity in Bracha Ettinger's constellation of subtle post-Lacanian, relational feminist psychoanalysis with aesthetic/po-
etic practice that also works through—mourning—the encounter with
mass death which is the traumatic legacy of the murderous twentieth
century. I hear their urgency, their despair, their conviction and their
hope through the intersection of thought and art. The phallic/Sky-
God cults that have come to dominate the globe through the major
universalist and proselytizing religions that account for billions of people's imaginative universes have gone on too long for human safety.
They do indeed proffer visions of ethical lives with many senses of the
sacredness of daily life, mercy and charity. But they have to confront
within themselves their preoccupation/fascination with death. They
have delivered much to value in thought and social order. But now they
are becoming ever more deadly. We have to think through history to a

futurity that really understands why beauty queens and assembled inter-national feminists aim to work for 'world peace'. This does not lie in domination, homogeneity, globalization, nor does it come from the weak notions of multi-culturalism and toleration. With the rising death tolls from terrorism, we see the shallowness of that defence.

We need to think the history of the sacred and see the sacred as ac-tive within the structuration of subjectivities; thinking through the his-tory of religions with the histories of the subject. We need to seek the poetic, creative, transformative model that will not imperialistically or phallically replace its other(s), but shift and supplement, allowing the generative play of masculine and feminine as principles of structural, sexual differences, not mirrors of each other in some dumb and ulti-mately asymmetrical equality. The feminine has been so censored that even feminists are afraid to think about it; insisting on only the social construction of gender, women stand by and allow the greatest revo-lution in thought of the twentieth century, feminism, to be put in the waste bin of past-their-sell-by-date fashions. The sacred and the femi-nine: the threshold between body and meaning, between life and thought are not willed away so easily—or we will pay the enormous cost of being left only the militarism of the Sky-Gods and their cultures of death.

Because the feminine is the figure of time and generosity to the other before and after me or birth/death/resurrection, the feminine is the figure of futurity.[62] Toward the end of his life, Bracha Ettinger solicited from Emmanuel Levinas, philosopher of the ethical, a statement on the feminine: 'the feminine is that difference, the feminine is that in-credible thing in the human, by which it is affirmed that without me the world has a meaning.'[63] Hedged with care so that he is not thought to be saying that we can get rid of women, Levinas is offering us another understanding of this profound rapport between the feminine and the sacred: life as the creative condition of both the other and the future. This finally links back to Kristeva's notion of maternity as the principle of generosity that transmutes the violence of eroticism—the instanti-ation of singular subjectivity—into the generosity that allows the other to live. If what she calls the maternal-feminine is the principle of life, it also offers something specific for our understanding of sustainable sociality in the terrifying conditions of this new age. That is why at our stage of cultural and social crisis we need to re-excavate, for our own future, the relations between the sacred and the feminine and even to dare to pose a specific feminine sacred through the profound extension offered by Ettinger's revelation of the Matrix: the matrixial being a path of wandering towards … never claiming a one and only—a path that can only be created in a weaving of several threads, strings with different histories, traumas, and desires, each ready to resonate with partialized elements of otherness and others in the unpredictable covenant of creation/life with all its unknown elements and dark places that are life and death.

# 2

# THE PRIESTESS OF ATHENA GROWS A BEARD
## Latent Citizenship in Ancient Greek Women's Ritual
### Barbara Goff

I take my title from the Greek historian Herodotus (Herodotus, *Histories* 1.175), where it is claimed of the people near Halicarnassus that they 'used to be warned of the approach of disaster to themselves and those nearby because the priestess of Athena grew a long beard'.[1]

When we study classical sources on women we are often faced with information that we struggle to classify. Is this the momentary eruption into history of a woman whose facial hair would nowadays be thought unfortunate? Is it the careful deployment of a false beard by a woman psychically equipped to sense danger? Or is it a total fantasy on the part of Herodotus or his informants? In the absence of an answer I shall suggest here that we can understand such references as traces of a particular conception of the female. I shall seek to show that such references construct women in ritual contexts as 'latent citizens', that is, as people who are not citizens and not identified with the projects of the city, but who may be called upon to operate as such and who will then perform, as the priestess does, to uphold the welfare of the city.

The topic of women's ritual practice in ancient Greece is a tricky one to include under the rubric of the Sacred and the Feminine, for a number of reasons. We have from antiquity hardly any literature or artefacts produced by women. Thus, because our evidence mainly comes from male-authored sources, the discussion of the 'feminine' is put under a question mark. Similarly, the notion of the 'sacred' is debatable in the ancient Greek context. Greek religion had no theocracy and very little theology, and was much more a question of practice than of belief—

what you did rather than what you thought.[2] This characteristic of practice leads many scholars to use a terminology of 'ritual' rather than of
'religion' or the 'sacred'. Yet this concept is also crucial to how I believe
women's ritual activity worked in its relationship to ancient Greek gender ideology. Within this ideology, women were constructed as permanent legal minors, unable to own property, to take serious decisions, to
exercise public roles, to express their sexuality or to give voice to their
concerns. Overall, scholars have often characterized women as secluded
within the domestic context and excluded from the public arena—this
is the ideological desideratum even when actual daily life does not con-
form. Moreover, a traditional figure like Pandora shows that women
are seen as inherently hostile to the projects of civilization and culture,
which must therefore be undertaken by men.[3]

In this context, Greek women's ritual activity was ideologically
charged, tasked with producing women who had internalized a version
of themselves geared to the needs of others, and who could, therefore,
function well in a male-dominated culture. Because ritual relies, however, on practice and action, women in the ritual context were endowed
with a certain level of autonomous agency. Since it is frequently women
who perform the rituals, they cannot be completely subordinate to the
rituals; they are the subjects of the ritual process as well as its objects.
Moreover, women's ritual practice is in pointed contradiction to the
prevailing tenor of their lives. In order to perform rituals women come
out of the house into the public arena, gather in social groups, and organize their own time and space, often in homosocial gatherings without the supervision of men. Women are visibly present to the
community, frequently performing rituals vital to the community's welfare. Quite often, certain women, like priestesses, are commemorated
in honorific inscriptions which would be put up in public spaces. While
ritual confirms a great deal of the normative ideological manifold, upholding the notions of female inferiority and malevolence, and incul-
cating a female identity that is confined to domesticity and certain kinds
of fertile sexuality, it can also contradict precisely these constructions.[4]

Faced with this complex situation, I shall concentrate here on a part
of it, and specifically on the way that ritual mediates between women
and the city to offer to women a quasi-political identity, a form of latent
citizenship. It is hard to exaggerate the importance of the city or 'polis'
in the classical period of ancient Greece; a self-governing political entity
of about 30,000, the polis was the primary unit of identification.
Athens, the city about which we are best informed, was democratic,
which in the Greek context meant total participation by all the citizens
in all the city's decisions. But citizenship in Athens and elsewhere was
restricted to the free adult male; the Greek city is often analysed by

scholars as a 'citizens' club' defined by the exclusion of women, children and slaves.[5] Yet it may not be totally appropriate to focus on such a legalistic definition of citizenship, because the polis also has other ways of relating to its members, of which ritual is one of the most important. Since women perform many of the city's ritual actions, the ritual context can and does identify them with the city, even though at other times it emphasizes that they are the 'other' by which the city is defined. In ritual, then, women's latent citizenship comes to the fore. Overall, however, we can see that the female constitutes a limit case for the city, a test of what the city can and cannot embrace and manage.

To discuss how women's latent citizenship emerges and becomes prominent in ritual I shall focus on the polis of Athens, although other cities will also feature briefly. Having considered a collective ritual and some ritual actions of individual women, I shall conclude by discussing an Athenian drama.

The *Thesmophoria* was an important ritual that involved all the women of the city. Although best known from Athenian sources, versions of this women's ritual are found in many locations throughout the Greek world, so that we possess quite a lot of detailed if confusing information. To the women who perform it, the *Thesmophoria* offers the contours of a kind of citizenship, although it can also be read to construct its female participants as the outsiders who define male citizenship by contrast.

For the *Thesmophoria* as celebrated in Athens, the free adult women— who would normally also be wives and mothers—leave their homes and congregate on the Acropolis, the hill in the centre of the city, where they live for three days in makeshift structures that we translate as tents. The first day is called *Anodos*, the Going-Up; the second day is *Nesteia* or Fasting; and the third is called *Kalligeneia*, the day of Beautiful Birth. At some point during the festival the women performed a particular piece of fertility magic involving dead piglets, but the festival was concerned with its female participants as much as with the agricultural territory of Athens. On the days of Fasting and Beautiful Birth the women are understood to replicate in their actions the mourning of the goddess Demeter when she thinks her daughter Persephone has disappeared, and her joy when they are reunited.[6] This narrative establishes a complex relationship to marriage, since the goddess lamented because Persephone had been snatched away for a forced marriage, but was eventually reconciled to her daughter's new status. While the women are thus clearly acting out their identity as mothers, they also exhibit themselves as chaste wives, in that they wear no floral garlands, eat garlic (which puts off potential lovers) and sit on branches of a plant that is renowned as an anti-aphrodisiac. The particular complex of female identities and activities in the ritual is said to promote the fertility not only of people but also of the land.

In their marital chastity, and in their contribution to the productivity of crops and herds, the women at the *Thesmophoria* work at preserving the polity, and as a result, the contours of citizenship begin to emerge within the ritual. In Aristophanes' comedy *Women at the Thesmophoria* the women meet in a properly constituted democratic assembly complete with herald, opening prayers, president, secretary, speakers and disputes over who gets to speak first. This is a comic gesture, of course, but it may well respond to a perception within Greek culture that this ritual brought forth the image of a 'city of women'. For instance, the site of the festival in Athens is generally agreed to have occupied the very spot where the citizen assembly met; in addition, normal assembly business was suspended during the festival, so it was indeed as if women had taken over the city. The *Thesmophoria* extends a form of citizenship to women in other ways as well. In one legal speech, women choose two of their number to be in charge of the *Thesmophoria* in an Athenian neighbourhood. The word used of the women's position of responsibility, which is also found in an inscription that concerns the festival, is *archousai*; this is the feminine plural of *archon*, the standard term for male Athenian officials.[7] A similar parallel appears in another inscription concerning a *Thesmophoria* in Greek Asia Minor. The inscription begins 'Thus the women decided …' where the word for 'decided' is *edoxe*, exactly that which appears in inscriptions recording the official business of the various Greek cities.[8] In such inscriptions, however, the wording is 'Thus the assembly decided …' reminding us that the women cannot be convened in an actual assembly or other analogous organization but remain simply 'women'.

The *Thesmophoria* has another important political or civic dimension, and that is to prove the status of the women who participate. Men who enjoyed a certain level of income were required to finance their wives' attendance at the festival and to provide a feast for the wives of their neighbours. If for some reason a wife does not receive this kind of maintenance, it can be taken in the legal context as a sign that she is not a legitimate wife but only a concubine (Isaeus 3.80). If she is not properly married, her children cannot be citizens and cannot inherit from a citizen father. Conversely, to be chosen as *archousa* could help to demonstrate a wife's legitimacy. It is notable that these legal cases on inheritance need to bring in the topic of women's ritual practice in order to prove the right or otherwise to the estate; a woman's demonstrable attendance at the *Thesmophoria* permits her to perform her proper role in raising legitimate children who can inherit.

I have suggested that because the *Thesmophoria* constructs women as good wives and mothers, it is also a site for the elaboration of their connections to the city and for the emergence of their latent citizenship. The festival, however, is not straightforward in its account of women as citizens; it also shows that women are not properly part of the city and so can be detached from it. The temple of Demeter, where the festival is usually held in cities outside Athens, is often sited in a slightly strange way, within the city walls but far away from other important buildings—or sometimes quite a long way outside the city walls. Its relationship to the other dimensions of the city is thus slightly tenuous.[9] The month in which the *Thesmophoria* is held is similarly significant because it also sees several rituals for men, which are implicitly contrasted to the *Thesmophoria*. Two festivals were held in honour of the legendary hero Theseus, of which one included young men dressed as women, a ritual event that has been plausibly interpreted as a type of initiation into manhood—young men act out the female in order to learn how to avoid becoming feminized in future.[10] Most explicit about making men is the third festival, the *Apatouria*, which is the occasion when young boys are registered into their fathers' kinship groups. This registration proves a boy's legitimacy and thus allows him to take his place in the life of the city.

We can understand the close proximity of these highly gender-specific festivals in different ways. We could say that the *Thesmophoria* is thrown into relief by the surrounding efforts to identify men with political roles, and thus that it emerges as an institution for elaborating parallel female versions of citizenship. Yet at the same time the festival's relation to its surroundings replays an important distinction between male and female identity. The males move through explicit, ritually delineated stages in order to attain an adulthood that will be politically authoritative. For the females on the other hand no amount of ritual work will position them as fully equipped citizens.

Other elements of the *Thesmophoria* can be seen to detach the women celebrating it from the city rather than to identify them with it. Some of the festival's components were interpreted as representations of a prehistoric, rather than civic, way of life. One source claims that the celebrants in Sicily 'imitate the ancient way of life' in their conduct of the festival (Diodorus Siculus 5.4.7), and as mentioned above the Athenian women at the *Thesmophoria* live in makeshift shelters and sit on branches rather than on proper furniture. The historian Plutarch asks, 'Why is it that at the *Thesmophoria* the women of Eretria cook their meat, not by fire, but by the rays of the sun?' (Plutarch, *Greek Questions* 298 b–c). Although he goes on to offer a practical explanation, we can see that this custom too could be interpreted as going back to a precivilized state. These elements of the ritual enact an imaginary era before the constitution of the city, marked by deprivation and the absence of the civilized arts. Feminist scholars have argued that male-dominated societies tend to produce myths that validate male dominance by invoking an earlier era of matriarchy which was primitive and inadequate.[11] If we can include the *Thesmophoria* under this rubric, we can see that its participants act out their exclusion from the civilized polis as well as demonstrating their latent citizenship.

In line with this notion of the primitive and brutal, we might note that the Greek imagination associated the *Thesmophoria* with violence by the massed females against the male, and so assimilated it to a favourite Greek nightmare, that of the women who get out of hand and get into positions of power. There are two narratives especially that speak of this violence. In one, Messenians attack Spartan women who are celebrating the festival of Demeter, but the women 'were inspired by the goddess to defend themselves, and most of the Messenians were wounded' by the sacrificial implements (Pausanias, *Description of Greece* 4.17.1). In the second, Battos the king of Cyrene is determined to penetrate the women's secrets, but is discovered and castrated with the sacrificial implements (Aelian fragment 44 ed. Hercher).[12] In Aristophanes' comedy already mentioned, *Women at the Thesmophoria*, yet another man infiltrates the proceedings, but in order to hide among the female celebrants he has to be depilated and dressed as a woman, and to hide his genitals—which when you are wearing the comic costume of a huge floppy red phallus, is not easy—and that kind of humiliation probably counted as castration for an ancient Greek male.

The *Thesmophoria* constructs a civic identity for its participants but also helps to reinforce the notion of the female as outside the parameters of normal human existence. In the case of ritual actions undertaken by individual women the 'latent citizenship' that I am investigating is often more clearly demonstrated. The individual women who are most likely to be identified in ritual with their cities are priestesses. To use the term 'priestess' to translate the Greek *hiereia* may be misleading, because a Greek priestess rarely wields sacred powers, nor is she in charge of sacred texts. How the *hiereia* appears in inscriptions, which constitute much of our evidence for Greek priestesses, is as the guardian of the temple precinct and of its activities, with what seem to us the secular powers to remove people from the precinct, for instance, and to fine them if they misbehave while there. The priestess is almost always said to act 'on behalf of the city'. In other texts, the priestess actually defends the city, and at Athens, intervenes in the city's history on two separate occasions.

In Herodotos (*Histories* 5.72) Kleomenes, a Spartan invader of the late sixth century, seizes the Athenian Acropolis and enters the temple. The priestess of Athena rises from her seat and says 'Spartan stranger, retreat. Do not enter the holy place. No Dorian [ = Spartan] is allowed to enter.' She is perhaps inspired by the sexually ambiguous figure of the patron goddess Athena, a female deity who is also a warrior; she is certainly empowered to make her defiant utterance by the authority of her cult position. Another priestess of Athena makes an equally significant gesture against the Persian invaders, in the early fifth century BCE. There was a dispute, roughly between conservative and radical factions, over whether to stay in the city and fight the Persians or to evacuate the city and rely on the newly built navy. The priestess of Athena announced that the holy snake on the Acropolis had ceased to eat the regular offering of a honey-cake, indicating that the goddess had abandoned the site and that the people should probably leave too (Herodotos, *Histories* 8.41). The priestess's utterance thus indirectly supported the radical party against that which may have included her natural allies, such as the treasurers of Athena, who voted for remaining on the Acropolis. The city was, in fact, evacuated and the Persians were decisively beaten in the ensuing sea-battle.

While it is unlikely that the priestess consciously espoused a radical political agenda, it is equally improbable that she had no idea of the potential of her statement. If we dismiss these episodes as part of the intense mythologizing generated by a critical period in Athenian history, we should note that our choice removes from history women who use their cult position to make interventions for the salvation of their city. To make this choice is thus to silence the priestesses even more effectively than has the male-dominated culture of classical Athens, since that culture at least imagined and sanctioned their interventions.

Some versions of priestesses defending the city involve the impersonation of a goddess. At Pellene, in the third century BCE, the invaders were routed by an apparition of Athena, but how did this apparition come about? In one source, (Polyaenus, *Strategemata* 8.59), the priestess of Athena, who is the 'most beautiful and tallest of the young girls' deliberately dons the goddess's helmet and panoply in order to perform the day's ceremony, and so terrifies the enemy. For the other source, (Plutarch, *Aratus* 31–32), however, the woman concerned is a war captive—also distinguished for beauty and height—who is forced to wear her captor's helmet as a sign that she belongs to him. When she emerges from the temple where she is being kept she terrifies the enemy with her resemblance to Athena. The difference between these two female figures seems to reside within an anxiety about whether women are or are not part of the city; while the war captive signifies that women's role is to be exchanged among men, and that, therefore, their allegiances can change, the priestess is installed at the heart of the city and her loyalty is demonstrated. Her ritual position allows her to take an initiative in order to save the city, whereas the hapless captive saves the city only by accident. Significantly perhaps, the Pellenians themselves prefer the version which relies on the priestess's initiative.

The latent citizenship of the priestess comes to the fore when she defends the city, which she can do by virtue of her ritual position. Sometimes we see a variant of this in which a ritual is said to be instituted after a woman or women perform an act that saves the city. In the early fifth century BCE. the women of Argos are said to have defended the city against the Spartans, and their prowess is commemorated in a ritual called *Hybristika* (Plutarch, *Bravery of Women* 245). The festival of Ares at Tegea similarly commemorates the women's valour against the Spartans (Pausanias, *Description of Greece* 8.48.4–5). Women are celebrated for saving the city, and their bravery is commemorated in ritual activities.

However, certain aspects of the rituals show that the situation is anomalous and disturbing. The *Hybristika* requires women to wear men's tunics and beards and men to wear women's robes and veils, thus upsetting the normal significations of gender; the festival of Ares is marked by a similar disruption of normal categories, because the women eat all the meat at the sacrifice and leave none for the men.[13] The women's latent citizenship, emerging in their military actions and in the rituals, can be a problem for the city as well as a deliverance, because if women participate in the city's preservation, men will inevitably begin to lose the signs of their participation and experience instead the feminine contours of exclusion. What is signified by these ritual anomalies is not simply an inversion of roles, but rather the zero-sum structure of Greek gender ideology; according to this uncompromising arithmetic, if women start to behave like men, men will become women. This equation is particularly clear at Tegea where the customary organization of sacrificial meat between the genders is not inverted, which would still provide both sexes with meat, but completely altered so that men receive none. Women's latent citizenship is important and necessary to the city but it is also undermining.

One way in which Greek women save the city is by sacrificing themselves for it. Human sacrifice is quite a pervasive figure in Greek culture, but as far as we can see there was no institution of human sacrifice in historical times—instead, there is a constant cultural elaboration on the image or fantasy of it.[14] This happens especially in the ritual context, where cults are often said to commemorate a sacrifice, especially one by a young woman. Why the victim is usually a young woman is, I think, because the female who is not yet married and reproductively active is marginal and expendable—but in her death her latent citizenship emerges and shows that even a marginal figure can successfully identify with the city.[15]

One such figure in Athens is Aglauros, the daughter of the early king of Athens Kekrops, who leapt voluntarily from the Acropolis to her death, in order to save the city from defeat. She was subsequently honoured not only with a cult but also in the oath taken by the young men who were about to finish their military training and become warriors. These *ephebes* swore in the name of Aglauros that they would defend the city. In her death the sacrificial daughter renounces the possibility of giving the city children, but acquires numerous paradoxical 'sons' in the ephebes, whom the city identifies with itself in her name. Their access to the position of citizen testifies to her latent citizenship.

There is a similar connection between sacrifice and ritual commemoration in the fragments of a tragedy by Euripides. Praxithea, the wife of another early Athenian king, willingly yields her daughter as a sacrifice to ensure victory over the enemy. The drama goes on to claim that Praxithea was subsequently installed by Athena as her first priestess, and we can deduce that ritual service constitutes a reward and recognition of a woman's ability to identify with her city. Interestingly enough we also know of a historical analogy to Praxithea's reward. The historian Plutarch claims that a woman, Xenokrite, helped to overthrow the tyrant of Cumae, and was subsequently elected priestess of Demeter by the citizens. The citizens apparently considered that the honour would be as pleasing to the goddess as it was appropriate to the woman (Plutarch, *Bravery of Women* 262).

So far I have discussed the notion of latent citizenship in terms of the *Thesmophoria*'s representation of good wives and mothers, and in terms of priestesses defending their city in different ways. Although my examples have mostly come from texts that are called historical, the ancient Greek notion of history is of course very different from our own, so that the histories may contain much more imaginative material than we might countenance. In terms that classicists use, there is not, so far, very much 'hard' evidence for women's latent citizenship in the ritual context. You cannot get much harder, however, than letters engraved on a stone, and I would like to close this part of my discussion with an example that is known to us only from an inscription. Dating from mid-fifth-century-BCE Athens, this inscription involves a historical case of election to the post of priestess.

The inscription concerns the selection process for the priestess of *Athena Nike*, Athena of Victory. Commentators agree that the decree seems not to establish the office but to modify it, so that we may posit a historical change in the method of selection, and it looks as if the change was in the direction of a more democratic process. Traditionally, the priestesses of Athena were drawn from a restricted field of prominent families with pedigrees going back decades, but this decree involves the words 'from all the Athenians', indicating that the traditional family was to take a back seat from now on and yield to a more inclusive form of organization. In Greek, 'from all the Athenians' could indicate all the Athenian men, or all the Athenian women, but because it is a priestess at issue, commentators agree that we must translate here 'all the Athenian women'. The word before this, in the Greek text, indicates that the selection is being made by lot, which was the usual way in which male political officials were appointed under the democracy. So, we can understand that the post of priestess is to be filled by an allotment among all Athenian women. We thus have a serious democratic alternative to the pre-existing restricted offices, and indeed many scholars have suggested that in fifth-century Athens there was a perceived need to bring ritual practice into line with developments in the sphere of politics, and thus to organize it along more democratic lines.[16] What seems to me utterly crucial is that this particular reorganization of ritual practice also aligns women, specifically, with the democratic procedures of their city—it in fact constitutes an unprecedented extension of democratic practice to women. The city deliberately rearranges an element of women's ritual practice so that it models the political practice available to the male citizens.

What I hope to have shown here is how ancient Greek ritual practice mediates between women and the city, presenting versions of women who are included by and identify with the city, even if sometimes problematically. For ancient Greek women, such inclusion is accomplished primarily in the ritual context, and I use the term 'latent' citizenship because such 'citizenship' requires the ritual context to become visible. The customary representations of women hold that the female is dangerously inferior, constitutionally hostile to the projects of civilization, and best confined to the silence of the domestic interior, so ritual practice can provide an account of female identity that offers a genuine alternative. Since ritual is, however, an ideologically charged practice, it tends to give with one hand and take away with the other; some rituals contradict themselves and show women simultaneously as included in the city and excluded from it. In connection with other elements of Greek culture this aspect of ritual makes it clear that the female is a limit case for the city, a test of what it can and cannot manage to include within its structures.

To close, I would like to feed these perceptions of ritual into a partial reading of one of the important literary achievements of ancient Greece, Aeschylus' tragic trilogy the *Oresteia*. This trilogy takes us from the aftermath of the Trojan war to the establishment of proper legal and ritual institutions in Athens. To ensure success in the war ten years earlier, Agamemnon, chief of the Greek troops, had sacrificed his daughter; now he returns home bringing with him a princess of Troy to be his concubine. For these two actions his wife Klytemnestra kills him, and she is supported in the deed by Aigisthos, her lover and Agamemnon's cousin with pretensions to the throne. Agamemnon's son Orestes escapes to exile, and in the second play of the trilogy, he returns in disguise to take revenge for his father's death, which in this perverted situation entails that he must kill his mother. Ordered on to this act of vengeance by the god Apollo, he is, nonetheless, pursued for it by the Furies, who are avenging spirits of his mother. They hound him to Athens where the goddess Athena convenes the first court to try him. Debating whether it is worse to kill a husband or a mother, the jury is split, and Orestes is finally acquitted.[17]

Over the span of the trilogy I read a move from women showing a dangerous autonomy in ritual to ritual peacefully mobilizing women in the service of the city. Klytemnestra devises rituals of homecoming for Agamemnon that are designed to lure him and the citizens into a false sense of security. In particular, she inveigles Agamemnon into entering the house by treading ceremoniously on a special carpet. But since the carpet is made of precious materials and should not be trampled underfoot, her ritualized gesture puts Agamemnon in a position of transgression and marks him out for retribution. Cassandra, the Trojan princess and Agamemnon's concubine, is a prophetess with a cultic relation to Apollo, but she has offended the god and is doomed to utter prophecies that are never believed. Thus when she is telling the citizens what will happen to Agamemnon inside the house, she seems to them to be raving. In the second play Orestes takes his revenge, supported by his sister and a chorus of Trojan slaves. The ritual activity consists largely of lamentation by these slaves for the dead Agamemnon. This may in fact be slightly problematic, because the women's lamentations help to push Orestes on to his highly questionable deed, and also because female funerary lament was restricted by law in fifth-century Athens.[18]

In the last play, when Orestes is acquitted, the city is threatened by the anger of the Furies, but Athena manages to deflect them and to transform them into the Eumenides, the Kindly Ones. Other females in the play are transformed as well. Instead of an apparently raving and doomed prophetess, the play opens with an appearance by the priestess of Apollo, the Pythia. She is a prophetess too but she is one installed and recognized by the community, and the prophecies she makes are clear and sanctioned by Apollo. The development of the trilogy robs the priestess/prophetess figure of her transgressive voice and energy, but succeeds in finding her a productive role within the confines of the city.

A similar move can be discerned, I suggest, at the end of the play, which is also the end of the trilogy. The trial concludes by finding the death of a husband far more reprehensible than that of a mother; Orestes' escape from the consequences of his action means that the female is downgraded. The Furies first rage at the injustice, but are then persuaded to calm down and stay in Athens, and they miraculously accede, even though they are required to go and live as underground goddesses, under the Acropolis. The play closes with a procession of Athenians to welcome the Eumenides to their new home. A number of different women occupy the most prominent positions in this procession; the goddess Athena mentions the women who tend her cult image, girls, wives and older women, and it is clear that their ritual activity in serving the Eumenides will contribute to the future welfare of Athens.[19] The dangerous autonomy of Klytemnestra is thus exchanged for the productive anonymity of women who serve the city in a ritual capacity. The play has reviled Klytemnestra and downgraded motherhood, but it needs the ritual capacities of women—and their latent citizenship—in order to build a fully-functioning city.

# 3

# THE SACRED, THE FEMININE AND FRENCH FEMINIST THEORY

*Daphne Hampson*

Invited to write on 'the sacred' and 'the feminine' in relation to French feminist theory, I find myself ambivalent. There is no question but that, given its Lacanian psychoanalytic context, French theory has cast light on the structure of Western religion. There is present an analysis both more profound and more subtle than has been achieved by Anglo-Saxon feminists. However, when it comes to questions of 'the sacred' and 'the feminine', I sense that Julia Kristeva and Luce Irigaray (whom I shall discuss) come from quite another cultural context, in which what it is to be a woman has been differently determined and symbolized. As compared with their French and post-Catholic, and in Kristeva's case also post-Orthodox background, I am aware that my Anglo-Saxon and post-Protestant position leaves me differently placed. Again, when it comes to a consideration as to how, given such an analysis, we should move forward, I have different emphases. I judge French theory not radical enough; too caught up with a particular understanding of the nature of language and the gendered speaking position of subjects. Moreover, although I have rejected Christianity as a masculinist and mythological system of thought, I remain in some sense a spiritual person. This also entails my arriving at a different point from two women whom I assume are to all intents and purposes atheist.

I commence with what I value about French thought; the insights it has given me. The heritage here goes back a generation to Simone de Beauvoir, to whom we as theorists owe so inestimably much. Translating Hegel's master/slave paradigm into the gender polarity of the man/woman relationship, de Beauvoir names woman as 'slave'. [1] Each party gains their self-understanding as the other reflects him or her back to him or herself. Moreover, taking on board Jean-Paul Sartre's insight into false-consciousness, de Beauvoir recognizes that the 'slave' sees the world through the eyes of the one who occupies the subject position, the 'master'. Thus she writes: 'Women do not set themselves up as Subject and hence have erected no virile myth in which their projects are reflected; they have no religion or poetry of their own: they still dream through the dreams of men. Gods made by males are the gods they worship.'[2] The second generation of French theorists, Irigaray and Kristeva, are furthermore influenced by Lacanian psychoanalytic thought, recognizing that our language, which is the 'symbolic' (gendered male), is fundamental to what we are. Hence women are up against a double predicament. Not only must they come into their own, ceasing to see the world through the eyes of men, but they lack a place other than the masculine construal of 'woman' in our received culture from which to do this.

A central pillar of that cultural construction which is the male symbolic has been transcendent monotheism, as both Irigaray and Kristeva so rightly see. Monotheism necessarily creates that which is 'other' to itself: when God is 'male' then that 'other' comes to be gendered 'female' in what is a hierarchical dichotomy. This is written into the structure of biblical thought. Take the book of Hosea (my example). JHWH (as 'male') takes the subject position in relation to the people of Israel (gendered female), paralleled by the prophet Hosea in relation to the prophet's wife Gomer. She, like Israel, is deemed to have gone astray, indeed depicted in lewd language and compared to a prostitute; whereas the presupposition is that she should be obedient to Hosea as Israel to JHWH. Man takes the 'female' position in relation to God, but he takes the subject position in relation to woman, who is always at the bottom of the heap. Kristeva points out that male saints have often seen themselves as 'female' in relation to Christ.[3] Further we may say the Church is designated the bride of Christ; while the Virgin Mary in Catholicism is said to represent the highest to which humanity can attain in relation to God. Incidentally we should note how these metaphors exemplify what Object Relations theorists term male 'splitting'. On the one hand woman is set on a pedestal, perfect and untouchable, both virgin and mother; on the other hand, she is cast out as slut, associated with the earth, nature, and sexuality.[4] Both projections, so one may conjecture, reflect the male fear of his own sexuality.

Julia Kristeva gives a brilliant depiction of this gendered, hierarchical dichotomy arising out of male monotheism. In a reading of the creation story she comments that the serpent and woman are separated from the transcendent God; polymorphic, they are associated with generation and eroticism, that which occupies the polar position to the singularity of the phallic One. She writes:

No other civilization [than the Western] ... seems to have made the principle of sexual difference so crystal clear: between the two sexes there is a cleavage, an abyss, which is marked by their different relationships to the Law (religious and political) and which is the very condition of their alliance. Monotheistic unity is sustained by a radical separation of the sexes: indeed, this separation is its prerequisite.

On the other hand, and simultaneously, [monotheism] represents the paternal function: patrilinear descent with transmission of the father's name centralizes eroticism in the single goal of procreation, in the grip of an abstract symbolic authority ...

The economy of this mechanism requires that women be excluded from the single true and legislating principle ... Eve has no relationship except with that—precisely because she is its opposite, the 'other race' ...

One betrays ... one's naiveté if one considers our modern societies to be simply patrilinear ... or capitalist-monopolist, and ignores the fact that they are at the same time ... governed by ... monotheism ...[5]

Consequently, in an interview published the same year as this passage, Kristeva speaks of Western women who are trying to get out 'from under the thumbs of ... monotheism'.[6]

For her part Luce Irigaray, in her magnum opus, *Speculum of the Other Woman*, considers how masculinist thought from Plato to Freud (or rather from Freud to Plato, for the book is constructed like a mirror) treats of 'woman'—strains of Hegel here—as that which reflects man back to himself.[7] Western thought is not cast in terms of multiplicity; it does not display relations of equality between men and women, each of whom occupies a subject position. Rather, for Irigaray does woman lack a coherent position from which to speak, to formulate her own being and essence. While the symbolic is gendered male, woman is associated with the semiotic, the realm of the mother; that which in our coming to language has been repressed. Her place in the symbolic is that which man has given her as the 'other' to himself. The only chapter in the book in which woman conceives of herself is that on mysticism, in this reflecting the point at which women have indeed 'contributed' to Western thought. Irigaray depicts a schizophrenic disorientation as woman tries to find some 'place' for herself in the symbolic ordering; for there is none.[8] What Irigaray's prescription may be to right this state of affairs is a matter to which we shall come.

French theory moreover gives us another insight, again over two generations and again with its roots in Hegel whose thought was so formative for French philosophy in the inter-war and post-war periods. Both Irigaray and Kristeva in their diverse ways recognize that man, separated from his mother (a journey no woman need undergo),[9] weaves her back into his transcendental: that in relation to which he understands himself, his God. Following Lacan, they conceive of man as depleted, restless, for ever searching for a completion which has been lost and which the mother represents. Irigaray reads the whole of culture no less—and perhaps incredibly—in these terms, writing of man's 'endless construction of substitutes for his pre-natal home'.[10] The Australian feminist theorist Elizabeth Grosz comments of Irigaray's position: 'One could go even further and suggest that the idea of God itself is nothing but an elaborate if unconscious strategy for alleviating man's consciousness of and guilt about this debt [to the mother].'[11] Kristeva meanwhile picks up on Freud's insight that the imaginary Father-God takes on the characteristics of both sexes. Freud referred to 'God' as the 'Father in personal prehistory' (*Vater der persönlichen Vorzeit*). This archaic image, she comments, is the guarantor of identity.[12] God is total love and care, corresponding to what Freud (following another) called the 'oceanic feeling' and which he analyses in the opening passages of *Civilisation and its Discontents*. For Sartre likewise we should note that 'God' represents that unreachable goal (for it is a contradiction in terms) which is a *pour soi/en soi*; at one and the same time *pour soi*, thus out-going and creative while incomplete—in Sartre's terminology possessing 'nothingness' (gendered male), yet also *en soi*, possessing completion if also inert (which conforms to his designation of woman).[13]

I turn however in the rest of this paper from the scene of my agreement with, and appreciation of, French feminist theory to those ways in which I find myself critical, or simply in another arena. The divergences are several, relating to both culture and religion. Whereas I think Lacanian-inspired thought useful in analysing what has been, particularly in the realm of theology, I do not wish to be trapped in a helplessness which suggests that the past dispensation is somehow inevitable. Were that the case one might as well throw in the sponge. Clearly Irigaray and Kristeva hold different positions from one another on this score. Kristeva believes that a reckless de-stabilizing of the male symbolic will run the risk of psychosis; the most that should be attempted is to enable the semiotic drives, associated with the female, to come to language and conceptualization in the symbolic. This takes place, as she thinks, primarily in the realms of art, religion and avant-garde literature. By contrast, Irigaray will step behind that mirror which is woman, through which man sets himself up as subject (she is A-Luce through the Looking Glass), that woman may create her own transcendental, allowing in like manner of her self-actualization. I shall return to this.

Nevertheless in common with Kristeva she too seems to think the task fraught, so determined are we by culture and language. By contrast Anglo-Saxon feminists, myself included, have often been perplexed by the extent to which the French seem to think gender set in stone. Not a little of the difference, as I shall suggest, may relate to the divergence of religious heritage.

It is significant here that, as French thought became popular among Anglo-Saxon readers in the 1980s, there was considerable puzzlement as to how the concept of 'the feminine' was to be understood. Even when it was grasped that this was not perhaps the biological essentialism that it appeared to be, questions remained as to the cultural concept. Anglo-Saxon feminism has tended to distinguish sharply between 'the feminine' (the masculine construct) and 'feminism' (the struggle for the equality of women or, equally, the different paradigms for thought or action which, whether on account of nurture or nature, women wished to promote). Indeed one could well say that the business of feminism was understood to be to dispose of the masculine construct! The notion of the 'complementarity' of man and woman has only too often served as a masculine ruse to avoid equality, its proponents frequently the most antagonistic to feminist ideals.[14] Not least may we think this to have been the case in the sphere of religion. By contrast, French feminists apparently have no difficulty with the term '*féminin*', connoting indifferently woman or that associated with the female. Central to both Kristeva's and Irigaray's *oeuvres* stands gender difference as a given, an untraversable bridge. It is in the context of this cultural difference that I turn to a discussion of 'the sacred' and 'the feminine'.

Reflecting as it does a number of these tangled threads, a good site to consider here is Kristeva's fascination with the cultural representation of the Virgin Mary. I think, in particular, of her essay, 'Stabat Mater', in which she weaves together a consideration of the famous medieval poem and a lyrical text on the birth of her own son.[15] The question to be asked of Kristeva is whether what she is about is cultural analysis pure and simple (in which case it may be very insightful) or she is also intending to be prescriptive. Kristeva suggests that the loss of viability of the cult of the Virgin has left woman without any public cultural representation of motherhood. But one wants to pursue the double question, firstly, as to whether that cult ever did women any good and, secondly, as to why women would wish to be represented *qua* virgin mother? Is this not a pandering to masculine sensibilities, a shoring up of that which man has desired woman should be, either in his eroticism or that she might assuage his fear? Kristeva thinks both to disturb and to increase the range of man's symbolic systems through allowing the *jouissance* of the semiotic, associated with the maternal and hence with woman, to take its place in culture and language. Hence the idyllic depiction of the mother cradling her son, her bliss at the child's birth, turned into poetry. But given that men have in any case associated woman with motherhood, poetry and sacrifice for others, how could it help women to idolize these things? This is hardly woman *qua* articulate agent, present in her own right in the hitherto masculine world and poised to change it.

Irigaray's position is somewhat other, in this correlating with her different endeavour. What delights her is to discover, in a museum in Italy, a statue of a woman resembling Mary, seated with the child before her on her knee, facing the observer. She writes:

> I was admiring this beautiful wooden sculpture when I noticed that this Jesus was a girl! That had a very significant effect on me, one of jubilation—mental and physical. I felt freed from the tensions of that cultural truth-imperative which is also practiced in art: a virgin-mother woman and her son depicted as the models of redemption we should believe in. Standing before this statue representing Mary and her mother, Anne, I felt once again at ease and joyous, in touch with my body, my emotions and my history and a woman. I had before me an aesthetic and ethical figure that I need to be able to live without contempt for my incarnation, for that of my mother and other women.[16]

It is of course the case that the mother/daughter relation (of no concern to men) is markedly absent in its celebration in Western culture. The Demeter/Persephone dyad is the only such which has come down to us from the mythology of the Ancient world. So far as I am aware the Bible never discusses it, by contrast with the endless focus on the father/son relationship. That which a woman is expected to deliver, a matter for rejoicing, as in so many cultures, is the birth of a son. The genealogy extends through the male line; so-and-so begat so-and-so, throughout the generations. Nor is female friendship celebrated, bar the interesting case of Naomi and Ruth in their common adversity. Jacques Derrida points to the double omission in the literature of friendship, from the ancient world to the present, of friendship between women and between a man and a woman.[17] It was indeed a revolutionary sentence when Virginia Woolf announced: 'Chloe liked Olivia.' So yes, Irigaray's pleasure is not mistaken.[18]

Nevertheless, I return to my questions. Why go for the Virgin and Christ child, or indeed St Anne and the Virgin? Is this not simply to remain trapped in the male religion, or to attempt to counter it through an identical female/female emblem? Woman is still present as 'mother', the child seated on her knee. Besides which, what kind of a mythical universe have we here? We know absolutely nothing of St Anne, while Mary, if a mother, was certainly not a virgin! In mammalian reproduction an equal number of chromosomes come from the female and the male; in the unlikely event of parthenogenesis the foetus would be female since no 'Y' chromosome would be present. Further, the idea of Mary as a virgin (which in turn gives rise to that of her immaculate conception as St Anne's child) comes from a mistranslation in the Greek Septuagint of Isaiah, where the underlying Hebrew simply implies a young girl.[19] As was his wont, Matthew (Matthew 1: 23) is attempting to show that an ancient prophecy is fulfilled in Christ. Early Christianity evidently knew nothing of any virgin birth; St Paul never mentions it. It is a clear importation from the paganism of the surrounding world. There are images of Isis, child on knee, which mirror early Christian iconography of Mary and Christ.[20] In reflecting on the image through which, pre-eminently, man has defined what woman should be in Western discourse, do we not as I say simply gratify the male imagination? Why not come down to earth, turn the page and force men to confront us as adult individuals and desist romancing 'woman' as a mythical mother?

We may well think that the representation of woman as the Virgin Mary in Latin, Catholic, culture has done much to determine the gender divide which has been so marked a feature of that culture. Kristeva certainly thinks so. She writes, in 'Stabat Mater':

Curiously and necessarily, when that balance [between Christ and Mary, man and woman] began to be seriously threatened in the nineteenth century, the Catholic church—more dialectical and subtle here than the Protestants who were already spawning the first suffragettes—raised the Immaculate Conception to dogma status in 1854. It is often suggested that the blossoming of feminism in Protestant countries is due, among other things, to the greater initiative allowed to women on the social and ritual plane. One might wonder if, in addition, such a flowering is not the result of a *lack* in the Protestant religious structure with respect to the Maternal …[21]

But is this quite right? It is not so much that the masculine desire for the mother lacks in Protestantism (in its Lutheran form at least) but that it was built into the conception of the Father God. It may well be that this configuration makes for less division between the sexes.

For what is justification by faith if not a being taken up into God? As Luther puts it in a famous passage the Christian lives *extra se*, 'caught up beyond himself' in God in Christ.[22] Faith, in the Lutheran context, is not (as in Catholicism) Latin *fides* but rather Latin *fiducia*, trust: a far more emotive concept. Catholics have failed to understand this: Lutheran 'faith' corresponds to Catholic 'love', except that it is not love for an 'other' but rather a living in, with and from God, surrounded by God. Here is Luther, employing feminine metaphors.

> The person who believes in Christ is righteous and holy through divine imputation. He already sees himself, and is, in heaven, being surrounded by the heaven of mercy. But while we are lifted up into the bosom of the Father, and are clad with the finest of raiment, our feet reach out below the garment, and Satan bites them whenever he can … Thus we are saints and children [of God], but in the spirit, not in the flesh, and we dwell under the shadow of the wings of our mother hen, in the bosom of grace … [But] you must draw your tiny feet with you under the garment, otherwise you will have no peace.[23]

And again: 'See how much labour women expend on making food, giving milk, keeping watch over a child: God compares himself to this passion. "I will not desert you, for I am the womb that bore you, and I cannot let you go."'[24] These passages precisely exemplify Kristeva's feminine *khora*; the sense of the womb (taken from Plato's *Timaeus*), to which she calls attention.

One may think that this difference as between Catholicism and Protestantism made for a radical difference in the relationship of women to the religion. It may also have helped to determine the cultural difference in the understanding of gender as between a Protestant Anglo-Saxon country and a Catholic Latin country. While both forms of Christianity appear to reflect the male's need for the mother, the fact that in Catholicism there is iconic representation of this through a separate female figure leads to a quite other sensibility. In Protestantism women, as do men, look to the one God (and there is in any case much less visual representation). I do not think women from a Protestant heritage worse off here; on the contrary. The Catholic cultural heritage has led to two separate genres of person, the division of sex absolute.[25] Now it is undoubtedly true that women have not been given equality within Protestantism. But rather than being another race, they have been counted lesser men, often allowed to prophesy or preach (that which is central to Protestantism, as is the celebration of the Mass in Catholicism). Again, the fact that Protestantism is a religion of the spoken word, the proclamation of the gospel, allows for a greater fluidity than the more static religion of vision with its iconography of 'woman' and of 'man'.

Certainly the difference in this regard is marked. I well remember the Italian feminist Adriana Caverero pointing out at a conference of the (British) Society for Women in Philosophy that, in a Catholic country, the Virgin was to be seen 'on every street corner'. It was on this account that she explained the importance of the concept of 'mothering' in (otherwise revolutionary and communist) Italian feminist theory. Catholics have frequently not grasped the chasm here. At a radical conference in 1980 I commented that, owing to its 'masculine' nature, Christianity could not encompass women. I recall my incredulity when Jon Sobrino, a Latin American liberation theologian, responded that while men should model themselves on Christ, women should look to Mary—as though therein lay the solution to my problem. That does not come within my purview, striking me as both offensive and bizarre. Again, at a conference on 'Women and the Divine' in Britain in 2005, Luce Irigaray devoted much of her paper to an attempt to retrieve what the Virgin might mean.[26] There is a failure to recognize that, for women coming from a Protestant background, Mary has never been on their horizon. I hold absolutely nothing in common with her or anything that she might represent. When I considered myself Christian I looked to the—in some sense 'male'—God who loved me; I now think in non-anthropomorphic terms of that dimension of reality which is 'God'.

Besides which this setting up of Christ and the Virgin as two divine persons, she equally with halo, must be the undoing of Christology and so of Christianity. (If I may momentarily speak up for Christianity which does not actually consist in the worship of a male human being as a god.) The Virgin's entry into Christian iconography may be thought in retrospect to have represented an acute danger to that church's new-found Christology of the fifth century. That Christology, elaborated within the context of neo-Platonism, understood God in Christ to have taken on the 'real universal' which is humanity. Of course to participate in the universal (humanity) there must be present a particular human being; a universal is not some abstract or umbrella concept. In becoming a unique individual, God in Christ took on what it means to be 'human'. It followed that by virtue of their humanity women bore the same relation as did men to Jesus *as the Christ*. Anything else and women would have been outside the scheme of salvation. If by contrast one sets up two genres of persons, men who look to Jesus and women to Mary, both Jesus and Mary being deified (or semi-deified) one has undone Christology in favour of a Jesuology. Now we have gods (or semi-gods); deified individuals.

At this point we may turn from 'the feminine' to 'the sacred'. Again my sentiments betray a different inheritance. I find myself writing simply that I am post-Christian, rather than post-Protestant, so strongly do I agree with the Protestant position in this regard. I want to say that Christianity is about overcoming the sacred. Yet again the revolution surely owes to Luther, that genius who set Western culture on another course. For Luther grasped, what it would seem was the earlier Christian stance, that in Christ sacredness was abolished. Christianity is not in this sense a religion, it does not set certain people apart as 'sacred'. One can for example read the *Letter to the Hebrews* as expressing the belief that in Jesus' death a final sacrifice has been made, such that the need for priests is done away with (Hebrews 10: 11–14). At his death the veil of the temple is rent. It owes to Luther that the German word for occupation is *Beruf*, calling. All occupations are equally a calling. Protestantism has been wholly suspicious of the pagan paraphernalia of sacred bones and relics, special feast days, or places in the church where the priest alone may go (as in Orthodoxy). It has thought these so much nonsense and mystification. A culture like the Scottish with its Presbyterian background is still marked by these sensibilities. On Good Friday there were always classes, just as on any other day, in the Theology faculty in which I taught. While Karl Barth—whatever one may think of his position, undoubtedly the greatest theologian of the twentieth century —sees human 'religion' as at 180 degrees to what it means to be Christian, the last subterfuge in which in its sin humanity tries to hide from God. Thus I find myself suspicious of the idea of the sacred; I think it 'medieval'. Of course were one to say metaphorically that the whole world is 'sacred' that is a different matter. But in that case there is no holy, for the word holy means chosen, set apart.

Those of a Catholic disposition have been prone to think Protestants unnecessarily iconoclastic and negative. An iconoclasm it may be, but it is an iconoclasm in favour of a cause; a recognition that all is filled with God's spirit and meanwhile a ridding of humanity of superstition. It is interesting in this respect that Catholic scholars of a former generation accused Luther of all sorts of perversion, himself a former monk who had taken to wife a former nun. But Luther was no sexual miscreant. His marrying was a theological statement: Luther did nothing if not from theology. His was a celebration of the world. 'Then shall all creatures laugh with thee and thou with them, even according to the body.'[27] The holy, the mystical was done away with. As we have said, this did not of course mean that women without further ado gained equality. Nevertheless one does have to wonder whether (male concepts of) sacredness has not been fatal for women. Indeed there may well be a connection here between the concept of 'the feminine' and that of 'the sacred'. The concept of 'the feminine' is a setting apart of woman as taboo, whether as mother, virgin or both. When there is this sense of holiness, of divinization (even though there be an un-reachable female figure present), actual women (as we have noted) come to be associated with the earthly, the flesh and sexuality. While men have defined the holy, women through their very bodies have only too often been seen as polluting it. Present in either male or female form, we may think the sacred to have done actual women no good at all.

I come then finally to the question as to how we might move for-ward, both to a renewed spirituality and to human equality, for I cannot imagine one without the other. Commenting on Schüssler Fiorenza's *In Memory of Her*,[28] Irigaray remarks that she 'describes what already exists without inventing a new subjectivity'.[29] I find the remark significant. I should want to say (and I am not sure what Irigaray thinks) that women already have a new subjectivity; profoundly different from two thou-sand years ago, advanced even from a generation ago—and quite other than the male construction of 'the feminine'. But it is for this reason that I can conjure up no association with women from the past; in many ways I hold much more in common with men in the past. Hence in re-sponse to Schüssler Fiorenza's well-known work I myself wrote a piece 'On Not Remembering Her'.[30] Thus also I do not credit that there can be a meaningful genealogy of women from past to present, nor think that we should concoct one. Women are in a novel place today. Until we challenge men to see us as we now are, the neighbouring sex, neither on a pedestal nor filth, we cannot progress. To suggest that women should be understood in conjunction with some past ancestry, for ex-ample by association with biblical women, is not simply unrealistic; it allows men to evade the fact that gender arrangements must be under-stood according to a radically other dispensation today.

If I have a somewhat different emphasis from Irigaray here, in rela-tion to Kristeva's project I want to say that I would hope we can bring about a far more fundamental change than simply disturb the male sym-bolic through allowing a certain *jouissance* to enter more fully into rep-resentation. We need forms of thought and commensurate metaphors which allow that there are two sexes present, as equals and agents in their own right. This will constitute a revolution. Religion has played a large part in creating the situation we have inherited: it is imperative that we counter its influence and deny the relevance of its symbols. Even in our seemingly secular society in Europe today religion remains some kind of over-arching transcendental. In Britain the Abrahamic religions, and basically Christianity, are taught in our schools by law. There is even talk of creating more 'faith' schools, funded in part by tax-payers' money. One must ask what is going on here? What does it tell us of the way in which men continue to conceive of women? We should not allow entrance to a creed which was anti-Semitic, nor one which was white supremacist, nor indeed today one which discriminated against those who find themselves homosexual. Yet religions, that is to say ideologies in which one gender is the norm, are taught along with ethics; while children's minds are formed by biblical stories which by no means show the gender equality we claim to acknowledge. What we should be aiming for is, clearly, a spirituality (if we are to have any such) in which all will axiomatically possess equal dignity. But that must entail a fundamental break with religion as we have known it.

It is here that the work of Irigaray is of interest. She sets forth in poetic language a kind of utopia in which there will be interchange between the sexes in their difference. Fundamental to her thinking would seem to be the influence of Feuerbach and this on several counts. A left-wing Hegelian and, the son of a pastor, acutely interested in religion, Feuerbach suggests that the human being (*der Mensch*, but the culture he is analysing is masculine) 'projects his being into objectivity' (*vergegenständlicht sich*: a *Gegenstand* is an object, thus 'makes his being into an object over against himself'), casting this object in the subject position, and then proceeds to conceive of himself as the object of this subject.[31] In other words, as we have seen, man takes up the position of 'slave' in relation to his God. Feuerbach's agenda is that we should re-appropriate that which we have projected, thus achieving our own self-actualization. This for Feuerbach must be a material re-appropriation; we must overcome the dichotomy of spirit over material which has, incidentally, so harmed women. Irigaray thinks likewise. In her case it is women who in self-appropriating their values are to become 'divine'. Again, in her case also the spirit/body dichotomy is to be done away with. The whole person is to relate, in a relation of equality, with his or her other; hence the sexual metaphors.

Consider here Irigaray's essay 'Sexual Difference'. Recognizing the place that God as his transcendental has played in man's self-realization, Irigaray wills that women too should come into their own. There will then be two sexes, not one and its 'other'. 'Why,' she asks, 'has sexual difference not had a chance to flourish, either on an empirical or transcendental level … why [has it] failed to acquire an ethics, logic or religion of its own … ?'[32] Why has this two-ness, this inter-relationship, not formed our transcendental and our empirical (everyday, actual) relationality? What we need, she thinks, is a sense of 'wonder' (*admiration*) between the two sexes in their difference, whereas the space between man and woman has been filled 'with attraction, greed, possession, consummation, disgust, etc.' As she writes: 'Wonder might allow them to retain an autonomy based on their difference.'[33] Taking the metaphor (or the reality) of sexual intercourse and sounding Hegelian, she suggests that the sexual encounter must be 'a double loop ... in which each can move out towards the other and back to itself'.[34] Then we shall have: 'a celebration, and not a disguised ... form of the master-slave relationship'. She adds, 'In this way it would no longer be a meeting within the shadow or orbit of a God the Father who alone lays down the law, ... the immutable mouthpiece of a single sex.'[35] Thus does she connect the overcoming of the religious situation which we have known with the renewed relationship between the sexes which she would have. Whether however it is necessary to conceptualize this relationship in carnal terms and whether we should simply be considering a particular man/woman relation, or rather a plethora of human relationships in which we are all involved, is another matter.

For myself I might want to think of this transcendental in somewhat different terms. It occurs to me that the feminist movement may in effect have both enunciated and practised a different 'transcendental' than that which we have known; understanding our 'transcendental' here as our over-arching paradigms, integral to our values and relationships. Hierarchy is replaced by relationality, singularity by multiplicity. Predicated upon this different outlook women have undertaken new practices: those of hearing-one-another-into-being, of valuing difference and applauding self-actualization. It can be no chance that it has been women who have come to these understandings, though whether on account of nature or nurture is a large matter which we cannot here consider. Increasingly one may think, though as yet insufficiently, these ways of thinking and of inter-acting have permeated our society as a whole. The ideals themselves need not of course be gender-specific: indeed the whole point is that women would that men inter-act both with them and among themselves otherwise than has commonly been the case. It is a political and social vision as to how society should function, and in that sense a transcendental. Here I find myself reminded of the work of Nancy Fraser, the American-Jewish political theorist and feminist writer. Criticizing Lacanian thought and extending her criticism to Kristeva's uptake of that thinking, Fraser suggests that theories of language which have an overdetermined notion of the symbolic are not useful. As feminist theorists, she suggests, we should rather think pragmatically about language and thus also consider how, through renewed praxis, change may come about.[36]

In concluding I turn to a consideration of religion, or spirituality.[37] It would seem that there is no way in which the Abrahamic religions can 'adapt': they are built upon the subordination of woman to man, as also man to God, through the gendered nature of their hierarchical

structure. Quite apart from which one may think incredible their re-
spective mythologies, indeed the idea that there could be a particularity
of revelation in history. This does not however preclude the possibility
of believing that, in whatever distorted form, these religions attempted
to express something of the human awareness that there is a dimension
to reality—which humans have then hypostasized (conceived of as a
definite entity), anthropomorphized and projected on high as 'God'.
If with Feuerbach (and Irigaray) we think that the form which 'God'
has taken has reflected man's own being, it may, nevertheless, be that
human beings have for good reason often manifested a marked spirituality. The destruction of the male idol, if one may call it that, need not
result in atheism. The question then becomes the interesting one as to
whether the paradigms and values to which we now hold may serve as
vehicles which can express that dimension of reality. My own conviction is that the paradigms which feminists have articulated are indeed
germane, given that we are speaking of something which takes place between persons, as for example that prayer or extra-sensory perception
is powerful, or that persons are healed and renewed. Whatever 'God'
may be, we may think God integral to that one reality to which we also
belong. Indeed, though it may not have been the dominant motif, God
has ever been understood as Spirit, integrally related with that life which
is ours. Such a shift in understanding would constitute the undoing, yet
also the renewal, of Western culture.

# THE FEMININE, THE SACRED AND THE SHARED
## The Ecumenical Space of the Sufi Dargah
### *Ananya Jahanara Kabir*

I begin with two quotations, from two sets of authors. First, from the book which has partly inspired this volume: *The Feminine and the Sacred*, comprised of the correspondence between Julia Kristeva and Catherine Clément. This correspondence ranges over Africa, India and medieval Europe: and yet, in the final letter written by Kristeva, a particularly glaring gap is finally articulated:

> As I think over all these months of correspondence, it appears to me that we are avoiding a question that has continued to preoccupy us nonetheless, and that, even recently, we mentioned only briefly on the phone. What about Islam in this journey through the sacred? Islam, whose fundamentalist version horrifies the modern world, to the point that the non-specialists—like you and me—have no desire to make subtle distinctions between the 'foundation' and the 'excesses'? … In black Africa and in India, you are confronted with a different Islam, and God knows how polymorphous Islam is. I would have liked you to tell me about its strange and multiple faces.[1]

Coming at the end of the book, this question continues to be avoided, with Kristeva herself moving on to China for a closing speculation on yin and yang and guilt-free bisexuality. Let us now turn to the second quotation in question: this one from a scholarly work interested in exploring precisely this gap that Kristeva has opened up: the 'strange and multiple faces' of Islam outside its Middle Eastern heartland. This book concentrates on Sufi practices across South Asia. Its editors, Helene Basu and Pnina Werbner, remark in the introduction:

> In studying Sufi saint cults as living, contemporary modes of or-
> ganising the sacred we seek to expose false dichotomies applied to
> the description, and hence theorization, of Sufi cults throughout
> the Islamic heartland and its peripheries. Such dichotomies deny
> the embodied nature of ritual and religious belief and practice by
> positing a series of spurious separation: between magic and reli-
> gion, between ritual and belief, between folk and official or nor-
> mative religion; between syncretic practice and Islamic orthodoxy.
> These separations have been imposed upon different facets of
> what is, we argue here, a single, total, symbolic reality.[2]

In this eloquent manifesto for the academic study of Sufism, too, we note a gap: the dichotomies mentioned do not include dichotomies of gender and sexuality. This gap is symptomatic. In this valuable, compas-sionate and learned set of essays on contemporary South Asian Sufism there is no discussion of how gender and sexuality might come into play within the performance of emotion at Sufi shrines.

It is within these gaps that I situate my chapter. On the one hand, we have the elision of Islam, especially the richly performative, expressive tradition of Sufi Islam, witnessed in Kristeva's and Clement's joint ex-ploration of the feminine and the sacred. On the other, we have the frustrating omission of gender from the explorations spearheaded by a new generation of scholars sympathetic to and interested in the con-tinuing vitality of Sufi cults in South Asia. I wish to fill in this doubly-incomplete picture by turning to South Asia's most sacred Sufi shrine, or *dargah*: that of Hazrat Moinuddin Chishti, founder of the Chishti Order of Sufism in South Asia.[3] This *dargah* is situated in the town of Ajmer in Rajasthan, India. It constitutes the centre of the sacred geog-raphy of South Asia, and exemplifies a particular intersection of geog-raphy, vernacularity and a performative, collective mode of expressing the sacred. As my title claims, I consider this experience of the Islamic sacred as being a shared, even ecumenical experience; furthermore, I consider these characteristics as intimately linked to a certain quality of South Asian Sufism that we may term, for the time being, 'feminine'.

I use as my 'data' the practices that occur at the shrine itself, but more importantly, I utilize, too, the memory of these practices, as trans-mitted and collectively and repeatedly felt through the musical genre of the *qawwali*, intimately associated with South Asian Sufism. In articulat-ing this affective interpretation of what (and how) the *Dargah* at Ajmer means, I have allowed myself two liberties. Firstly, in moving between the twelfth century, when these cultural phenomena began to crystallize, and the present moment, which continues to see their proliferation and ramification, I have not worried about 'scholarly accuracy'—providing sources, dates, secure lines of transmission, avoiding anachronisms. I have responded instead to the non-linearity, the achronicity, the anti-telos and the stubborn persistence of the sacred. Secondly, and, inevitably, this analysis is born out of my personal history as a South Asian Muslim, who stands at the intersection of many roads through which the sacred has been transported and localized down the centuries, and who has used the *qawwali* to revive old connections with Ajmer Sharif. In the process, I focus on a collective subjectivity that emerges out of performing the sacred at the *Dargah*—the phenomenon of men taking on a 'feminine' persona in response to the demands of the sacred. From a Western perspective, this subjectivity could be termed bisexual, homosexual or even androgynous. I will attempt, however, to extract from it a greater conceptual fluidity than these categories and labels suggest: a fluidity of experience, expression and emotive response to the sacred. By examining the *Dargah* as a 'feminine' space, which compels men to assume 'feminine' traits, I shall not ignore the question that Kristeva herself gestures towards:

> I like that Islamic idea of a poetics of beings in the time of their absoluteness, and I really want to believe that the whirling dervishes represent a pinnacle of that poetic subjectivity. Composed of dance, of sound, of meaning—both exalted in the magic of a passion and mastered, purified, bleached out like the gleam of the mirror reflecting a place beyond. Granted. At the same time, I am worried that so little space is reserved for a woman in that sublime sublimation.[4]

In fact, my entire chapter can be seen as an implicit answer to this question. Through it, I attempt to make sense of the 'sublime sublimation' that the *Dargah* and *qawwali* offer. Yet through it, I also stake a claim to that 'sublime sublimation'.

## Sufism in South Asia

As a pan-Islamic phenomenon, Sufism emerged very early in the history and outward spread of the religion. Over the centuries, it developed two faces. The first is an abstract, philosophical and discursive face, which evolved in the classical Islamic heartlands during the European medieval period. This Sufism is associated with Neoplatonist thought, subtle theological discussion, and treatises on the relationship between embodied desire (*nafs*) and the eternally rational soul (*ruh*), between the exoteric (*zahir*) and the esoteric (*batin*), between divine love (*ishq*, *mohabbat*) and its human manifestations.[5] The second face of Sufism is a performative, embodied, expressive one, which can be found wherever Islam took local roots: the Middle East, South Asia, Africa, South-East Asia. This performative Sufism can be seen as the enactment and transformation, under local conditions, of those basic principles that were formulated within what subsequently became discernible as 'learned, treatise-based Sufism'. Take, for instance, 'the core of classical Sufi mysticism: divine love conceptualized as inner experience of growth and realization in the relationship between individual worshippers and a saint, and can be interpreted as a model for all human dialogical interaction.'[6] Divine love is central to and universal within the Sufi episteme. Yet the actual expression of this love continues to generate Sufi practices that diverge in their performative and embodied forms, in accordance with local languages of love, longing and desire, and with local sacred geographies.

In considering contemporary Sufism as the product of a long dialogue between pan-Islamic discourses and local vernacularities, we cannot forget the legacies of colonialism and its aspirational modernities. Despite the onslaught of Enlightenment discourses on rationality and superstition, colonial programmes of ruthless modernization and the corresponding drive towards Weberian disenchantment, and, most importantly, despite pan-Islamic reformist traditions (e.g. Wahhabism), these embodied, localized Sufisms live and thrive, particularly across South Asia.[7] South Asian Sufism is as deeply contested as are all strains of South Asian Islam; yet, unlike its fate in the Middle East and Central Asia, Sufism has continued to offer a viable, lived, participatory sacrality to South Asian communities and individuals. 'Throughout South Asia, shrines of Sufi saints appear juxtaposed to other complex, postmodern and postcolonial realities',[8] plotting a sacred geography that transcends postcolonial national borders. These shrines or *dargahs* offer resistive spaces where the binaries of colonial and postcolonial modernities can be shed and alternative subjectivities allowed momentarily to emerge. Enabling these transformations is the all-powerful body of the charismatic saint, whether living or dead, in conjunction with the *dargah* as the repository of sacred memory centred on the saint's grave. Accruing around this conjunction is what has been termed the 'hardware of sanctity' that binds together the devotee, the *dargah* and the saint.[9] The body of the saint, the perpetuation of the saintly lineage (*silsila*), the physicality of the shrine—all together induce certain behavioural modes in the devotee which interpellate the individual into a larger collective.

Whirling dervishes notwithstanding, South Asian Sufism possesses a myriad such modes of performing emotion, all informed by a rich regionalism and a deep-rooted vernacularity. These vernacularities, while necessarily divergent, share a generic similarity arising from South Asian Islam's long coexistence with Hindu expressive practices, especially those concerning the relationship between the worshipper and a morally, ethically or deontologically higher being. The 'Islamicization of the indigenous'[10] that resulted means that most South Asian *dargahs* include regionally-inflected rhythmic music and dancing that express the semiotics of bodily abjection, submission, self-abnegation, longing and separation, the best-known kind being the *qawwali*.[11] Here, the lead vocalist sings a couplet, whose second line is taken up and iterated by the backing group; strong rhythmic accompaniment is provided by collective hand-clapping as well as traditional Indian percussion instruments. The strongly iterative quality of the music and the lyrics binds performers and listeners into an organic whole, charging the space with a sacred aura and encouraging members of this new collective to lose themselves in trance-like states. Musically, the *qawwali* is embedded in South Asian systems of *raag* (melodic scale) and *taal* (rhythm cycle); lyrically, it shares the idiom of Hindu devotional songs, for example, the *bhajan* detailing love for Krishna. While acknowledging the shared aspirations of South Asian performative mysticism, whether Hindu (Bhakti) or Islamic (Sufi), and the shared musical and emotive idiom of the Hindu devotional *bhajan* and the *qawwali*, I nevertheless foreground the *dargah*'s affective difference from a Hindu temple, and the hermeneutic autonomy of the *qawwali*. We may thereby appreciate the specifically 'feminine' nature of Sufi ecumenism, invested in the emulation of those who have blazed individual trails of self-abnegation because of the unbearable weight of *ishq*, of divine love. Pre-eminent among these is Hazrat Khwaja Moinuddin, whose *Dargah* at Ajmer I focus on here.

### Ajmer Sharif: the localizing of Sufi emotion

Hazrat Khwaja Moinuddin came to India from the border of present-day Afghanistan and Iran in c. 1190, bringing the message of Islam after being inspired by the teachings of his own spiritual leader, Harun Usmani, and also by the Prophet Muhammad in a series of dreams.[12] He lived in Ajmer until his death in 1232, and was buried there; over the centuries (and especially under Mughal patronage) the *Dargah* as we now know it accrued around his grave. Today it is a labyrinthine structure, accessible through a narrow network of lanes that lead, through a succession of imposing gates, mosques, open courtyards, offices of the *khadims* or hereditary shrine keepers, to the beating heart of the complex: the grave itself, embellished richly with gold, silver and enamel work. The *Dargah* throngs with devotees/pilgrims of all kinds, including Hindus and Sikhs (although their relationship to it is different from the Muslim pilgrim), and Muslim visitors from Bangladesh, Pakistan and the diaspora. Many of these pilgrims stay with particular *khadims* (hereditary shrine keepers descended from Hazrat Khwaja Moinuddin), whose hospices ring the *Dargah* complex. The *Dargah* is especially and unbelievably crowded during the annual *urs* festival of Hazrat Khwaja Moinuddin: the ten-day celebrations marking his death as the moment of his symbolic union with the divine. These surging crowds externalize the reverence, love and affection with which Hazrat Khwaja Moinuddin is remembered among South Asian Muslims: as his appellations declare, he is *Sultan-e-hind* (emperor of India) and *Garib nawaz* (protector of the poor), where the 'poor' constitutes all those who come to his shrine; often, he is simply, and rather sweetly, *Khwajaji* (where 'ji' denotes respect) or *Khwaja piya* (khwaja darling). Supremely charismatic, he is, like other Sufi saints, *waliullah* (friend of God) who can 'intercede' on behalf of those he loves;[13] to be thus loved, all that the individual needs to do is long for the saints' love.

The manner of Khwajaji's memorialization offers a striking counter-narrative to dominant accounts of Islam's spread in twelfth-century India through the rapacious sword, as emblematized in the plundering figure of Mahmood Ghazni, contemporaneous to Khwajaji.[14] At the same time, the emphasis on Khwajaji's intercessory powers and the thin line between respecting his grave and worshipping it, have been disapproved of strenuously by reformist Muslims. Yet, despite these theologically valid disapprovals, the turn to Ajmer remains a collective reflex among South Asian Muslims irrespective of social class and regional differences. In consonance with the general remarks about South Asian Sufism that I made earlier, our perceptions of Ajmer Sharif's sacrality seem not to have diminished with the onset of modernity, postmodernity and pan-Islamism. This persistence would seem to confirm 'the common perception of Sufism as a realm of Islamic emotional discourse opposed to the "cold" and "technical" constructions put forward by theologians and judicial scholars.'[15] Islam, that most juridical and praxis-oriented of religions, appears minimalist in the channels of emotive self-expression that it permits. In contrast, Sufism seems the space par excellence of emotion and unrestraint, the space of charisma and response to charisma, the space of liminality and wildernesses, the space of nomadism and vagrancy—of a gamut of divinely inspired madnesses as embodied in the figures of the *dervesh*, the *malang*, the *qalandar*, the *majzoob*, the *mastan*—all categories of 'sufi madmen' local to the deserts straddling Pakistan and Western India. Ajmer, situated in the Thar Desert of contemporary Rajasthan, is a fitting location for the flamboyant Sufi asceticism that traditionally developed away from the urban mercantile networks within which early Islam was born and flourished.[16]

It is equally possible, however, to read this emotional history surrounding Ajmer Sharif as evidence for the 'other within' that Sufism represents for Islam: not a competitive but a complementary otherness. Sufism's cultivation of charisma and emotion, which Khwajaji exemplifies, can be seen as a continuation of the original charismatic moment of Islam that was grounded in the body and behaviour of the Prophet Muhammad, and in the sacred centres of Mecca and Medina.[17] As a *qawwali* celebrating the *urs* of Khwajaji states in its successive verses: 'the lanes of Ajmer are fragrant during the *urs*; they are fragrant with the perfumes of Medina; bowing my head at your threshold, I am overcome by the memory of the black-shawled one (the Prophet Muhammad); to quench the flames of love fanned by the *urs*, cool breezes from Medina are blowing through Ajmer.'[18] A Sufi saint such as Khwajaji does not compete with the Prophet for the hearts and minds of Muslims—rather their relationship asks to be read as a series of metonymic transfer and perpetuation of the prophet's ur-charisma. Ajmer and Khwajaji are relocated within the charismatic lineage of the Prophet, his son-in-law Ali and his grandsons Hasan and Husain: 'I have seen all manner of saints strolling through the lanes of Ajmer/I have seen Ali himself emerge from Khwajaji's room.'[19] Sufi shrines such as Ajmer Sharif metonymically replicate Islam's sacred centres of Mecca and Medina; they do not aspire to replace them. From this perspective, Sufism appears the space within Islam that permits certain modes of emotional expressivity which would otherwise be deemed transgressive: a space conceptually and affectively interlocked with orthoprax Islam.

## Sacred transgression and the shifting feminine

As a *qawwali* commonplace iterates: 'mohabbat hi shariat hai' (love itself is the law). This 'permissive transgressiveness' of South Asian Sufism is rooted in the ways in which what we might term gender roles, or gender expectations, are deployed at the *Dargah*. Let us begin with the central rite performed at the *Dargah*—*chaadar chadana* or mounting the *chaadar* (where *chaadar*, 'cloth covering' signifies a multitude of referents: the veil worn by women, especially brides; a sheet covering the bed, the winding sheet for the corpse). In the context of a *dargah*, it is the grave of the saint on which the *chaadar* is mounted, signifying the transformation, through death, of the saint into the bride of God. What may be considered the *sanctum sanctorum* at Ajmer certainly foregrounds these associations: it is no less than a very ornate bridal chamber, at the centre of which is the grave, literalized as a four-poster bed in solid silver. On this bed *khadims* place, on behalf of the pilgrims, *chaadars* of velvet, silk and *zari* (gold braid) and shower heaps of red and pink rose petals, whose heady scent mingles with that of incense, and combines with the glitter of lamps, chandeliers and candles and the press of bodies to make the *sanctum sanctorum* an intensely haptic, collective space. Within this space, and through the iteration of the *chaadar chadana* ritual the body of the saint is continually reaffirmed as that of the eternal bride. It is this status of the saint as bride-in-perpetuity that is celebrated, in fact, at the *urs*—which is nothing less than the equivalent of a marriage ceremony between the saint and god.

The feminized saint, the saint as bride rather than groom—is the first of a series of gendered role-play associated with the *Dargah*: the pilgrim, too, adopts a posture of idealized femininity vis-à-vis the saint. If the saint is feminized vis-à-vis God then the pilgrim who longs for the saint, longs for him and his favours as a woman—as communicated most obviously by the classic phrases associated with exalting Khwajaji and his powers. *Qawwals* (singers of qawwalis) beseech Khwajaji to fill the laps of supplicants ('godi bhar de', where idiom predicates the meaning of filling the lap with child). Thus the granting of favours is metaphorized as guaranteeing fertility and childbirth. Frequently, however, this association works more subtly: for instance, the phrase 'godi bhar de' (to fill the lap) is often recalled through the rhythmically identical idiom, 'jholi bhar de' (to fill the sack, with connotations of mendicants, nomads, and wandering ascetics whose sole possession is that sack).[20] The gender of these ascetics conjured up thereby is rendered female by the corollary act of 'aanchal phailana' or spreading the end of the sari, to receive alms, which the devotee is seen as performing. To clarify, then: the idiom of supplication articulated especially through *qawwalis* for Khwajaji typically interpellate the devotee/pilgrim as a female ascetic, who comes to his threshold, supplicating for alms by spreading the ragged end of her *aanchal* or sari end; by idiomatic association her supplication for favours is compared to that of a barren woman begging for a child.

The composite figure evoked is that of the *jogan* (female ascetic) and the *deewani* (madwoman). This figure has strong resonances with Meera, a historical figure from medieval Mewar in present-day Rajasthan, who has gained mythical status as the paradigmatic *jogan/deewani* who left her princely husband for the love of Krishna.[21] Arising from the same desert topography of present-day Rajasthan, Meera, the *deewani* for Krishna, segues into the nameless *deewani* for Khwajaji. Like Meera, this *deewani* too sets out from home, barefoot, clad in the ochre robes of the mendicant, hair loose and unbraided. Unmindful of rank, family, status or marital femininity, she wanders through the desert responding to the call of her beloved and stumbles, abject, into Khwajaji's threshold. This madness is incomprehensible to the non-inspired ('mere deewangi ko hosh wale behes farmaye/magar pehle usey khud deewana banne ki zaroorat hai': the sane cast aspersions on my madness, but first they need to become mad themselves).[22] The *jogan/deewani* figure combines abjection, self-surrender, and irrational longing, funnels it through a feminine form and directs it towards the sacredness radiating outward from Khwajaji. This role demands that Khwajaji emerge as an all-powerful dominant figure. When the devotee as *jogan/deewani* supplicates to Khwajaji, Khwajaji's response is mysterious, unpredictable, capricious but ultimately loving: 'yeh dil ko behelne ki ab ek hi surat hai/agar voh mujhse keh de aa tujhse muhabbat hai' (now there is only one countenance that can soothe this heart/if he should happen to say to me, come, I have fallen in love with you).[23] The devotee is granted the leeway to demand, almost flirtatiously—'if you don't listen to me, I'll tell everybody to come to your door to beg for alms'—but this permission to flirt is also a favour granted by Khwajaji. His power over the abject devotee forms part of the everyday vocabulary of Ajmer Sharif: it is frequently asserted that Khwajaji 'pulls' the devotee towards Ajmer ('kheech letey hai') as and when he pleases, and when the call comes, it is impossible to ignore it.

The sacred as feminine within the space of the *dargah* is thus a shifting signifier. The saint is feminized as the bride of God; but he is masculinized as king of Ajmer (*shah, raja*) vis-à-vis the feminized devotee as *jogan/deewani*. Furthermore the *deewani* is not the only feminine mode that the devotee can adopt: the role of bride-to-be or adorned woman is also available (though this association is more frequent in *qawwalis* associated with the Delhi *Dargah* of Hazrat Nizamuddin Auliya, fourth in the Chishti lineage following Khwajaji). These *qawwalis* are in the tradition of Amir Khusrau, the early fourteenth century poet and friend/follower of Hazrat Nizamuddin.[24] Here, the figure of the adorned young woman conveys the disarray in which Nizamuddin's assertive love throws her: 'Chhaap tilak sab chin mose naina milaike— gori gori baiyya hari hari chudiyan … baiyya pakad kar deen mose naina milaike' (you snatched away all my adornments by locking my gaze with yours … my fair arms adorned with green bangles—you grabbed hold of these arms, locking my gaze with yours). If the ascetic beseeches for *sukoon* (spiritual peace) through her very disarray, the bride beseeches the saint to ensure her modesty to the outside world by being mindful of her veil ('laaj rakho more ghunghat pat ki'):[25] the *ghunghat* is created by pulling over one's face the end of the sari (the *aanchal*). As the *jogan* recalls Meera, the adorned bride as young woman recalls Radha, Krishna's mythical beloved, whose clandestine meetings with

Krishna in the forests of Brindavan are always in danger of being thwarted by the taunts of her mother-in-law and sisters-in-law: these obtrusive female relatives are also invoked in qawwalis centring on the devotee as bride. Invoked, too, are other iconic moments of encounter between Radha, her female companions, and Krishna as playful lover: for instance, at the well, where Krishna breaks their earthen pots with well-aimed stones, shattering more than just their composure in the process.[26]

## Degrees of separation

Such moments from a vernacular repertoire of feminized approaches to the sacred/divine become reincorporated, via *qawwali*, into the feminized devotee of the sufi saint and the masculinized, playful saint himself; thus, 'mai to gayi thi paniyan bharan ko—daur jhapat mori matki phatki' (I had gone simply to fill water at the well; but in the sudden commotion, my pot was shattered); such an image also becomes stamped by the ceaseless movement between the exoteric and esoteric levels, the quotidian and the spiritual, that vivifies the hermeneutics of the Sufi sacred. The multiplicity of roles, the possibility of role reversal, and the oscillation between ascetic and bashful young girl—all point to the fluidity with which the feminine operates within this hermeneutics. This fluidity is heightened, even made explicit, by the fact that *qawwals* are all-male groups, whose use of first person feminine pronouns and verb endings heightens the contrast and conflation while generating a peculiar thrill, on the part of the audience, through recognition and appreciation of the contrast. One might read this adoption of grammatical gender and its concomitant adoption of feminine postures as an appropriation of the feminine by men. That is, by feminizing themselves, male *qawwals*, male *khadims* and lay male devotees edge out the space available to women to participate in the sublime sublimation (to return to Kristeva's grouse). I would, however, offer a somewhat different assessment and interpretation of this collective feminization, based on the idea of longing and inaccessibility.

The 'feminine' operative in the *Dargah* space and memorialized in and through *qawwali* need not be a gender reversal whereby men appropriate the feminine and cordon it off for themselves at the expense of real women; rather I consider it as a mode which signifies self-abnegation, self-surrender, and potential annihilation of the ego, which is open to all those drawn to Khwajaji (or indeed any other saintly figure), irrespective of gender; and which, moreover, is also used for the saint as he relates to God. The only difference is that Khwajaji, as bride, has attained symbolic union with the divine, while those drawn to him long to win his favours. This longing does not lead to the resolution and certainties of closure: the devotee longs for Khwajaji's gaze to alight on him or her, the gaze from which radiates benevolent love (*chashm-e-karam*), but the moment that he or she as *jogan/deewani* will be granted the ultimate favour of that glimpse, is seen as an apocalyptic one: 'jis din mai tumhe dekhoon us din hi qayamat hai' (the day I finally see you—that day itself will be the Day of Judgement);[27] it will be the end of the story as well as the end of the world: 'tumhare chasm-e-karam ho to kaam ho jaaye/adah se dekh lo—qissa tamaam ho jaaye' (if your benevolent eyes manifest themselves, all work will be complete—look on me just once with desire—the story itself will be complete).[28] Drawing conclusions from within the logic of narrative, the feminine is a screen on which men and women project their longing for access to a sacrality whose pivot is Khwajaji, in acknowledgement of the sacrality that he, similarly feminized, has already accessed. But it is acknowledgement, not emulation. The longing is not aspirational, tending towards closure; rather, it stands outside of narrative in a space of the irrational, anti-teleological and emotional excess.

The connection between the feminine, the abject, and the ceaselessness of longing is confirmed by the rituals leading up to the moment of *chaadar chadana* (mounting the chaadar). Under the guidance of a *khadim*, the lay pilgrim, who has finally arrived at Khwajaji's threshold, places on his or her head a shallow cane basket bearing the *chaadar* and rose petals. This posture, which mimics that of the carrier of a heavy load—either for manual labour or in performance of feminine domesticity, can induce in the pilgrim an overwhelming awareness of the abject self. This abject self recurs in the other classic *Dargah* posture expressive of physical surrender to the saint and metaphysical inability to reach him: half-lying, half-kneeling, clutching at the filigreed marble screens that run the perimeter of the *sanctum sanctorum*, and looking into it through them. The role of the *khadims* in the ritual also emphasizes the necessity of separation and therefore of mediation between the pilgrim and the saint: guiding the pilgrims with their head loads, they insert themselves in between the two parties by occupying the space in between two sets of silver railings around the tomb. The pilgrims stay outside the second railing. Together they shower the tomb with the petals, but only the *khadim* can throw the *chaadar* on to the tomb. Standing in the mediating space, he places an edge of the *chaadar* over the pilgrims' heads while uttering prayers. The gender gears shift yet again: at this moment of the maximum possible closeness to Khwajaji, his bridal role coalesces with his masculine, regal one: the veil becomes the edge of the royal robe (*daaman*), offering figurative protection to the abject-as-subject.

## Femininity, androgyny, and reaching beyond

One is tempted at this stage to substitute the 'sacred and the feminine' with the 'sacred and the androgynous' as a way to understand what goes on at Ajmer Sharif. These labels, however, seem puny and constricting in comparison to the fluidity they seek to define. This is a fluidity which uses the feminine as an outward signifier for an excess of reverence, love and longing towards the sacred, and for a move, ultimately, towards the transcendental. It is available to both men and women, to both saint and pilgrim, and to anyone, of any religion, who may be so predisposed towards the sacred. Of course, the contemporary politicization of religion in South Asia may not make such ecumenism always possible in praxis. Shrinking spaces such *dargahs* may be, but they are still viable as spaces of refuge and resistance. And, because of the ceaselessness of longing the *dargah* predicates, it is possible to feel part of its power simply through the force of longing, across the distances, until Khwajaji himself pulls the individual to arrive physically at his threshold. It is in this light I should like to discuss a short clip by Qasim Riza Shaheen, a British Asian performance artist based in Manchester, whose repertoire contains an installation/performance, 'Being in Love'. One of its components is a two-minute video loop, 'Tore Surat ke Balhari: A Translation.'[29]

This sequence shows Qasim dancing to a *qawwali* performance at a Pakistani *dargah* of the same Chishti order that Khwajaji brought to South Asia. The *qawwali*, 'tore surat ke balhari' (Beholding your countenance, I offer myself in sacrifice) is one of the most beloved of the Amir Khusrau tradition that I described earlier. It describes the devotee of the Chishti saint as an adorned young woman, whose girlfriends taunt her for her dirtied veil: this spring, she asks the saint, please come and dye my veil anew. One of its most powerful verses, which we also hear in this video, imagines the saintly lineage as the groom's marriage procession, welcoming Khusrau, the ideal devotee, as the king's darling. As these verses are sung by a group of *qawwals*, Qasim dances, with matted locks and beard—the sign of the world-renouncing ascetic— and vermilion and henna, the sign of the world-embracing bride-to-be; he wears a richly decorated bridal costume. In thus literalizing and combining the different roles of the feminine which we have noted in this paper, Qasim's response to the Sufi sacred is profoundly familiar and defamiliarizing. It links a frustration with gender labels inherited while growing up in the West, with the pressures on young British Muslims as indeed Muslims everywhere today. In a world which not only promotes, but operates—indeed, thrives on—segmentation, the boxing of identities, and anti-humanism, one young man turns to the 'remembrance of a Sufi mystic who, centuries ago, took to dancing in women's

clothes in order to win the favours of his beloved, even if it meant becoming a whore'.[30] Born out of an internalized longing for 'a number
of shrines of saints that [he had], over the years, developed an imaginary relationship with', and one, in particular, he 'wanted to be married
to', he admits that 'judging from reactions, it seemed as though something of this nature had not been done before or, at least, as explicitly
as I was proposing'. Yet he insists that the Sufi elders at the shrine in
question were ultimately supportive of his venture. Unsurprisingly,
Qasim has never been to Ajmer himself, and does not want to verbalize
why he is waiting: for the time being, he is content to have brought
Manchester, his home town, into the compass of the sacred geography
of which he feels spiritually part.[31]

## Of liminality and alternative texts

I end by articulating that which is obvious, but the restatement of which
is burningly needed in today's increasingly constricted global-local mi-
lieux: the *dargah*, the saint and the devotee/worshipper/pilgrim together
create an embodied space of liminality and ambivalence. This ambivalence enables the generation of love, of amity, of egalitarianism, of ecumenism. The alternative ethical order that is thereby enacted expresses
the inexpressible under conditions of ecstasy. The adoption of the
'feminine', both in the language of speech and the language of the
body, can be seen as a marker of a moment of permissive transgression, when the boundaries between the exoteric and the esoteric worlds
are breached to irradiate the former with the lucent charge of the sacred. In and for an instant, the boxing of our lived experiences into
'gender' categories is used to overcome the limitations of such 'gender',
and also of other hierarchies and boxes. Through such transformations
are created 'alternative texts—utopian experiential imaginaries of other,
possible world orders'.[32] These alternative, older, always-existing world
orders pull us towards them, inviting us to defy the quotidian constric-
tions of gender, nation, geography, history, and identity itself, releasing
our universal potential to become something other than ourselves.[33]

# THE SACRED AND THE FEMININE

## An African Response to Clément and Kristeva

*Molara Ogundipe*

The title selected for this collection, *The Sacred and the Feminine*, is a conscious inversion of the title of the book by Catherine Clément and Julia Kristeva, *The Feminine and the Sacred*, a work that functions as a catalyst to the papers assembled here. The latter book's title implies and states the objectives of the conversation of the two scholars as women and their relation to the sacred.[1] Our collective concern in this book is articulated as *The Sacred and the Feminine*. This can be read as emphasizing the sacred and how it relates to women, appertains to women, or how it is located in the feminine. Here lies an important distinction.

In my chapter, I shall focus on the concept of the sacred from an African point of view, and then delineate how the sacred is located and manifested in and by the feminine among the Yoruba, ending with the conceptualization of the Yoruba creation myth and the role of the female deity or *Orisha Osun*. Although African cultures are not monolithic, similar patterns of thought can still be traced in the endogenous religions that an African woman theologian has named 'primal' religions, and I have called in other places, 'indigenous' in West Africa.[2]

The Yoruba conception of *Osun* shows that the feminine is not always 'ecstatic', 'hysteric' or mentally deranged as it is often theorized in the West. Evidently women all over the world are 'not one', to borrow the syntax of Luce Irigaray, for as we now say and as articulated by Simone de Beauvoir: 'One is not born, but rather becomes a woman.'[3] Womanhood is, therefore, culturally determined. Consequently, when we speak of the feminine, what do we mean? Throughout this chapter, I will use *the feminine* to refer to the biologically female person. The use of the word, 'woman', to mean exclusively the feminine in Africa and in Yorubaland would be problematic since womanhood sometimes crosses physical and gender borders. Womanhood is determined and defined by gender roles, not only by the female body among the Yoruba and other African groups; that is, womanhood is not tied to the female body.[4] As in other African cultures, a woman can be socially constructed and defined as a man after menopause; a *sangoma* (endogenous doctor) can be greeted and typecast as a man; the male healer in the Senegalese rite is visually represented as woman in the N'Deup rite discussed by Catherine Clément in the text in question here; and the Rain Queen of the Lovedu in South Africa can have official wives.

A response from an African scholar, cultural critic, and feminist is called for by the book put together by a French/Bulgarian feminist, Julia Kristeva, whose experience, ideas and examples are clearly and admittedly located in Europe from which she theorizes exclusively, and by a French/Jewish anthropologist, Catherine Clément who has clearly travelled in Africa and strives valiantly to be universalistic in her thinking. Kristeva asks 'if the ancestral division between "those who give life" (women) and "those who give meaning" (men) were in the process of disappearing' as if the distinction were viable, accepted and acceptable in the first place.[5] Then they both proceed to use this view of life as a basis for their own theorizing, as a given which could now be being undermined by 'technology' and 'life bearing meaning' in 'this third millennium', no longer 'dominated by the sacredness of the Baby Jesus'. [6] They do not challenge the dichotomy and the theory in itself which is then generalized to the world at large.

Let us ignore here the historical fact that much of the world has not been dominated by the sacredness of the Baby Jesus. Despite her brilliance and careful thinking, Julia Kristeva seems to be very limited to 'the world as Europe', presenting theses that are arguable because Eurocentric and not borne out by the lives of all women and in all world cultures. Much as I share some of her views on motherhood and life from African perspectives, the 'ancestral' view that she traces back to the Greeks and forward to Hannah Arendt is meaningless in most African and African Diaspora cosmologies as well as in the particular cosmology I am going to present here: that of the West African Yoruba. In these African and Africana systems of thought, life and meaning can neither be separated nor ascribed separately to one sex or the other as I shall make clear later.

The interpellation of the book by my response can again be said to be demanded by the very interesting fact that the two scholars begin their intellectual inquiry of women and the sacred with a wide ranging discussion of what Kristeva describes as 'the three enigmas: the feminine, the sacred and the various fates of *Africanness*'. She writes:

[B]ut here we find ourselves fixed on a 'sacred' that is increasingly 'black'! Black women, black religions: our journey continues to link the three enigmas—the feminine, the sacred, and the various fates of *Africanness*—in a metaphor that becomes more substantial as we write, and which further complicates, if need be, what Freud in his time called the 'dark'—that is, the black continent.[7]

Shades of Conrad and *Heart of Darkness*! Kristeva's discourse, in a regrettable way for the years 1998/2001 (the dates of the first edition of the book and its translation) links brutality and blood-thirstiness to Africa even when she is discussing Proust.[8]

For the reason that the first 27 pages of the book discuss Africa substantially, I shall begin my response there, including necessary corrections of important factual, historical, and interpretative errors. The first letter of the book is from Clément to Kristeva. She makes clear to Kristeva her presence in Dakar, Senegal in Africa at the time of her writing. In connection with their theme of women and the sacred, Clément reminds Kristeva of Freud's comparison of femininity in general to 'the dark continent'. This perhaps explains why in their discussion they continually refer to the 'id' in relation to the feminine, a very problematic concatenation for me. Clément then attempts to identify the sacred from her description of a scene of possession at a Catholic mass in Senegal. The black Senegalese women of the laity go into screaming possession that she identifies as a 'trance'. Clément states that the event took place in Popenguine, twenty miles from Dakar; 'the women are black and Catholic' and 'born on the coast of West Africa where the first Portuguese colonizers and the first Muslim preachers arrived at the same time in the fifteenth century'. The introduction of Islam and African Catholicism, she says, dates from that era.[9]

For the sake of informing the world correctly about Africa, about which not enough is known, even among scholars, and in the interest of transnational feminism, good research, and the intercultural women's discourse that both Kristeva and Clément called for in their introduction, it will be necessary to make the following corrections here. Popenguine is more than twenty miles from Dakar; it is at least two-and-a-half hours and about 75 kilometres by car. It therefore represents a different milieu from the highly urban and international city of Dakar, capital of Senegal. The Portuguese did first arrive at that West African coast in the fifteenth century but were not colonizers then. They were merely traders and frustrated sailors looking for a way to reach India by going east, unlike Christopher Columbus.

Islam was introduced into West Africa well before the fifteenth century. In fact documented presence of Islam in the region can be dated back to the eighth century CE. Eminent Arab historians have written about the epoch, notable among whom are Al-Bakri, Al-Masudi, Ibn Batutah and Ibn Khaldun. Besides these scholars, we can also cite local scholars whose works have come down to us, for example *Tarikh al-Sudan* (*The History of the Sudan*) by Al-Sadi and *Tarikh al-Fattash* by Muhammad al-Kati. This misreading of the history of Islam in West Africa, that often occurs in the works of Africanists and others, has often been attributed to the burning of Kumbi-Saleh, the capital of the medieval African kingdom of Ghana by the Muslim fundamentalist, Abdullah Ibn Yasin and his followers, named 'El morabetin' (the men of the monastery), but in the West called the 'Almoravid'. He waged a 30-year 'jihad', a holy war, on Ghana ending with the fall of Kumbi in 1067.[10] However, Islam was already in Africa well before then, at least as early as 650 CE. The Ghana empire flourished from 750–1076 CE. Africans in the Mandingo zone had been writing and setting up *madrassa* schools before the fall of the Ghana capital and the arrival of the Arab Almoravids.[11] It is also generally known that Muslim indigenous preachers were all over West Africa before the arrival of the Arabs; in fact, West Africans were mainly Islamized by other West Africans. Notably, the arrival of writing in Arabic in the Mandingo zone is often dated as between the tenth and eleventh centuries.

Catherine Clément is right to have dismissed the naming of the trance as hysteria by the middle class, Gallicized Senegal official sitting next to her at the ceremony, who snobbishly dissociates himself from the event by the naming, probably to impress Clément by such dissociation. Furthermore, he may have been trying to show her that he is also of the culture of the *metropole*, as often happens with the colonized and post-colonial middle classes who are also referred to in Francophone Africa as *Negropolitan*. She is correct in her reading of him and her linking of the possession to its manifestation in Brazil. The Senegalese, however, would call the event 'spirit possession', not a trance. There is also a significant difference between the Senegalese event and the Brazilian possession of the Yoruba tradition of the *candomble* to which Clément refers, as I will indicate later.

Nonetheless, it is not the term, 'trance' or 'possession' that is important but the concept that is behind the observed behaviour. Regarding this, Clément makes serious errors about the reasons for the behaviour and her theory about its etiology. The event is forced onto the grid of her theory that the possessed state of the women is caused by a psychological revolt against their class origin. It is probably difficult for her as an etic observer to know without close and detailed research that the phenomenon of possession is not an expression of the class oppression of the women whom she assumes are all maids. Though she puts a finger correctly on the event when she says 'the African trance' emerges from under the glaze of the foreign religions that have come into the area from 'the Marranos, Jews, Protestants and Catholics' (Islam should have been in her list too), her factual guess does not fully apprehend the events happening before her.[12]

Indeed the Serer religious expression of the encounter with the sacred or accession to the level of possession is not a pathological expression of a reaction to class oppression. Rather the traditional energy of the Serer religion breaks through and perverts the Catholic liturgy but to a different end than is problematized by Clément. It is explained and known by emic members of Senegalese society that the Serer culture is one of the cultural universes that have survived in its integrity in Senegal, despite all the waves of other cultures. It is, therefore, viewed as still very strong and powerful in modern times, seen as having no tension in contemporary Senegalese society. Women are also very powerful in Serer culture and religion both of which they totally control as women and priestesses. They are the healers, as Clément correctly tells us, and they use various ritual procedures, but what they spit over the possessed woman is not saliva as Clément reports. It is water projected from the mouth in a process the Wolof call *boussou* (the verb to spread, meaning 'that which is spread'), water that the woman healer absorbs and keeps in her mouth. She now ritually 'spreads' the water over the possessed woman to purify her spiritual body as a patient. Since the water has come through the mouth of the initiated healer/priestess, whose mouth is now sacred, the water also is considered to have become sacred from having gained power and force through the healer.[13] I shall address definitions of the sacred in more detail later.

The Serer are a matrilineal people, like the Wolof and other peoples in the Mandingo zone of the West African Sahel, who now have to process the overlays of androcentric and patriarchal religions in their world, namely the Abrahamic religions, one of which is Christianity that Kristeva describes as 'a paternal cult' and a 'cult of the father and son'.[14] Very perceptively she disquisitions at length on Mariology, the cult of the Virgin Mary, and shows that the Virgin Mary is constructed in such a way by the Church that she is finally not a woman at all, despite her motherhood, and not a human either, due to her ascension in Catholic doctrine. As she does not experience sex or death, Mary is beyond being human. Due to the vital survival of Serer religious culture where women are actual, human women, however, the women at a Roman Catholic mass still try to worship their Supreme deity, *Rokh*, as they express their humanity in incantations, screaming and possession, if that state of consciousness is attained.

What transpires, therefore, is that the Serer women superimpose their *Rokh* consciousness over the Catholic liturgy, in a manner similar to

the process that can be observed in voodoo—the African Diaspora indigenous religion of Haiti in which the African deities are superim-
posed on Christian saints as was also done in Brazil. The
superimposition in Senegal is done in a way that raises the women to
the level of possession. For instance, the Lord's Prayer in the Christian
service may be chanted in the tones present and used only in the liturgy
for Rokh worship and then raised to decibels where possession takes
place.[15] It is as subtle as this—expressing a Serer religious consciousness
over Catholic substance, and not necessarily about being maids, through
the adaptation of the intonation of a Serer liturgy to a foreign one in
a manner that may appear as screaming to an outsider, which the
French Senegalese official himself might well be. That is, he may not
himself be a Serer.

This brings us to the question of ethnicity that Clément herself proceeds to raise in relation to class. She says the women were villagers
and servants after which she makes one of her usual blanket statements
about 'Africa': that 'in Africa what is so easily called "ethnic group" also
depends on the caste system—very concealed but still extremely present—as well as on social roles'.[16] To say that what are so easily called
ethnic groups in Africa depend on caste systems is a mystifying sociological statement. There may be caste systems in Senegal but they do
not define ethnic groups because different castes are found in the same
ethnic group, i.e. the concept of *gnegno* (low caste that includes all workers such as griots, poets and chroniclers who service families and aris-
tocratic lines, blacksmiths, carpenters, jewellers, and leatherworkers etc.)
and *gueer* or *bueer* (the royal or kingly line) among the Wolof can also be
found among the Toucouleur and other ethnic groups. In a discussion
of caste in Senegal, several levels of the caste system were identified as
common to various ethnic groups: the *bueer* or *gueer* which is the
king/ruler and relatives, the *garmi* who are noble men and women, the
commoners who are freeborn known as the *baadoolo*, below which come
the *gnegno* who work with their hands thereby including musicians, verbal and plastic artists (as stated before) and at the lowest level, the *jaam*
who are of slave ancestry, consisting of family slaves or nobles who
lost rank as captives in war.[17] Others among my interviewees confirm
the sociological fact that Serer maids are frequent in the country today
but this is not to say that all Serer are, therefore, in the servant class.[18]
Marieme Gueye, however, confirms that there is a popular notion
among the Senegalese that the Serer make the best maids because they
are hardworking and are, therefore, preferred. Gueye also indicates that
the image of the maid is a Serer among the Senegalese themselves, but
not, in my deduction, for the reasons that Clément adduces in her text.
In fact, in this letter and section of her observations, Catherine Clément

makes some of her most incorrect statements about the Serer, their sociology in modern Senegal, the reasons for their existence as servants and their possible psychological states, considering what is generally known about their culture and sociological roles, ambitions, and achievements.

Contrary to Clément's supposition that the Serer are a disadvantaged group in Senegal, the world-renowned Léopold Senghor, president of the country for half of its independent life, was a Serer. Moreover, the Serer and the Lebou whom Clément also discusses in another connection and who are both matrilineal peoples, form the highest number of Senegalese in the modern administrative class with regard to their percentage in the Senegalese general population. Such social placing contradicts Clément's picture of the Serer as being disempowered and 'not one of the powerful'. In addition, the Serer in the past were a self-sufficient agricultural people who, following the economic travails of the post-independent history of the country, had to migrate into the cities, like the Wolof of Joloff, Walo and Baol for specific jobs. They are nationally known to prefer only temporary jobs which will permit them to return to their farms in the rainy season. They choose domestic labour in the cities where they have no urban skills, education or non-agricultural work to do. The Serer are said to have pioneered in Senegal the temporary job situation that provided them with mobility, working four months in the dry season in the cities as house servants after which they return to their farms.

Sembene Ousmane dramatizes this experience of the illiterate house-maid taken to France by French employers in his early film, *The Black Girl* (1966). Not having the mentality of a slave and feeling devalued, the housemaid commits honorific suicide in Paris to protest her treatment by her employers. The temporary job situation pioneered by the Serer is said to have crossed ethnic lines these days. As such, it is no longer the monopoly of one ethnic group because people born and raised in the cities dedicate themselves to these activities. One of my interviewees, Babacar Mbow, further reminded me that there are no inter-ethnic problems in Senegal of a kind comparable or similar to what obtains in countries like Nigeria and Côte D'Ivoire today.

It may be admirable in a humanist vein to be universalist in one's approaches as Clément usually is. Both Kristeva and Clément identify themselves as daughters of the European Enlightenment. Yet in making parallels in her insights, as between the Serer women, the Ethiopian and Egyptian *zar*, the N'Deup in Dakar, Mother Teresa and the Brazilian *candomble* Santeria women for instance, we must be careful not to generalize practices whose manifestations and goals are different. For instance, Brazilian *macumba* in Rio or the *candomble* rites, though deriving from Yoruba religious heritage and consequently African, as rightly noted by Clément, have different objectives. The Brazilian rites are not psychiatric in intent as is the secular N'Deup rite of Dakar that Clément describes at length and parallels to the divine and non-secular rite of the Serer possession. The *macumba* rite in Rio, because intended to obtain good deeds from the gods, is directed towards a different and spiritual end. This explains the difference in the manifestation of the rite. For instance, no possession is used for healing. It is not the patient who becomes possessed, as in the Serer ritual; the priest in Rio becomes possessed as the transmitter of divine power, for being the one who propitiates the gods. In the Senegalese Lebou psychiatric healing rites of N'Deup, the priest does not become possessed; rather the priest as healer channels the sacred energy directly to the patient who may become possessed as she or he struggles with her demons or psychosis.[19]

In the interest of researchers of Africa and medical professionals who might benefit from a better understanding, I shall discuss further here the N'Deup, described as 'a spectacular therapeutic rite' of the Lebou by Catherine Clément. It is a therapeutic rite, I am told, for secular and psychiatric healing, not a sacred rite. It is also confusing that Clément uses terms such as 'genie' or 'jinns', Arabic terms borrowed through Islam to refer to Lebou concepts. The 'jinn' is not maleficent in both Islam and Senegalese culture, but the spirit 'deum' in Lebou thought, that is being exorcized, is maleficent and malevolent. The 'jinn' in the Qu'ran and Islam are otherworldly creatures of the spirit world in general that can be good or bad. In the Qu'ran it is written that Allah created three sets of creatures: humans, jinns and animals. The word 'jinn' therefore is a floating concept in Senegalese culture. Jinns are phantasmagoric personages transported in language from Islamic concepts but who do not play a particular role in the Wolof cosmogony that includes the Lebou. In contrast, the term 'deum' is definite. It refers to a living person with maleficent and supernatural powers who could be your neighbour or your boss.[20]

The N'Deup is enacted for two reasons: firstly, when one encounters, depending on one's locality, the powerful spirit of *Raap* or *Mame Coumba Lambaye* among the Lebou of Rufisque Senegal (that became *macumba* in Brazil). *Raap* are powerful spirits of the sea and waters; secondly, when one is caught by 'deum', the consequence of which is the loss of a state of consciousness which is being possessed or a status of insanity from the shock and trauma of meeting the malevolent, maleficent and supernatural powers. This is when the Lebou N'Deup is required. It is a therapeutic practice designed to address the psychiatric mental status of an individual who has encountered the situation described above. Possession in itself here is not designed to cure. Singing songs of acclamation of new spirits alone can cause one to be possessed. It takes eleven years of apprenticeship to learn all the hymns to be sung to a *Raap*. Participation is not voluntary and the singing of one's family songs can lead one into possession during which one is considered to have released one's troubling spirit. One appeases the spirit and reestablishes one's status as a woman and a person with sacrifices.[21] That this important medical practice, which might interest Julia Kristeva because of her profession, entailing the most complex form of knowledge, is concentrated in the hands of women is very significant. The science of N'Deup is developed by women and is completely in their hands. The N'Deup is a space for women and for women as healers. Only the drum players and the killers of animals are men.[22] That is why the male healer has to be dressed as a woman as noted by Clément. It is not about the 'bi-sexuality of therapists' in the Western sense. It is about the recognition that the male healer is in feminine territory, the territory of women, and he therefore has to acknowledge and fit into its imperative by dressing as a woman. The highest priestess of this profane and secular science of psychology, developed by women as N'Deup, lives in Rufisque. She is named Adia Fatou Seck commonly referred to as Fatou Seck 'N'Deupkat—*N'Deup practitioner*'.[23]

If the Serer possession event is sacred and N'Deup is secular and profane, what then constitutes the sacred in this part of Africa? The commonalities in African religions and the similarities in their undergirding epistemologies have been well established in the scholarship of African theology. These similarities, to be found in the cosmogonies of African cultures in general and West African cultures in particular, make it possible for me to also intervene from a Yoruba perspective. We can establish at this point a definition of the sacred that tries to examine the word itself from its Latin root of *sacer* which means 'held apart or set apart'. It is necessary to point out from the onset that to be set apart in the African and Yoruba spiritual sense is not a factor of inferiorization, contempt or rejection. Rather it is a distancing, born of respect and veneration in the sense of that which is holy. The African 'apartness' is in marked contrast to the biblical tradition set forth in Leviticus about various aversions and prescribed reactions to what were considered 'unclean' or unholy such as illnesses and discharges from both men and women. Obviously one of these discharges is the woman's monthly flow, her *menses*, regarding which being set apart is firmly enjoined for the woman in that condition. This matter will be taken up later.

The concept of the sacred pertinent to the Serer women in the Clément text derives from African concepts that have also survived in the African Diaspora, namely, that there are two levels of reality that determine the universe and its contents including the human person. The two levels consist of the physical and the spiritual or the numinous, the visible and the invisible. This double reality is also present in practice, space and objects, for instance, the passed-down clothes of departed elders that become sacred heirlooms; the elders themselves rendered sacred from wisdom, experience and suffering—surviving this vale of tears—and being close in time to joining the ancestors; babies from being newly arrived from the spiritual world of the ancestors, which fact makes their fetal hair sacred, the umbilical cord binding the child and the mother and also binding the baby to the spiritual world; beads worn by priests and priestesses etc.

The Yoruba believe that each person has a dual being too, a spiritual second that follows that person through life, death and reincarnation. This means living beings who are themselves sacred can confer sacredness on objects. Everything has its double in the spiritual world: the person is double, being the material creature we see in constant conjunction with a spiritual version of the same person that may be invisible without being necessarily absent. Toni Morrison says it well in her novel *Beloved* when she makes one of her narrators argue that invisible things are not necessarily not here.[24] The sacred is, therefore, that which has demonstrated itself as able to manifest itself at these two levels and enclose in itself the power that resides in the Supreme Being, the final source of all that is sacred.

All power is considered as resident in God; therefore, all reality including so-called deities is merely manifestations and patrons of aspects of the power of God. God or God-ness, so to speak, infuses everything in the universe. This is why African theologians today, and scholars in the past, have tried to make the world and the West (the Western intellectually central tradition or intellectual grand narrative) that love dichotomies understand that African religions were monotheistic basically with patrons or representatives of aspects of the power of God abounding in the universe and relating to humankind. It is actually a vision of a polytheistic monotheism. Unfortunately the West in this domain seeks parallels with its own experience or history as usual rather than trying to understand the new, the different, and the Other—the much theorized but elusive Other.

The parallel the West makes here is with the Greek experience and their own Nordic or Celtic traditions. It is assumed that if there were polytheisms there, surely there must have been polytheisms in pre-Jewish, pre-Christian or pre-Islamic Africa and they have to be of the same kind or they do not exist. Yet somehow the existence of the Christian concept of the Trinity, Satan, Lucifer, angels, and genies in these religions does not seem to interfere with the rationality of naming these

Abrahamic religions monotheistic. I also think that a simplification derives from a Christian consciousness that denigrates African and most other pre-Christian cultures by making parallels between them and the religions and gods of the biblical Canaanites who were reproached for and said to have worshipped gods of wood and stone. Wood and stone may be considered sacred in African cultures because they represented the power and force of divinity, but they were not worshipped in themselves, even when rites and rituals were performed on or around them. Symbolic behaviour sometimes seems very difficult for some interlocutors to grasp, not to speak of grasping the abstract and the numinous.

As has been described *ad nauseam* by African culture workers, theologians, and scholars, there was always the idea of an omniscient and omnipotent God, a Supreme Spiritual Being in many African cosmologies. Often that presence was neither male nor female, and was the force of justice and good that controlled everything in the universe. This Being had the power to do and undo, and created everything—so also a Creator God. Being good and concerned with making everything right and successful, that Presence does not undo; h/she leaves events and actions to be products of choices made by humans, leaves events as outcomes of human choice, human error or chance which is also an aspect of the numinous that has to be placated and sometimes deified for its power and effect on existence. All reality is managed by lower level deities who carry out the intentions of God. The Supreme Being is considered too vast and awesome to relate to us, relating is, therefore, done through his/her representatives who are myriad. This is probably why the argument is made that such a cosmology cannot be monotheistic.

To return to the question of the Supreme Being, it is argued that his/her awesomeness is a reason the Presence is not represented or worshipped in shrines or temples. No shrines and temples are built to the Creator/Supreme Being who is very present in many African epics, folktales and other oral traditions. Contending arguments, however, also exist from some opposing African scholars who think the preoccupation with Supreme Beings is a predilection of the mentally colonized and their anxiety to equate African religions with Christianity. Certainly among the Yoruba *Olorun* or *Olodumare* was this sacred and supreme power in the universe that encompassed everything. Feminist theologian Mercy Oduyoye describes similar conceptions in other West African religions.[25] *Olorun* is not just a sky god as some anthropologists believe; to respond to their suggestion from the fact that literally the word translates as 'the owner of *Orun*'. *Orun* means the sky, as well as where the dead go to live—the place accessed by those who have transitioned to the other existence since death in the Yoruba cosmology is not a tragedy. Death is a transition to become an ancestor who will be reincarnated as a living baby at any time, in the permanent cyclical movement of life between the spiritual and the material world. Death is only tragic if one dies young and does not fulfil one's potential. That is why funerals are celebrated among the Yoruba and most West African cultures.

Everything is philosophically sacred for being objects of the Creator of the universe; humans are sacred for being life-bearers, possessing their double that is in spirit, and the essence of the spiritual infuses everything. That does not mean that everything has to be worshipped, though it does mean that everything has to be treated with the respect due to its essence. That is why in the endogenous way of life, trees were propitiated before they were hurt by felling, why hunters have rites and poetry to be chanted about and to animals, why human blood is sacred as the earth herself is, for being our mother. Unfortunately, it is also because humans are sacred that they were sacrificed, not for blood-thirstiness as depicted by foreigners, but from the positive belief that only the most sacred and precious things and beings should be given to God and his/her deities. The nearest to the world-feeling described here for Westerners is probably that of the Native American.

It is this idea of a sacred that permeates everything that is misunderstood as animism. The word, 'animism' comes from the Latin, *animus*, meaning 'mind'. Animism assumes a belief that there is a mind in nature. Africans do not believe that there is a mind in nature. The mind is in the human beings who think about nature and construct it as sacred. African spiritual thought does not think that wood and stone and everything else have life or are alive; rather it conceptualizes a sense of the numinous in space, objects and practice without worshipping the space, the tree or the river in itself. The river is a symbol of the spiritual that infuses it and resides there. The sacred infuses the river; that does not make the river alive in itself. The patrons or embodiments of the divine power that makes rivers possible—and do what rivers do (and the same goes for other aspects of God) have been translated as deities; the word in Yoruba is *orisa*, sometimes spelt *orisha*, the name for these patrons, representatives or embodiment of aspects of spiritual power who are accessed and propitiated through prayer, song and dance, the arts, and sacrificial offerings. They are not nature gods but gods of aspects of human functioning in the universe—e.g. the art of drumming, medicine, dance, the achievement of wealth, the protection and maturation of youth, that power and beauty of nature's functioning expressed through animals and plants, the science of knowledges etc. These *orisa*, named deities, are sacred for being venerated. Manifestations of aspects of God, they can also be anthropomorphic, as well as be former extraordinary and outstanding persons in history and society, but God, the Supreme Being, in this universe, is never anthropomorphic.

The idea of the invisible world being a physical world that can be accessed through prayer, propitiation, ritual, the arts and even magic, is one that eludes and confounds post-Enlightenment Europe such that primal African religions have been reduced to animism or, as Kristeva suggests, endogenous animism. This reductionism may also flow from the covert idea that the autochthonous African is incapable of abstraction.

At this point, we may ask what is sacred about women. What constitutes the sacred and the feminine in and consequently from endogenous African and Yoruba thought today? Women were empowered to carry and manage the most important rites and rituals either as priestesses or as deities or *orisa* themselves. To reiterate, an *orisa* is more like a sacred patron of some aspect of existence, all within God's power, and there are female *orisa*.

Women, moreover, are considered sacred because they possess that which is considered the highest power, that is, the power to give life, which only God, the Creator and Supreme Being has, whether that presence is *Olodumare*, *Amma* (Dogon), *Nyame* (Akan) or *Rokh* (Serer). At this point, I find a coincidence with the thought and position of Julia Kristeva when she relates the sacred in women to the power to give life.[26] In his narrative of the ancient Dogon religion of Mali, Ogotommeli informs us that there were no male priests allowed to serve in the ancient religions built around the Supreme Being, *Amma*, who is a woman among the Dogon of West Africa.[27] As women are endowed with the ability of God through their power to give life, they are considered sacred. They become more so, when they produce twins or more in some cultures and especially among the Yoruba who are said by reliable sources to produce the highest incidence of twinning in the world. A materialist rejoinder often is that men also produce children, but the pragmatic position at the back of this African thought is that only the identity of a child's mother is sure.

Furthermore, the visible creation of the child in her body for nine months is also found more impressive and awe-inspiring than the male contribution to reproduction. The mother is, therefore, also accorded the sacred power of absorbing or diverting the malevolent forces unleashed against her progeny without her suffering from it. Such extraordinary spiritual power that demonstrates that the mother-figure, for instance, lives powerfully at both levels of the spiritual and the this-worldly, and can use and embody power in both worlds effectively, is called the sacred. Regarding space, there can be sacred forests, groves, houses etc., but the *sine qua non* in the African concept of the sacred is the giving of life.

The woman or the feminine is also considered sacred because of her direct connection with spirits and the spiritual world. For this reason, she predominates in priestly roles and other basic existential rituals, domestic and public, social and political. This fact explains my rejection of the initially discussed ancestral tradition from the Greeks that Kristeva evokes: that women give life and men give meaning. Woman is considered among the Yoruba and other Africans as both a giver of life and a giver of meaning through doing. In fact, she is considered primarily a doer because the spirits do not come down without the power and blessing of the woman. As priestess, in some West African cultures, the woman blesses and interprets the code of the spirits and thus interprets existence to the village. She interprets the meaning of life to her village.

It is a common belief as well as a social and political practice among the Yoruba that whatever is not blessed by a woman will not succeed. History, oral and written bears witness to situations as important as prosecuting war, offering initiating rituals and practices in the town or in the king's palace, engaging the family in events and issues that needed the sanctifying decision or prayer of the womenfolk. A woman is in this way too both a giver of life and a giver of meaning. Finally, giving life and giving meaning are not antagonistic in the African world of primal religions. There is no life without meaning and no meaning without life. The dichotomy is again another example of a Western grid and love of self-exclusionary dichotomies.

Yet in view of this touted sacredness of the woman in Yoruba and other African cultures, one may ask why women are not powerful in modern day Africa and Nigeria? Perhaps their conditions are due to perversions caused by the Abrahamic religions, the insertions and distortions of the Victorian and patriarchal colonial powers, and the modern-day gender politics of struggle between men and women over power in the new constructions of the family, the administration of the society and the nation state. Sometimes this gender politics is attributed to a deep-seated fear of women; at other times to a desire by men to continue the androcentric colonial heritage that is more in the interests of the male population. Still at other times we name as cause the collapse of primal or endogenous cultures or their rejection and suppression due to a sense of shame and embarrassment about those cultures. These reasons could all be coincident and are certainly not exhaustive.

As the woman is sacred in endogenous thought, her body is also sacred. Similarly her body as the house of life, parts of her body such as her hair and nail clippings (the sacredness of which became problematic with the ever-materialist reactions of both Clément and Kristeva in their book), women's discharges such as her milk, menses, tears, sweat, and even saliva are considered sacred. They can and are used as blessings, curses, and potions for power—social, material and supernatural. It is notable that analysts of the Jewish proscription on menstruation do not discuss it in the context in which it was advocated in the Bible —that of surrounding all human discharges including male ones with regulations for ritual purity. Apparently these caveats were not done against women as such in Leviticus, but in the health interest of a nomadic and mainly illiterate group of religionists marching through deserts on pilgrimage to their Promised Land.

I have written at some length about the sacredness of the woman's body—her body, her nakedness, breasts, vagina and discharges (in Nigeria and among the Yoruba in my book, *Recreating Ourselves: African Women and Critical Transformations*).[28] Menstruation is considered sacred and powerful, believed to have the power to interrupt, interfere with, and cause to happen. This conception of menses is prevalent in West Africa, if not in the whole of the continent. The Soce of the Senegambia, another Mandingo subgroup, hold that the highest point of a woman's power is during her menstruation. No matter the mystical power of a man, it is crossed and disempowered by the woman. That is why men in Africa generally avoid sexual interactions with women in that period. In the medieval epic of *Sundiata*, a protagonist and invincible hero, Susamgoro Keita was said to be only conquerable if the beak of a cock was put in the vagina of a menstruating woman for some time, to be seasoned in sacred power, before attaching the beak to the arrow that will be pointed, just pointed, at the invincible Susamgoro to achieve his inevitable death. The vagina is, therefore, not simply a place of pleasure for most African men but a site of power and good luck, consequently an explanation for some of the fear of women.

It is also believed in contemporary times that if a merchant woman puts her hand in her vagina and then touches her goods before she goes to market, she will sell every item.[29] The uterus is also considered sacred. As recently as the 1980s, my family had some land dispute in which the men of the woman's line began to farm the land. In the basically male-administered inheritance system of the Ijebu, my subgroup of the Yoruba, this was not done, though women could inherit directly from their patrilineage if a male member willed the possession to them in his lifetime, as my father did with me regarding some land. It was considered improper that this nephew took the use of land as of right.

My father was outraged and, breathing fire and smoke, summoned a family meeting urgently. The young men, his nephews through his sisters, however, had a plan for him. As soon as the meeting began, they broke into song about the children of the vagina and the power of the vagina in a scene that was quite Achebe-esque, as I thought at the time.[30] They sang about the power of the vagina that links families and blood. My formerly fuming father, a retired Christian bishop, a church-planting and school-founding missionary, broke into tears there and then, weeping about his deceased sisters. He went on to say his hands were tied for he had been reminded of unshakeable sacred laws, and that was the end of the dispute. He declared that the young men could go ahead and use the land.

It is this sacred concept of the body of the woman that is found potent in political struggle all over Africa and has been recorded by political scientists. Not only do I write about it in my book quoted above, but, in a personal communication, Griselda Pollock reminded me of the use of the female body in a documentary about an episode in Apartheid South Africa made in 1990. The film documents African women protesting the demolition of their home by the apartheid state who removed their clothes to stop the soldiers and bulldozers.[31] Among the Yoruba, stripping and the threat of it was used effectively by the women of Abeokuta protesting taxation in the 1940s—a struggle that finally led to the exiling of the king.[32] Women used the same invocation of the sacredness of women against military governments in Nigeria and as both threat and actual happening as recently as the 1990s and thereafter, in protests in the Nigerian Niger delta against the oil companies polluting and destroying the environment, without any care for the surrounding population. Such remembrances of the sacredness of the woman's body are positive; regrettably, this concept can and has led to the unfortunate murders of women and their mutilation in the pursuit of using their bodies for powerful magic and potions, even in contemporary times.

We shall now consider motherhood that makes women sacred and implicates the *sine qua non* of sacredness which is the giving of life. Mother-love is just as sacred for it is also creative, implying another life-giving power of the mother in action—the ability to create the other, through mother-love. Considering that these ancient African ideas occur also in Kristeva's text, it underlines for us that the world is more interconnected than we wish to think sometimes. It behoves us to promote intercultural studies, for concepts considered deep and brilliant emerge or have existed for millennia in the so-called Third World. Even when we misread, we can unlearn our findings and attain correct understandings. The Yoruba iconize their ideas of motherhood in the legend of *Osun*, a female *orisa* who appears in the creation myth of the people. She is the only woman member of the pantheon of gods who were sent by the Supreme Being to effect the creation of the world.

The Yoruba in Western Nigeria are about 30 million pre-colonially town-dwelling people who had an empire spreading to modern day Benin and Togo, an empire that historians speculate collapsed with the slave trade in the eighteenth century. The culture of the Yoruba has survived in Brazil, Cuba, Trinidad, Guyana and the United States of America. The political centre of the Yoruba Empire was in Old Oyo which was more of a Sahelian or savannah culture while much of modern-day Yorubaland is in the rain forest. Due to political strife, the Yoruba capital is believed to have moved down to the southern and forest area city of Ile-Ife that became its spiritual and cultural centre and has been carbon-dated to the ninth century CE. Historians have also tried to establish, through oral history, dramatized rituals, festivals and traditions of conquered kings being reduced to priestly functions, the hypothesis of an immigrating group of Yoruba who found and integrated with an indigenous people.[33]

Contemporary Yoruba are primal/endogenous religionists, Muslims and Christians. Islam came into Nigeria among southerners before Christianity. Religions and their supporting arts are very often syncretized today. A powerful middle-class elite that is adjudged to be economically and politically dominant in Nigeria today is said to be constituted by majority Yoruba men and women. The Yoruba cultures in Nigeria have also been noted for their economically active and independent women with traditions of authority and autonomy that predate colonization or encounter with the West. The strong and respected positions of the women and the self assured attitudes of the women are partly traced to the sacredness of the feminine in that culture. These in turn can be located in the culture's metaphysic; in the cosmology that places womanhood and motherhood at the very beginning of time where, without them, creation and life itself would have been impossible.

In one of the myths of origin preserved in one of its versions in the Ifa and related systems of divination poetry or corpus,[34] 17 deities were sent to the earth to effect the creation of the world, 16 men and one woman, *Osun*.[35] She is supposed to have invented and taught the knowledge and science of divination to the male god, *Orunmila* who is now remembered as its architect, depending on one's source and the gender politics of the raconteur or the context. The Ifa corpus is introduced by Wande Abimbola as:

an important system of divination found in many cultures of West Africa. In Yorubaland where Ifa is a major divinity, this fascinating system of divination has been closely identified with Yoruba history, mythology, religion and folk-medicine. The Yoruba regard Ifa as the repository of their beliefs and moral values. The Ifa divination system and the extensive poetic chants associated with it are used by the Yoruba to validate important aspects of their culture. Ifa divination is, therefore, performed by the Yoruba during their important rites of passage such as naming and marriage ceremonies, funeral rites and the installation of kings. In traditional Yoruba society, the authority of Ifa permeated every aspect of life because the Yoruba regard Ifa as the voice of the divinities and the wisdom of the ancestors.[36]

In the interest of African Diasporic research and archaeology of knowledge, it is important to note here that the Ifa worship and studies are more welcomed and promoted in the worldwide African Diaspora countries than in Yorubaland that is locked into fundamentalisms of the Abrahamic religions. In the United States and among African Americans in particular, Ifa enjoys much respect, following and engagement. Ifa describes the origin of the world and how the world was created among other contents. It sings the coming of the deities to create that world. I say it 'sings' because the verses of Ifa are often chanted, that is, performed and incantated by the priest/priestess in a manner that can rise to song, very evocative for me of the style and tradition of the African-American sermon. Perhaps this is a cultural survival, for the Ifa priest was/is a religious, community and knowledge leader as the preacher was in the days of the plantation and slavery when the church was also a site of knowledge and the consolidation of the community ethos. The preacher was, after all, at that time also, a kind of transatlantic babalawo/Ifa priest, healer, spiritual diviner, doctor, cultural leader and community psychologist/psychiatrist.

As one of the most erudite scholars in the science of Ifa, and perhaps the most published in Anglo-Western terms, Wande Abimbola strongly attempts to recuperate the rightful position of *Osun* in the origins of the Ifa Divination and as a 'bag of wisdom'. He writes in the same chapter that 'his purpose in the essay is to examine the intimate connection of *Osun* with Ifa divination ... in her own right as a person ...' He starts with 'the popular view ... that she got to know about Ifa through *Orunmila*, her husband ...' In later pages of the essay, he makes the claim that *Osun* has much more to do with the origins of Ifa divination than the babalawo (Ifa priests) are ready to admit. Says he: 'I will indeed put forward the hypothesis that the entire divination system of Ifa started from Osun from whom it got to Orunmila and not the other way around.'[37]A bold and self-redemptive position for a Yoruba male scholar to take!

From my studies of Ifa, I had encountered versions of Ifa verses and stories that acclaim *Osun* for inventing the Ifa science and from whom her husband stole or plagiarized it. What is new considering modern revelations about the role of wives and women friends in the work of acclaimed geniuses across the centuries! Ifa Divination poetry, being oral and memorized, is not monolithic and does not proceed through time seamlessly as is sometimes mistakenly suggested. As the various priest/priestess narrators include or exclude items from their repertoire, basic stories, adages and philosophical bents remain, though gendered perspectives may be affected by the politics of the narrator. The myths of Ifa have always had variants depending on factors such as cult interests, as well as the social and power interests of the context of the narration. The corpus or corpi, to be more exact with a plural term, also incorporates new wisdoms and insights as the Yoruba en-counter other cultural influences such as Islam, and Christianity, such wisdoms and insights that are often integrated into the texts or into the use of language and metaphor and tropes as the Yoruba language itself evolves in time, as all languages do. Therefore the Ifa corpi themselves move in time with a moving Yoruba culture that includes encounters with other peoples such as other Africans, Arabs and Europeans. It is still, however, a knowledge system of the Yoruba and a philosophical record, testimony, and encyclopedia of their culture as it evolves.

Abimbola proceeds to discuss verses that are relevant to his project, showing verses of how *Osun* saved the life of *Orunmila* when all the deities were summoned there by God, *Olodumare*, and then threatened by the female power of women named *aje*, whose cannibalizing ten-dency and ability derive from their choice to pervert for negative uses the power of women described earlier. One may give life or destroy it; the *aje* are given to destroying when they please. The cosmology recog-nizes that good can become evil, and power can be used perversely. After *Osun* saved *Orunmila*, on their return to earth, they become closer than before. They become lovers and a marital couple who did not live together, 'because it was not the custom to live together at the time'— a pre-feminist recognition of the possible independence of women in Yoruba originary vision.

Other verses from other sources of Abimbola tell of a bag of wis-dom that was thrown down from heaven by *Olodumare* for the use of humankind. All the *orisa* were required to look for it with the promise that whoever found it would be the wisest of them all. *Osun* and *Orun-mila* being intimate decided to look for it together. *Osun* found it, put it in her pocket but 'the bag slipped through the broken pocket of her garment', described as an 'agbada', a male and huge garment. Notably, these deities were not conceived of as naked. '*Orunmila* accidentally stumbled on it and kept it.'[38] Sound familiar?

Finally, an Ifa story that I find pertinent is that of the first arrival of the deities on earth. Seventeen *orisa* had been sent from heaven by *Olo-dumare* with instructions on 'how to make the young earth a pleasant place to live'. They ostracize *Osun*, 'carrying out their instructions without involving *Osun* in any of their activities'.[39] This sounds like modern practices of governance and development in Africa today. As a result, nothing was achieved by them; rain does not fall while 'illness, bitterness and restlessness' occupy the earth for their exclusion of *Osun* who has been taking care of them *and all things*. '*Everything they did came to naught.*'

> Osun ni i si ma toju won
> Lonje, niwa, leyin
> Gbogbo ohun ti won se, ko gun.

> [*Osun it was who took care of them*
> *For food, in all matters pertinent*
> *All that they did came out wrong.* (Author's translation)][40]

So in desperation, they send *Orunmila* back to *Olodumare* to ask where and how they went wrong since they had carried out his instructions to the letter. *Olodumare* then asks them if they involved the only woman among them in every action of theirs to which they say no. *Olodumare* then responds in verses that say he/she is a 'creator who does not make people twice'. *Orunmila* is told to return to earth and make sure that *Osun* has a hand in everything they do, in which case everything they do would be successful. Later, after the resolution, in which the story turns interestingly patriarchal and cleverly makes *Osun* institute the patriarchal laws binding women in repressive rites, *Osun* still ends her final proclamation chanting that in everything else apart from the male women-controlling rites, 'anyone who tries to do anything, must imitate/resemble *Osun* in knowledge'. [41]

> A fi imo jo t'Osun o
> A fi imo jo t'Osun o

> [*Must resemble Osun in knowledge*
> *Must resemble Osun in knowledge.* (Author's translation)]

*Imo* is the Yoruba word for knowledge, unsatisfactorily translated as 'deliberations' in Abimbola's recorded text here, and a rather half-hearted way of acknowledging what is ascribed to *Osun*. It is knowledge as opposed to wisdom, which is *ogbon* that is ascribed to her; wisdom was the issue in the story of the lost bag. Knowledge, wisdom and wealth therefore were ascribed to *Osun*, this originary female archetype in the Edenic days, in the imaginary of the culture. She could also be a fierce warrior as well as a benevolent mother of the Yoruba people/humanity.

*Osun* worship is one of the few religious activities that have survived in modern Nigeria while the *Osun* festival in Osogbo is one of the biggest and the most modernized and accepted despite inroads of Christianity, Islam and other aggressive cultural and religious conflicts to suppress the worship because it is considered heathen, gentile—a favourite word of the born-agains in Nigeria—and ungodly.[42] Other opposition comes from internalized cultural colonialism in Nigerians themselves in their own despising of and shame about their indigenous cultures. Regarding *Osun*, her motherhood tends to be more emphasized in male patriarchal reportages and analyses of her. Both male and female in Yorubaland and perhaps all Africa accept the sacrality of motherhood. No cult of matricide exists in Yorubaland and other West African cultures, contrary to the generalization that Kristeva and Clément make about its universal existence. Where matricide occurs as an event in folktales, it is not in approval but as an ironical statement of extreme absurdity, extreme evil and perversion of character, underlined as that which is unthinkable and not done. *Osun*'s significance touches other areas of existence and practice in addition to motherhood; it, in fact, appertains to the female principle cosmologically.

The woman or the female principle is seen as a symbol and icon of all life and that which is good. In the language, we say something is female meaning it is good; male, meaning that which is hard and given to bad luck. The woman or female principle also symbolizes the whole town, city and people. These symbols populate the visual manifestation and representation of kingship in Yoruba culture, patriarchal or androgynous as it has been claimed to be. The paraphernalia of the king/ruler called *oba* in many forms represents the female principle. It is, in fact, inadequate to translate 'king' as *oba* because *oba* in Yoruba is genderless; it does not refer to the sex of the person but to his/her role. Where you have female kingship or female regency, the person in the role could be male or female and still be called an *oba*. There have been female *kings* (a contradiction necessitated by the very patriarchal nature of the English language itself that forces one to translate oba as king), in ancient times of Ile-Ife. A female king is said to have paved the streets of Ile-Ife with potsherds.

The paraphernalia of the *Oba* of Owo, similar to that of the *Oba* of Benin, has been analysed, as follows, by a distinguished African and Yoruba artist and art historian.[43] The parrot feathers in the *oba*'s crown represents the power of women because they also have the power of transmigration and flying if they choose to have recourse to it, and the *oba* needs the support of women for his/her reign to succeed. Hence the feathers are on his/her head. The *oba*'s blouse that is white recalls water which is also female because it is the source and sustainer of life. His huge white skirt moves like the waves of the sea (*okun aragbarigbi*), making his waist pregnant-looking, because as *oba* h/she is also pregnant with the town and its people—he carries them inside him like a mother. The *oba* is full of children as the plantain or banana bunch is covered with plantains/bananas (*ogede so to to*), in this manner again identified with female principle in nature and life. The water imagery recurs throughout the culture just as the bowl shape does, evoking pregnancy, protection and the stability gained from a mother—in the shape of the Ifa bowl and many other votive utensils and iconography.

The very language in which the *oba* is greeted encodes female symbolism for not being gender specific. Hailed as *Kabiyesi*, the *oba* is greeted in a word that is an elision *of Ka bi o, ko si*—that means 'Questioning you does not occur/cannot exist'.[44] The titular and boundless power of the king is thus being hailed even when, in reality, the king-makers actually rule and his/her life depends on them and on the population who could ask him to abdicate by committing honorific suicide that is part of the Yoruba constitution.

*Osun* is portrayed variously as the mother of knowledge (thus meaning-giver), power, creativity and wealth as well as female independence. As a female deity, she has liaisons with the different gods, is said to have married some or left them as needs be in various tales of the gods, showing that marriage and divorce were known and accepted among the Yoruba before Western colonization. This point also relates to the one I emphasize in my writing on the status of African women—that women are generally adored or divinized as mothers, but oppressed only as wives or within marriage. Needless to say, the wife is somebody else's daughter. Furthermore, the independent and self-sufficient woman was also conceived in the ethnic imaginary well before the feminist movements of the twentieth century. That is why an Africanist scholar, Diedre Bádéjò has rightly and, in a very original and insightful move, suggested her as the archetype and symbol for African feminism.[45]

Does the woman in Yoruba culture come into the subject area as sacred? Evidently, from the foregoing, she can. Is there anything sacred that can be considered strictly feminine as Catherine Clément and Julia Kristeva ask? Definitely, yes, from the argument and examples given in this paper. Is the Yoruba culture itself a male construct? Are the myths and verses of Ifa Divination Poetry produced by men or women? The jury is still out on these two questions while they offer themselves as very interesting and imperative areas of research. To what extent have women as subjects constructed Ifa concepts and texts? There is a tendency to assume or even affirm that women are not *babalawo* (priests) of Ifa though much evidence supports the fact that women are and can be. Some corrections of such phallocentricity are recently being made by male scholars in the area. Is the conceptualization of God and the Yoruba pantheon, and so *Osun*, the product of male minds? I cannot answer this question here; I can only hope that more research will be done on the issue for it will also partially answer the question of the construction of Yoruba culture solely by men or not. Whether or not this is the case, the versions of culture that we have indicate that the woman as a feminine person is given, not just an important role, but a central one in the Yoruba cosmogony, in the culture and self-defining Ifa Divination Poetry where she originates knowledge, wealth, and wisdom in general. She is also present as one of the deities to whom creation on earth has been delegated. The woman, life-giver and meaning-giver to life, also embodies life and is, therefore, sacred both ideationally and corporeally.

What does this say of a culture like the Yoruba, one that is read as being outwardly patriarchal? Yoruba culture may be patriarchal and male-dominant in certain practices and ideological statements. Yet it also emphasizes, very frequently and importantly, the androgyny of reality and existence, making central the importance of the female principle as life's mainstay. Yoruba culture tends to integrate the sexes and gender roles. Such conceptualization makes the culture balanced, at least at the conceptual level, while it puts seniority and gender roles before sex in the question of status between men and women. It succeeds in making Yoruba culture one of the human cultures that respect women outside their physicality and the sexual act. The failure to punish women for sex and coitus in the Yoruba ontology may be related to the important fact that there is no concept of original sin in the culture, as there is also none in most indigenous cultures of Africa. There was no serpent in a garden to give rise to a femininity that is the mother of all evil and, by that token, definitely no longer sacred.

# THE BECOMING-WOMAN OF THE EAST/WEST CONFLICT

## The Western Sacralization of Life and the Feminine Politics of Death

*Maria Margaroni*

### The return of bare life in Western politics

In *Homo Sacer: Sovereign Power and Bare Life* Giorgio Agamben draws attention to the separation in Western Metaphysics of simple natural life (*zoe*) from *bios*, a life validated in the rational discourse and communal action of the polis. According to him, this separation has functioned as the unacknowledged foundation of Western politics, a foundation exposed to view only at 'the threshold of the modern era' when natural bare life returns to the polis and Western politics turns into what Michel Foucault has called a 'biopolitics'.[1] Pursuing Foucault's thinking in the introductory volume of his *History of Sexuality*, Agamben attempts to draw out the implications of the concern with the living human body that Foucault traces at the heart of modernity. As he argues, this concern points to the normalization of what until that time was only a state of exception: in other words, that sovereign zone of indistinction where 'the realm of bare life ... gradually begins to coincide with the political realm'.[2] At the point of convergence between these two realms, Agamben (re)inscribes 'an obscure figure of archaic Roman law' which, in his view, might offer us the key to a more nuanced understanding of the workings of contemporary bio-power in the West.[3] This figure is that of *homo sacer* (sacred man) who, Agamben explains, may be killed (without his death incurring a punishment) and yet not sacrificed.[4] Abandoned at the borders between human and divine law (his death is neither a homicide nor a sacrifice), *homo sacer* constitutes for Agamben the paradigm for all of 'us' today who have 'entered into an intimate symbiosis with death', exposed to 'a violence without precedent precisely in the most profane and banal ways'.[5]

It is because death in the West is experienced as 'profane' and 'banal' that we need to rethink the ban imposed on the figure of the *homo sacer* with regard to a sacred form of violence. What is more, we need to rethink this ban in conjunction with the resurgence outside the West of a sacrificial practice that is currently turning into the most serious challenge to Western politics.[6] My contention in this chapter is that a recourse to nationalism and religious fundamentalism is not sufficient to do justice to the historical specificity of a practice that is not simply the return of the old (i.e. the ancient sacrificial myths of Shiite Islam) but, as Christoph Reuter insists, a 'quintessentially modern phenomenon'.[7] As I shall argue, the contemporary development of a political culture of death (one emerging in the 1980s in the context of the Iran-Iraq war and expanding to places as different as Palestine, Chechnya, Sri Lanka and very recently Iraq) can only be appreciated if seen in light of the sacralization of life in the West. Drawing on Agamben, Foucault, Alain Badiou and Jean Baudrillard, I am going to understand this 'sacralization' as the institution of a biopolitics that seeks to administer and control life and the parallel establishment of a 'bioethics' that renders the protection of bare life its privileged object. As we have seen, Agamben has grounded the modern sacralization of life in the figure of the *homo sacer* whose necessary complement, according to him, is the sovereign, the one endowed with the right to take decisions of life and death, the one with regard to whom all humans are *homines sacri*. By contrast, I want to shift the emphasis away from this juridico-political doublet, drawing attention, instead, to the *ethico*-political dynamics of another (equally mortal) pair: that formed by the *homo sacer* and the figure of the hostage. Whereas the former's life is dispensable, the latter's is a life to be protected at all costs. In both cases, however, the life in question remains unsacrificeable. If a martyr's life is neither to be simply *taken* (as the life of the *homo sacer* is) nor to be jealously *kept* (as that of the hostage) but expended, offered as a gift, then the contemporary reinvestment of the rituals of martyrdom may be seen as a timely response to the emergence of this ethico-political doublet whose figures (the *homo sacer* and the hostage) are still in tight (and deadly) embrace.

Thinking about martyrdom in this light may help us appreciate the role of the *oikos* in the context of this phenomenon. Going back to Hegel and his reading of *Antigone*, the *oikos* is the space of bare life and the rituals of death. It is no wonder, then, that women have become the privileged agents or mediators of this sacrificial culture of death. What I will be arguing is that martyrdom is a feminine practice that is currently minoritizing the East/West conflict. But before I focus on the actual practice of martyrdom and its production of a minor history, I want to illuminate further the ethico-political doublet which I intend to place at the heart of the most pressing dilemmas we are facing today.

## The elimination of death in the West

> But there is nothing to be done; just where we hope to drive out death, it surfaces again through all the protective screens, extending to the furthest reaches of our culture.[8]

In his analysis of a distinctively modern power 'whose highest function was … no longer to kill, but to invest life through and through', Foucault points to the parallel 'disqualification of death,' reflected in the waning 'of the rituals that accompanied it'.[9] Writes Foucault: 'That death is so carefully evaded is linked less to a new anxiety which makes death unbearable for our societies than to the fact that the procedures of power have not ceased to turn away from death,' which is now reduced to a mere consequence of the decision to 'disallow' life.[10] This is why, according to him, when death (in its singularity) erupts ('at the borders and in the interstices of [a] power … exercised over life'), it marks 'power's limit, the moment that escapes it'.[11] It is because politics in modernity redefines itself as the production of knowledge on and technologies of life that 'death becomes the most secret aspect of existence, the most "private"'.[12]

In a recent collection of journalistic essays published between 1987 and 1997, Baudrillard diagnoses a similar demise of death in the West. Like Foucault, he attributes the 'elimination of death … as a singularity … the most singular of singularities' to what we have traced as the sacralization of life in Western modernity, the increasing preoccupation with understanding, administering, protecting, fostering, prolonging life.[13] 'Our humanitarianism and ecological ideologies', he writes, 'all speak to us of nothing but the human species and its survival. Seen in terms of survival, or, in other words, of life superstitiously prolonged and protected from death, life itself becomes a waste-product we can no longer rid ourselves of, doomed, as it is, to indefinite reproduction.'[14] In his view, the Western desire for survival at all costs has produced a 'funereal' ideology, in the context of which two paradoxical figures dominate.[15] On the one hand, the figure of the victim—always other—whose sufferings 'we' follow through the protective screen of our TV.[16] On the other hand, the figure of the virtual soldier, whose destiny, he suggests, is 'the destiny of the civilized [the Western] man'.[17] Although these figures appear at different moments in Baudrillard's analysis of contemporary Western society, it is worth thinking them together (which is what I am venturing to do here), as they may throw light on that ethico-political doublet of *homo sacer* and hostage that I introduced earlier.

If victimhood, according to Baudrillard, has become the 'primal scene' of our contemporary existence, this is because Western society is unable to deal with the thought of 'an unthinkable violence against itself'.[18] For the Western spectator, then, it is always the other who is caught in the 'real' experience of death and whose life has become dispensable. And it is, indeed, the other (the non-Westerner, the non-citizen) who risks true abandonment in the face of human as well as divine law. It seems to me, therefore (contra Agamben),[19] that there is today one *clear* figure of the *homo sacer*, which is far from paradigmatic of all of 'us'—irrespective of where we are situated. This is the figure of the victim-as-other or, more accurately perhaps, that of the other (the refugee, the illegal immigrant, the Bosnian Muslim) as the quintessential victim—since the terms 'victim' and 'other' become interchangeable for the well-meaning Western spectator. Both Baudrillard and Agamben draw attention to the function of current humanitarian discourse in the production of the other-as-victim whose 'imploring eyes' 'we' are invited to heed.[20] In his book on ethics, Alain Badiou also takes issue with the passivization of the 'marginalized', 'excluded' or 'Third World' subject, his/her consistent reduction to bare life, 'the haggard animal exposed on [our] TV screens'.[21]

The reason why I insist on qualifying Agamben's figure of the *homo sacer*, foregrounding (through Baudrillard and Badiou) its subaltern nature lies in the necessity to appreciate the complexity of contemporary bio-power, a complexity manifesting itself, according to Agamben, in the production of a divided subject: namely, the 'people' as referring to both 'the constitutive political subject and the class that is, *de facto* if not *de jure*, excluded from politics'.[22] My aim is to understand the divided subject Agamben discusses in terms of the growing rift between East and West, a rift opening no longer around the control and possession of wealth but around the value of life. What is at issue here is the line dividing a life that is consecrated as the ultimate goal and privileged object of politics and a life that is not worth living, a bare life that is admitted into the political only through its vulnerability, its exposure to the risk of death. In my reading of contemporary experience, suicide bombing marks the arbitrariness of this line. At the same time, it throws into relief the colonial underpinnings of the technologies that seek to stabilize it, rendering bare life the indisputable and unacknowledged essence of the Third World. As my references to Baudrillard and Badiou suggest, there are no oppositional representations of the other in the West, for all existing forms of humanitarian politics or other-directed ethics take an interest in the subaltern, Third World subject only in so far as this is perceived as a *homo sacer*, a victim bearing the weight of a death that is deemed too heavy for the Western subject. As Foucault himself acknowledges, contemporary bio-ethics may constitute 'a political response to the new procedures of power', but, in taking life at face value, promoting it as the highest good, it cannot but remain complicit with them.[23]

For Badiou the epitome of contemporary bio-ethics is the postmodern ethics of the other, which has its origins in Emmanuel Levinas's influential philosophical work. According to him, the problem with this form of ethics is that it conceives the other as 'a fundamentally passive, fragile and *mortal* entity—as a potential victim to be protected ... by a dutiful, efficient, and invariably "Western" benefactor/exploiter'.[24] It is, indeed, true that in Levinas the other approaches me always from below—she is the widow, the orphan, the beggar. It is also true that if her life is more precious than mine this is because it is seen in all its bareness, in the flesh of its humanity. Yet it may be objected that the twist Badiou gives to Levinasian ethics fails to do justice to his thought, in the context of which passivity is the supreme quality not of the other-as-victim but of the ethical subject, while the other's destitution is precisely what assaults and traumatizes the self, what renders it a helpless captive rather than a self-satisfied benefactor. In fact, I would argue that, if Levinasian other-directed ethics offers an uncanny articulation of the double-bind in which 'we' (citizens of the West and our others) are caught today, this is not because it reproduces the familiar pattern of exploiter and victim. It is rather because it suggests (and we need to take this suggestion seriously) that the self obeying the call of the other *qua* victim can only do so as a hostage. 'To be oneself', for Levinas, is synonymous with 'the state of being a hostage', which he understands as a state of absolute passivity, an existence in the accusative that weighs the self with an excess of responsibility, 'the responsibility for the responsibility of the other'.[25]

Allow me to translate this thinking in terms that throw into relief both its political significance today and its historical context, for we cannot ignore the fact that Levinasian ethics is the product of the concentration camp, the space where, according to Agamben, 'politics becomes biopolitics and *homo sacer* is virtually confused with the citizen.'[26] It seems to me, therefore, that if (as the history of the camp has taught us) the other in the West has consistently been interpellated as a victim (a bare life that can either be killed or saved but is deprived of political voice or status) then the self cannot but be guilty 'in its innocence' and can be accused 'of what the others do or suffer'.[27] Is this, then, why suicide bombers and organizations that support them in the Middle East insist that there are no innocents?[28] And might the reign of terror we are currently experiencing be interpreted as a state of ethical haunting: i.e. a haunting that is 'ethical' in so far as it forces a vigilance and responsibility upon us, preventing our subjectivity from 'closing itself off in its peacefulness'?[29] In an interview given after 11 September 2001 Shaykh Muhammad Husayn Fadlallah condemns the murder of civilians who had nothing to do with the American administration quoting a precept from the Qur'an stating that 'no bearer of burdens should bear the burden of another'.[30] Yet our growing realization today is that 'we' in the West are precisely the bearers of another's burden. According to Jacques Derrida, this is the strange law of hospitality that turns the host into the guest's hostage, binding her by an oath that she never swore.[31]

I think this is what Baudrillard means when he suggests in *Screened Out* that, like the virtual soldier, we in the West are currently occupying 'the dead man's place'.[32] For, in our complicit production of the other-as-victim, we are condemned to carry 'the fault of another'[33] and, as the increase of the threat of terrorist attacks reveals, we are all potentially hostages even before we are actually captured.[34] The most 'profane' and 'banal' death that haunts us, then, is not, as Agamben argues, that of the *homo sacer* (the man whose life is dispensable and whose death is, as a result, unpunishable), but that of a man protected 'in his impotence with the whole legal panoply of human rights'; the one whose life is precious in so far as it is a pledge, a token of trust, a promise for the fulfilment of somebody else's contract.[35] 'We are in a strange situation,' writes Baudrillard, 'neither dead nor alive,' but ('paralyzed, immobilized') 'standing in for the dead'.[36]

The double bind I am trying to articulate takes us beyond the traditional understanding of the East/West conflict in terms of a war waged between cultures that are radically different and politically unequal. In other words, it takes us beyond a discourse that opposes the powerful and the powerless, the rich and the poor, the oppressors and the oppressed. If, in my reading of this conflict, I have foregrounded the figures of the hostage and the victim, instead, this is because I wish to throw light on the distinct forms of powerlessness on both sides. If power needs to be located somewhere, this is neither 'here', nor 'there', neither with 'them', nor with 'us', but in the complicity established between these forms of powerlessness, in the mortal embrace I have been tracing that binds together a life that is dispensable and a life that is to be protected at all costs. My contention is that the contemporary practice of suicide bombing is the offspring of this embrace.

## A feminine politics of death

> Because it is only as citizen that he is real and substantial, the individual, when not a citizen, and belonging to the family, is merely unreal insubstantial shadow.[37]

In his historical analysis of suicide bombing Reuter draws attention to the shock with which this practice is received in the West. 'For us,' he writes, 'there is something unnerving, something disturbing, about the notion that human beings would sacrifice their own lives in order to kill others, in the belief that their lives have value only as a weapon.'[38] The shock derives from what appears to be an impassive flouting of the two basic tenets of modern Western politics: on the one hand, the conviction that life is the supreme political object and, hence, no longer the affair of a single individual; on the other hand, the seemingly resistant affirmation of every individual's right to life and one's body.

In giving up the 'natural' will to survive and testifying 'to the individual and private right to die, at the borders of … [a] power … exercised over life', the suicide bomber refuses to take life at face value, either as a political object or as a natural right, the distinct marker of humanity and valuable possession of the hostage.[39] To the minute care of life in the West s/he opposes a love of death[40] and a tradition of ritualized practices around a body already consecrated to dying (from the training of the body in military camps to the washing/cleansing rituals before the attack, the videotaped testimony and the burial/celebration rites after the sacrifice). Situating her/himself at the limits of Western biopower, the suicide bomber (re)inscribes her/his death as a moment of 'astonishment' within it,[41] the eruption of an absolute singularity that smashes all the West's protective screens, forcing it to open up to what can no longer be kept outside. If the main casualty of her/his act is the Western citizen (this paradoxical fiction of normalizing technologies and inalienable rights), this is because it uncannily gives flesh and blood to the 'unreal insubstantial shadow' that haunts the Western citizen since Hegel (at least), threatening to eliminate the universality of his consciousness in 'the abstract universality of mere existence' and natural decay.[42] Significantly, for Hegel the shadow following on the footsteps of the citizen (as Eurydice does Orpheus) exposes the polis to the challenge of a rival ethical law (the law of the family) and of an 'everlasting irony' that he identifies with 'womankind'.[43]

Would we be justified, then, were we to suggest that the development of a culture of death in sites where Western identity remains in crisis

marks the entry of *oikos* into the polis and the becoming-Woman of the
East/West conflict? It is interesting I think that all analysts of this culture foreground the significant role the family plays in its sustenance
and reproduction. In most cases, the individual martyr acts as a representative of a particular family, determined to continue a tradition, preserve the family honour or, sometimes, atone for a father's failure or
mistake that jeopardizes the status of the family.[44] After the act, it is
the family that receives all credit (in the form of financial help or a
martyr's certificate) and that becomes the immediate target of revenge
(the houses of immediate relatives of suicide bombers are demolished
by Israeli authorities). Even the organizations that indoctrinate prospective martyrs and take responsibility for their acts consciously adopt a
family structure, urging their recruiters to play the part of a father, an
uncle or an elder brother.

Analysts have also emphasized the important contribution of the female members of the family in the organization and promotion of the
rituals that make up this culture of death.[45] Indeed it is the mothers,
wives or sisters that have become the privileged mediators in these rituals. Their role is particularly valuable after the sacrificial attack for they
are the ones in charge of giving back to the deceased their death by in-
terpreting it, providing a representation of and a destination for it.
While, according to interviewers of martyrs' families, the fathers and
brothers adopt a resigned silence, the sisters, wives and, especially, the
mothers assume the task of justifying and explaining the act. As Hegel
argues, the function of 'womankind' is to prevent their loved ones from
being reduced in death to 'a mere thing'.[46] By taking upon themselves
the act of destruction that death is ('the passing into mere being'), they
re-signify it 'by adding to it,' according to Hegel, 'the process of consciousness'.[47] They are the ones who transform death from 'a bare
something' that happens to the deceased by 'chance' to 'a work of their
own doing'.[48] The result is, and I am quoting Hegel again, that 'bare
existence … gets also to be something willed, and thus an object of
gratification'.[49]

The significance of the above can only be appreciated if we remind
ourselves that 'bare existence' is precisely the destiny of the subaltern
subject, a destiny imposed on him/her and over which s/he can have
no control. What the practice of suicide bombing and the rituals surrounding it point to is the subaltern subject's determination to assume
responsibility for his/her death, to take on his/her destiny but re-signify
it in terms that cease to render him/her a '*homo sacer*'. The contribution
of 'womankind' is crucial in this context for women are the ones who
keep the memory of the deceased and his/her sacrifice alive, preventing
him/her from being reduced to empty particularity. Even when the re-

mains of his/her body are not recoverable or not released to the family, the role women play remains central. Their task here is to raise what for Derrida is 'the question of … the foreign woman'.[50] The question relates to the interminability and impossibility of mourning for one who, like Oedipus, has died in a foreign land; one who, in making a gift of his dying person ('this is my body, keep it in memory of me,' Derrida writes[51]), renders the recipient of his gift 'a retained hostage, a detained addressee'; one who, because of this, has 'only a secret burial, an ungrave invisible even to his family';[52] one, finally, whose death is not a homecoming (a return to an earthly or heavenly home) but 'the absolute of his becoming-foreign'.[53]

In an essay on 'The Israeli racial state and feminist resistance' Ronit Lentin argues that after 11 September 2001 'the West's enemy is … increasingly feminized'.[54] This process of feminization is, needless to say, not separate from the passivization of the subaltern other that we traced earlier for, as Lentin suggests, if 'wars continue to be waged on the symbolic battlegrounds of women's bodies' this is because 'as symbolic tropes [and, may I add, as idealized bearers of life] women are constructed as those who must be protected'. This is precisely what leads Jenny Edkins in her book *Trauma and the Memory of Politics* to argue that whereas 'Agamben's emblem of modern sovereign power, the *homo sacer,* is a male figure … if we examine crises involving human rights violations, zones of indistinction or emergency, the figure that we come across there is female'. She adds, it is 'the person of the female' that 'seems to occupy a fundamental place in the imagery of the humanitarian international'.[55] In this light, the practice of suicide bombing seems to oppose to this process of feminization a culture that invests in an understanding of the feminine that remains incomprehensible in the West.[56] This is an understanding of the feminine as the literal or metaphorical bearer of death, the privileged mediator in the realm of shadows, the hostess of an event that takes her hostage, the agent of a mourning which, like Antigone's, turns into a 'terrible weapon'[57] or, finally and again like Antigone, as the 'mother of what remains'.[58]

What is it that we are witnessing here, then? The *culture of an other feminine* emerging in opposition to the growing feminization of the subaltern other? A *minor politics of death* erupting as a response to the Western minoritization of the other's life? I am using the Deleuzian term 'becoming-woman' to signify precisely this culture in the feminine, this minor sacrificial politics. For Deleuze 'becoming-woman' is synonymous with 'becoming-minor', a term encompassing the following three processes.[59] To begin with, a process of deterritorialization, the deterritorialization of dominant norms with the effect of opening them to their lines of deviation; secondly, the process of challenging the separation of the personal and the familial from the socio-political sphere; third, the process of initiating new collective enunciations and forms of group solidarity. I want now to argue that the emergence outside the West of a ritualized politics of death marks the becoming-minor of the East/West conflict.

I have already traced this becoming-minor in the martyr's conscious flouting of the norms of modern Western politics, norms that, as we have seen, privilege life as the paradoxical object of no less totalitarianism than humanitarian discourse and that transform 'the entire population of the Third World into bare life'.[60] I have also tried to understand it as the entry of what, according to Foucault, is most 'private' (i.e. death) into Western bio-politics, the convergence in the ritualized culture developed around martyrdom between the personal/familial and the socio-political and the re-investment in the context of this culture of distinctly feminine values. But there is one additional sense in which suicide bombing might be read as the becoming-minor of the East/West conflict for, we may suggest, it literally deterritorializes this conflict, re-staging it on the ground and according to the terms of the one deprived of everything (human rights, status, voice) but his biological life. As Mohammed Sid-Ahmad, an Egyptian political analyst argues, 'what we are seeing [today] is the politics of impotence … not just a clash of Islamic terrorism and the world, but the dispossessed against the mighty.'[61] Indeed, martyrs have repeatedly been called the 'poor man's bombs' or, to borrow Reuter's words, 'the "psychological atom bomb" of the weak against the powerful'.[62] In his interview with Davis, Abdel Halim Izzidene, political leader of Islamic Jihad in Jenin makes this clear: 'In this world of modern warfare, we need methods that will have a real effect. To fight the jets and the bombs, we have something called human bombs. It's a different kind of balance of power.'[63] In a similar vein, a Palestinian leader tells Reuter: 'We don't have tanks or F-16 jets. But we have something better: our exploding Islamic bombs. All they cost is our lives, but nothing can beat them— not even nuclear weapons!'[64] What we need to note here, of course, is the subaltern subject's attitude to the Western value of life. As another Palestinian tells Reuter, 'our lives are cheap', for life is 'the only commodity' that the subaltern possesses 'in abundance'.[65]

It is because life in the West is never enough whereas, outside it, it is always in excess that the becoming-minor of the East/West conflict has taken the form of a sacrificial offering, a care-less spending, an *expenditure* of life. It is in this sacrificial offering that a new collective enunciation becomes possible. In my reading, this collective enunciation can neither be extricated from nor reduced to the nationalist and religious discourses that inform this sacrificial practice. It needs therefore to be perceived as catachrestic, in other words, as signifying more than such discourses allow for, as Judith Butler suggests, political catachresis is inevitable when 'the less than human attempts to speak as human'.[66] It is to this catachrestic enunciation that I now wish to turn.

## Witnesses of History

The witness is on his own. He speaks. The judges listen and say nothing.[67]

As we have seen, in his account of the sacralization of life in Western modernity Agamben singles out the concentration camp as the space *par excellence* where the citizen (potentially *any* citizen, according to him) can be reduced to bare life. This is why he reacts against 'the wish to lend a sacrificial aura to the extermination of the Jews by means of the term "Holocaust"'. As he argues, the killing of the Jew is the 'actualisation of [his/her] mere "capacity to be killed"'. 'The dimension in which this extermination took place is neither religion nor law, but biopolitics,' he insists.[68] It is no wonder, in this light, that the emergence of the concentration camp as the paradigmatic biopolitical space made possible what Thomas Flynn calls a 'history without witnesses',[69] a history, that is, whose very unfolding depends on the elimination of narrative. As Edkins emphasizes, the aim of the Nazis in the camps was to produce an inhuman form of life (the Muselmann qua *homo sacer*) 'separated from every possibility of testimony'.[70] 'The Historical reality of the Holocaust,' Shoshana Felman and Dori Laub write, 'became … a reality which extinguished philosophically the very possibility of address, the possibility of appealing, or of turning to another'[71]—be it a divine or human other.[72] In my view, this is what is at issue in Agamben's figure of the *homo sacer* whose distinct identity consists not merely in his/her exposure to a most 'profane' and 'banal' death but also in his/her production as a 'mute' body,[73] a body deprived of the possibility of discourse (i.e. that 'in our humanity' which, according to Anne Dufourmantelle, '"promises" us to another'.[74] This is, then, why the Jew in Nazi Germany is for Agamben the paradigmatic *homo sacer* whose death remains unpunishable and whose life can neither be shared in communal speech nor offered in sacrifice. 'The Muselmänner', Edkins insists, quoting Agamben, 'were intended to be … "bare, unassignable, unwitnessable life"'.[75] I want to suggest that, in explicitly staging the ritualistic offering of a mute body as the sharing of a narrative, the contemporary development of a *thanatopolitics* mobilizes precisely the possibility of address extinguished in the Nazi camp.

Although the narrative, the martyr's farewell video, precedes the sacrificial act of death, it paradoxically seeks to provide testimony for it, to affirm its truth, one strengthened by the video's foregrounding of the fact that the subject communicating this truth is, at the moment of viewing, dead: 'I who have now become a martyr,' the voice addressing us says. What is the value of this truth that can only be safeguarded in death? What is the meaning of this other history in the process of unfolding here, a history determined to create its witnesses *before* the event?

In his critical engagement with contemporary ethical discourses of the Other *qua* victim, Badiou emphasizes the necessity of opening the 'haggard animal' that such discourses promote to its potential for transcendence and, hence, immortality. As he argues, the human animal's potential for immortality is awakened the moment s/he succeeds in rising above the 'perseverance of being', rendering him/herself a vehicle for the passing of a truth-event.[76] 'I call "subject",' he writes, 'the bearer of a fidelity, the one who bears a process of truth.'[77] It is because this process exceeds and displaces the subject that transcendence is made possible and 'the human animal is convoked to be the immortal that he was not yet'.[78] We may choose to remain suspicious of Badiou's subtle recasting of existentialism. At the same time, however, he offers us a framework within which we can begin to understand the practice of suicide bombing as a politically invested reaction against the 'funereal' ideology developed in the West that casts the Other as a potential or 'natural' victim. Hence the significance of the narrative that precedes the martyr operation and that aims to pre-inscribe the 'mute' body involved in it within both human and divine law.

As suggested by the root that both the word for martyr (*shaheed*) and the verb 'to witness' or 'testify' (*shahida*) share in Arabic, the narrative is an integral aspect of the act of martyrdom, for both the sacrificial act and the narrative that frames it aim to function as *testimonies*. In his essay on '*Testimonio* and the politics of empire' John Beverley emphasizes that 'what is at stake in *testimonio* is ... the truth *of* the other.'[79] According to him, in testimony 'we are in effect interpellated from the other.' The voice addressing us, he writes, 'comes to us from the place of' the other, 'an other repressed or occluded by our own norms of cultural and class authority'. Yet, as he argues, 'it is not the intention of this voice simply to display its subalternity.' This is why I insist on reading into the event of martyrdom a desire to re-cast the subaltern other as an 'I', a 'someone' in Badiou's terms who holds him/herself responsible and accountable for a history that is yet-to-come. It is this desire that I see as epitomized in the spoken testimony that the prospective martyr offers for, as Hannah Arendt contends, 'the doer of deeds is possible only if he is at the same time the speaker of words.' 'Speechless action,' she tells us, 'would no longer be action.'[80] Sufferer as much as actor (this is the double sense of the word 'martyr'), the subject of the narration identifies him/herself as an agent or, as Arendt puts it, a 'who' addressing the members of his/her community, announcing his/her intentions and stating the reasons behind the violent act s/he is about to commit. Re-inscribing him/herself into the text of human law, s/he positions him/herself in front of a tribunal as a conscious defendant or an invaluable witness—the only one with privileged access to the truth of the event. At the same time, s/he promises him/herself as a sacrificial lamb whose body is singled out to become the site for a future communal bond, one opened by the implicit address that a gift, an offering, cannot fail to carry. It is because this bond is 'futural' (and is, thus, not to be reduced to existing national or religious bonds) that suicide bombing becomes the signifier of what I would call a *minor* history. Let me conclude by explaining how I understand this minor history.

To begin with, this is a history that unfolds in reaction to the *nomos* Agamben has traced in the concentration camp, a *nomos* that is currently replayed in a variety of other spaces from the refugee camp to the immigration detention centre. For not only does it reclaim the life of the Muselmann (as a life worth dying, a life worth offering as a gift) but it also seeks to close the gap opened in the camp between the biological body and the speaking body, the inhuman and the human, the Muselmann who, according to Primo Levi, is the 'true witness' but who does not survive to give testimony and the survivor who can only be a 'pseudo-witness'.[81] This is why, as I have suggested, this is a history that creates its witnesses *before* the event and that seals the truth of its testimony with their death.

Because it is the history denied to the Muselmann, this is also a history narrated in 'a small voice' (as Ranajit Guha might put it),[82] a history, in other words, that is barely audible, for its subject is one who (by definition) is deprived of a voice. It is the history of a mute body (the mute body we have traced from Agamben to Baudrillard and Badiou) that speaks its singularity—albeit from the site of death. According to Derrida, death is precisely the 'place of my irreplaceability', my singularity as a subject.[83] At the same time and because of this, it is the site from where 'I feel called to responsibility'.[84] In this light, it seems to me that, if suicide bombing constitutes the enunciation of a minor history, this is because it suggests (*pace* Levinas) that we can only take responsibility for the *death* of the other; but we can only do so from the site of death ourselves, what Baudrillard has called 'the dead man's place'. In her novel based on the current situation in the Middle East Amy Wilentz appears to make a similar suggestion. Ari Doron is one of the three protagonists of *Martyr's Crossing* whose voice we hear in the course of the narration. Ari is an Israeli soldier considered responsible for the death of a Palestinian toddler when, obeying orders, he refused him and his mother entry to Israel and thus access to medical help. As the novel unfolds, Ari comes to the decision that the only ethical course of action he can take is to offer himself to the child's family as a hostage, to expose himself to the risk of death, assuming a responsibility which he knows is not *his* ('He was here to take responsibility as an Israeli soldier'[85]) but for which he is ready to become the willing bearer.

Does such an assumption of responsibility (inextricable, as it is, from a certain 'hospitality toward death')[86] open up a space for a new politics, an alternative form of solidarity, what I have called a futural communal bond? For Beverley the new politics opened by *testimonio* begins 'with the recognition of … an authority that resides in the voice of others'.[87] The question, then, for 'us' today (the question raised in the contemporary context of the East/West conflict and lying at the heart of the minor history I have been tracing) is no longer the one articulated by Gayatri Spivak in 1983 (i.e. 'Can the Subaltern Speak?'),[88] but *how, indeed, do we* listen *to the subaltern's voice, given that we increasingly find ourselves interpellated by this voice as both its response-able addressees* and *its hostages?*

# ENUNCIATING THE CHRISTIAN *DIEUE* AND OBSCURING THE OTHER

## A Québec Perspective

*Denise Couture*

In the framework of the general problematic of the sacred and the feminine, I propose to analyse a Christian theological symbol that occupies a paradoxical position. I am referring to the term *Dieue* created by the suffix of the feminine 'e' added to the spelling of *Dieu* (God) in French. Women in Québec have been employing this term for around 15 years. The designation does not refer to a feminine image or characteristic of the divine, such as God the Mother, or an allusion to compassion, for example. It constitutes a feminist feminization of *Dieue*. It points out that there is femininity and there is divinity. An 'e' is placed on to the end of a word, not just any word, but on to that which is powerful enough to carry the weight of a socio-symbolic system.

Voicing the feminine spelling of *Dieue* itself expresses a critique of the neutrality of discourse. In the theological field, feminists and womanists argue that theological discourse is not devoid of gender, nor is it colourless, neutral or apolitical.[1] This discursive criticism falls within what is known as a political theology of location, which examines the conditions of the enunciation of discourse.[2] From this perspective, theological truths are analysed in conjunction with their provenance. Rather than developing a discourse based on a precarious focal point, the position of enunciation is being problematized.[3]

This is applied indeed to discourse on *Dieue*, located in, emerging from and voiced in Québec, in a Catholic Francophone context.[4] The term was first proposed in 1988, by the Christian feminist collective *L'autre Parole* (The Other Word). This collective, formed in 1976, has since operated, in relation to feminism, in the form of a group composed of small cells of realization and action, and, in relation to theology, in the form of an originally Christian community which has developed a theology and its own rituals. The women of *L'autre Parole* have chosen to use the term *Dieue* to speak of and to pray to the Christian divinity as an act both of deconstruction of a masculine tradition that no longer made sense, and as an act of construction of a spiritual relationship between women and the divine without the mediation of the masculine being necessary. The feminine *Déesse* (Goddess) was not appropriate. It would have implied a turn in the direction of a different, non-Christian tradition.[5]

Since the 1990s, the feminine spelling of the Christian *Dieue* has been well received amongst Christians in Québec. It is commonly used in ritual celebrations organized by women belonging to various theological movements; it is also adopted in academic discourse.[6] Certain men and certain groups sometimes employ the term: *Dieu-e* (with a hyphen), to convey that there are not only female but also male enunciators of a word whose effects on gender relations should be looked at more closely. The term was neither adopted in France nor in the Francophone countries, to my knowledge, partly because of the degree of cultural receptivity in terms of language.

As a member of *L'autre Parole*, I have come to address *Dieue* in the feminine in my prayers and I no longer pronounce the name in the masculine (ending in 'u') apart from in group prayers. For some including myself, the feminised term has become an element of a construction of female identity. As an academic theologian, I belong to the white Catholic majority in Québec, which itself belongs to the dominant Western powers, remaining, however, a minority in terms of being a French speaker in North America and struggling to keep the language alive. I occupy the paradoxical position of thinking in my maternal tongue, Québecois French, about an Anglo-Saxon sort of problem since, as we know, the question of the feminist feminization of the Christian divine is part of a corpus of English language texts. In France, however, it remains almost non-existent. I am aware of a discrepancy between the language and the problem of the present article.

The symbol of *Dieue* has not emerged in Québec by chance. It represents a feminist, Christian and Québecois specificity. Closely linked to its geopolitical context of origin, the term should reveal as many of the possibilities as the difficulties inherent in the construction of a relationship between the feminine and the divine in a *phallologocentric* linguistic system. I would like to situate it in three domains: the linguistic, the theological and the feminist, and to highlight, consequently, different aspects of the paradoxical position held by this enunciation.

## Linguistic considerations

In the last thirty years, a strong tendency has emerged in Québec to feminize titles, jobs and words, which has included several cases of the addition of the grammatical feminine 'e' suffix to the end of a noun such as teacher ('professeur*e*') or writer ('auteur*e*'), to choose examples linked to the academic world. In a recent piece of research, Marie-Eva de Villers compared the words and expressions used in the Québecois newspaper *Le Devoir* and the French newspaper *Le Monde* published during 1997. In terms of the results of the research, interestingly, eighty five per cent of these words and expressions are common to both lexical groups, French and Québecois. The *auteure* of the *Multidictionnaire* of the French language has classed the words specific to *Le Devoir* in three categories 'in accordance with the typology of *The Exposition of a Linguistic Policy on Québecisms*, published by the French Language Bureau in 1985'.[7] Firstly, for those which are classed as 'Québecisms of French origin'—that is, old French words that are no longer in common usage in France, such as '*batture, brunante* [dusk], *croche* [quaver], *écornifler* [to scrounge], *ennuyant* [boring], *épivarder*'—they represent 8 per cent of the words specific to *Le Devoir*.[8] Secondly, 'borrowed Québecisms' form 11 per cent of the words and expressions specific to the Montreal newspaper. Indeed, these words are most often borrowed from English. The third category of Québecisms, the one that is the most important and which concerns us here, represents 68 per cent of the corpus. These are 'created' Québecisms.[9] The *auteure* comments: 'It is innovation which constitutes the principal differentiating factor between the Québecois and the French nomenclatures, a lexical creativity which draws fundamentally on the French sources. Derivation plays a key role,' as in *téléavertisseur* (*récepteur de recherche de personne* in France), or *déneigeur* ('snow-remover', for which a French equivalent is perhaps not necessary).[10] The researcher stresses that 'The new feminized words represent three per cent of the lexical forms specific to the Québecois daily.' Notably, feminization has been 'clearly increasing' recently in *Le Monde*, as a 2003 study affirms.

It is not by chance that the term *Dieue* has been coined on Québecois soil, where two strong linguistic tendencies are in evidence: lexical creation originating from the possibilities offered by the French language, on the one hand, and the feminization of nouns, on the other hand. The potentiality of feminizing the word '*Dieu*' by adding an 'e' is provided by the French Québecois language. As Gayatri Spivak writes, on the subject of the mother tongue, 'although it's unmotivated, it's not capricious.'[11] A linguistic operation is performed. It falls within the given range of potentialities. It is particularly interesting to observe that, in French, the word '*Dieu*' with the masculine ending cannot easily accommodate the addition of a feminine marker. If the new term, *Dieue* with the feminine ending, surprises, destabilizes and inspires, one cannot fail to notice that such a word, holding such power, is expressed by a silent 'e'. By manipulating the word *Dieu* in this way, the French language undermines all its rules. The feminine marker remains silent. There is an imposed silence, existing even under the pressure of a very strong assertion. This paradox of the formalized feminization of *Dieue*, appearing in the context of the trend of development of the French language in Québec, corresponds to the status of the word 'she' (*elle*) in the language. To restate Spivak's point, Echo, who replies to Narcissus, is 'incapable of speaking for herself … in her own autonomous and independent voice. She can speak only in the language of the other, moreover, by repeating that language'.[12] Transgression is possible, but is not far removed from repetition. The insertion of the feminine is effected by the addition of a voiceless vowel.

### Theological considerations

In the corpus of feminist Christian theology in Western academia, there is a broad consensus on the necessity of counteracting the implicit masculinity of the Christian God.[13] A divergence exists in viewpoints regarding alternative ways of speaking of the divine. Various ways of getting around the problem are in evidence: recourse to the terms deity or divine, alternate use of a feminine and masculine pronouns (She/He) when speaking of God without feminizing the very word itself, writing *G-d*, multiplying the images associated with God, such as those of love, life-giving power, creative energy, pure vitality, and others.[14] Authors propose the use of various non-exclusive images and metaphors for saying *Dieu-e*, (either masculine or feminine), some of which are feminine, such as Goddess, She, She Who Is, Mother, Friend (*Amie*) or Lover (*Amante*), both of the latter being in the feminine.[15] Still others suggest that the divine be thought of in the feminine or that monotheism be questioned.[16]

One book on Christian theology that is recognized in the world of academic research in the United States, concerning the feminist feminization of the symbol of *Dieue*, is *She Who Is* by Elizabeth A. Johnson. This expression feminizes the interpretation given by Christian tradition of the answer received by Moses before the bush, to the question of Yahweh's name (Exodus 3: 14). Notably, the book was translated in Paris in 1999 by Cerf editions, under the title *Dieu au-delà du masculin et du feminin: Celui/Celle qui est* (*God beyond the masculine and the feminine: He/She who is*).[17] The modification of the title for the French audience confirms the French reluctance to feminize expressions regarding *Dieue*. This editorial choice weakens, however, the questioning nature of feminization. Elizabeth A. Johnson uses the word '*God*'. She writes:

It may be that the decision to preserve the word 'God' is only a temporary strategy, valid only until a new word emerges, which refers to the ever-inexpressible intelligence of the holy mystery, an intelligence which incorporates the reality of women, like that of the whole creation. In active anticipation of this, we are employing a feminizing language (She-God), which aims to open up new semantic avenues for expressing the divinity …[18]

It is worth underlining that Johnson's project consists of a reconsideration of the divine from a feminist perspective with reference to the resources already provided by Christian tradition. The theologian argues that the feminization of the names of the Christian *Dieue* fulfils one of the possibilities of this tradition; her argument is that the feminization of *Dieue* conforms faithfully to traditional Christianity. As regards method, she speaks of 'building a link between the edges of classical Christian wisdom and those of feminist Christian wisdom', and of 'building a hermeneutic bridge between these two fulcrums …'[19]

In terms of the theologian's position on the gender of Dieu-*e*, it can be seen that the Parisian editor's translation of the title of her book was not inappropriate. Following the tradition of Karl Rahner's transcendental theology, our *auteure* understands God first of all as the sacred Mystery.[20] She writes: 'the mystery of God transcends the feminine-masculine duality in a way which we cannot imagine.'[21] In this sense, therefore, there is not a feminine dimension and a masculine dimension to *Dieue*, for this would mean projecting human categories onto the deity. Also, she adds, 'the recourse to feminine metaphors in discourse on God should never be interpreted as the attribution of a feminine dimension to God, as is manifest in Mary or other women.'[22] Indeed, the feminist feminization of *Dieue* in North American feminist theology neither aims to express certain minor feminine qualities of a God who remains masculine, nor to say that God's gender is feminine. On the contrary, Elizabeth A. Johnson again explains, 'The images and names of God are not aimed at designating 'parts' of the divine mystery, presuming that this were possible. They evoke … the divine mystery in its totality. The feminine images in themselves refer to God as such …'[23]

In light of this, it is important to use various images and metaphors to enunciate *Dieue*, some masculine, others feminine, some cosmic and others metaphysical. According to the theologian, since

the mystery of God transcends all possible images … only a symbolisation of God that integrates the full reality of women and the full reality of men, along with the world of nature, will allow the idolatrous fixation on a single image to be shattered.[24]

In today's climate of a readjustment of the situation of women, there is scope for a 'generous' usage of feminine symbols for speaking of the divine.

Thus, among various ways of speaking of *Dieue*, in its entirety, drawn from the resources of Christian tradition, the *auteure* chooses the symbol of Sophia, taken from the First and the Second Testament. Sophia does not correspond to only one dimension of God, to a character whose function would be to mediate between the divine and the human; she represents the divine in its entirety. The *auteure* declines the symbol of Sophia, in terms of the trinity, as Mother-Sophia, Jesus-Sophia and Spirit-Sophia; she reveals a feminine-feminist trinity: a creative, liberating and inspiring *Dieue*. The Christian *Dieue* can also be named She who is, Mother, Christa, friend, she who gives sustenance.[25]

In terms of feminist Christian theology, the women of *L'autre Parole* who have coined the term of *Dieue* with an 'e' in Québecois French, share overall Johnson's methodology. I will summarize this in five elements: 1) The enunciation of *Dieue* does not mean that *Dieue*'s gender is feminine. 2) It expresses the divine in its entirety. 3) It is one appellation of the divine amongst others. 4) It represents an authentic rereading of Christian tradition for today: it is faithful to that tradition. 5) It is part of a feminization of the names of *Dieue*, which has become necessary for Christian women of today.

I find a particularly interesting aspect in the appellation of *Dieue*, as it is proposed in Québec. In the same breath it says '*Dieue*' and it says 'the feminine exists'. The term effects a meeting between a Christian theology and a feminist approach in an extraordinarily synthetic manner. It provides a space for different ways of building links between the two. If it is true that the feminization of *Dieue*, in Québec, is closely linked to the thought of US theologians who are reinterpreting Christian tradition for the present day. For Québecois women, *Dieue* also refers to French feminism, to the tradition of the Goddess or to that of feminist spirituality.[26] The feminine spelling of *Dieue* refers to a feminist position on enunciation in theology, in its strategic diversity, which could include a diverse range of experiences and interpretations.

## Feminist considerations

The question of *Dieue* is part of the linguistic problem with which feminism is particularly concerned. According to the latter, it is necessary for *her* to gain the opportunity to function as a subject in the language that has produced her as an object.[27] Feminism thus understood does not aim for the inclusion of women in an existing system, but for the experimentation with new modes of being. It manifests itself as a construction of feminist-feminine subjectivities. It prepares the way for new ways of living and speaking that do not yet exist.[28]

The act of speaking of *Dieue* can be analysed as a feminist strategy that is both political and linguistic, and which consists of creating a *she-subject*, a feminist-feminine subjectivity. In this light, speaking of *Dieue* does not signify primarily that God's gender is feminine (we have seen this with Johnson). It reveals the feminist position of the enunciator.

This approach requires a few explanations. It belongs to the field of post-structuralist feminism. The sense of the term 'post' in post-modernity, post-structuralism and post-colonialism should be distinguished. Following Rosi Braidotti, we can understand post-modernism as an historical period, post-structuralism as a philosophical approach developed in Europe and post-colonialism as an interdisciplinary approach, appearing on the periphery of Europe and North America and which has theorized the emergence of situated subjects.[29] The post-structuralist approach problematizes the subject-in-becoming by considering it both as multiple points of emergence of a production and as multiple points of effect of a socio-symbolic structure. Alongside Rosi Braidotti, we can understand post-modernity as a process of globalization and fragmentation, linked to the death of 'man'. In these late post-modern times, two things can be seen to happen: the effacement of what belongs to 'man' and the emergence of his shadows, his others, those whom he has subordinated in order to become confident of his own identity. These 'others' of modernity are woman (the sexual 'other' of man), ethnic others, autochthons and people of mixed race (the other subjects of Eurocentrism and United States imperialism) and nature or the earth (the 'other' of techno-science).[30]

In line with this vision, feminism can base its action on the category of the (impossible) group of women as a complex collective subject that includes the multiplicity of differences between them and within them. In this late post-modernity, the emerging subjects, including women, are undergoing an increasing reification, in certain respects. They also produce discourse, in increasing quantities. They occupy a liminal position: women are powerless and they have power. They have no space from which to speak from themselves, but they speak from themselves. Brown, black and white women lean on the identity of 'woman' in its diversity, to lead a collective struggle, but this collective identity does not exist. At the frontier of a potential new formulation, this feminism consists of a strategic inscription of the feminist-feminine element in discursive and non-discursive formations, a movement in which I am placing the speaking of *Dieue*. This incorporates the (impossible) category of the group of women in the term *Dieue* itself. Suddenly, speaking of *Dieue* can function as a fulcrum for developing feminist subjectivities in their multiplicity. Hence the great interest of the term, which effects the insertion of *her* into the language, by means of a grammatical *e*. It records that which will remain: a trace, written (and silent, as we have seen). Not in just any word, but in that which symbolically carries the weight of a system.

The Canadian theologian Marsha Aileen Hewitt argues that the feminization of the divine serves interests contrary to feminism because women achieve it within the framework of a theological theory which, in itself, is not brought into question, but which, by other means, participates in the construction of the subordination of women.[31] Hewitt is right in saying that the theological system (linguistic) is unchanged. We must, however, answer her with the fact that there is no 'right place' for women to occupy. A feminist strategy that works at the same time both for and against women remains insurmountable. From the viewpoint of a post-structuralist feminism, such as I am putting into action here, the different theological approaches which have been influenced by feminism's treatment of the problematic of *Dieue* (especially existential theologies, theologies of correlation and theologies of liberation), are all partly right and partly wrong places to occupy. All remain paradoxical for the construction of a feminist-feminine subjectivity. It is relevant that feminists occupy these different positions or that a female theoretician can move from one to the other. The post-structuralist approach favours an ability to move between one theory and the other, from one position to the other, so as to struggle against 'the simultaneity of potentially contradictory axes of oppression'.[32] It encourages a type of analysis that leads to the mapping out of the different positions.

We might ask ourselves whether it even remains relevant for women to continue to speak of the divine. On the one hand, the current geopolitical context favours the circulation of religious fundamentalist discourse and powers, which set out a reductionist vision of the condition of women based for instance on Christian or Muslim theologies.[33] On the other hand, the majority of feminists have rejected *God* and religion. *Dieu*, with an 'u', acts as foundation and guarantor of a system of domination and exclusion that has reached the limit of its own possibilities. Some women theoreticians have thus welcomed the death of such a God.

The *Dieu*, with an 'u', *acts*: by disappearing, he opens up new possibilities of freedom for subjugated voices. In speaking of *Dieue*, women appropriate a discourse that is created by themselves and for themselves, in a theological guise, as a strategy for giving a geopolitical answer to the religious discourse that legitimizes their confinement to a position of inferiority. This strategy operates as much on the personal level (a spiritual experience) and the political level (a strategy of change carried out by a subversive play with language), as on the academic level (the insertion of a problematic, a written trace, into the subject).

## Conclusion

I understand the voicing of the Christian *Dieue* as the experimentation of a feminine-feminist enunciation at the heart of *phallologocentric* language. Adding the feminine 'e' suffix in *Dieue* emphasizes the masculine character of *Dieu*. It brings female enunciators into the light, along with a position of enunciation of *she* subjects. It is appropriate that the term is appearing at the present time, that is, at a time which is an in-between period, between what is no longer and what is not yet. *Dieue* is a symbol of transit, which enunciates, in a single word and a single movement, the feminine and the divine. It expresses the weaving of links to be built in different ways between the two, for the present and for the future. It occupies a paradoxical position, a moving space where what is not yet is being built.

This paradoxical position should be analysed in different lights.

Firstly, as a possibility offered by Québecois French, it lies at the intersection of Anglo-Saxon and French discursive formations. Being polysemous, it opens up a space for a diverse range of experiences and interpretations. As regards the relationship between the divine and the feminine, it is able to evoke the contents of the American approach to feminist theology, but to refer, as well, to those of what is called French feminism.

Secondly, by a remarkable trick of the French language, the very strong affirmation of the feminization of the divine is expressed by a *silent* 'e', by an 'e' that is unheard. *Dieu* with a 'u'—the foundation of a socio-symbolic system of domination—resists with all its strength the material insertion of a position of feminine enunciation. A second contradiction lies in the fact that the powerful assertion of *Dieue* remains voiceless.

Thirdly, in terms of academic theology, there is no good place for feminists to stand. The enunciation of *Dieu* or *Dieue*, either one or the other, is part of the framework of an anthropological theology that has already constructed *she* as the *other*. Hewitt is right. The feminization of the divine is accomplished within a linguistic system that it fails to question. At the same time, it inserts into that theology a trace of the feminine, which will remain; it creates a fissure in the foundation. The third contradiction is that the enunciation of *Dieue* works both against and for the interests of women.

Fourthly, I have analysed the strategy of insertion of the feminine, of the vowel 'e', in the word *Dieue*, as the construction of a feminine-feminist subjectivity which supports itself with the impossible category of the collective of women, those glimpsed in their diversity of brown, black and white women. The fourth contradiction lies in this reliance on a category which we know to be an impossibility.

To conclude the present analysis with a new question that will return us, in a critical manner, to the Québecois context from which the term in question has emerged, we can draw a link between these few paradoxes and another expressed by Gayatri Spivak. This *auteure* has taught us that modern Western philosophical discourse bases the autonomy of the subject on a construction of the other: that the other that 'woman' represents is argued explicitly in this discourse, whilst the other whom the subaltern represents is obscured.[34] The feminine Christian *Dieue* has emerged from a homogenous background of white Catholic women, who have still had little experience of meeting women from different ethnic and spiritual groups. A subsequent question would be to establish how the Québecois enunciation of *Dieue* helps to obscure the difference between women. A fifth paradoxical position consists of occupying the opposite position, in which women subjects are made visible, while at the same time obscuring the difference between women and non-Western ethnic groups.

# SRINGARA RASA

The Feminist Call of the Spiritual/Erotic
Impulse in Indian Art

*Ranjana Thapalyal*

*Sringara* is one of the eight essential emotional states in Indian dramatic and visual art theory. It covers the depiction of a range of states from romantic separation and longing to the visualization of sexual union and ecstasy. The experience of these states is also widely accepted as an allegory for the individual soul's longing for union with the ultimate consciousness—Brahman, God, or True Reality. *Sringara rasa* illustrates particularly clearly the way in which metaphors for complex spiritual ideas sit alongside sensuous imagery in ancient Indian thought, which celebrates human beauty, male-female relationships, and the bounty of nature in general, even as it defines these phenomena as not real.[1] Some of these sensuous and often symbolically sexual images are also objects of veneration, such as the *sivaling*, a popular sculptural form representing the body of Siva.[2]

Within this aesthetic is found the multi-dimensional and powerful presence of the Hindu feminine, which has shaped and influenced women through time. From *apsaras*, the intellectually and culturally refined celestial nymphs of mythology, to flesh and blood historical *devadasis*, dancers who were 'married' to temple deities in south India, women have enjoyed strength born of association with creativity and the regard of society, alongside extreme vulnerability. While women professionals and performers abound in modern India, and Indian history has recorded many examples of women participating at every level of society, the expectation of conforming to traditional marriage and child-rearing roles is an ever-present reality, as can be the loneliness of attempts at breaking these bounds. Actresses, dancers, and performers in general can fall into a particularly ambiguous position, in which their art is celebrated, while their integrity as individuals is held in doubt.

Yet the recognition of opposing and co-existing tensions within human emotional experience, and a theoretical base for reconciling apparently opposite impulses, is a fundamental part of the Hindu outlook. In this paper it is proposed that, particularly because of the flexibility of realities it affords, a re-examination of the feminine in Hindu thought can reveal possible directions for contemporary feminism. In asserting this, there is a danger of being seen to perpetuate undue subservience to tradition, and of becoming associated with culture in its revivalist or fundamentalist forms. In evading engagement with ancient ideas, however, lies the danger of missing a unique opportunity to empower women's lives today with concepts whose resonance with current realities belie their chronological data. Among such concepts is that of *sringara rasa*.

## The theory of rasa

The emotional mood or experiential essence to be conveyed by any form of art is a fundamental part of ancient Indian aesthetic theory. In a theatrical performance, the performer invokes the eight *rasas*, or fundamental emotional states. Each piece of literature or work of art has a dominant emotional 'flavour'. In drama, it is the job of the playwright and performers to imbue the audience with the meaning and experience of the chosen dominant emotion. *Sringara* is one of the fundamental eight. The *Navarasa* theory is expounded in the *Natya Sastra*, written between 100 BCE and 100 CE from oral tradition.[3] This treatise is attributed to the legendary Bharata Muni. To this day, it serves as a guide to traditional performers, craftspeople and artists of India. Through the centuries, it has also engendered scholarly commentaries and interpretations, and continues to be a source of contemporary debate amongst theoreticians and performers alike.[4] The *Natya Sastra's* chapters on *rasa* have always held particular fascination. This is possibly because, as the renowned scholar Kapila Vatsyayan states,

> The theory of *rasa* is developed as a psycho-somatic system by establishing correspondence between the motor and sensory systems. The psychical manifests itself in the physical and the physical can evoke the psychical.[5]

The theory deals with universals readily recognizable and shared by all cultures, its specific quality lying in Bharata's elaboration of techniques for presenting these feelings through body and language into a shared aesthetic experience.[6]

The pairing of eight emotions into four sets evidences Bharata's keen observation of the human condition. An excess of one is said to lead to the other, and they are paired in the following manner:

Love/Humour (*Sringara/Hasya*)
Valour/Wonder (*Vira/Adbhuta*)
Anger/Sorrow (*Raudra/Karuna*)
Disgust/Fear (*Bibhasta/Bhayanaka*)

By transferring these pairings into any contemporary or historical setting, one begins to see the degree of insight into human psychology they represent. Uncontrolled anger does indeed lead to sorrow and often regret; disgust or prejudice is usually a reflection of fear. Valour or bravery in the face of practical or spiritual ordeal induces a sense of wonder and admiration; love, *sringara*, is indeed accompanied by laughter and the letting down of one's guard to be able to experience humour. *Sringara* is often referred to as the 'king of *rasas*' because love is the one emotion that, by definition, encompasses all the others. It can also take many forms and operate at both physical and metaphysical levels. The Bharata Natyam dancer V. P. Dhanajayan states,

> The common concept is that *sringara rasa* refers to love between man and woman and its consequences. A much deeper sense is actually conveyed by this term. The meaning of this term, *sringara* is beauty, *soundarya*. That is why *sringara lahari* is also known as *soundarya lahari*. Beauty is that which attracts the mind or appeals to a particular penchant of the mind. That is love; love is not just *rati*—the amorous attitude. There can be love between a child and its mother, between friends, between a teacher and disciples and, of course, love towards God. The beauty in Man is love and this love is what distinguishes Man and makes him supreme in all creation. Hence, love is beauty, that is, *sringara* is truth.[7]

The most vivid examples of *sringara rasa* in both art and dance are the Radha Krishna legends. As romantic stories, they describe the birth of Krishna (an incarnation of Vishnu the preserver), his childhood, in which he is portrayed as mischievous but endearing, his youth as a cowherd, and later his rule as powerful and just king. At first glance, his relationship with the milkmaid Radha during his youth seems odd given the otherwise clear indications of the sanctity of marriage. Radha was said to be a married woman, though one would hardly guess it from her adventures with Krishna. Paintings and dramatic dances abound in which the Radha-Krishna relationship is presented in a very human way, displaying longing, jealousy, union—at times coy and, at other times, joyously bold, and suffering the grief of separation.

Metaphorically Radha represents the individual soul—the house-holder—who longs to escape the cycle of rebirth, to be united in time and space, with Truth. Krishna represents this cosmic state—or the Godhead. The popularity of Krishna worship from the second century BCE is significant as it reflects an extension of Hindu practice from the ritualistic Vedic eras, and mystical renunciate tendencies of the Upan-ishidic outlook, to a more personalized devotional form of religion.[8] In the *Bhagavata Gita*, Krishna philosophically reconciles the path of ac-tion/duty, and the path of meditation/intellectualization towards self-realization.[9] By doing so, he also establishes the validity of devotional action as a route to salvation, and opens the way to popularizing a sense of intimacy with the deity. Hence the Radha-Krishna stories as told in the *Bhagavata Purana* are allegorical in intent and usually treated with piety in the listening, painting or enacting.[10] Portraying a very different Krishna to the one from the *Gita*, however, their explicit mortal refer-ences are unmistakeable. These are emphasized in texts such as the twelfth century *Gita Govinda* by Jayadeva that concentrates on the ro-mantic, erotic or *sringara* aspects of the relationship between Radha and Krishna, and is the subject of many miniature paintings especially after the fourteenth century.[11]

In literature, a fully elaborated example of the multiple layers of *sringara rasa* is the Sanskrit play *Abhijnana-sakuntalam* (Sakuntala and the Ring of Recollection) written by the poet and playwright Kalidasa (c.500 CE). It is based on the story of Sakuntala, the mythological daughter of a celestial nymph and an ascetic hermit. Among the earliest appearances of Sakuntala is in a passage of the epic *Mahabharata* (c.300 BCE, added to up to 300 CE). The best-known version of the tale, however, comes from Kalidasa's play, which is also considered one of the finest of classical Sanskrit dramas. It is ideally suited to an inquiry about the spiritual and sensuous in Hindu thought. In the barest out-line, the narrative is a love story involving two protagonists from very different worlds.[12] The evocation of *sringara* is present throughout the play, not only in descriptions of the maiden and her suitor King Dusyanta, but also in the poetic re-creation of the forest in which Sakuntala lives, and even in her relationship to it. She is described as the sister of the gentle deer she feeds, and the vine-entwined mango tree for which she particularly cares is referred to as an embracing couple. Overall in the play, there is a general mood of romance and contem-plation of exquisite but vulnerable beauty. True to the *navarasas*, love as well as humour are conveyed, as are the attendant experiences of sor-row, anger, disgust and disillusionment. Serving its literary intention, and creating a lyrical human drama, the play runs the gamut of the many deeply felt aspects of love that fill a lifetime.

Some extracts of Kalidasa's play from Barbara Stoller-Miller's translation give us a taste of the *rasa* created. On first spying Sakuntala, Dushyanta is immediately attracted to her:

Act I (14)
*King:*
Is this Kanva's daughter? The sage does show poor judgement in imposing the rules
of the hermitage on her.

The sage who hopes to subdue
Her sensuous body by penances
Is trying to cut firewood
With a blade of blue-lotus leaf.

When Sakuntala eventually accepts her feelings for Dushyanta and agrees to write to him, she is equally clear about the physicality and intensity of her feelings. As no writing materials are available, she uses her nails to press her message on a lotus leaf.

Act I (30)
*Sakuntala* (singing what she has written on the leaf):
I don't know
your heart
but day and night
for wanting you,
love violently
tortures
my limbs,
cruel man.

The King, on learning he must see to some duties, thereby interrupting his efforts to win Sakuntala over, describes the pain of separation:

Act I (22)
*King:*
My body turns to go,
my heart pulls me back,
like a silk banner
buffeted by the wind.

When Sakuntala is to leave for her husband's home, her friends and the very animals of the hermitage and forest are heartbroken:

Act IV (5)
*Priyamvada* (to Sakuntala):
You are not the only one who grieves. The whole hermitage feels this way as your
departure from our grove draws near.

Grazing deer
drop grass,
peacocks
stop dancing,
vines lose
pale leaves
falling
like tears.

Kanva too, though an ascetic, who has renounced material attachments, suffers the sorrow of parental separation.

Act IV (5)
*Kanva:*
My heart is touched with sadness
since Sakuntala must go today,
my throat is choked with sobs,
my eyes are dulled by worry—
if a disciplined ascetic
suffers so deeply from love,
how do fathers bear the pain
of each daughter's parting?[13]

## Sringara and duality

In *Abhijnana-sakuntalam*, another very human situation is recognized—a genuine struggle between social obligation, and the natural and passionate leanings of youth. There is in Sakuntala's presence a charged sense of awakening nature, of potential fertility and, at the same time, spiritual calm. There is a constant polarity at work between structured social morality with all its boundaries, and the ultimate knowledge that these codes will always be broken. In this respect Sakuntala's rescue by her mother from the indignity of having to prove herself through her unborn baby's identity is very striking. In Kalidasa's play, Sakuntala is portrayed as good and worthy of respect. She is, however, rescued ultimately not by the good and noble around her but by her mother, the *apsara* who abandoned her at birth, who conceived her in order to ruin a powerful male ascetic and who is still a beautiful, sensual and celestial being. The polarity between the physical and the spiritual takes another turn at this point in the play, as all the apparent wisdom of the sages who have raised Sakuntala fails to allow them the humanity of empathizing with her at her most vulnerable. Yet Menaka, the symbolic opposite of the renunciate contemplator, steps forward to protect an innocent young woman, thereby also reasserting her mother-daughter bond. This event cannot be seen simply as the union of societal outsiders, for Menaka does not retreat to a secret hiding place, but to a heavenly abode where the very founders of the divine world reside, and where she and her daughter are welcomed. While Menaka's celestial origins allow her the freedom to rebel against the conservative outlook of the hermits amongst whom her daughter resides, her ultimate acceptability within the cosmic order allows her to bring Sakuntala to a space between the two worlds. It is in this space that the lovers are eventually reunited when Dusyanta's memory returns and he comes to seek forgiveness.

In relation to the acceptance and celebration of the sensuous and erotic, *apsaras* are intriguing members of the Hindu and Buddhist cosmic world. Flying divinities originally associated with water, they are portrayed in Hindu and Buddhist art and literature as highly skilled in the arts of music, dance, language and seduction. In sculptures and paintings they appear totally immersed in whatever they are engaged in—dancing, singing, at play, and attending others, but seeming to celebrate and be at peace within themselves.[14] Yet the codes of conduct by which they are governed clearly apply only to *apsaras*, and not to mortal women. Like a human courtesan, the *apsara* is *expected to* behave outside the norms of society, and often does so at the bidding of a male ruler. In the case of Menaka, she seduces Vishwamitra as a favour to the god Indra who has grown jealous of the ascetic. Yet the *apsara* is very much a creature of power, far stronger than mortal men, able to fly between different realms of reality. She is appealing as an icon of female achievement, drawing strength from her physical and mental femaleness, as well as her spiritually feminine dimension.

The *apsara* has at times been interpreted as symbolic of the tension between *kama* (love/eroticism) and *tapas* (austerity) as yearnings within the human condition.[15] While this construal does fit the Menaka/Vishwamitra scenario, it also posits a polarity that misses the fundamental inter-connectedness posed by the theory of *rasa* and particularly of *sringara rasa*. In the Hindu cosmos, love itself can become a vehicle for self-realization. As mentioned earlier, sexual union between male and

8.1    Ranjana Thapalyal, *Lady Lotus*, 2000, colour transparency. Copyright Ranjana Thapalyal.

female has been used in ancient Hindu symbolism of the *sivaling* or joined *yoni* and *lingam*.[16] In later Tantric traditions, sexual practice itself is presented as a valid form of awareness raising.[17] In this context, it is possible to see in Sakuntala's abandonment of tradition in order to marry her suitor in the un-witnessed Gandharva fashion—a valid but frowned upon convention in ancient India—both the recklessness of youth, and at the same time the reasoning of a mind which does not see physical love, sexual union, as vulgar or irreligious (8.1).

What inferences can be made from this tale? One opportunity is to see in the depiction of Sakuntala's character, and in that of her mother Menaka, the possibility of existing with dignity on the edge of traditional social codes. The story and personality of Sakuntala encourage an acceptance of the many aspects of being a woman, and of a spiritual dimension to beauty, love, and survival. In the past, however, real women who have tried, or have been forced by circumstance, to live between boundaries have not fared as well as the fictional Sakuntala. The historical figure of the *devadasi* focuses our attention on the social implications of treading between the spiritual/religious and the world of *sringara*. One of the oldest dance forms of India, *Bharata Natyam*, was nurtured in its original form as ceremonial worship in the temples of South India, and handed down through generations by *devadasis*. Following scriptural precepts of the *Saiva Agamas*, a young girl could be dedicated to a particular temple and at sixteen 'married' to its deity.[18] Together with male priests, many of whom also would have been dedicated to the temple as children, the *devadasis* fulfilled various ceremonies aimed at evoking the *shakti*, the female energy of the male deity. As in so many aspects of Hindu ritual, a multiple vocabulary of prayer was employed. Alongside the priest's recitation of *mantras*, sacred phrases, the *devadasi's* conduit was song, and a highly structured dance form incorporating mime, rhythmic composition and symbolic *mudras*—hand-gestures. The *devadasi* was an officiate of the temple, and, in what seems in contemporary eyes a remarkably liberal recognition of her needs as a human being, and of the possibility of devotion without asceticism as such, she was allowed to have an emotional and sexual relationship with one devotee or priest of the temple. The relationship was monogamous, and offspring were accepted by temple and society.

Ironically, it can be said that it was modernization that exposed the *devadasi* to social opprobrium rather than the institution of temple dancers.[19] With the outlawing of the *devadasi* system in 1948, the same women who would have been considered auspicious guests at weddings were officially declared to be immoral. Some were driven to prostitution, a way of life of which they had been accused by Christian missionaries and Western-educated Indian reformers who classed them with courtesans and dancers of the Mughal courts. Others languished under governmental rehabilitation efforts. These attitudes, rooted in a nineteenth century Western moral code, entirely out of tune with the complexities of traditional India, continue to inform the general perception of the significant function of the *devadasi* system.

While the system had no doubt the potential for exploitation, late twentieth century interviews with surviving *devadasis* offer a glimpse of the concept as empowerment through devotion, and enunciate the deep hurt felt by the *devadasis* at finding themselves suddenly reviled by the society they had hitherto served.[20] The system was significant also because it embodied several fundamentals of Hindu thought. It linked the practice of music and dance with the religious path. It created a female position of spiritual authority or benevolence. It offered a socially accepted possibility of non-domesticated existence for women; *devadasis* were expected to devote their entire time to their arts and to rituals, not to household chores. Through the system of partnering one priest or devotee, the perpetuation of sacred arts was also ensured, through generations of children brought up and trained by the *devadasis*.

The banning of the *devadasi* system, however, while projecting disgrace on the women, did have the effect of bringing their dance form into a wider public domain as a performing art. In its repertoire, it still carries the devotional imagery, content and layered symbolism of the original. Two women dancers Rukmini Devi (1904–86) and Balasaraswati (1918–84) were key figures in the revival and evolution of *Bharata Natyam*. Balasaraswati, whose mother and grandmother were both learned temple dancers, was one of a few *devadasis* who agreed to dance on stage. Others declined as they felt the secular performance space was inappropriate for what was essentially a form of worship.

Remembered today as a sublime performer and important cultural figure, associated also with the era of early assertions of Indian self-rule and self-knowledge, Balasaraswati's determination to dance and teach others conjoined with a new breed of post-Independence dancer. While one set of modern Indians was discarding Hindu rituals and the arts associated with them, another was attempting to retrieve and conserve them, as exemplified by upper class, educated Brahmin women who studied dance as fine art and established it as both respectable and tied to a scholarly tradition. Rukmini Devi's contribution in this regard culminated in the founding of *Kalakshetra*, an academy of dance and music in Chennai that continues to teach these disciplines within their religious context and emphasizes their devotional aspects.

### Saraswati and Vak

At the roots of contemporary Hindu society's dichotomous positioning of the feminine as both divine and in need of control, as well as the possibility of escape from it, is the Hindu concept of the universe. The three causal forces, Creation, Preservation, Destruction, in their persona as Brahma, Vishnu, and Siva, each have a female counterpart.[21] It is she who provides the energy to spark the actions of the male aspect, and this idea as the basis of the *devadasi's* symbolic purpose in temple worship especially of Siva. Vishnu's consort is Lakshmi, who is associated with well-being and prosperity. Siva's consort is Parvati who is associated with primal energy, or nature itself, in both its benign and destructive aspects. Brahma the creator is the consort of Saraswati who is, therefore, linked with learning, the arts and speech.[22] The causal factors of creation, preservation and destruction are manifestations of what can be described as a universal formless intelligence/consciousness called Brahman, who is not active, but causes creation to occur. The first step towards the creation triumvirate occurs in the personification of Brahman as Sara—a deity-like being—more like God in the monotheistic religions.

Brahma can be described as the creative aspect of Brahman, but the two are distinct entities. Brahma's four heads, signifying *manas* (mind), *buddhi* (intellect), *citta* (conditioned consciousness), and *ahamkar* (ego), are all required for the act of creation. The significance assigned to Saraswati as the female counterpart of Brahma is crucial and fundamental. In Hindu creation myths, it is through the mind of Saraswati that Brahma created the Vedas—the first Hindu texts. The concept is evidenced even in her name, which incorporates the words *sara* (as essence) *swa* (self), making Saraswati the giver of self-knowledge.

Saraswati is depicted as one who has not only the experience of
the supreme Reality but is also the embodiment of the philosophy
of the Upanishads. These are the essential qualities of a guru, a
spiritual teacher.[23]

*Manas, buddhi, citta* and *ahamkar* are represented by the arms. Saraswati's
*chitta* hands hold the scriptures, or prayer beads; her other two hands,
mind and intellect, create music with the *veena*.

Each deity in the Hindu cosmos has an animal vehicle, *vahana*, also
symbolic in some way of the way in which the deity is to be understood.
Saraswati's *vahana*, the swan, being symbolic of discrimination, in the
sense of differentiation between truth and falsehood, indicates the cen-
trality of the concept of knowledge in Hindu thought as something
that requires discernment as well as mental capacity. The mythological
*hansa* is said to be able to separate milk from a mixture of milk and
water. This reinforces the message that Saraswati is a bringer of light
and knowledge, and more significantly, she is the source and purveyor
of *gyanasaksha*, the eyes to see/recognize knowledge. As compared to
the overt powers of Durga and Kali, both representing the primal energy of nature, Saraswati's power is of a more cerebral kind, but equally
potent in implication.[24] She is the giver of knowledge, creativity, speech,
which are all vehicles for self-realization. Hence the female ascetic as
well as the bejewelled dancer can take inspiration from Saraswati.

There is also another earlier form of Saraswati, the female entity
Vak, the voice of speech itself. Unlike other members of the Hindu
pantheon, Vak is disembodied. She is speech, or the essence of
sound—the fundamental creative impulse.

According to the Yoga and Sankhya system, sound is the root of
all other sensory potentials. It is the sensory quality that belongs
to ether, the original element. Hence through it all the elements
can be controlled. The mind itself is composed of sound. It is the
reverberation of our words and the ideas they represent which
forms the pattern of the mind.[25]

Vak is not associated with any male gods, but is an independent entity,
all-pervasive, all knowing. In Sanskrit drama, her voice is constantly
used as a theatrical device to give important information, to explain
off stage events, and to act as a voice of authority.[26] Thus in drama, Vak
bridges the gap between mortal and divine worlds. In a philosophical
sense, she is a manifestation of pure Consciousness. In Saraswati, who

contains the concept of Vak, we find a female being who is the embodiment of clarity of mind, as well as physical beauty. What is central to engaging with Saraswati in the context of this paper is the fact that the two are never seen as negating one another. Saraswati's bodily beauty can be seen as metaphor for the sublime knowledge contained within her mind, and her intellect can be said to manifest the luminous quality of her appearance.

In modern as well as traditional works, especially but not only in Western traditions, women's voices have all too often been associated in literature and in the popular imagination with vanity, gossip, nagging, ignorance, fear and guile. In refreshing contrast, there exist powerful entities such as Vak and Saraswati in older ideologies with which we can choose to align ourselves. In doing so, one is not obliged to accept all the baggage of ancient Indian thought and its multifarious interpretations. Just as characters and ideas have evolved through time to support the current ethos in which they are retold, so the journey continues. If women today can find spiritual sustenance in reworking and extracting potent ideas such as Vak and Saraswati, and find self-expression through concepts such as *sringara*, why should this opportunity be lost?

One of the possible difficulties in the attempt to extract feminist nurturing from Hinduism may lie in the fact that the male-female power dynamic is often expressed in what can appear to be unequal allegorical terms. In essence, male and female, as concepts of universal law, are placed in an inextricably interlinked and equal status. In the analogies used through time to demonstrate the essence, however, male and female *roles* can seem to be hierarchically placed. For example, in the allegory of individual soul in search of mergence with the higher consciousness, as seeker and sought, the seeker is almost always female, and the ultimate consciousness portrayed as masculine lord. This is manifested in the Bhakti (devotional) cults as a whole, and takes a more secular overtone in the romantic allegories of Radha and Krishna. While Radha and Krishna both desire each other, in the most popular stories, frequently performed in many dance styles, it is Radha who is depicted as lost in longing, angry at being apparently rejected, being consoled by an inevitably forgivable Krishna.

Yet if we are able to apply a holistic approach to the subject of empowerment of, and from, the feminine, without too polarized a separation of male and female, a meaningful engagement, and the grounds for a contemporary empowerment from ancient Indian ideas, can emerge. This is not to say that we should ignore the andro-centric ways in which Hindu philosophy has often been interpreted through the ages. As in all histories, the feminist recognition of these factors is a prerequisite to unravelling them, and very often, a return to the philosophical roots of aesthetic imagery can illuminate strands that lend themselves to integration with contemporary thought. The theory of the *navarasas* is a manifestation of a belief in the inter-related nature of all opposites, which is a basic tenet of all the schools of Hinduism. It is applied also to conceptions of male and female energies.

The theory of creative energies in the form of complementary opposites of *purusha* and *prakriti* has been expounded in *Samkhya* philosophy from 400 BCE.[27] *Purusha* and *prakriti,* primal universal powers beyond ordinary perception, are manifested in ordinary life and in nature. The term *prakriti* means matter in its germinal state, or, primeval matter containing and bestowing vitality, diversity, and energy. It is *prakriti* that activates nature with all its dynamism of form and function, its abundance and its terrifying manifestations. In the male/female analogy of creation, *prakriti* is identified with the female principle, also known as *sakti*. When *sakti* interacts with *purusha,* the male principle, the material world is created. Both would, in a sense, be inert without the other. In some Hindu schools of thought, it is *prakriti* that is active while *purusha* is inert; in others, it is the opposite. *Purusha* is also seen as primeval man, human beings, both men and women, while *prakriti* is the world that they inhabit and by which they are ensnared.[28] In the same vein, Brahma is usually shown seated on a lotus, which emerges from the navel of Vishnu, symbolizing the ultimate interdependence of creation and preservation. Vishnu's *prakriti* is *Maya*; Brahma's knowledge that it is created and therefore unreal is *purusha.*

Here again is potential for both feminist concurrence and dissent. One could argue that the positioning of knowledge of the ultimately illusory nature of phenomena in the male principle *purusha* is a way of privileging it over the female principle of *prakriti*. Yet in the tacit interdependence of the two principles lies potential for an application to male-female dynamics in contemporary life that could bypass the traditional battle of the sexes.

This assertion does not negate the power imbalance in most societies that has given rise to articulations of revolt and calls for rethinking and restructuring traditional male-female roles. It does suggest another strand in the argument, another way out of the impasse of emphasis on *difference* between men and women. Could the idea of primal, psychological, spiritual interdependence be freed from the constraints of some historical interpretations, yet remain aligned to others that allow for a useful societal evolution? And most startlingly, could a theory of love and beauty, thousands of years old, be a formative part of such a development?

To return specifically to the idea of *sringara*, perhaps in the ancient Indian grasp of the sensuous and its relation to the spiritual, some bal-

ancing forces can be located for women today. Exposed for some years
to the notion of girl-power or ironic girlishness in an ostensibly post-
feminist age, perhaps we are lacking a theoretical base for the assertion
of femininity as a self-defining action. Whose ideas of the feminine do
we adhere to? Celebrating the female body and all its potential for giving and receiving pleasure need not mean putting oneself in the hands
of commercial forces which are ultimately still largely controlled by
men, or at least uphold a male-dominated society in which violence
against women seems a perennial factor. Perhaps it is only when women
are able to define beauty in their own terms, drawing from the precedents of their own choosing and applying these in empowering ways
will we be able to activate as *prakriti* a *purusha* of a more palatable order.

   The reinterpretation of ancient Indian ideas on morality, sensuality,
and spirituality are in a sense in a nascent stage. In an interview, Kapila
Vatsyayan recalls her first encounter with the sculptures of the tenth
and eleventh century Khajuraho temples in central India, whose façades
and interiors teem with sculptures, many of conjoined couples, depicting life and love in all its manifestations. The erotic imagery set in the
context of the other scenes of everyday life of the Candela period came
as a revelation, making apparent the Victorian quality of the outlook on
art to which she and her friends, all trained in prestigious American
and European universities, had hitherto been exposed. Khajuraho also
brought about the realization that fundamental to Indian art was the
conviction that sacred and secular were not opposite, but part of each
other.[29] In Vatsyayan's writings on Indian art and philosophy lie many
keys to the multi-layered vision of reality that they present. Her explanation of the significance of *rasa* in ancient Indian thought as operating
in, and communicating physical/psychical realms, has already been
mentioned. Such understanding of the interrelated nature of supposedly different aspects of human experience and ability echoes the ancient Indian science of medicine, *Ayurveda*. In the theory of *rasa*:

> Without stating it explicitly, [Bharata] implies an adherence to the
> notion of five elements (*bhutas*) and the humours … According
> to the *Ayurvedic* system of medicine, equilibriums and disequilibria
> are created by the balance of *Agni, Vayu, Prithvi, Jala*, and *Akasha*
> (fire, air, earth, water, ether). Indeed the types of characters enu-
> merated in the *Natya Sastra* could emerge only from tacit accept-
> ance of personality types outlined in the system of Ayurveda etc.[30]

Further, Vatsyayan remarks that ideas about art and drama on the sub-
continent, stemming from what today seems an unusual *multidisciplinarity*,
have continuously responded to philosophical and scientific debates.

8.2 Ranjana Thapalyal, *Menaka*, 2000, colour transparency. Copyright Ranjana Thapalyal.

The views of early commentators on the *Natya Sastra* have to be under-stood against the background of the evolution of distinct schools of Indian philosophy, principally Mimamsa, Samakhy, Yoga, Vedanta, and Kashmir Saivism. Each of the commentators was investigating Bharata's exposition of *rasa* and *styyibhava* from the tacit assumptions of their particular schools.[31] The discourse on the nature of aesthetic experience, creation, presentation, expression, and the evocation of an analogous experience in the receiver is also a dialogue in the philosophical schools, on the nature of the phenomenal world. [32]

It is evident that a generous understanding of human nature is implicit and expounded in ancient Indian thought. As in the theory of *rasa*, with *sringara* as supreme example, so in the paralleling of philosophy and medicine, Hindu art and philosophy is permeated by multidisciplinarity and creative slippage. Such an outlook requires of us the same suppleness of mind, and will reap rich rewards (8.2).

# 9

## *STABAT MATER*—A NAMELESS PLACE
### Film, the Feminine and the Sacred
#### *Nina Danino*

*Stabat Mater* (16 mm, 8 mins, 1990) opens with shots of blue spacing, and on the soundtrack the voice speaks the lines below.

> Spoken Voice: *The voice in each woman is not only her own, but springs from the deepest layers of her psyche: her own speech becomes the echo of the primeval song she once heard, the voice, the incarnation of the "first voice of love which all women preserve alive … in each woman sings the first nameless love."* [1]

The first images of the film follow—a palm tree and a statue of the Virgin—and over them a woman's voice sings a *saeta*.

My mother sings; she sings in Spanish to the Mother, the Mater. She sings a form which is archetypal, a sung lament. I ask her to sing two improvised laments, which, in the rise and rise of the voice, reach for an impossible register of virtuosity and feeling. These improvisations are based on the form of the *saeta*—meaning an arrow—a song without music for the solo voice. The *saeta* is a vernacular form of sacred song—a low form, sung from the street, balconies and pavements, sung to the agony of Christ or to His Mother during Passion Week. That is, to the Stabat Mater, who is the Mother at the foot of the Cross—an iconic emblem of sorrow.

The *saeta* traditionally consists of a short, two or three line poem sung by a single unaccompanied voice, in which the flow of the lines is broken up, disjointed and repeated to enable the voice to stretch in an ever-upwards pitch, reaching a crescendo at its highest peak of emotion, and coming to a sudden or even abrupt end. Now elevated to a

9.1 Nina Danino, *Stabat Mater*, 1990. Still.

specialist art form, it is performed by highly paid professional singers around the streets of the procession in scheduled appearances—like virtuoso star performances. The *saeta* is a trope which, in the soundtrack to my film *Stabat Mater*, stems from a cultural and religious specificity, but which also has a trans-cultural charge, linked to the universality of the woman's voice and to the body that it engenders in the viewer, in the body of the film and in the performance of a disembodied subjectivity.

*Stabat Mater* is also the title of Jacopone da Todi's Latin hymn, which has been set to music by many composers, including Pergolesi, Palestrina and Rossini; in their hands, it is a high cultural form of sacred music. Only the popular form of the *saeta* is heard on the soundtrack, but by association, two streams of music flow through the film—high and low—two forms of enunciation. Pasolini thought that the dialectical tension between the high and the low had the character of a sacred operation, as of 'two languages in free indirect discourse … the correlation between two asymmetrical proceedings, acting within language'.[2]

Another kind of song is heard in the opening lines of the film, spoken by a woman's voice, describing the power of the woman's voice as 'the first voice of love which all women preserve alive', which evokes a connective space, a shared feminine space, because 'it is not only her own', but also a link to a previous order, 'an echo' of another type of song which 'she once heard': 'the first voice of love', a nameless love. It is a voice 'mixed with milk'.[3]

Milk and tears, as Marina Warner has pointed out, are the mark of the Virgin.[4] The Stabat Mater is the sorrowful Virgin *par excellence*. The Virgins of Passion Week are also Mater Dolorosa, and embody suffering, pain and sorrow as forms of popular knowledge and devotion, emblematized through the crowd's own joy and sorrow, as the Sevillian people call out to her as she passes in her veils and static tears,

'*Guapa!*'—these are wolf whistles for a young woman. Exultation and sorrow are one. The famous Sevillian Macarena is also a crying Virgin, with her tears of diamonds, but like all Virgins (who follow the Christ and are in fact alone), and like the Stabat Mater herself, this sorrow is silent; no cries or hysterical wailings are heard. Her surrogate cries are found in the responses from the crowd and in the laments sung by the singers. For Kristeva, these silent tears are the metaphors of non-speech, 'a "semiotics" that linguistic communication does not account for'.[5]

So, is this figure of a nameless love an idealization, which, as Kristeva seems to say in her personal essay 'Stabat Mater', stands over an empty place, and in which, in Western and Christian culture, is embodied the emblematic representation of Virgin and Child? 'This motherhood is the *fantasy*, that is nurtured by the adult man or woman, of a lost territory; what is more, it involves less an idealized archaic mother than the idealization of the *relationship* that binds us to her, one that cannot be localized.'[6] It is a nameless place.

How can one represent this nameless place in film? How can film represent the sacralization of absence? One thinks of film as having content, and so the sacred in film is thought of in terms of representation, as, for example, the subject matter in Carl Dreyer's *The Passion of Joan of Arc* (1928). On another level, the experience of the Transcendent, or remnants of the sacred, as Paul Schrader says in his specialist study of the sacred in *auteur* film, can only be enunciated through the mediation of a style which is not *itself* the Transcendent, but a representation of it through form: 'Because transcendental style is fundamentally just that, a style, it can be isolated, analysed and defined … Transcendental style uses precise temporal means—camera angles, dialogue, editing—for predetermined transcendental ends.'[7]

9.2  Nina Danino, *Stabat Mater*, 1990. Still.

Perhaps the closest that the register of the sacred approaches to us beyond the frame of the religious is through aesthetics, and there are perhaps styles and forms which convey a sense of the sacred, and that can even be experienced as sacred in themselves. One can think of sacred music, which can cross religious cultures, especially via the hybrid spaces of what is categorized as 'world music'.

S. Brent Plate suggests that the experience of the religious or sacred in art also happens at the level of form, practice, aesthetics and medium (i.e. when inscribed within the art work, as in Pasolini's notion of the operation of the forces hidden in production). On another level, this experience can occur in the interaction between the object and the viewer, such as might be the expected experience of a viewer in front of a Rothko painting.[8]

For each of us, particular works of art may be imbued with a sense of the sacred, or we may be acculturated to understand particular aesthetic forms as being imbued with a near-sacred aura; for instance, consider the notion of the aesthetic sublime, which in modernism is often represented through aesthetic formalism. Art works can even be read as touching on the edges of the sacred—one can think of the works of contemporary male artists such as Bill Viola, Anish Kapoor and James Turrell, which are often underscored critically in these terms. But the sacred cannot just be a relative, cultural, aesthetic or subjective matter, for it is also a matter of belief.

With the exception of religious art with explicit religious content and/or the aesthetic power to carry it, such as that of Caravaggio, for example, in aesthetics it is very difficult to experience the 'live', immersive, awesome quality and transformative power of what is generally understood as the sacred, in the interaction between the static art object and the viewer. Film, however, which has a number of dimensions, such as time, and contains combinations of the aural and visual and of colour and pace, can affect and stimulate the emotional and bodily senses more directly.

Film is the most perfect medium (so far) for the enunciation of diverse registers, tensions and drives. It is a medium that can 're-site' or 'transport' the viewer or audience, through the multiplicity of its dimensions of time, sound, image and spatiality, and by way of its linear and expanded forms. Film is a phenomenological medium (though not without its historical and political contexts), but it is also a medium and a material. It is this material and, at the same time, ephemeral quality of film, with its complex relationships to the temporal, which can create the possibilities of an 'other place' within its habitat-space of the cinema. This also happens, in a different way, in the simulacra of the cinema-like spaces in the gallery. Experimental film, with its self-con-

9.3 Nina Danino, *Stabat Mater*, 1990. Still.

sciousness as material and as art, has always situated itself as what Bellour terms the 'other cinema', which 'has never stopped haunting the great representational cinema' by lurking on the borders of its master dominant discourse, inhabiting the liminal or 'semiotic' spaces of representational cinema and also migrating into the spaces of the gallery.[9]

Experimental forms perhaps aim to do two things: to expand and challenge the dominant discourse, and in so doing, perhaps to create sites for the enunciation of what was previously foreclosed. Far from being an empirical project, I see experimental or art film as a form of feeling or perception without the limitations of codified structures, often struggling to enunciate the unsaid or the unperceived. This struggle may be played out in the use of verbal language itself and of the place of the subject and of the feminine within it. For this reason, many women artists, especially in film (with its strong dominant master discourse), have tried to create visual alternatives to the representational codes of dominant cinema, and sometimes this has involved the rejection of spoken language altogether, in favour of the purely visual (although the banishment of the verbal and acoustic, and the privileging of the purely optical also has a hierarchical place in the male canon of experimental work, albeit for different reasons).

Perhaps the experimental always has a feminine dimension which is outside language (the language of film codes) and is perhaps, like Lacan's psychoanalytic notion of the feminine, something 'other', a form of absence.[10] As art, it is perhaps a form of practice which cannot be entirely represented or fully embodied in linear language, neither by the codes of representation in film, nor by symbolic language. If so, it also occupies a privileged place that cannot entirely be colonized by language, a place which is enunciated through the dialectical tensions— in Pasolini's terms—of a free indirect discourse of different registers, which nevertheless must come together and cross in (aesthetic) discourse—otherwise there would be no communication. How can a film such as *Stabat Mater*, a physical object and a material product, represent this absence or nameless place? This sacred place? How does the film language of *Stabat Mater* attempt to convey to the viewer the possibility of experiencing such a place through its forms, rhetoric and aesthetics?

We have to employ language: visual language as well as audio language. Film, as a material and a language, is physical, and editing can order or disorder time and space. 'In order to convey fleeting glimpses of that which the camera cannot capture, the film is quickly edited to a sequenced rhythm of hand-held-images.'[11] Close-up hand-held images of flowers, graves, trees and panoramas are inter-cut by a skipping, walking hand-held camera. All framing is a form of decision-making, and in cutting off the world so decisively, the close-up frame can be a form of idealization; for that too is a process of mother-making. At the same time, the act of framing, as S. Brent Plate points out, of dividing or cutting, is also a ritual act which is embedded in the act of creation, with its imperative to separate in order to create anew, for we are not replicating a place in the documentary genre (although it is a real location as well), but re-rendering it in a new, re-created world.

The film combines these close ups with wider, hand-held moving images, shot as the camera skips forward in sequences of streets, roads, road signs and panoramas, ending in a view of the open sea and a lighthouse. The cutting and inter-cutting creates an unstable space.

> The back and forth oscillations of images and associations, echoing the framing and re-framing of the hand-held camera, with shots connected in an unpunctuated torrent, build and construct the spectator's experience as chiasmic. The corporeal vision of the spectator, seeing from where the camera is in a shifting unsteady swoon, in some kind of effusion, is devotional, poetic, erotic, melancholic—even sacrificial?[12]

9.4 Nina Danino, *Stabat Mater*, 1990. Still.

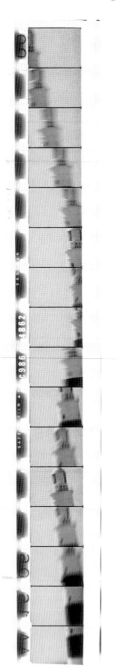

9.5 Nina Danino, *Stabat Mater*, 1990. Film strip.

In my films I have used my own voice on the soundtrack. The woman's voice reads fragments of the end of James Joyce's *Ulysses* at fast speed—a canonical text which inscribes, in its end chapter, the eternal female principle, which is centred, cosmological and sexually devouring. Yet, the skipping and moving camera leads us inexorably forward, driven in the pure abandonment of child-like joy: *my mother, yes the fun we had running along Willis road to Europa Point.*[13] It takes us to a place where pronouns merge or are relinquished, where the feminine swallows all differentiation into the blue film spacing which ends the film. Is this regression? I don't think so, because the viewer is both taken forward by this torrent of images and sound, but never allowed to be completely absorbed into the fictive space. These are the forces hidden in the production of *Stabat Mater*: the voice plays a part, as do music and song. The feminine, and perhaps even the sacred, is attempted through a dialectics of practice; association, framing, pace, rhythm, content, sound, voice, reference, location (with its ephemeral and sensory qualities of colour and light) and fast editing. These elements combine, and do not allow the viewer to hold on to fixed points of identification, nor to characters or actors who stand in for ideas, nor to the story or plot, because all these things are absent; yet all around us the aural and symbolic film language, constructed in the viewing, creates a rhetoric for the representation of this sorrowful/ joyful absence.

A lush garden ... a stone virgin ... the mother's garden ... a stone grave ... a flower ... the virgin bridge ... an artificial flower ... a mother's voice ... a deserted street ... the veiled virgin ...

9.6 Nina Danino, *Stabat Mater*, 1990. Still.

a blue sky ... the virgin's lament ... the voluptuous voice ... the Madonna ... the sorrowful mother ... a torrent of words ... the apotheosis of virginity ... the rhetoric of a realist image ... a syntax of *jouissance* ... the hollow of a blue bay ... Infinity ... the rose ... the madonna's flower ... the lover's blossom ... the flower of the cross ... a dead God ... a spiritual veiling of castration ... all stinking tatters ... melancholy ... blue spacing ... the mother's body flowers ... the stony tower ... a pagan lament ... palms ... the opening and closing of an eye ... irises of sphincters and camera apertures ... the flower of the madonna's body...the unveiling of the veiled one ... the flowers of the body of the mother ... the resuscitation of a stony ideal ... something base ... the Infinite.[14]

The film's end mirrors its beginning; the words below are spoken over a sequence of blue film spacing, followed by a sequence of images of palm trees and the same statue, over which the solo voice sings a second lament.

Spoken Voice: *Voice: inexhaustible milk. She has been found again. The lost mother. Eternity: it is the voice mixed with milk.*[15]

Saeta: *Esperanza Macarena, tu eres la Madre de Dios Y Estrella de la Mañana*

# KATHLEEN RAINE
## Poetry and Myth as Constructions of the Sacred and the Secret
*Céline Boyer*

Kathleen Raine, poet and essayist, was born in London in 1908 and died in 2003. In her book *Women in search of wisdom*, Anne Bancroft devotes a chapter to the greatest living English language poet of the day, whom she describes as a 'natural mystic'. Raine was the great poet who wrote, 'I have read all the books but one/Only remains sacred: this/Volume of wonders, open/Always before my eyes,' and 'What is our country but a dream/That we have told each other page after page,/Golden branch and golden flower,/Fountain, tree, river,/this invisible Paradise.' She was co-founder of the journal *Temenos*, and of the research academy of the same name, an organization dedicated to the teaching of the imaginative arts. Since understanding of the sacred is universal, *Temenos*' research draws on all traditions. In Western civilization, Plato and Plotinus are acknowledged by Kathleen Raine as the sources of the philosophy of the sacred. For this poet, the pursuit of the sacred was a reflection of the violent rejection of modern materialism, and, through her eloquent and profound work on William Blake, she saw a philosophy of mystery and hierophany emerge in her own poetic creation. Regarding the *Temenos* academy, she emphasized that:

> Our goal is clear: to publish only those works which are founded on an imaginative vision of the sacred, with no link to religion, but starting from the principle that a vision of the sacred is innate, that it is the necessary foundation of all art and of all knowledge coming from the mind.[1]

The sacred is not an easy concept to define: Rudolf Otto, in his work *Das Heilige*, analyses the modalities of religious experience. He believed that this experience is specific, and created the term 'numinous', which comes from *numen*, meaning 'the divine', or 'divine sovereignty'. To Rudolf Otto, man is naturally endowed with a religious sense. He describes the feeling of terror before the sacred, before that *Mysterium tremendum*, which René Girard also describes in *la Violence et le sacré*.

Mircea Eliade, professor of History of Religions at the University of Chicago, has dedicated all of his research work to the dimension of myth, the religious and initiation. In his analysis entitled *le Sacré et le profane*, he writes:

> The modern Westerner feels a certain unease before certain manifestations of the sacred: it is difficult for him to accept that, for certain people, the sacred can manifest itself in stones or in trees. The sacred stone and the sacred tree are not worshipped for themselves: they are so precisely because they reveal something that is no longer stone nor tree, but the sacred, the *ganz andere*.[2]

The sacred manifests itself as a new reality, another order of things—sadly it encounters an insufficient linguistic terminology—how can words express that which exceeds and eludes us? How can metaphysical mysteries be expressed? According to Kathleen Raine, poetry is able to express this sacredness: poetic writing also transgresses the order of things; it probes the heart of things and beings and thus recreates the world's invisible force. She stresses that 'Nature represents the sacred places of the power of the imagination, symbols of the loftiest meanings and values to which man can aspire.'[3]

The sacred is therefore an experience and not a quality of an object—the poet envisages nature as a theophany, a hierophany. For Raine, her own mother represents the magician's voice that grants access to holy realms: thus that idea is associated with the feminine in her imagination—the sacred is made feminine, the feminine is made sacred. She combines the maternal figure with concepts of the 'magical and irresistible beauty of the sacred'.[4] As a poet, she decides to make herself into the echo of that process of feminine creation par excellence—gestation—and procreates by creating. She becomes the voice of the explorer, a new magician in her turn, creating feminine writing whose poetic quest opens up new paths. She adventures in spheres of the unknown, those regions of consciousness that are still dark, and traces a cartography of the sacred laid bare. William Blake remarks that poetry, painting and music constitute the three powers which man has at his disposal for conversing with paradise; as Raine puts it, 'Poetry, to a certain extent, aspires to and participates in the sacred vision of the Word.'[5]

In Kathleen Raine's work, nature becomes the promise of an encounter with the sacred—she turns the world into a metaphor and sings the mystery of the cosmos though poetic rhythm. It is a form of pantheism. The Greek roots *pan* and *theos* form the following concept: Everything is in God; God is in everything. We find ourselves here on the exclusive level of a pattern of immanence where the universe is presented as the body of one great multi-faceted unity, with no beginning and no end. Everything is sacred, nothing is profane; man is immersed in the divine even if he does not perceive it. As a creature he carries within him, along with all other living things, from a blade of grass to an elephant, a divine fragment that links him to the Great Totality by means of fusion. In the poem *Semence/Seed* Raine writes:

> From star to star, from sun and spring and leaf
> And almost audible flowers whose sound is silence
> And in the common meadows, springs the seed of life.
> External and innate dimensions hold
> The living forms, but not the force of life
> For that interior and holy tree
> That in the heart of hearts outlives the world
> Spreads earthly shade into eternity.[6]

This nature often becomes a feminine womb: it is associated with fertility rites and vegetation cycles. The outside and the inside, the 'external and innate dimensions' are connected by osmosis in the experience of the sacred: poetic ecstasy allows that globalizing vision to be reached, where unity becomes possible. Kathleen Raine emphasizes art which, being the city of the soul and couched in the conscious and rational faculties of the psyche, tends towards unity, thanks to that faculty of union with the cosmos and with the collective unconscious that is the imagination. Poetry makes possible this osmosis between man and the world through the means of the imagination. It is the power to imagine absent forms in an almost intuitive fashion. Integrated in perception itself, combined with the workings of the memory, opening around us the horizon of the possible, the imagination is much more than a faculty for evoking images, it is a power of creating distance and *mise-en-présence*. Poetic images and metaphors allow the sacred to be captured, and to make visible the invisible.

There is a poem on the way
There is a poem all round me
The poem is in the near future
The poem is in the upper air
Above the foggy atmosphere
It hovers, a spirit
That I would make incarnate.
Let my body sweat
Let snakes torment my breast
My eyes be blind, ears deaf, hands distraught
Mouth parched, uterus cut out,
Belly slashed, back lashed
Tongue slivered into thongs of leather
Rain stones inserted in my breasts
Head severed
If only the lips may speak
If only the God will come.                    'Invocation'[7]

The writing of the poem approaches the ecstatic experience—the symbolic sacrifice of the body allows the sacred illumination to be glimpsed. The coming of the poem is synonymous with the coming of the god, and therefore of the sacred. The woman poet describes her female body—her breasts and her womb, her uterus—as receptacles of revelation and ecstasy. This way, the woman poet discovers modified states of paroxysmal consciousness. This transgression leads to the contemplation of certain modified states of extreme consciousness—mystic ecstasy, psychedelic trance, intoxication induced by summits or depths, alcoholic fits—as transitory psychotic states that permit the crossing of thresholds and the visualization of the invisible. Poetic ecstasy is reached through that female body that goes into a mystic trance in anticipation of the divine, of hierolatry or of the epiphanic vision. The 'controlled disorder of all the senses' advocated by Rimbaud leads to that state of opening up to the sacred, to the mysterious and to the abyssal. The poet, like a shaman, enters into a trance of inspiration and dis-covers what is hidden. The myth permits that intrusion towards the numinous, towards the emotional and towards the encrypted; poetic mythic writing becomes a progression towards the sacred, as Yves Bonnefoy emphasizes:

To live 'poetically' on earth is to presume first of all that the earth lives. It is that instinctive solidarity between poetry and nature that the myths of the golden age, and in fact all myths, bore witness to.[8]

For Kathleen Raine, myth is a catalyst for the sacred: it allows us to accede to a totality of which our individual existence is only a part. At the heart of the profane and quantitative modern world, she envisages man as living in exile from the realities of his imagination. It falls to the poet to perform the role of awakening profane man by weaving personal myths to unveil the secret of a life, and collective myths to unveil the sacred in life itself. It is a necessary function of the *ars poetica* to transpose individual vision into a common language: the poet unveils the *secret*, (the interiority of his own consciousness) and he unveils the *sacred*, (the interiority of the world). Kathleen Raine thus considers 'poets to be the prophets of the modern world'. Myth recounts a sacred history; it relates an event that has taken place in primordial time, in the mythical time of beginnings. The poet weaves images in order to create for herself a paradise in modern civilization as much as to reduce the profanity linked to a non-sacred time, a time of *banal everydayness*. In her use of myth, Kathleen Raine refers to hierophants who guide us towards that sacred, and who are essentially feminine figures such as Persephone, known later on under the name of Kore, 'the young girl', queen of the underworld but originally goddess of wheat. The return to life after burial is symbolized by the myth of Persephone, taken away and then restored, and it gave birth to the Eleusinian mysteries. Kathleen Raine sees in these female hierophants mystagogues of rebirth, the palingenesis that signifies resurrection. The Egyptian goddess Isis is one of the central sacred figures in the poet's work: as Osiris, her husband and twin, has been cut into fourteen pieces by his brother Seth, Isis will gather together the fragments of her dismembered loved one and resuscitate him in her wings for three days. Kathleen Raine entitles one of her collections of poetry *Isis Wanderer* in order to bring to light that feminine figure of unification and sacred mystery:

> I piece the divine fragments into the mandala
> Whose centre is the lost creative power,
> The sun, the heart of God, the lotus, the electron,
> That pulses world upon world, ray upon ray
> That he who lived on the first may rise on the last day.
>
> 'Isis Wanderer'[9]

Kathleen Raine combines the mythologies of the emblematic figures Isis and Persephone, and another, Aphrodite, who for Lucretius, in the introduction to the poem *de natura rerum*, represents the supreme life-giving force. The myth of dismemberment and rebirth, called a 'monomyth' by Joseph Campbell, is an initiation into an understanding of the sacred: Osiris is dismembered then resuscitated, like Dionysus,

whose name means 'who is born twice', or like Adonis, Tammuz or
Jesus. But Kathleen Raine reads the monomyth through feminine figures—she explores the numinous dimension of the magicians:

> And I who have been Virgin and Aphrodite,
> The mourning Isis and the queen of corn
> Wait for the last mummer, dread Persephone
> To dance my dust at last in the tomb.
>
> The Transit of the Gods'[10]

To reach the *ganz andere*, or 'mysterious sacred', song and dance induce a trance through which the sacred vision of the world is seen. For
the poet, mystic incantations lead to musical iterations and rhythmic
echoes—the song or *hyporcheme* is initiatory—it is the symbol of the
word that reconnects the creative power to its creation; poetic writing
thus becomes polymelodic through a ritualization of language. It is
what the poet T. S. Eliot calls 'the acoustic imagination'. Music then
becomes an initiatory investigation: it constitutes the fundamental
rhythmic pattern of our imaginative universes as well as the movement
beyond our rational modernity, in order to return us to the primitive
roots of our collective unconscious. Kathleen Raine assumes the role
of *rhapsode*, a word that comes from the Greek *rhaptein*, 'to sew', and *ôdé*,
'song'. A *rhapsode* was, in Ancient Greece, a singer who went from town
to town, reciting epic poems, especially Homeric ones. In her poetry,
Kathleen Raine combines voices, songs and whispers which are often
of a rarely identifiable supernatural origin, belonging to the sphere of
the sacred and the mysterious—sirens, totemic animals, angels and
trees, where enigmatic characters deliver coded messages and initiatory
magic formulas to induce a quasi-sacral exaltation. The work of the
bard resembles that of Thoth, Egyptian emblem of the invention of
writing and of the lyre, who must restore the initiatory power that in-
trinsically links writing and music. Raine's poetry is alliterative, like
mantra-poetry; her musicality leads towards a new order of things because it allows for a better expression of the self (Heidegger refers to
it as primitive language—*die Ursprache*).

The other initiatory process is dance—or *kommoï*—which creates
movement while seeking to mirror the cosmos. In Kathleen Raine's
poetry, to dance for God is to perform a sacrificial dance, it is about an-
nihilating profane man, victim of the historic time described by Mircea
Eliade, in order to become sacred man, who is himself made in the
very image of displacement and surpassing. All civilizations have used
dance to describe the rhythm of the seasons, the mysteries of life and
death and the alternation of day and night, of sun and moon. Kathleen

Raine uses the figure of the dancer who, since the furthest reaches of time, has always used a necessarily sacred space to mark in this way her own interior evolution, in a search for resonance and harmony. She writes on this subject:

> In the *Ion*, Plato writes about the sacred knowledge of inspiration. Like the Corybantes dance only when they are outside of themselves when they compose those beautiful songs we know; but once they have entered into the movement of the music and rhythm, they are transported and possessed like Bacchantes. The poet is light, winged, sacred.[11]

For inspired poets, the rhythms of song and dance constitute the magical means of transporting their audience and themselves out of commonplace reality to that other kingdom, according to Raine. Dance is therefore initiatory in her poetry, as René Lachaud points out, because 'we want to be initiated, not in order to become a god but to discover the divine spark without which we would know nothing.'[12] The *kommoï* and the *hyporcheme*, dance and song, are catalysts of energy that lead to shamanic flight, ecstasy and the sacred. Kathleen Raine seeks to adopt an eidetic poetry, a Heideggerian expression which signifies that there is no arbitrary rupture between words and things. Exaltation leads to a reconciliation with the sacral, in order to depose degrading profanity. But as a woman, Kathleen Raine depicts the numinous equally in the notions of creation and procreation.

In their work *Le Féminin et le sacré*, Catherine Clément and Julia Kristeva stress that maternity is inherently an experience of the self and of the sacred:

> We have each explored, you and I, in our own fashion, the apparent 'returns to' in the forms that the sacred takes: the return to childhood, the return to the body, inside and outside, in the precise lyricism of the mystics; the return to maternity, which you are right in saying is the source of the sacred.[13]

The poet weaves recurrent metaphors of maternity leading to the sacred—the moon is often associated with the luminous round belly of the mother, the *Magna Mater*. The images of germination multiply, everything sprouts and grows like an ode to life and its sacred dimension. In her poem *Embryon*, she compares the microcosm and the macrocosm, creating a miraculous osmosis—the infinitely small (the embryo) and the infinitely large (space) bear life and make sacred the principle of existence and presence.

Spun in the womb's cradle, veins
And nerves that weave the skein of thought
Behind new eyes unborn, in dreams
Float into senses delicate,

And open, slowly to unfold
In gentle flower, sheltering wings
That brood above the painful world
And screen the open doors of space.          'Embryon'[14]

For Kathleen Raine, childhood becomes the source of myth and retains a numinous and luminous aura. Myth and childhood merge together, moreover, in this return to origins, in the same feeling of exile
within profane modernity. Poetry becomes a form of reminiscence, of
anti-amnesia, in the Platonic sense; it chases headlong towards that
wonderment linked to childhood, which leads to a vivid vision of mysteries, through a deeply simple gaze.

Kathleen Raine's poetry is thus the reflection of the magic of Isis: it
uses rhythm and rhapsody, dance and ecstasy, the enthusiasm of a
child's gaze and the enchantment of the maternal gaze, in order to reach
an exhilaration leading one towards the sacred, towards that *ganz andere*.
She stresses that the sense of the sacred is something that we can experience without ever being able to define it. It is from this mystery, situated, by its very nature, beyond all comprehension, that the prophetic
voice is born. Maternity, the unique experience of fusion with the other,
is a metaphor that haunts her writing. It is associated with 'the sublime
language of nature, bearer of sacred meaning'. To conclude this discourse on the writing on the feminine and the sacred in the poetry of
Kathleen Raine, I will quote two visionary writers, Christiane Singer
and William Blake:

If in this world where it threatens to disappear we do not reawaken
in ourselves the dimension of eternity, of contemplation, of welcome, the dimension that is feminine and sacred, if we do not create those enclaves of silence where the frenzy is suspended, we
will have forgotten our vocations as men and women.[15]

Arise you little glancing wings, and sing your infant joy!
Arise and drink your bliss for everything that lives is holy.[16]

# PAULA REGO'S (HER)ETHICAL VISIONS

*Maria Aline Seabra Ferreira*

In this essay I wish to analyse Luso-British artist Paula Rego's series of paintings which deal with the Virgin Mary (2002), looking at them in the context of other representations of pregnant Madonnas in art, as well as comparing them with additional examples of anti-clerical and icon-oclastic paintings by Rego, who uses Christian iconography abundantly throughout her work, often in an unorthodox, satirical vein.

Paula Rego, who was born in Portugal in 1935, can be said to be re-covering a mostly muted and submerged vision of the 'virginal mater-nal', to borrow Julia Kristeva's words, and of the physicality of the Virgin Mary's body, so forcefully repressed and hidden in traditional Christian imagery, a body which, in Rego's work, is seen to be going through the physical changes of pregnancy like other women.[1] In 'Sta-bat Mater', Kristeva provides a detailed and critical look at the image of the 'virginal maternal', associating it with notions of essentialism and motherhood—which are problematized in the parallel columns of text —and considering the manifold paradoxes attached to the concept of 'virgin motherhood'.[2] Drawing on Marina Warner's *Alone of All Her Sex: The Myth and Cult of the Virgin Mary* as a privileged intertext, Kris-teva ends her piece by calling for a '*herethics*',[3] a notion that would fuse the kind of ethics that is specifically feminine, 'hers', with the subversive notion of heresy, of transgression.[4] Subversive and 'heretical' is preci-sely what we could call some of Rego's paintings, and the transgressive drive that criss-crosses these pictures is precisely a form of Kristevan 'herethics'.

Rego's series of paintings on the Virgin Mary were commissioned by the President of Portugal, a personal friend of the artist, to be placed in eight small niches in the private chapel of the Palácio de Belém in Lisbon, his official residence. Although not a religious man himself,

Jorge Sampaio entrusted to Rego—herself not a practising Catholic, and indeed critical of many Catholic teachings and dogmas—the task of producing paintings with religious themes.[5] Even though, as Rego explains, what she did was follow the storyline of the Virgin Mary's life suggested in Jacobus de Voragine's *The Golden Legend*, compiled about 1260, and even though she insists that she had not intended to produce shocking or scandalous pictures, she could not help being provocative in her work, and judging from visitors' reactions to the paintings, some of which I witnessed, they do provoke strong reactions, including feelings of repulsion, horror and abjection in seeing such sacred themes being visually dramatized in ways that might be considered by some as blasphemous and irreverent.[6]

In Rego's work, the religious and the profane have always been wedded. Religious iconography has been a recurring presence in her paintings, and although Rego did not have a religious education, she explains that, when you have been brought up in Portugal, you cannot help imbibing the images attached to Roman Catholicism.[7] Reflecting on religious art, Rego observes that:

> There's a certain kind of feeling in looking at religious art that you don't get out of anything else; and this area of feeling has something to do also with sin and eroticism. It's something very peculiar to Catholicism and I would like to be able to translate it into a more modern situation, because the emotions involved are so strong, because they tell a very strong story and they're to do with love, with loss, with sorrow and all these things, and that's best told in religious pictures than anywhere else.[8]

That is precisely what Rego does with her series of paintings on the Virgin Mary, as well as in other recent works, such as *As Meninas a Brincar às Missas*, a work with a conspicuously subversive topic, which depicts an almost sacrilegious scene from the Catholic Mass, where a woman is giving the host to a genuflecting woman in what could be considered a blasphemous, transgressive appropriation of the role of the male priest, with the implication that women should play a more active role in the Church hierarchy.[9]

Paula Rego's image of the pregnant Virgin Mary, *Nativity* (11.1), emphasizes the female, carnal, sexual facet of the Virgin's body, which has been virtually occluded in art and literature. In *Art and Lies* , Jeanette Winterson writes that the 'Blessed Virgin is not a woman', since she was not allowed full humanity like other representatives of her sex.[10] Rego recovers and accents the human, physical side of the Virgin Mary, retrieving the biological and spiritual being of the Mother of God.

11.1 Paula Rego, *Nativity*, 2002, pastel on paper mounted on aluminium, 54 × 52 cm. Copyright Paula Rego. Photograph courtesy of Marlborough Fine Art Ltd., London.

What these pictures share, I wish to argue, is a desire to make conspicuously visible what the Church, and androcentric society in general, have striven to keep under a veil, due to the heretical and transgressive potential of the scenes under examination.

Representations of a pregnant Virgin Mary are few and far between, constituting a subject that was considered potentially sacrilegious and best left unrepresented. This early image of a pregnant Madonna in painting occurs in a fresco from the ninth century, in the crypt of Santa Prassede, in Rome, which depicts the Virgin surrounded by two angels, with her hand pointing to her swollen belly. Other early instances of this religious trope are *Maria in attesa del Bambino* (c.1335), by Bernardo Daddi, in the Museo dell'Opera di Santa Maria del Fiore, in Florence, followed by the *Madonna del Parto con le Personificazioni della Virtù* (c.1375–80), by the Scuola Fiorentina, in the Pinacoteca, in the Vatican Museums.[11] Rossello di Jacopo Franchi's *Madonna del Parto* (c.1420), in the Museo di Palazzo Davanzati, in Florence, is a close precursor of Piero della Francesca's *Madonna del Parto* (1467), which is probably the most famous example, being strikingly unusual in its revelation of the pregnant Madonna.[12] Two angels are portrayed drawing apart the richly ornate curtains to reveal a heavily pregnant Virgin Mary, shortly before giving birth.[13] As Marilyn Aronberg Lavin explains:

> The central figure's grand scale identifies her as Maria Ecclesia, symbol of the Church itself … With a gesture of infinite grace, she touches her womb and alludes to her own fecundity. The popular name of *parto*, which means 'delivery', is thus something of a

misnomer since she is pointing not to the birth of Christ but to her pregnant state. She belongs to a class of images of Mary standing by herself without the Christ Child that developed in Tuscany in the fourteenth century and were surely votive altar pieces commissioned for pregnant women. In such images … Mary frequently wears a high-placed belt which emphasises her enlarged abdomen while also symbolising her virginity. The hand placed across the womb was part of this tradition as was the pointing gesture.[14]

In *Food, Sex and God: On Inspiration and Writing*, Michèle Roberts describes Piero della Francesca's *Madonna del Parto* as 'surely one of the most beautiful and powerful, sexy and numinous paintings of the Christian era'.[15] As Roberts notes, the painting 'evokes female divinity through acceptance of maternity, just as in the old folkloric images the Goddess could be worshipped throughout Europe as a pregnant woman'.[16] Piero's Madonna, then, as Roberts goes on to add, 'fuses and reintegrates the physical and the divine … Piero's woman is both maternal and sexy, both connected and free, both queenly and ordinary', words which could also apply to Rego's pregnant Virgin Mary who, unlike Piero della Francesca's, is represented in labour, a much more scandalous, indecorous and indeed unprecedented image in religious iconography.[17] Mary Jacobus, in related vein, engages with the figure of the pregnant Madonna in her analysis of Freud's case study 'Dora', offering a fantasy of her own as a way of approaching Freud's text.

Imagine Dora confronting, not the Sistine Madonna, but Piero della Francesca's 'Madonna del Parto', or 'Pregnant Madonna' … The fresco makes outrageously visible what Raphael's painting represses, the Madonna's corporeal implication in the Virgin Birth.[18]

With reference to Dora's phantom pregnancy, Jacobus remarks:

Christian tradition in Western art sanctifies the feminine body by making it a maternal body. The imaginary inflation of the Madonna's stomach before Dora's eyes seems profane not miraculous because it reminds us that the maternal body isn't virginal after all.[19]

This is a condition that is also applicable to Rego's own pregnant Madonna.

Another example of a pregnant Madonna is *Maria in Erwartung*, by Matthias Grünewald, in the Isenheimer Altar, in Colmar (Alsace), which is part of an allegory on the Nativity painted in 1512–16.[20] Similarly, in Willingham Church (St Mary of All Saints), which dates from Norman times, there is a large painting known as *The Visitation*, from the mid-fifteenth century, which shows the pregnant Virgin Mary meeting Elizabeth, herself pregnant with St John the Baptist. Also in England, at the Church of St Thomas in Salisbury, another fifteenth-century painting of the Visitation shows the heavily pregnant Virgin and her cousin Elizabeth touching each other's swollen bellies with delight. The theme of the Visitation, which of necessity represents Mary and Elizabeth as pregnant, was also considered by many members of the church as indecorous and improper, so, unsurprisingly, paintings which address that topic are very uncommon in English churches. Although pictures representing the Biblical Visitation might be expected to portray the Virgin as conspicuously pregnant, that is clearly not always the case: the Virgin's belly is typically modestly hidden under large robes. Paintings of the Visitation, nonetheless, constitute the most important and numerous cluster of pregnant Madonnas in art.[21]

As far as statues are concerned, some early examples date from the first half of the fourteenth century. Two such statues stand in the Pazo de Ximenez, the cathedral museum of the Santiago de Compostela. One is 'Anunciación: Virgen de la Esperanza o de la 'O' Y San Gabriel Arcángel' by Mestre Pero, Coimbra (first half of the fourteenth century), representing a hugely pregnant Virgin, with an enigmatic but not sad look on her face.[22] The other is 'Anunciación: Virgen de la Espectación Y Arcangel S. Gabriel', also from the first half of the fourteenth century, by an unknown artist, showing the Virgin, heavily pregnant, holding a book in her right hand, while the left rests on her belly. Her long hair falls on her shoulders, and there is a smile on her face. Also in the Santiago de Compostela, on the façade of the Iglesia de la Salomé, there is a statue of another pregnant Virgin. There are also some examples of statues of pregnant Madonnas in Portugal, including several so-called *Nossa Senhora do Ó*,[23] in and around Aveiro, in Coimbra, as well as in the Cathedral in Évora, a cluster of images that bespeaks a popular devotion to the pregnant Virgin.[24]

Marina Warner notes that in 'fourteenth- and fifteenth-century Europe, the statues of the *Vierge Ouvrante*, a fetish-like Madonna whose belly opened to reveal the Trinity concealed within, became objects of devotion'.[25] Kathleen Gomes, in turn, points out that while statues of pregnant Madonnas were relatively popular in Portugal in the early Middle Ages, typified by the statue of *Nossa Senhora do Ó* by Mestre Pêro (c.1330–40, Museu Nacional Machado de Castro, Sé Velha de Coimbra), they were gradually taken away from altars during the Counter-Reformation, since it was considered inappropriate to show the Virgin during her pregnancy.[26] Interestingly, the statues of pregnant Virgins in Santiago de Compostela contrast sharply with Piero della Francesca's *Madonna del Parto*.[27] While the latter's face shows her anxiety about her condition and fearful anticipation of the birth to come, two of the pregnant Virgins in the Santiago de Compostela seem positively happy and radiant in their advanced stage of pregnancy.[28]

Paula Rego's painting of a pregnant Virgin Mary about to give birth can thus be inscribed alongside these few examples, which bring to the fore the Madonna's prominent and protruding abdomen.[29] Rego's representation of the expectant Virgin, unashamedly fleshy and corpulent, however, deviates sharply from traditional depictions of her. Even though the artist keeps the traditional blue dress, she goes a step further in her depiction of the Virgin: while other images of pregnant Madonnas usually depict the Virgin in an upright position, and not in the act of parturition itself, Rego shows the Virgin Mary in labour, lying on the floor of the manger, her legs wide open, and, in a further subversive gesture, with her head reposing on the Angel's leg. Indeed, while other images of pregnant Virgins, like Piero della Francesca's, emphasize the stately, venerable role played by the Virgin Mary in Church iconography, Rego's brings her down to earth, showing her as a woman with labour pains, whose face, however, betrays, in a line of continuity with Bernini's statue of St Teresa (1647–52, Santa Maria della Vittoria, Rome), swoons of mystical and physical ecstasy, a certain pleasure in bodily pain, contiguous with spiritual rapture. Rego's depictions of scenes from the Virgin's life conspicuously stress the connection between the sacred and the profane, the divine and the earthly, the pain and *jouissance* that are an inextricable part of everyday life.[30]

Another subversive detail in Rego's series of paintings about the Virgin has to do with the introduction of a female or androgynous angel instead of the traditionally male one. Indeed, in *Annunciation* (2002), instead of the conventional angel Gabriel, Rego has painted a very down-to-earth female angel, herself looking vaguely pregnant in her unangelical stockiness, seemingly with the body of a woman and a masculine face, occupying a prominent position in her role of announcing the good news of the Virgin's pregnancy and helping her when about to give birth. As Rego herself explains, she believed it did not make much sense to have a man explaining to Mary the mysteries of pregnancy, and since the angels are traditionally thought not to have a definite sex, she felt at liberty to choose the sex of her angel.[31] Rego believes that the angel she painted is really Mary's Guardian Angel: 'Gabriel é um agente, mas este é o guardião dela!'[32]

Angels occupy a prominent place in Paula Rego's iconography. Both Rego and Luce Irigaray recover and valorize the figure of the female angel (or in Rego's case, that of an androgynous one), as helper and agent, not just as mediator. In *Sexes and Genealogies*, Irigaray notes that angels have been 'misunderstood, forgotten', words to which Rego, I believe, would subscribe.[33] Indeed, angels abound in Rego's work. One of the most salient examples is her amazing *Angel* (1998) a seemingly phallic, castratory female angel bent on revenge, an imposing female figure. Gail M. Schwab considers Irigaray's reflections on angels 'one of the most puzzling and profoundly original aspects of Irigarayan thought', noting that Irigaray

> has appropriated an image that had already been highly elaborated philosophically, theoretically, and artistically in the Western cultural order, and she anchors it in the female body, from which it had been carefully cordoned off before, since angels are supposed to have no sex. She relates it to maternity through the placenta and to feminine desire and sexuality through the mucous.[34]

This is a nexus of ideas that we can also see at work in Rego's paintings, which emphasize the close proximity between the Virgin and the Angel during the various stages of her life. Irigaray maintains that 'if we do not rethink and rebuild the whole scene of representation, the angels will never find a home, never stay anywhere. Guardians of free passage, they cannot be captured, domesticated, even if our purpose is to see ourselves in them.'[35] For Tina Chanter, in turn, the angels, as 'Rilkean figures, read through Heidegger … bring together in a disjunctive, impossible-to-think union the religious transcendence of spirituality with the material immanence of bodies'.[36]

Irigaray's reflections on the role played by the Virgin Mary in the Church hierarchy, and the question of the development of a potential female divinity, shed light on Rego's paintings. Indeed, I see Irigaray and Rego, in their different media, moving in similar terrain. In many ways what both Rego and Irigaray are doing is trying to recover, verbalize and represent in visual terms an ignored, disregarded, *imaginary* layer, 'what our culture has chosen not to take up and symbolise', in Gail M. Schwab's words.[37] In the case under investigation, this refers to the neglected procreative matrix of the Virgin as well as the role of the angel. According to Schwab, Irigaray 'continues to take previously unsymbolised aspects of feminine existence, female corporeality, and sexuality, aspects that had been lost in the silence of patriarchal taboo, and bring them to the cultural order through the creation of images and symbols present to consciousness', a recuperative praxis which finds a strong counterpart in Rego's paintings of the life of the Virgin.[38]

These new scenes of representation, then, which in many ways amount to alternative primal scenes—such as the Annunciation and the Nativity reinterpreted from the perspective of the Virgin Mary and the angel—evoke new spaces for the feminine divine, closely wedded to the profane, and suggest new, germinal perspectives for rethinking the sacred and the feminine in contemporary times.

In *Marine Lover*, Luce Irigaray muses on the mystery of Jesus's birth and conception, suggesting that Jesus 'is brought into the world by a teenage virgin pregnant by the Holy Spirit. Begotten, not made ...This mysterious conception leads, first of all, to the repudiation of the woman in which it takes place'.[39] Irigaray comments on the elision of the female reproductive organs, noting that the 'matrix that engenders this man without a father remains invisible'.[40] For Irigaray, the Virgin's consent to carry Jesus in her womb constitutes the foundation of Christianity, since without the Virgin's acquiescence Jesus would not have been born. According to Irigaray, the Virgin's

'yes' subtends Christian culture, which would not exist without her. And if the nature of this fiat were questioned, perhaps the basis of centuries of Christianity would need to be re-evaluated. Because, according to the traditional interpretation, her 'yes' is equally a 'no': a no to her own life. To her conception, her birth, her flowering. No to everything, except the Word of the Father.[41]

In Rego's contemporary rendition of the Annunciation, the adolescent Virgin, dressed like a schoolgirl, seems overpowered by the large, bulky, androgynous-looking angel, and gazes at her/him in utter disbelief, perplexity and scepticism. The Virgin's wondering, questioning look might easily be read in the way that Irigaray does in *Between East and West*, where she ponders the Annunciation scene from the Bible, and observes that the angel Gabriel's words to the Virgin Mary leave out what she considers a fundamental question, namely whether Mary wishes to be the Mother of the Saviour.[42] Without this question, Irigaray notes, the Annunciation is liable to invoke the imposition of a patriarchal order, Mary being thus left as the 'simple vehicle at the service of giving birth to the son of God-the-Father'.[43]

For Penelope Deutscher, Irigaray offers a critical reading of the Western tradition of representing the feminine as mediator between Jesus and God. Her interpretation is also recuperative and interventionist. She believes that biblical stories can be read otherwise, so as to offer the possibility of the invention of a new imaginary.[44] As Deutscher further notes, Irigaray proposes that

Jesus's birth be retold as a story of how Mary participated in and consented to the conception. The advent of the angels is to be seen not as an announcement but as an interrogation of Mary's aspirations.[45]

Rego's series of paintings about the Virgin Mary can clearly be seen as inscribed in precisely this kind of subversive, irreverent, interrogative impulse.

While Irigaray has repeatedly called attention to this placing of women as mediating vessels, and not subjects in their own right, Julia Kristeva, in a related vein, reflects on the desirability of founding an alternative feminine sacred place, 'other spaces for questioning the sacred'. Kristeva even goes so far as to question whether women shouldn't leave the Church, 'since it develops its own logic and would not know how to transform itself without destroying itself'.[46] The paintings by Rego that I have been examining here participate in precisely this kind of religious inquiry, implicitly interrogating the role of women in the Church hierarchy and simultaneously suggesting other realms where a sacred feminine could be developed, a religious spiritual practice distinct from the traditional patriarchal one. As Michelle Boulous Walker observes:

> patriarchal systems of representation repress the (carnal) knowledge that the mother's body is a sexual one … In the light of this, Christianity gives us the domesticated image of the Virgin Mary, the mother devoid of sexual desire. Mary literally embodies the fate of the virgin mother, existing only in relation to her perfect product, Christ.[47]

Rego provided illustrations for a recent edition of Eça de Queirós' series of novels *O Crime do Padre Amaro* (*The Sin of Father Amaro*) (1876), in which there is a clear continuity between the account of Amélia's pregnancy, which includes a scandalous, heretical representation of her as the pregnant Virgin Mary, and Paula Rego's later picture of the Virgin about to give birth.[48] Rego's images of the pregnant Virgin Mary, and de Queirós' depictions of Amélia, can both be said to bring to the fore precisely those female, carnal, sexual facets of the Virgin's body which are deliberately repressed and concealed, indeed, are even clandestine, in traditional Christian iconography.[49] The visibility of the Virgin's pregnant body bespeaks, and can be read as an integral component of, the attempt on Rego's part to rethink religion in the feminine, from a Kristevan 'herethical' perspective, as well as to satirize and critique some of the politics and iconography of patriarchal religion.

In analogous fashion, Father Amaro dressing up Amélia as the Virgin Mary, as depicted by Rego in *Ambassador of Jesus* (1998) is another provocative, subversive image, a blasphemous painting liable to provoke and scandalize, as is *The Cell* (1997), in the same series, which portrays Father Amaro lying down on his stomach in bed, masturbating over an image of the Virgin Mary under the bed, while listening to Amélia undressing in a room above him.

Turning now briefly to the penultimate painting in Rego's series, *Pietá* (2002), what strikes me is the extreme, poignant vulnerability of Rego's adolescent Madonna,[50] holding her dead or dying son, her eyes lifted up to heaven in desperation and disbelief, highlighted by the menacing, fiery sky in the background, which finds a pictorial echo in the Virgin's burgundy skirt and the brownish-red earth. What is stressed here is, yet again, the plight of an adolescent girl who becomes pregnant without quite knowing how, gives birth, and then has to go through the Calvary of watching her son die a painful, slow death. Rego, then, eschews the traditionally idealized, glorified visions of the Virgin Mary for a more down to earth, humanized, secular version, linking physicality and transcendence, with which women can better identify in the various stages of their lives.

Another subversive aspect of Rego's series on the life of the Virgin Mary is the very fact that it was painted by a woman artist. Some critics, analysing Rego's sequence on the Virgin, have commented on the fact that almost for the first time we have a woman painting the story of the Virgin, from a feminine point of view. Rego herself notes that 'Eram sempre homens que pintavam a vida da Virgem e aqui é uma mulher. Tem um ponto de vista diferente. Porque a gente identifica-se muito mais com a história dela. Aliás, isto é uma homenagem e uma história da Virgem.'[51] This idea that only male artists devoted themselves to painting the life of the Virgin is, however, hardly true. There have been, throughout the ages, many examples of female artists who concerned themselves with religious themes, and in particular with interpretations of the Virgin Mary. The list includes Caterina dei Vigri (Saint Catherine of Bologna, 1413–63), Lavinia Fontana (1552–1614—considered the first professional woman artist), Barbara Longhi (1552–1638), Artemisia Gentileschi (1593–1653), Michaelina Woutiers (1600–59), Josefa de Óbidos (1630–84), Elisabetta Sirani (1638–65) and Elizabeth Siddal (1829–62), to cite only some of the most salient examples.[52] In an interview, Rego further revealed that the question she was faced with was how to continue an established tradition of religious iconography and simultaneously to update the story. The solution she came up with was to revisit the Biblical narratives from a woman's point of view: 'Uma mulher a contar a história—em rigor, Maria a contar a história.'[53]

In addition, as Rego clarifies, she was acutely aware of the need to accent the corporeality of the Virgin Mary, asserting that: 'O mais importante de tudo é que Jesus foi um homem e Maria foi uma mulher a dar à luz—ele vem de dentro dela. São pessoas! Não vêm do espaço sideral. São de carne e osso.'[54]

### No longer alone of all her sex

In a different but related context, the Virgin Mary can be seen as the mother who gives birth on her own, without male agency. In Rego's art, I wish to argue, the Virgin's pregnancy can be equated with a positive vision of feminine autonomy from men. With the introduction of human cloning, women would be able, if they so chose, to procreate on their own, without male intervention. The Virgin Mary, then, in this scenario, would no longer be alone of all her sex, to borrow Marina Warner's words, and no longer the only woman to have given birth on her own, since other women, given the advent of human cloning, might also reproduce by circumventing male agency.[55] Indeed, cloning might be seen as enabling a recovery, and simultaneously a deconstruction and repossession, of the icon of the Virgin Mother as a positive representation for women, a source of empowering fantasies.[56]

In 'Stabat Mater', Kristeva claims that 'motherhood … today remains, after the Virgin, without a discourse'.[57] With cloning, however, the fantasy of a virgin mother might come to be fulfilled, providing a revolutionary new vision of the concept of motherhood and potentially enabling new feminine discourses to arise, alongside Kristeva's call for a '*herethics*'.[58] As Toril Moi similarly stresses in relation to 'Stabat Mater', 'there is … an urgent need for a 'post-virginal' discourse on maternity, one which ultimately would provide both women and men with a new ethics', a discourse to which I believe Paula Rego is contributing in visual terms with her series of paintings on the Virgin Mary.[59]

At the end of *Alone of All Her Sex,* Marina Warner remarks that 'as an acknowledged creation of Christian mythology, the Virgin's legend will endure in its splendour and lyricism, but it will be emptied of moral significance, and thus lose its present real powers to heal and to harm.'[60] It seems to me that, contrary to Warner's predictions, the impact of human cloning for women in particular is likely to add a renewed vigour to the iconic figure of the Virgin Mary, turning her into a potent symbol of stimulating and reinvented potentialities for women.

### Conclusion

We might ask at this stage how future Madonnas are likely to be represented, in the wake of Paula Rego's strongly physical and iconoclastic images. I am reminded of an early short story by Henry James, 'The Madonna of the Future', published in 1873, about an American artist, Theobald, who is working in Florence and whose aspiration is to paint a Madonna that would measure up to Raphael's *Madonna della Seggiola*.[61] Theobald's craving for perfectionism, though, makes him postpone the execution of his painting for so long that his model, a young woman, becomes middle-aged, rough, stocky and sexual, a 'Madonna of the Future', as the narrator of James's story calls her.[62] This Madonna, who never gets painted, could be Rego's, in her powerful physicality, a different Madonna who, unlike Theobald's, was painted with all its scandalous potential.

In 'In Parenthesis: Immaculate Conceptions and Feminine Desire', Mary Jacobus argues that the Virgin Mary figures 'in a discourse of maternity that is bound to reproduce the Law of the Father'.[63] On the contrary, I believe that the figure of the Virgin Mary can be identified as the initiator of a new space for the feminine, a much more autonomous space which might also include a 'becoming divine' of a feminine subjectivity', in Irigaray's words.[64]

# FROM LEDA TO DAPHNE
## Sacrifice and Virginity in the Work of Ana Mendieta
### *Anne Creissels*

Ana Mendieta is an artist of Cuban origin who carried out her first performances in the early 1970s, after completing her studies at the University of Iowa in the USA.[1] Using her own body in what were often violent actions inspired by Santeria (a religion blending Catholic elements and Afro-Cuban rituals), Mendieta reveals the link between the creative act and sacrifice. At the same time she aims to make her body sacred through rituals of purification in which she becomes bodily at one with nature. She thus appears to adhere to a Christian, patriarchal and essentialist conception in which, as Bataille, above all, shows us, the woman's body constitutes both the privileged object of sacrifice and the promise of redemption. As a female artist, Mendieta occupies a paradoxical position: between desire for autonomy and reification, between feminist affirmation and dissolution of her own body.

Rape, which appears more or less explicitly throughout her performances, constitutes a crux in this respect, crystallizing the ambiguity of her position and fundamentally posing the question of the body's limits, which is central in Mendieta's work. Beyond Santeria, I therefore propose to link certain of her performances to myths portraying metamorphosis, rape and virginity, such as the myths of Leda and Daphne. Through this reading I want to suggest that Mendieta is questioning that concept which assimilates the sacred with violence, and which confers on virginity a value that is ambiguous to say the least. I shall examine, through her work, the possibility of any affirmation of a female artist in this cultural framework.

## From sacrifice to animalization

The notion of sacrifice features explicitly from Mendieta's earliest performances onwards. *Feathers on a Woman* (1972) shows her covering a young woman's body with white chicken feathers. As Donald Kuspit has remarked, through this transformation the woman loses her humanity, her identity.[2] The (supposed) sacrifice of the animal effectively echoes the (figurative) sacrifice of the woman, reduced to the state of sacrificial animal. We can see, from the fact that the pubis alone is not covered with feathers, the affirmation of the link between sacrifice and sexuality. In addition, the use of white feathers links sacrifice and virginity. In that respect this work seems to be part of a 'Bataillesque' conception, associating religious sacrifice with eroticism. In these terms the woman's body is both the object of transgression and that which permits the experience of the sacred.[3] According to Bataille, 'the male lover disintegrates the woman he loves no less than the bloodstained sacrificer does the sacrificial man or animal.'[4] Mendieta is, moreover, influenced by Octavio Paz, who is himself close to Bataille.[5]

*Feathers on a Woman* is one of the rare performances in which Mendieta uses a body other than her own. The portrayal of the artist transforming a woman's body into an animal seems to me to describe quite literally the creative act as animalization. If the fact that here it is a woman who proceeds to animalize another woman can be seen to override the man-woman, active-passive opposition, then the link between sacrifice and creation, far from being criticized, is, on the contrary, affirmed. This affirmation raises the question of the position that Mendieta occupies with regard to myths. The wish to deconstruct entrenched myths, which we can see in her work, comes up against the essentialism that structures her oeuvre. The shifting of identity present in this performance does not really put into question the Christian conception of the opposition of the sexes, to which Mendieta seems, fundamentally, to adhere.

In *Death of a Chicken* (12.1), a naked Mendieta holds by its feet a white chicken whose neck has just been slit. Still convulsing in its

12.1 Ana Mendieta, *Untitled (Death of a Chicken)*, 1972, performance, University of Iowa, photographer unknown. Courtesy José Bedia, Miami.

death throes, it spatters the artist's body with blood. For Kuspit, Mendieta's identification with the chicken seems clear, and the action is a
metaphor for sexual initiation undergone as a traumatic experience. According to him, Mendieta portrays herself in this performance as both
man and woman, active and passive, both perpetrator and victim of
sacrifice.[6] At the heart of this action, there is indeed a tension between
decapitation (referring to castration) and deflowering. On this point,
Julia Kristeva (1998) has shown, by drawing on Freud's text 'The Taboo
of Virginity',[7] how penetration, and to an even greater degree deflowering, could be experienced by the woman as a rape and could lead to
a desire for vengeance.[8] Through these readings a link emerges between
victimization and seizure of power, between sacrifice and transfiguration.

As regards the first performance, we see here a process of victimization of the artist through the dispossession of her role as executioner;
it is the artist who is now animalized. The spectator, as Merewether observes, becomes implicated as the executioner by participating in this
act.[9] If she does not animalize the other woman, Mendieta instead
brings about the animalization of the spectator, through the spectacle
she presents of her own animalization. This latter dimension has been
particularly developed in a performance entitled *Rape Scene* in which the
artist seems to me, paradoxically, to rape the spectator, inflicting on him
or her the intolerable sight of her body tied up and spattered with blood.

*Rape Scene* is part of a series of works on the subject of rape, relating
to a particularly striking news story: some female students had
been raped and killed one year earlier on the campus of the University
of Iowa, where Mendieta had been a student. For this performance the
artist invited some students and friends to her home: on arrival they
found the door open and, in the half-light, the body of Mendieta tied
to a table, as if she had been the victim of a rape.[10] By putting the spectator in the position of perpetrator (the voyeur becoming equivalent
to the rapist), her aim is to bestialize him. The performance-viewer relationship is thus described as a violent and damaging bodily interaction, modelled on conflict-ridden male-female relations, and as an
animalizing sexuality. From the artist (or man) animalizing the woman's
body to the female artist animalizing the spectator, an inversion of the
roles of executioner and victim is all that is in operation: an inversion
which merely contributes to the perpetuation of a system of opposition.

## Leda, or surpassing the limits of the body

Mendieta's work, because it is based on the passage through extreme
states by metamorphosis, poses in exemplary fashion the question of

limits, or rather the absence of limits. The idea of rape, which appears recurrently in her performances in more or less explicit form, seems to show an acute awareness of the tension, running throughout the whole oeuvre, between a vulnerable body whose limits can be pushed and a body that is all-powerful because it knows no limits. Bringing these performances together, even if they refer to the rituals of Santeria, of the myth of Leda and the swan, should allow me to introduce what the notion of metamorphosis implies as far as paradoxes are concerned. Mendieta's actions present, in addition, a certain formal resemblance to some performances of Viennese actionists, explicitly relevant to this theme.[11]

In the myth, which has inspired numerous representations, Zeus (Jupiter) metamorphoses into a swan in order to approach Leda and take advantage of her (12.2). The woman thus becomes the object of an animalization through the violence of the mating with the swan. At the same time, the god (or creator) is supposed to be animalized himself, to become bestial in the true sense (through metamorphosis) and in the figurative sense (through the violence he exerts). Through this bestial rape, it is a specifically erotic bestiality which reaches its height, as Régis Michel was able to demonstrate. According to him, rape in general, and of Leda in particular, crystallizes the violence inflicted on woman in an art which he describes as misogynistic. In this conception of eroticism (evidently Bataillesque but, more broadly, Western and Christian), the aim is to reify and humiliate the female body, a supplementary stage in the transgression and profanation of the act of love.[12]

The fusion of woman and animal which Mendieta's performances stage seems to constitute a sort of condensation of the myth. In the

12.2 The Painter of Louvre MNB 1148, attributed, *Leda and the Swan*, c.350–40 BCE, Apulian red figure ware loutrophoros, 86.AE.680, The J. Paul Getty Museum, Malibu, California.

12.3 Ana Mendieta. *Untitled (Blood and Feathers)*, 1974, Raquelin Mendieta Family Trust Collection.

identification of woman with animal, as in the mating of the female body with the animal, what is at stake is the loss of identity by the surpassing of limits. *Blood and Feathers* (12.3) thus depicts Mendieta literally becoming one with the animal, pouring animal blood on her body and covering herself in feathers. The power of metamorphosis appears clearly here as transcendence of hierarchies and limits.[13]

This leads us to consider Mendieta's affirmation that, had she not been an artist, she would have been a criminal.[14] In an attempt to create a theoretical foundation for Mendieta's work, Merewether demonstrates how the assimilation of art with crime and the critique of society's repressive conventions occurs just as much in Foucault as in Marcuse or Bataille. He considers the notion of 'expenditure' to be central in Mendieta's work, and suggests that the masochism perceptible in her work be viewed as part of a transcendence of limits, following the example of crime.[15] Foregrounding masochism in this way forces us to question the ambiguous value Mendieta accords to rape, as the transgression it constitutes can be seen as giving structure to the female identity. This transgression, crystallized by metamorphosis, allows the passage from one state to another and clearly marks the power of the artist. Liberating but also dangerous, in Mendieta's work it resembles a form of exorcism.

This is why, between the reclaiming of her own body and the renewal of the conditions of submission, Mendieta's performances raise an element of doubt, even of unease. This attitude marks at best a conflict, if not an incapacity, to surpass a patriarchal Christian concept not only of sexuality, but of femininity. Consequently the feminist affirmation, transmitted through violence and sacrifice, appears paradoxical. Passing from sacrificial object to subject-object of sacrifice does not in this sense constitute a critique or radical deconstruction of a system founded on the difference between the sexes. The adherence to this concept, which makes the creative act a form of animalization, is in effect underwritten by the idea of a feminine specificity, which takes shape in a heightened manner in the following works.

## Identity and the sacred

Mendieta's work from 1973 onwards is increasingly related to nature, and the notion of sacrifice is no longer so explicitly linked to sexuality. The assimilation of the body to the earth marks the series *Siluetas*. Here Mendieta leaves an imprint of the form of her body in the landscape, an imprint either hollow or formed by the assembly of natural elements. These works illustrate in singular fashion the link between the construction of myth and the search for an identity, highlighted powerfully by Lacoue-Labarthe and Nancy in *Le mythe nazi*.[16] In paradigmatic fashion, by creating a fusion with nature, Mendieta affirms, through their common fertility, a feminine specificity. The Earth-mother in this respect constitutes an all-powerful, truly mythical generality, in which Mendieta's body literally melts, and in a certain sense becomes lost; the affirmation of a collective identity so clearly implying the dissolution of personal identity. The rituals of purification, which her performances stage, underline to what extent this dissolution of the body is associated with the idea of transcendence.

By assimilating the female body to nature, Mendieta affirms a female specificity, a difference in essence between man and woman. This has the disadvantage of contributing to the perpetuation of a system of domination founded on the opposition of the sexes. Nicole Dubreuil-Blondin, in an essay on women's Land Art, aims to deconstruct a certain feminist interpretation inspired by the alliance of Land Art with nature. This position, held by Lucy Lippard, consists of viewing Land Art as marked by the feminine, the communion with nature recalling a primordial state which preceded the advent of the patriarchal society. Women's Land Art would thus denounce the rape of the earth, in an ecological affirmation. As Dubreuil-Blondin points out, this concept presumes a double transcendence: that of the sacred site, cut off from the world, and that of an immemorial female order. In her opinion, proceeding in this direction amounts to emphasizing the idea of a determining feminine.[17] This conception seems to accurately characterize the work of Mendieta, who is indeed a contemporary of an essentialist feminism. Lippard and Mendieta have, moreover, been in contact with each other, and the art historian has played an important role in the feminist commitment of the artist.[18] The identification of Mendieta's body with nature clearly corresponds to an affirmation of power. This rallying to the abstract, limitless, all-powerful body that is Mother-earth takes place however at the cost of a reification; it implies the negation of the self as subject and a loss of one's own identity.

The notion of identity, be it cultural or social, implies the body, and leads inevitably to a questioning of sexed and sexual identity. Because it supposes a differentiation, the identity quest forces us to question the difference between the sexes, that paradigm of all difference. On this point Mendieta's work contains elements to reflect on, and obliges us to state certain theoretical points. The ambiguity of Mendieta's propositions, between feminist claiming and negation of the body, relates to the constituent ambiguity of the myth: it is both dangerous and liberating when it is a question of pushing the limits of the body, of the human, of life. So the quest for identity can thus be seen to coincide with a wish to transcend human identity, that which crystallizes the figure of the martyr, very latent in the work of Mendieta, which is echoed by the equally ambivalent figure of the androgyne. In this respect, Pontalis has shown how the myth of androgyny, and more broadly, any myth of bisexuality, constituted both an affirmation of the transcendence of the man-woman opposition and the effacement of the desiring subject.[19]

As regards the difference between the sexes, the myths of androgyny and essentialism seem to coincide in the idea of an incompleteness, an initial separation of the human. The idea of a primordial union, an all-powerful entity, a uniqueness or a lost eternity, is at work deep down in Mendieta's oeuvre, which clearly displays a desire to transcend the condition of human mortality. Mendieta shows herself to be incapable of renouncing omnipotence, paradoxically doing so in the very staging of dissolution and death. In this way, her work illuminates the link between creative force and narcissistic wound, and more broadly between transcendence and fear of death. Her claim to identity leads to a loss of identity, a paradoxical refusal of all uniqueness. Here the line is drawn between the quest for identity and the fear of the other, or fear of being other. In this sense, the sacred constitutes the site of exteriority and foreignness par excellence, at the same time as it constitutes the fantasized site of uniformity and lack of differentiation.

The fusion of the artist and her work illustrates, in her case, the idea of an absolute creation at the same time as the total loss of the self. To escape the inevitable destruction of the body, Mendieta stages destructions of herself and her work. In her desire to escape her condition, she has recourse to sacrifice and its representations; between transcendence and loss, that which supposes the body is made sacred. Her work thus displays the very strong desire to construct a virginal body, which constitutes both an absolute affirmation and a total reification.

## Daphne, or the alienating virginity

From her first performances to the incorporations of her body in nature, Mendieta's work is centred on her female body, its destruction and its reappropriation. From the outset, this line of work creates a tension between a defensive position (of retreat and victimization) and an offensive position (of affirmation of autonomy). Mendieta's works clearly have a cathartic function. Across these performances we see either a renunciation of virginity (by the staging of a penetrable and vulnerable body, animalized and soiled), or a reclaiming of virginity (by the construction of an impenetrable, powerful and limitless body in nature's image). If the figure of Leda marks the first performances, certain subsequent works seem to replay the myth of Daphne. The passage from Leda to Daphne, or from animalization to vegetalization,

can be read as the passage from description of sexuality as rape, to the means of escaping this by a retreat into the self. In Ovid's narrative, the metamorphosis of Daphne (effected by her father whom she called to help her) effectively results in the preservation of her virginity, and the escape from a sexual relationship with Apollo who is pursuing her.

In the version by Bernini (12.4), who has produced one of the best-known representations of the myth, a piece of bark tries to cover Daphne's body from the feet upwards, making her impenetrable, as Mieke Bal describes in detail.[20] This sculpture gives an exemplary form to the metamorphosis, the female body (supposed to take root by becoming a plant) finding itself literally turned to marble, as if becoming mineral. The mimicry, fusion and disappearance, as well as the incarnation linked to the metamorphosis of Daphne, are echoed in the artistic practice itself. Through this, the notion of virginity takes form in all its ambiva-

12.4 Giovanni Lorenzo Bernini, *Apollo and Daphne*, 1622–25, marble, Borghese Gallery, Rome. Copyright 2006 Photo Scala, Florence/Luciano Romano.

lence: as value linked to creation, subject for the artist to work with, art material. Between loss and gift, destruction and reconstruction, virginity finds itself clearly linked to the exercise of art, the power of creation. By considering certain works of Mendieta in relation to the myth of Daphne, I want to show how Mendieta, giving a value to virginity, occupies a position that is both liberating and alienating. Bringing to light the link between virginity and rape should also enable the deconstruction of what appears to be the keystone of both patriarchy and matriarchy.

Making the body sacred is an essential part of Mendieta's work. In her desire to transcend the body, and in the process her own female body, the artist has recourse to the notion of virginity. A religious concept, virginity is synonymous with purity and constitutes the condition necessary for achieving redemption. It is also a patriarchal concept aimed at establishing masculine domination and perpetuating the primacy of the phallus, reinforcing and legitimizing phallic power. In effect, if virginity is woman's virtue par excellence, it also marks the negation of her desire.[21] It even justifies and underlies the violence of sexuality. Linked to rape, in that it suggests a possible violation, it works to put the woman's body in the position of object. In this sense, virginity is indeed a phallic figure, one of the forms (paradoxical, of course) that phallic power takes. In this case, to oppose the notion of virginity to a male power constitutes only a feminist claim under male control, or the emphasis on a female determining factor in place of a male, which amounts to the same thing. For the very acceptance of this value already implies the adherence to a system of thought founded on the difference and opposition between the sexes.

I will focus here on two of Mendieta's works: *Old Man's Creek* (12.5), depicting the artist becoming one with a tree, and especially *First silueta* (12.6), performed on an archaeological site, which stages a naked Mendieta, lying down and covered with white flowers which seem to grow from her body. The white flowers springing up from the prostrate and dead-looking body, laid to rest on this zapothic site, quite clearly symbolize death giving birth to life. The link between woman and earth and, more broadly, nature, is also affirmed: the female body appears literally fertile. This piece, if it does not refer explicitly to the myth of Daphne, seems nonetheless to echo certain figurations of the myth, particularly ancient ones. While fairly distant from Bernini's representation of the myth, Mendieta's piece is however very close to a Greek sculpture of Daphne.[22] In both cases, vegetation seems to grow from the body (and not to cover it), particularly from the pubis.

This affirmed link between vegetation and fertility could give rise to a metaphoric interpretation of the figure of Daphne. The latter might

12.5 Ana Mendieta, *Old Man's Creek or Tree of Life*, 1976, performance, Iowa city, Iowa, Raquelin Mendieta Family Trust Collection.

12.6 Ana Mendieta, *First Silueta or Flowers on Body*, 1973, performance, El Yagul, Oaxaca, Mexico, Hans Breder Collection.

symbolize giving form to a work independently of man, and signify the power of creation more than that of procreation. This idea of depicting artistic power through fertility seems all the more pertinent in Mendieta's piece, as it is the artist's body that is shown to be literally fertile. However, we can well imagine that the myth of Daphne, rather than showing woman's power of creation, constituted in the Greek world precisely a warning for young women of a marriageable age, who wanted to escape marriage and their only socially recognized condition as mother. Daphne's liberty is achieved at the cost of being turned to vegetation, no doubt synonymous with immortality but also marking a return to the earth.

Affirmation or retreat, displacement or fixation, transcendence or death, power or admission of powerlessness, these two works crystallize the ambiguity in Mendieta's work, and the paradoxes inherent in the position she has adopted. If Mendieta lays claim to a strong feminine identity in the link she has established between herself and the earth-mother through their equivalent fertility, she incarnates at the same time a phallic figure. By excluding man, there is in effect a reclaiming of phallic power for the self. No doubt this deadlock marks the failure of an essentialist position, but, beyond an admission of failure, Mendieta's work poses the question of the possibility of an affirmation as woman artist in a framework of male domination, and therein lies the interest in her work. The claiming of identity in effect implies the integration of the idea of a difference in essence between the sexes. But to adhere to this essentialist concept leads at the most to an inversion of patriarchy and matriarchy. The question is how to avoid renewing the same structures, and to take up a position without joining with any form of power which necessarily relies on the exclusion of the other. This is the question that Mendieta's work leaves hanging, constituting a limited and ambiguous case of feminist affirmation through sacrifice, and a paradoxical, and for that very reason exemplary, case of adherence to the myth of the creative artist, suspended between transcendence and dissolution.

# 13

## *INSIDE-OUT*
### Sculpting Sacred Space in Bernini and Bourgeois
#### *Victoria Turvey Sauron*

Bernini's extraordinary seventeenth-century sculpture group *Saint Teresa in Ecstasy* (13.1), usually taken to be an illustration of one of the visions of the Spanish mystic Teresa of Avila, is the quintessential Baroque sculpture, spectacularly transgressive of the traditionally-conceived boundaries between the sacred and the erotic, body and soul, but also inside and outside.[1] Like its later 'sister' sculpture the *Blessed Ludovica*, depicting the reclining holy woman supposedly in the throes of both ecstasy and death, the remarkable folds of *Teresa*'s robe paradoxically both cover all her skin (except for her face, hands and feet), and also exaggeratedly display a fantasized body, the dark crevices of marble suggesting the intimate surfaces of the female body.

In another sense however, the agitated folds forming the surface of these sculptures not only index the layer of skin hidden beneath the drapery folds, but also reveal something much deeper. It may be possible that the sculpture's surface visually realizes, externally, the inner experience of religious ecstasy. In one convincing argument to try to explain the work, Giovanni Careri attributes to the extraordinary folds of the *Ludovica* an independent, signifying power. Calling it a 'surface for the inscription of pathos', he continues, 'Bernini has created, on top of/beyond Ludovica's body, a "performing" body (or a body on display), composed of a "real body" and an "imaginary body" in the throes of spiritual passion.'[2]

While the folds, in their excess, therefore signify and over-signify the female sex, *Ludovica*'s drapery also paradoxically negates the physical body. The interior experience of the saint's encounter with her God, undecidedly oscillating between the deeply sacred and the deeply erotic, is dramatically exteriorized in an extraordinary ecstasy of marble, beyond, *au-dessus*, any possible 'real' body.[3]

13.1 Giovanni    Lorenzo Bernini, *Altar of the Cornaro Chapel (Ecstasy of St Teresa)*, c.1645–52, marble, height 350 cm, Santa Maria della Vittoria, Rome. Copyright 1990 Photo Scala, Florence/Fondo Edifici di Culto.

In the chapter entitled 'Beckoning Bernini' from *Louise Bourgeois' Spider*, Mieke Bal sees the *Teresa* sculpture group very much in terms of fire, that the *Teresa*'s body is a burning flame. This metaphor permeates her text and also colours the particular characterization of the sculpture which sparked off my inquiry in this paper. Bal writes that 'her body's inside cannot be distinguished from its outside'.[4] She also notes that:

> the ecstasy is due to, or rather consists of, literal ec-stasy: the propagation of the fire of love from inside out, so that *Teresa*'s skin, that outer limit of the body, partakes of it; hence, her body's limits are themselves no longer limits … Her whole body becomes a flame: each part of it, of its cover, its surface but beneath which nothing else remains, becomes a flame; fire comes to overrule previous shapes.[5]

In a sense, Bal is saying that *Teresa* (13.1) is already inside-out, or that such a concept has no relevance for a sculpture consumed with flame, inside which nothing remains. When Bal moves on to discuss one of Louise Bourgeois' sculptures, the *Homage to Bernini* (13.2), she writes that 'this work turns Bernini's painterly surfaces inside-out.'[6]

In this paper I wish to further problematize and question the consequences of this almost throwaway phrase of Bal's, so suggestive and problematic for not only the nature of sculpture, but also about the nature of body and spirit, the experience of the sacred, and of the body, sexuality and femininity. Bourgeois and Bernini are here thrown together into a conceptual space formed by the specific physicality of

13.2  Louise Bourgeois, *Homage to Berni-*
      *ni*, 1967, Bronze, 54.6 × 49.5 ×
      58.4 cm. Courtesy Cheim &
      Read, New York. Photograph:
      Peter Bellamy.

their sculpture, but which also pulls together debates and discourses of visuality in general; an indescribable, sacred space, where, I will argue, their encounter across the centuries has the potential to interrogate and realign visual discourses of the female body throughout western art history.

Bal presents the *Teresa* (13.1) sculpture as Bernini's masterpiece of layering. Her conception of the interior of the sculpture is, however, problematic—we remember she wrote about 'its surface … beneath which nothing else remains'.[7] What troubles me about this metaphor is the void at its centre. When this body is inside out, for Bal it is demystified: the saint's experience is known completely because *nothing else remains*. In fact, it seems to me that Bernini attempts to represent Teresa of Avila's entirely 'interior' experience of ecstasy, but in doing so, negates and transfigures her actual body so that only a fetishistically excessive 'outside' remains. It is visualized and at the same time neutralized. Before asking whether there is an alternative to Bernini's interpretation, it is important to ask why a female 'interior' is so threatening that its visualization results in the simultaneous and cataclysmic bodily negation and excess which we find in the *Teresa* (13.1).

The threat represented by the interior of the female body in particular has, in Laura Mulvey's words, 'haunted representations of femininity through the ages, not consistently manifest, but persisting as an intermittent strand of patriarchal mythology and misogyny'.[8] Nowhere is the inside of the female body construed as more disturbing than in the misogynistic texts of the early Church fathers. There we find a recurring theme of the horrific nature of the female body, and in particular a strong and strangely angry revulsion at the thought of the treacherously beautiful exterior, a semblance of purity, hiding the horrors dissembled under the skin. I cite here only St John Chrysostom:

> The whole of her body is nothing less than phlegm, blood, bile, rheum and the fluid of digested food … If you consider what is

stored up behind those lovely eyes, the angle of the nose, the mouth and the cheeks you will agree that the well-proportioned body is only a whitened sepulchre.[9]

Similar texts can be traced up to late medieval times.[10] Bernini's sculptures come at the climax of this cultural impulse, at the end of the Renaissance, where the despised body had become an ambiguous sign in a visuality which now had incorporated the pagan into the rediscovery of the antique, in particular in the visual language used for the mystical aspects of Christianity.

This female body, constructed in that discourse precisely in terms of the horror of the inside, is also mentioned by Freud, where he anatomizes the fear of castration, informing in turn the mechanism of fetishism. As Laura Mulvey summarizes,

> Masculine desire is caught in an oscillation between erotic obsession with the female body and fear of the castration that it signifies. It is, of course, the fear of castration, and subsequent disavowal of the woman's body as castrated, that Freud saw as the cause of male fetishism.[11]

If erotic desire in women is not enabled by the resolved Oedipus complex, then the defence mechanism of fetishism comes into play, where the object of desire is displaced away from the woman's body or genitals, onto an object or item of clothing for example. In misogynistic early Christian writings neither mechanism seems to operate in a context where women are not valued as objects of desire, and this deeply-felt fear is dramatically unveiled in these texts.

A Freudian psychoanalytical approach forms the theoretical basis for the book *Ouvrir Vénus* by Georges Didi-Huberman.[12] Referring to Kenneth Clark's famous separation of 'nude' and 'naked', Didi-Huberman argues that this separation or distancing, and associated idealization, of the female nude in art history is a form of obsessional neurosis which operates a defence mechanism against the sexual desirability of these nudes, and in particular against a desire tinged by the fear of a nudity which is by definition threatening, according to the author, because nudity suggests and leads towards the horror of the body's insides and internal organs.[13] He bases his argument around a dense text of Freud's from 1926, 'Inhibitions, Symptoms, and Anxiety', which focuses on forms of defence, amongst which Didi-Huberman focuses on *isolation*.[14] He is interested in isolation because of how the touch taboo functions. Because the act of touching simultaneously incorporates the possibility of physical aggression and of erotic pleasure, it contains the paradoxical 'oscillation' between erotic desire and fear, which, as mentioned by Mulvey, characterizes the visual economy of the female nude in art. Touching could equally be a caress or an attack, just as opening (the larger concern of Didi-Huberman's book) could equally be a liberation or a wound. Referring to the work of both Aby Warburg and Walter Benjamin, Didi-Huberman argues that images of nudes are a *dialectique à l'arrêt*, or 'halted dialectic', a status quo of disparate and balanced tensions: nudity is fundamentally 'impure'.[15]

Although intended to track the operation of the 'isolation' defence mechanism and thereby to explain the unnameable threat the sealed nudes convey, Didi-Huberman's analysis opens for me quite another can of worms about the operation of fetishism in art history. In his model, interior and exterior are stringently kept separate; in this way, he writes, 'Organic images would thus be … double sided.'[16] What is more, the interior is invariably characterized in terms of violence and horror—'To open a body is surely to disfigure it, to destroy all its harmony.'[17] Just as *all* nudity is seen as mortally dangerous, so, he writes, 'it is impossible to isolate or to be unaware of the mortal unease which is created by any nudity of the flesh,' but the nature of the universality of this danger is not further investigated.[18]

For Didi-Huberman, the threat posed by the unified, sealed nudity of a female body, is perhaps that as defined by Freud: the threat of castration. Didi-Huberman's text reinforces rather than breaks down the binary split between inside and outside, which itself operates the fetishism defence, and defends the male child against the horror of the primal scene, but which, at the same time, problematizes depictions of the female body throughout the whole of society as well as in art history. For Lynda Nead, fetishism creates 'an aesthetic that has structured the representation of the female body in western art since antiquity'.[19] She argues that, as a result,

> one of the principal goals of the female nude [in art] has been the containment and regulation of the female sexual body. The forms, conventions and poses of art have worked metaphorically to shore up the female body—to seal orifices and to prevent marginal matter from transgressing the boundary dividing the inside of the body and the outside, the self from the space of the other.[20]

Many of the central concerns of Nead's seminal book *The Female Nude*, from which this extract is taken, arise out of Julia Kristeva's *Powers of Horror*, the English translation of which appeared ten years previously.[21] In it, Kristeva develops the concept of the 'abject', primarily a psychoanalytical concept, but a concept which also has consequences in a semiotic sense for the functioning of power systems in society. To attempt to summarize the abject would necessarily be to misrepresent the complex argument of *Powers of Horror*, but in the simplest terms the abject could be described as the borderline between subject and object. Psychosis is the result of the inability of the subject to identify an exterior object, resulting in the failure to construct its own identity: the subject cannot be autonomous without identifying with an Other. Desire is impossible because it requires a clear concept of an Other, therefore desire is expressed in terms of abjection (breaking down of boundaries). Lynda Nead returns to this idea to explain why the female nudes in art history are perfect, sealed, idealized:

> What seems to be at stake … is the production of a rational, coherent subject. In other words, the notion of unified form is integrally bound up with the perception of self, and the construction of individual identity.[22]

An interesting element of *Powers of Horror* is the way Kristeva visualizes abjection in architectural terms. The reason for the failure of the subject is a lack of awareness of the body's limits, paradoxically causing the subject to become sealed within those limits, a 'fortified castle', with the ego sealed off, with no possibility of the Other outside.[23] This image reminded me of Teresa of Avila's book, *The Interior Castle*; Teresa was another theorist who was also a figurative architect.[24] In *Louise Bourgeois' Spider*, Mieke Bal posits a theoretical framework of architecture as a rich metaphor for body and art, critical theory and psychoanalysis. As a figurative as well as literal space, architecture is an obvious site of articulation of inside and outside. Art historians of the Baroque such as Wölfflin and Jean Rousset have specifically characterized Baroque architecture in terms of the scission between the lavish style of the façade and the serenity of the interior.[25] In *Le Pli*, Deleuze sees this as quintessentially Leibnizian, expressing it in terms of the theory of the 'monade': 'The monade is the independence of the interior, an interior without exterior. But its correlative is the independence of the façade, an exterior without interior.'[26] For Deleuze, the ideal Baroque architecture is *un pur dedans*—a pure interior—not even hinting at an exterior; for example, an interior with external light sources disguised.[27] An example of this can be found in the Cornaro chapel housing Bernini's *Teresa* (13.1), where the golden rays above the sculpture conceal a source of light which seems supernatural.

There is a marked insistence on purity in Deleuze's text, and on the fact that there should be no confusion between inside and outside, reminding us of the discourse of Didi-Huberman. Referring to Bernini's sculptures, Deleuze discusses the relationship between clothes and skin as being 'publicized, extended, and enlarged' in the Baroque.[28] The scission itself is being privileged, as is indeed later the very space between clothes and skin, a euphoria of surfaces which for Deleuze is embodied by the elements: fire for *Teresa* and earth for *Ludovica*. Mieke Bal makes a similar characterization in the quotation we saw earlier: 'Her whole body becomes a flame: each part of it, of its cover, its surface but beneath which nothing else remains, becomes a flame; fire comes to overrule previous shapes.'[29]

Ironically, in a chapel which is a masterpiece of interior architecture, *Teresa* is a masterpiece of exterior surface: there is no interior because everything is exterior—body and spirit alike are represented in the play of light and shade on marble. Fire, embodying surface for Deleuze, *is* body for Bal—but a burnt body, negated in a dancing flame which, since it consumes and moves and overrules shapes, traps the gaze in innumerable surfaces. *Teresa* is transgressive and liberating in many ways, but surprisingly Bal's reading, which on first sight appears enabling, seems to also reinforce and remain integral to a fetishistic visual economy, where excess of surface denies and represses an interior, enabling the reality of the body to be completely subsumed in the all-consuming fire. For Perniola, 'Saint Theresa's body disappears in the drapery of her tunic'—her body is 'engulfed' and 'transformed into fabric'.[30] This characterization of being 'engulfed' surely becomes suggestive of Kristeva's characterization of the function of religious rituals to defend against the abject; 'to ward off the subject's fear of his very own identity sinking irretrievably into the mother'.[31] There is also a certain element of the fear of castration inherent in the idea of being engulfed in this substance which seems to be shaped like female folds. Not coincidentally portrayed forever poised just before receiving the penetration of the angel's golden dart, the saint becomes a cipher of a masculine psychosis where sexuality and desire are either diverted or abjected via the mechanism of excessive surface.

The ruched, creased, folded marble of the fully-clothed *Teresa* seems to be operating in a similar way to the sealed, perfect, smooth female nudes which Lynda Nead is attempting to deconstruct. Smoothness or folds, the difference here is irrelevant, as both can operate in the same way—the insistence on surface operates a visual detour enabling the interior of the body to be negated. The discourse of interior and exterior is not only put to work, however, by literal representations of female bodies. A parallel with several works by British artist Anish Kapoor from the last two decades can help shed light on the way in which the *Teresa*'s folds uphold a fetishistic visual economy.

The first awareness of a point of view, Bal notes in *Quoting Caravaggio*, seems to be articulated in Baroque art.[32] That is, the gaze can now be situated outside the self; it becomes non-monolithic and multiple. This means that the subject is put in danger: its position is no longer certain, as it can be inherent in the object. In what are, for me, very Baroque sculptures, Kapoor's *Inside-out* and *Upside-down*, from 1995 and 1998 respectively, the supremely reflective surface not only diverts and disallows the gaze focused upon it, but in turns sucks self, Other, and gaze into the indeterminate space of its 'interior'.[33] It is a mirror which is simultaneously deeply self-absorbed, just as an excess of reflection is an excess of the self-image, but also deeply self-alienating. Unlike the mirror in Lacan's theory of the mirror stage, where the image of seductive unity allows a 'self', albeit an illusory one, to be conceived of, the mirror in the work of Kapoor operates in a different way. The curved, impossible surface refuses, controls and possesses the false self-image until it is put in doubt. Viewers of the 2004 sculpture *Cloud Gate*, designed for Chicago's Millennium Park, feel compelled to search for their own image in the bewildering swoops and curves.[34] This all-surface is both fascinatingly beautiful and profoundly threatening, profoundly implicating the subject's gaze while threatening its very coherence, by suggesting that both subject and gaze are being sucked inside an interior which cannot be known or imagined, the sense of surface is so overwhelming. It is a metaphor both for the primal scene and for the mechanism of fetishism, which destabilizes the subject/object relationship.[35]

The tradition of the depiction of the female nude is a form of art which, I suggest, is sited in a fundamentally masculine aesthetic. Bernini's *Teresa* and the three sculptures by Anish Kapoor are but two examples, from vastly different contexts, of the ways in which this masculine discourse can be present throughout Western visual culture. Such images, by articulating the particular threat posed to the masculine psyche by the abject through the transgression of boundaries, uphold a psychosis within visual culture, which attempts to close off boundaries of the body and reinforce fetishism: a neurotic form of sexuality, characterized by the fear of the wounded and wounding woman.

Identifying the 'agenda' of such artworks is a deeply problematic pursuit. Laura Mulvey, for example, draws on a series of photographs from the late 1980s by Cindy Sherman to illustrate her larger project to defeat the damaging power of fetishism.[36] The series entitled *Disasters* includes very difficult images, involving blood, vomit and suggestions of human excrement of different types, where the eye cannot fix on one point; disturbing and upsetting pictures which are tremendously provocative in their absolute refusal of the type of clichéd, masquerading female body which Sherman plays with in her earlier photographs.

For Mulvey, in these photographs 'the topography of exterior/interior is exhausted'.[37] I feel, however, that while these photographs oppose fetishism in one sense, they are also working within its economy, reinforcing the same 'horror' associations of femininity. Rather than removing or exhausting questions of exterior/interior, they are, on the contrary, pigeonholing femininity into an excess of interior. Although the boundaries of the body are transgressed, they are still operating; we are merely on the other side. These works are therefore still functioning within the same psychoanalytic/sexual model. Having identified a discourse of visuality working within fetishism, I want therefore to conjecture about a form of art, and a form of art history, which does not think in terms of inside or outside, and which escapes from the visual model of the feminine imposed on women by fetishism.

We might approach these issues by taking yet another step further away from the *Teresa* and its universe, to evoke the mathematical figure of the Klein bottle. Very reminiscent of the shape and concept of the sculptures by Anish Kapoor, the Klein bottle is a conceptual, four-dimensional figure developed in the field of topology, which is visualized by a three-dimensional shape, but is itself able to be represented, via perspective, in a two-dimensional plane. Felix Klein's original conception for the bottle, which he developed in 1882, was as a shape where 'outside and inside meet'.[38] Mathematician Konrad Polthier provides a summary description. 'The bottle is a one-sided surface—like the well-known Möbius band—but is even more fascinating, since it is closed and has no border and neither an enclosed interior nor exterior …' and, unlike a torus or 'doughnut' form, 'the Klein bottle does not bound a volume—in other words, it has no interior.'[39] The Klein bottle is literally and mathematically all surface. The philosophical enigma posed by this hypothetical form brings into focus the play of concepts in the artworks maintaining fetishism: there is no interior, it is all surface. However, the concept also opens up new possibilities. The bottle cannot 'contain'—yet it is still called a 'bottle'. The notion that a bottle does not have to contain, might open up a space where skin does not have to contain.[40] Another description of a Klein bottle reads, 'Its inside is its outside. It contains itself.'[41]

Kristeva's *Powers of Horror*, while grounded in Freud, sets out to move away from Freud's masculine-centred incest model to return to the negated sign of the woman and mother, and the misunderstood sign of the feminine, throughout Freud's writings. Kristeva does this by focusing on the potent image of the transgression of the boundary between the masculine and feminine realms. The moves made in *Powers of Horror* have been extremely enabling for subsequent feminist theorists. To look backwards instead, among the writers whose work enables Kristeva's own, I find a textual trace of a possible solution to the visual problem in the thread Kristeva picks up from Georges Bataille. Kristeva writes:

> Georges Bataille remains the only one, to my knowledge, who has linked the production of the abject to the *weakness of that prohibition*, which, in other respects, necessarily constitutes each social order ... Bataille is also the first to have specified that the plane of abjection is that of the subject/object relationship (and not subject/other subject) and that this archaism is rooted in anal eroticism rather than sadism ... [the prohibition] does not seem to have, in such cases, sufficient strength to dam up the abject or demoniacal potential of the feminine.[42]

For Kristeva, the importance of Bataille is his awareness of the interdependency between systems of power and the limits of the body, and the revolution inherent in the possible erosion of those limits.

In ideas initially set down in 'The Notion of Expenditure', Bataille modifies the Freudian view of the symbolic relationship between gold and excrement as transposition, retention to defecation, inside to outside, to imagine 'a world without transposition'.[43] For Bataille, as Yve-Alain Bois summarizes in *Formless*, gold and excrement 'share a condition of pure loss (the jewel is economic waste by definition). The jewel, shit, and the fetish are all on the level of sumptuary expenditure'.[44] Crucially, ecstasy, tears, laughter and sexual pleasure are the sites of what Bataille calls 'strong communication', or 'moments of pure loss ... when identity abolishes itself'—for example, referring to the sexual act, he says, 'No communication is more profound; two creatures are lost in a convulsion that binds them together ... binds them only through wounds where their unity, their integrity disperse in the heat of excitement.'[45]

In a world without transposition, just as gold and excrement are indistinguishable, so are subject and object: a true space where questions of inside and outside are set aside. This text is from a lecture, and similar ideas permeate Bataille's non-fiction writing, but the true articulation of the search for the loss of identity, for this 'strong communication' which is also the space of ecstasy and of the sacred, is in fact found in his fiction. Bataille's understanding of the 'sacred' is that which is wholly other: excrement, tears, ecstasy, laughter and sexual pleasure occupy the same conceptual space, a space which is defined by Rosalind Krauss in *Formless*. Krauss moves towards a definition of the formless which I feel moves within this very space, operating as a space of loss of self which is essentially postmodern: not a threatening destabilization of the subject as in Kapoor's *Cloud Gate*, but the specific form of *entropy*, a term which refers to the space where hot and cold water meet and become tepid, the space where a camouflaged insect can no longer differentiate between its own body and the leaves around it—not so much a lack of boundaries between self and other, as a profound putting-into-question of the place of the self within space at all.[46] Krauss also draws upon Robert Caillois's metaphor of the Praying Mantis, the body of which, after death, automatizes the appearance of life to such an extent that the creature is still capable of 'playing dead', and therefore can be in a position to say the unsayable, 'I am dead':

> Reflexive modernism wants to cancel the naturalism in the field of the object in order to bring about a newly heightened sense of the subject, a form that creates the illusion that it is nothing except the fact that 'I am seeing it.' The entropic, simulacral move, however, is to float the field of seeing in the absence of the subject; it wants to show that in the automatism of infinite repetition, the disappearance of the first person is the mechanism that triggers formlessness.[47]

Georges Bataille depicts this space very powerfully in a paragraph from his novel 'Madame Edwarda', an at once concise and poetic evocation of a *jouissance* of loss of self, intense but strangely calm and without fear, passing beyond questions of limits and surfaces.

> Her naked thigh caressed my ear: I seemed to hear the sound of sea swell, the same sound you hear when you hold a large shell against your ear. In the darkness of the brothel and in the confusion which surrounded me (I felt choked, my face was red, I was sweating), I was strangely suspended, as if Edwarda and I were lost one windy night on the seashore.[48]

It is not only the imagery of the lovers being suspended together in an indefinable space which is important here, but the fact that this is associated with hearing the sound of a seashell pressed against the ear, a sound which of course is none other than the pulsing of your own blood reflected back. This is an infinite reflection of self, Krauss's 'automatism of infinite repetition', at the moment of oral sex; a moment when, inevitably and powerfully, the masculine is visually confronted with the feminine Other.[49]

Kristeva uses this very phrase, *confrontation with the feminine*, in *Powers of Horror*, when she comes to the essence of the difference between the two forms of art I am articulating. She writes:

I shall set aside in this essay a different version of the confrontation with the feminine, one that, going beyond abjection and
fright, is enunciated as ecstatic … a coming face to face with an
unnameable otherness—the *solid rock of jouissance* and writing as
well.[50]

In this strikingly sculptural term, Kristeva names the space, the matter,
of the sacred and the ecstatic, refusing the ethereal 'primeval essence'
of femininity and using writing to sculpt out of formless, threatening
*jouissance* nothing less than solid rock. And this is finally where I come
back to Louise Bourgeois. In a 1983 sculpture, part of Bourgeois' series
*Femme-Maison (*13.3), questions of femininity, architecturality and the
nature of sculpture and matter are being engaged with. Something similar is happening in *Homage to Bernini* (13.2), the bronze sculpture of
which Mieke Bal wrote that 'this work turns Bernini's painterly surfaces
inside-out'.[51] If 'nothing remains' inside *Teresa* (13.1), then for Bourgeois to represent *Teresa* inside-out is a contradiction. Bourgeois' homage to Bernini is not a rejection or updating of his work, but rather an
affectionate nod to another theorist of the feminine, to a sculpture
which offers a compelling theory and debate of femininity, but at the
same time to suggest an alternative
theorization which has indeed perhaps only become possible in
sculpture thanks *to* Bernini's intervention. Bal entitles her chapter
'Beckoning Bernini', emphasizing
the temporal relationship between
past and present art, not seen in
terms of influence. Bourgeois'
sculpture is seen as 'enfolding' and
'debating' that of Bernini.[52] Perhaps Bernini and Bourgeois meet,
paradoxically, in the Baroque fold.

Bal's own writing already moves
beyond 'turning inside-out'. She
first characterizes the sculpture as
an egg, then goes on to write:

13.3 Louise Bourgeois, *Femme-Maison*, 1983, marble, 63.5 × 49.5 ×
58.4 cm. Courtesy Cheim &
Read, New York. Photograph:
Allan Finkelman.

the object *is* bark, just as coarse,
but solid, massive. There is no
inner wood that it hides. Yet the
object is not entirely solid; it is
also hollow. And inside, where

you least expect it, is a tiny bit of Berninesque smoothness. Multiple, like the master's folds; but then again, inside-out. No suggestion of hollowness here.[53]

The result of the debate is an apparent paradox; an eternal suspension between whether or not the sculpture is all-surface, a mass of tree-bark, or hollow. This is for me the brilliance of Bourgeois' work. Centuries of art are enfolded within the softness of the marble: not contained by it, but part of its shape and structure. The suspended movement, travelling beyond inside-out, pays homage to Bernini to move beyond the visual economy of fetishism, and sculpt the solid rock of *jouissance*.

# THE WORD MADE FLESH

Re-embodying the Madonna and Child in Helen
Chadwick's *One Flesh*
*Leila McKellar*

Ideas of the sacred and the feminine are at the heart of many of Helen Chadwick's artworks. Her innovative work in the 1980s and 1990s in photography, sculpture and installation became well known for explorations of identity, femininity and desire, often through the use of controversial materials and subject matter. Archival materials have recently revealed the extent of the meticulous research and planning that Chadwick undertook in the production of her work. Previously unseen writings from around 1985 document the production of a piece that reworked one of the most iconic images of Christian art, that of the Madonna and Child. In contrast to many narratives of the virgin birth, Chadwick's *One Flesh* (14.1) draws attention to the radical nature of Christ's conception, in which the Word became flesh, as it highlights the way that this becoming disturbs thresholds between the bodily and the spiritual.

### Reworking the image of the Madonna and Child
To make *One Flesh*, Chadwick pressed the warm flesh of her neighbour, Paula, and Paula's newborn daughter, Caresse, against the cold glass of her photocopier and allowed its gliding bar of light to form paper indexes of their enfolded bodies.[1] She took these flimsy paper traces, with their rudimentary tones of light and shade, and coloured and collaged them to create a pentangular tableau with the intense jewel colours and gilded panels of a Renaissance altarpiece or stained-glass window. The central figures of the resulting portrait echo those of so many images of the Madonna and Child, in which a mother in flowing robes holds a naked baby to her breast. However, this is where the sim-

14.1  Helen Chadwick, *One Flesh*, 1985,
photocopies, 160 × 107 cm.
Copyright Helen Chadwick Estate. Courtesy of Leeds Museums & Galleries (Henry Moore
Institute Archive).

ilarities end. The infant in *One Flesh*
is female, not the male child we are
accustomed to seeing in the arms
of the Madonna. Indeed, here the
mother's finger points to the infant's female genitalia.

The scene appears to be a domestic one. A pair of woollen
bootees lies on a wooden bench
before the figures, and behind
them green patterned wallpaper
adds to the homely impression.
However, this air of domesticity is
deceptive. Formed in a period of
much radical feminist artmaking,
*One Flesh* is an embodiment of
Chadwick's stated intention to
'subvert [the] docile domestic
image' of the mother and child.[2]
Chadwick was one of a number of
artists who were engaged in projects of appropriating and rewriting
images of women from the history
of art, including the Madonna,
who is a recurring figure, for example, in the pieces by Rose Gar-
rard exhibited as 'Frameworks' in 1982–83.[3] Chadwick's subversion
becomes evident in the golden halo above the figures, which upon
closer inspection is revealed to be a gilded placenta. Above it float disembodied labia threaded through with rings.

*One Flesh* also finds a place within an interrogation of the maternal
that was taking place in feminist art of the 1970s and 1980s. In *10
Months* (1977–79), for example, Susan Hiller used diaries and photographs to document the ten lunar months of her pregnancy, while Mary
Kelly's *Post Partum Document* (1973–79) traced the artist's relationship
with her son during the first six years of his life through texts and indexical records. *One Flesh* is one of several of Chadwick's works that
treat the themes of birth, motherhood and female fertility. She explored
the subject of her own premature birth in a series of sculptures entitled
*Ego Geometria Sum* (1982–83), which included a replica of the incubator
in which she spent the first few weeks of her life. She also looked at her
relationship with her own mother in the *Lofos Nymphon* series of projections (1987), which depict mother and daughter embracing. As I will

go on to suggest, *Lofos Nymphon* may be viewed as a counterpart to *One Flesh*, forming a Pietà to *One Flesh*'s Nativity.

Around the time that Chadwick produced *One Flesh*, a shift away from the autobiographic treatment of the artist's life and body occurred in her work. She had suffered criticism for the use of her own naked body in *Ego Geometria Sum* and in her 1986 Turner Prize-nominated installation, *Of Mutability*.[4] She now began to move towards an exploration of more general issues surrounding motherhood and the body.[5]

## The Virgin Mary and the Word/flesh opposition

Chadwick became interested in the ways in which representations of the Madonna have provided a model of ideal femininity after reading Marina Warner's 1976 book, *Alone of All her Sex: the Myth and the Cult of the Virgin Mary*. The foundational narrative of Christian belief tells of the coming together of the human and the divine in Mary's womb, where the Word became flesh. The Gospel of John tells how 'the Word was made flesh and dwelt among us' (John 1:14). Chadwick noted that this account is at odds with the type of Christian thought described by Warner in her study of Mariology, which holds that the realms of the body and the spirit must be separate. Spiritual fulfilment may conventionally only be achieved through detachment from earthly pleasures, while the divine may only be present in events like the Virgin Birth, which suspend the laws of nature.[6]

By 1985, when *One Flesh* was produced, feminist and deconstructive theory had rendered the concept of the Word ideologically suspect. This was due to its alignment in Western logocentric thought with masculine-rationalist concepts, including the Idea, the Law and the Father, and its perceived opposition to the material, feminine realm of the flesh.[7] According to the Gospel of John, the Word is identical with God the Father: 'In the beginning was the Word, and the Word was with God, and the Word was God' (John 2:1). The notion of the Word made flesh suggests a union of matter and spirit that disturbs apparently 'natural' distinctions. Chadwick's desire to draw attention to this disruption of binary categories in *One Flesh* is evident in her assertion that the piece should act as a 'resolution of [the] quarrel between body and spirit'.[8]

Warner documents a process by which, since the time of the early Christian Church, a gradual accretion of myths, which have little or no basis in the gospels, occurred around the story of the Virgin birth and acted to preserve distinctions between the spiritual and fleshly realms. One of the most powerful of these myths, which was eventually pronounced dogma by the Catholic Church, is that of the perpetual virginity of Mary.[9] Chadwick researched the account, originating in the ideas

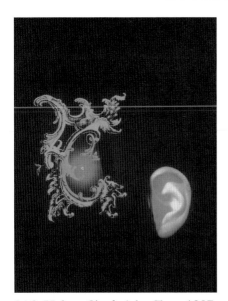

14.2 Helen Chadwick, *Ecce*, 1987, leather, plywood, electric light and slide projection, 150 × 150 cm. Copyright Helen Chadwick Estate. Courtesy of Leeds Museums & Galleries (Henry Moore Institute Archive).

of the third-century Greek exegete Origen and celebrated in mediaeval poetry, that Mary's virginity was maintained by means of conception through the ear, by the Word of the Holy Ghost.[10] Chadwick was intrigued by the story and made a lightbox entitled *Ecce* in 1987 (14.2). 'Ecce' is the word used by Mary to the angel Gabriel at the annunciation, 'Ecce ancilla domini', 'Behold the handmaiden of the Lord' (Luke 1:26–38). Like *One Flesh*, *Ecce* is formed of photocopies, here depicting the ear that is the receptacle of the Word.

The doctrine of Mary's unbroken hymen, left intact during Christ's conception and even while she was giving birth, suggests that anxieties about feminine fertility have revolved around the permeability and leakiness of the feminine body. Boundaries that are uncertain, that allow the passage of bodily fluids, are unsettling in the case of the Virgin Mary, who was chosen for her purity. In order to account for Christ's apparently impossible birth from a seamlessly sealed body, in certain accounts the baby emerges like a ray of light through glass.[11] Appropriately, this is precisely the way a photocopy is produced, a fact to which I will return below.

In contrast to the story of the virgin birth, Chadwick's work has never made any attempt to conceal the physical processes of childbirth. Her 1993 photograph, *The Birth of Barbie* (14.3), makes an explicit connection between the images of women that contemporary Western society teaches from an early age are acceptable, and the bodily reality of the reproductive process. *One Flesh* may be less explicit, but continues in the same vein. There is no suggestion that this female baby's conception and birth were anything other than earthly. The mother holds scissors poised to sever the umbilical cord that links her with her child. Even the halo that floats above the pair takes the form of the placenta that Chadwick described as a 'square halo of the living'.[12] As the organ that conducts nutrients from mother to child, the placenta exists at the

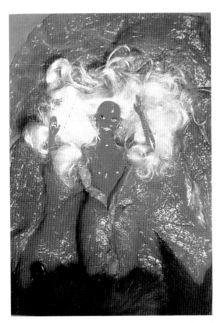

14.3 Helen Chadwick, *The Birth of Barbie*, 1993, c-type photograph, 15 × 10.5 cm. Copyright Helen Chadwick Estate. Courtesy of Zelda Cheatle Gallery.

boundary where one ends and the other begins. Chadwick's working notes describe it as a 'vessel of love' and emphasize the way that 'Mother and child [are] linked by the placenta and umbilicus'.[13] Above this halo are positioned the labia through which both placenta and child have passed.

The removal from the nativity story of these elements, which physically link the infant God with his mortal mother, has the effect of diminishing the power of Christ's human birth. The radical message of the Gospels, according to Christianity, was that the divine assumed human form and was subject to the frailties of the flesh, including suffering a human death. If Christ did not have a human birth, but appeared by supernatural means, his humanity is called into question and the power of his sacrifice on the cross decreases significantly.

One of the reasons that the Virgin escaped the normal processes of childbirth was that these were part of the curse of Eve that all women must endure as a punishment for her original sin, which theologians interpreted as being sexual. Warner's contention is that, positioned on the side of the Word, Mary stands directly opposed to Eve, who has symbolized the sins of the flesh, passed down to all women. Since Mary conceived without intercourse or pleasure, she was exempt from the pains of childbirth. Mary, then, by her exceptional maternity, points up the normal identification of woman with the sins of the flesh.[14] In contrast to this image of motherhood as a curse rather than a blessing, Chadwick writes of *One Flesh* as 'a celebration of the curse of Eve' that depicted 'Birth as "original joy"' rather than original sin.[15]

## The mother-daughter relationship

As a site for the coming together of the Word and the flesh, and for the struggle between the two, the body of the Madonna that *One Flesh* depicts undermines the association of the Word with pure spirit. *One Flesh* also undermines logocentric power as, while the Word gains its authority from its ability to convey the thoughts and ideas of a unified sovereign subject, the paradoxical separation and togetherness of the mother and child suggests a divided or doubled subjectivity. Furthermore, as I will go on to argue, the Word here is subject to the alternative logic of bodily meaning that is present in the sensations of the maternal embrace.

The images of the Madonna and Child and the Pietà that bookend the narrative of the Virgin's life with Christ find echoes in Chadwick's *One Flesh* and *Lofos Nymphon* (14.4). In contrast to representations of Mary and her son, however, these two works explore the kinds of complex bonds and anxieties of the mother-daughter relationship that the powerful Oedipal drama with a parent of the opposite sex may overshadow. Mary Kelly's *Post Partum Document* explores a relationship between mother and son in which Oedipal issues entail a castrating loss, with the child's entry into language and the Law of the Father.[16] By contrast, in their depictions of mother-daughter relationships, *One Flesh* and *Lofos Nymphon* hold out the possibility of the continuation of a state of narcissistic wholeness, in which the bond between mother and daughter may not necessitate a separation between the object of identification and the object of desire.

The *Lofos Nymphon* series depicts Chadwick and her mother against backgrounds showing the view from the home in Athens that should have passed down the maternal line to Chadwick, but did not. In these images mother and motherland intersect, as the poignant pose of the Pietà speaks of grief for both the loss of home and the loss of the maternal body. Both *One Flesh* and *Lofos Nymphon* are images of paradoxical unity and separateness, a state which characterizes the mother-child relationship and which is central to the way it troubles the boundaries of a notional self. In relation to *Lofos Nymphon*, Chadwick wrote:

> To return to the mother might be engulfing and precipitate a fatal loss of self … what a solace it would be to construct a haven for the disembodied memories of pleasure at the mother's breast—a chamber where the oscillations of dread and longing merge together and I might resurrect this lost archaic contact safely, quelling my fear of her depths.[17]

It thus appears that the body of the mother may be both welcoming and threatening to a daughter who is subject to, yet fearful of, mutually overwhelming longings.

14.4  Helen Chadwick, *Lofos Nymphon*, 1987, installation with canvases, oil
paint and slide projections. Copyright Helen Chadwick Estate. Courtesy
of Leeds Museums & Galleries (Henry Moore Institute Archive).

Here the mother-daughter relationship is one of narcissistic involve-
ment in which, as Rosemary Betterton has suggested, the two women
are positioned 'body against body', or *corps à corps*, a phrase which Luce
Irigaray adopts in her essay 'Body against Body: In Relation to the
Mother'.[18] Irigaray uses the phrase to denote contact that may be understood as simultaneously struggling and embracing.[19] In Chadwick's
images, the maternal embrace may be both nurturing and smothering,
the maternal body both the same and frighteningly other. In this light,
it is possible that the scissors that cut the umbilical bond in *One Flesh*
may provide welcome freedom. On the other hand, as the generic form
of the image sets up the expectation of a male infant, initial shock at
the absence of male genitals may lead the viewer to interpret the scissors as the threat of castration wielded by the all-powerful mother.

### Portraying *jouissance*

Understood as the vessel for the Word made flesh, Mary's body stands
at the intersection between bodily meaning and linguistic meaning. According to Julia Kristeva, it is precisely on this borderline between sensation and language, between the semiotic and the symbolic, that
*jouissance*, which she describes as 'this indeterminate passion-anguish-
melancholy-joy', becomes possible.[20] Sensory feeling and desire were
at the heart of Chadwick's ideas about her art. She describes *One Flesh*
as an 'affirmation [of the] love of life and pleasure'.[21] The notion of
*jouissance* thus became a touchstone for Chadwick as she developed
these ideas through her work.

Kristeva suggests that the sacred is located at the same boundary between sensation and signification at which *jouissance* exists. In *The Feminine and the Sacred* she positions the sacred 'on the borderline between
nature and culture, the animalistic and the verbal, the sensible and the
nameable', and contends that the difference between religion and the

sacred lies precisely in the notion of *jouissance*, which, she argues, religion denies.[22] In the light of this, I would suggest that while Christian religious tradition may focus on original sin, the 'original joy' that Chadwick proposes may be a form of sacred *jouissance*.

Chadwick had studied Kristeva's psychoanalytic explorations of depictions of the Virgin and Child painted by Bellini. Her annotations to Kristeva's 'Motherhood According to Bellini' show her particular interest in the contrast between Bellini's representations and those by, for example, Leonardo, in which the Madonna's gaze centres upon her child, suggesting complete absorption in the baby. In Bellini's images, in particular those produced between 1450 and 1480, the mother's gaze is invariably averted, her expression distant. For Kristeva this suggests 'ineffable *jouissance*'.[23] Chadwick's Madonna, too, averts her gaze. Her eyes close and her face turns away, intimating an ecstasy that is inaccessible to the gazes of both child and viewer. However, whilst Bellini's mothers appear distant, their bodies unavailable to their babies' touch, Chadwick evokes a *jouissance* that is felt by a very present body.

As I have noted, Chadwick had been criticized for the use of her own naked body in her work. She insisted at the time that her images were not representations of a particular body, nor objects of a desiring gaze, but rather showed the body as a site of feeling, as the subject of its own desires.[24] In *One Flesh*, too, sensory feeling appears inseparable from the body, as to explore one is necessarily to depict the other. As well as presenting the viewer with a portrait of *jouissance*, it is my contention that *One Flesh* may also evoke *jouissance* in the viewing body. The mind's ear hears the murmur of suckling child and rumpled silks. The mind's skin senses their heavy embrace and feels the softness and weight of infant skin against the crook of the arm, against the breast. I would argue that the Word is not evaded entirely here. Rather it is incorporated, or incarnated, and subjected to an alternative fleshly logic.

*One Flesh* contains an intimacy that is not present in Bellini's images. His Virgin's face is invariably separated from the arms and hands that hold the baby by voluminous folds of fabric, which seem to render the maternal body absent even while it is at the centre of the painting. Chadwick's image, too, contains swathes of fabric; however, these envelop both mother and child in an almost fleshy embrace. While haloes around their heads often visibly define the distance between Bellini's mother and child, Chadwick's placental halo crowns both as one being. Rather than being cut off from her mother's body, therefore, in *One Flesh* the child cleaves close to it, body against body, skin touching skin.

Evoking just such a touch of skin against skin, Chadwick wrote in her book *Enfleshings* that 'touch cannot be in opposition to itself, can never be perceived as surface or source, but an acknowledgement that actual is mutual—a conjoining of two.'[25] Chadwick's words echo Jacques Derrida's assertion that touch disturbs thresholds between self and other, for to touch is always also to be touched by the other that one touches.[26] One might read the image of mother touching child, therefore, as depicting precisely this blurring of boundaries at the surface where mother-skin and child-skin become indistinguishable, as the title, *One Flesh*, suggests.

On the other hand, the touch of skin against skin may also be a means by which the child differentiates itself from the body of its mother, as this touch makes sensible a previously unfelt separateness. Catherine Clément speaks of a transitional moment at which the child first becomes aware of its own 'sack of skin'.[27] As I become aware of my own separate selfhood and leave the maternal embrace, it is my skin that embraces me, that holds me together, that defines my limits. The paradoxical unity and separateness of the mother-child embrace may thus inhere most intensely in the membrane of the skin, which *One Flesh* sensitizes in the viewing body, and which acts as a cleavage in the double sense, the surface where self and other both separate and cling together.[28]

### The photocopy: where earthbound and ethereal meet

Just as the subject matter of *One Flesh* troubles the thresholds between the mind and the body and between mother and child, Chadwick's use of photocopies as an artistic medium has a particular relation to the work's representation of subjectivity. Chadwick was always interested in new technologies, so when Canon introduced new models of photocopier that could print in blue and brown, she soon began to explore their creative possibilities in works including *Ecce* (1987) and *Of Mutability* (1987). As I have mentioned, in certain accounts of Christ's birth, the baby is described as appearing like light through a pane of glass. Light passing through glass is precisely the way in which the photocopied image is produced. While this version of the story has the effect of defining Christ's difference from his human mother, as they are not joined by any umbilical cord, for Chadwick, the use of light to create a portrait had the opposite effect, blurring rather than sharpening the boundaries of subjectivity.

In her notebooks, Chadwick mused that 'At the speed of light, matter/mass no longer exists ... At the speed of light, I no longer exist.' She went on to describe a consequent 'Dissolution of [the] boundaries of [the] self'.[29] Just as the separate togetherness of the mother and child is a form of reproduction that troubles the sense of where one ends and the other begins, in the process of being photocopied, multiple copies of the self can be created. Furthermore, it is clear that the transformation from mass to energy acts, for Chadwick, as a means of interrogating the limits of the subject. She describes the way the photocopier 'traps or locates ghostly images [as the] Earth-bound and ethereal meet'.[30] Just as the body of the Virgin forms the intersection where Word and flesh conjoin, therefore, so the body pressed to the photocopier exists on the boundary where the fleshly body and the spectral light-trace that will outlive it meet.

The photocopier is a more direct way of producing a portrait than the camera, as it requires the direct contact of the body on glass. Chadwick was drawn to the immediacy of mechanical reproduction and wrote of the appeal of the 'Naturalism [and] crude truth to life of [the] machine-made image'.[31] The automatic nature of the photocopier avoids the problematic presence of the intentioned artistic author within the artwork. Furthermore, the fact that the photocopy is not usually linked with artistic production distances it from more ideologically loaded media such as painting. While a painting of the Madonna and child is able to preserve their exalted distance from mortal viewers, in *One Flesh* the photocopied bodies appear as accessible as if they were pressed against glass in front of the viewer.

Chadwick disagreed with Kelly's famous assertion that 'To use the body of the woman, her image or person is not impossible but problematic for feminism.'[32] *Post Partum Document* avoided figurative representation of the body through the use of indexical bodily traces, including stained nappies and clay handprints. Although *One Flesh* is, unlike Kelly's work, a direct representation of the maternal body, I would argue that the photocopies of *One Flesh* are also effectively indexical rather than iconic. Chadwick defined *One Flesh* as 'photocopies from life', explaining that in such a description she aimed 'to be precise, to try and make people realise that what had happened hadn't happened through the lens of a camera, that somehow it was much more direct'.[33]

Paradoxically, although it may be more direct than a photograph, the use of the photocopy avoids photography's claim to be a reproduction of the world that is unmediated by the language of representation. In its seductive apparent transparency, the photograph promises access to the Real, the register that exists prior to symbolization.[34] The photograph never ultimately succeeds, however, in closing the rupture with the Real that is opened up when signification takes the place of sensation with the entry into language. The crude marks made by the photocopier, on the other hand, make no claim to transparency. Rather, in the photocopies of *One Flesh*, the Real is present in a different way. It erupts in the sensory *jouissance* felt by the mother, which produces an experience of the maternal body as Real. Furthermore, as I will shortly conclude by arguing, when evoked in the viewing body, this element that resists signification interrupts the negotiation between viewer and sign.

### A new icon

Working notes on *One Flesh* that have recently come to light speak of the creation of a 'new icon'.[35] It has been my contention that, while conventional icons have erased the fleshly aspect of the nativity, this new icon draws attention to the radical way in which spirit is transmuted into matter at Christ's conception and birth. In addition, Chadwick's notes suggest a reading of the photocopy as a medium that enacts this becoming in the opposite direction, as flesh becomes light and the subject becomes a ghostly trace. *One Flesh* thus performs a double movement between the body and signification.

As I have argued, it is at this limit of signification that *jouissance* occurs. Kristeva suggests that *jouissance* eludes representation. It is 'beyond discourse, beyond narrative … beyond figuration'.[36] My assertion is that, in addition to offering a visual image of a maternal *jouissance* that will always exceed its representation, *One Flesh* works to engender sensation in the viewing body, evoking the touch of skin against skin, the sound of the suckling child, the faintly sweet smell of the newborn. Kelly has written that it is precisely the encounter with the Real in the form of 'the corporeal reality of the child's body' that allows an experience of the maternal body as Real.[37] I would argue that, by synaesthetically evoking such an encounter with 'corporeal reality', a visual image like *One Flesh* may be able to produce the viewing body as Real as it arouses sensory feeling in that body. Such an interpenetration of representation and the body means that, in contrast to conventional representations of the Madonna and Child, which subordinate the flesh to the power of the Word, the dynamic between Word and flesh in *One Flesh* bears more resemblance to that of the mother-daughter relationship: a state of continuously struggling embrace.

# 15

# SOMETHING TO SHOW FOR IT?
## Notes on Creativity and Termination in the
## Work of Tracey Emin
### *Vanessa Corby*


May Dodge—My nan Shes 92 I call
her Plum she calls me
Pudding

She made me the most beautiful baby clothes—white crochietd
[*sic*]
She made them for me a few years ago—she said at the time
'I've made them for you now because by the time you have a baby
—I'll be making clothes for angels'

Dear Nanny I'm not afraid anymore—life's fantastic—who'd have
thought I could make Angels—
for you
Theire [*sic*] waiting XXX

Tracey Emin, May Dodge, My Nan, 1963–93

## Introduction

*May Dodge, My Nan* (15.1) is a mixed-media artwork currently on display in Tate Liverpool. Until I encountered it during a visit to Tate Britain in February 2005[1] I had only seen one of Tracey Emin's works in the flesh: *My Bed* (15.2) installed in the Saatchi Gallery, formerly the headquarters of the GLC. I purposefully sought out these displays of Emin's work, yet until late 2003 I had been indifferent to it and the media furore that followed it. Or perhaps it is more accurate to say that I had switched off from, what seemed to me to be, personal broadcasts

15.1  Tracey Emin, *May Dodge, My Nan*, 1963–93, framed memorabilia in five parts, dimensions variable. Copyright the artist. Courtesy Jay Jopling/White Cube (London).

to 'all and sundry'. Never mind expressionist precedents and post-modern pre-occupations with the banality of the everyday. I approached Emin and her work as a classed subject. The compulsion to 'air dirty linen in public', was, to the upper-working-class codes of conduct that had shaped my upbringing, a contemptible characteristic of the lower working classes. Families like mine aped what they perceived to be middle-class values; pride and privacy were synonymous. Emin, I thought at the time, practised 'showing herself up'.

This selective inattention to the spectacle Emin made of herself went further than working-class snobbery however. To be honest, I just didn't get it. I had only a passing familiarity with *My Bed*, in spite of its high profile during the 1999 Turner Prize. I knew the piece had something to do with abortion, and had heard the infamous phrase 'emo-

15.2  Tracey Emin, *My Bed*, installation Turner Prize Exhibition, Tate Gallery, London, 20 October 1999–23 January 2000. Copyright the artist. Courtesy Jay Jopling/ White Cube (London). Photograph: Stephen White.

tional suicide'. In contradiction of earlier analyses of the unmediated, confessional nature of Emin's practice, the work's indebtedness to the vocabulary of the women's art movement was clear.[2] But my engagement with Emin's reference to termination went no further than to cynically align *My Bed*'s references with the shock-tactics of Hirst and Harvey. Why else would a woman make art out of this particular gendered trauma?

Six years later, standing in Tate Britain, I found viewing *May Dodge, My Nan* to be a profoundly moving encounter.[3] This piece locates Emin's art practice beyond a straightforward negotiation of the realm of aesthetics and art history that nevertheless gives permission to it. Duchamp did not have a monopoly on punning. Embroidery, crochet and appliqué are not the *product* of the Woman's Art Movement in the 1970s; it must not be forgotten that they were the reclaimed territory of 'make do and mend' crafty grandmothers and great grandmothers. Home-made blankets, bed spreads and antimacassars embroidered a generation of women's childhoods that witnessed the slow extinction of a special kind of womanliness; a classed, capable kind of femininity defined by baking, sewing and cleaning.[4] Heaven help the woman who presented her husband with 'shop-bought' cake. Yet this new interest in Emin's work has not been generated by a nostalgic identification at the level of working class genealogy otherwise blinded to the sexual oppression at the heart of such creative yet labour-intensive femininity.

For women, feminism is still, as Shoshana Felman suggested in her now classic text *What Does A Woman Want?* 'among other things, reading literature and theory with their own life'. It is a life, she added, however, 'that is not entirely in [women's] conscious possession'.[5] As a product of a secularized society living out the patriarchal legacies of its religious beginnings I did not, until recently, even realize that I did not possess the means to encounter Emin's engagement with the subject of termination. Those works by Emin that negotiate abortion, it is possible to suggest, defy the accessibility that Julian Stallabrass believed to be central to Emin's making.[6] I will suggest that the continuing hyperpoliticization of abortion negates the possibility of the psychological and corporeal dimensions of that act/event entering cultural consciousness. As *Abortion: Loss and Renewal in the Search for Identity*, written by Eva Pattis Zoja in 1997, argues:

> The written word seems yet to have been invented with respect to this event, as if the event itself has no real existence outside the moments in which it takes place, and could never be the subject of a narrative.[7]

15.3 Tracey Emin, *Homage to Edvard Munch and all My Dead Children*, 1998, single screen projection and sound, shot on Super 8, Duration: 2 minutes 10 seconds. Copyright the artist. Courtesy Jay Jopling/White Cube (London).

My desire to seek out Emin's work is the product of a new awareness of, and respect for, the courage and creative means by which Emin articulates a hitherto 'unsayable experience'. Termination is an act/event that occurs in a 'non-place', in the liminal space of the taboo that at present precludes any knowledge of it other than to those who have experienced it.[8] What was now discernible within *May Dodge, My Nan* and *My Bed* was the mourning for and negotiation of the denial of a familial and still societal expectation that women will 'naturally' become mothers. The 'angels' Emin made for her Nan, I presumed, were her own 'dead children', referenced in her *Homage to Edvard Munch and all My Dead Children* (15.3). Emin's compulsion to air her dirty laundry in public hadn't changed, I had.

An awakening consciousness of the negative representations of termination that pervade popular culture is crucial to the following reading of Emin's art practice. The aim of this paper is to situate selected works by Emin in relation to termination as an event whose *experience* is currently absent from cultural memory. In so doing I will suggest it becomes possible to de-pathologize the present understanding of Emin's emotional reaction to termination in her work. For the pathogen does not only come from the lack of a common discourse within which to articulate this experience, or the need, for some, to grieve. Rather, it is augmented by the diametric opposition of this lack to the existing representations of women who abort that entirely preclude a model of mourning. This paper will argue that it is the chasm between the experience of women and its politically motivated cultural representations that is profoundly traumatizing. Let me be rightly understood however: any reference to the trauma that can follow termination, to the feelings of anxiety, guilt and depression, are *dependent* on the circumstances that shape the experience of the procedure and its aftermath for the woman

concerned.[9] As an articulation of that experience, the cultural and political value of Emin's work for other women transcends the gallery
space, for it marks the beginning of that very discourse whose absence
it testifies to. The work does make a spectacle of the artist, but crucially
it is Emin that makes herself so; she makes or brings something into
the visible to offer it for the audience's scrutiny. She gives the viewer
something to show for her experience.

'Showing', in its colloquial sense in the North of England, and I suspect elsewhere, describes the early stages of pregnancy first made visible by the rounding of the belly: a woman begins to 'show'.
Termination is a procedure for which, eventually, there is nothing to
show. For 'the pregnant woman' who signs her consent to the procedures made legal by the 1967 Abortion Act, life, it is presumed, can go
on as before, as if no-thing had happened. The key question of this
paper, therefore, widens: why would a woman make works of art that
persistently bring her back to the moment of that act/event, its agency,
responsibility and legacy? Wouldn't that in someway defeat the object
of the procedure? Why make something to show for this experience in
a culture whose only means of coping with it is silence or vilification?

### Speaking silenced experience

*The Art of Tracey Emin,* published in 2002 and edited by Mandy Merck
and Chris Townsend, is the most substantial critical text published on
this artist so far. It reads for the connections between the body of the
artist and her practice beyond the notion of the confession.[10] The fundamental significance of Emin's practice is marked as that which, as
Rosemary Betterton states, puts her own body and experiences centrally
in the work to pose 'questions about the relationship between representation, lived experience and the construction of self in art'.[11] *Exploration
of the Soul* (15.4) is one such artwork. It presents a hand-written account
of key episodes in the artist's biography on 32 sheets of A4 paper, in-

15.4 Tracey Emin, *Exploration of the Soul*, 1994, hand-written text and photograph on paper, overall display dimensions variable, unique.

cluding her early sexual experimentations with her twin brother Paul and their own entry into the world:

> She [Emin's mother] told us she loved us—that she would do anything for us. Strange to think we were an accident—strange to think—she'd booked out a clinic—to have us aborted
> And strange to think she talked herself out of it—
> It was 1962—she was married—dad was married—but of course not to each other …[12]

Displayed in Tate Britain, *Exploration of the Soul* gives context to *May Dodge, My Nan* on the opposite wall. Emin's dry wit does not negate the power of this text to place her at once in the shoes of the 'angels' she made for her grandmother. She too, like them, might not have been. To conceive of Emin as a woman whose pregnancies were made 'invalid' by medical intervention is thus insufficient. Rather, a profound sense of empathy and identification marks Emin's relationship to her aborted foetuses. Her 'dead children' constitute her as a mother-not-to-be. Concomitantly, therefore, Emin's courage is of a different order to that of her mother's.

To draw creatively from *Narrative Means to Therapeutic Ends*, written by pioneering Australian therapists Michael White and David Epston, is to illuminate the way in which Emin organizes and gives meaning to her experience in *Exploration* by 'storying' it.[13] Put simply, a dominant narrative is constructed by the artist via key incidents that are consciously or unconsciously selected for their ability to lend weight to the coherence of the 'Emin' plot. White and Epston's practice builds on Gregory Bateson's theory of 'part for whole coding'.[14] 'Not only,' Bateson argues, 'is the interpretation of an event determined by its receiving context but those events that cannot be "patterned" are not selected for survival; such events will not exist for us as facts.'[15] The viewer is thus confronted with a paradox. Emin's experience of termination is clearly crucial to the storying of 'poor Tracey', yet this is not the case for those texts that have been written for her and her work.[16]

Whilst it can be said that abortion is acknowledged both by popular culture and the discourse written about Emin, neither sphere adequately represents its gravity or complexity. In the case of Emin its specificity is assimilated within what Merck and Townsend identify as the 'cut, the wound … the suppurating incision into body and soul' that is proffered to the artist's audience.[17] In *Exploration*, the disparate and difficult events in the artist's adolescence and early adulthood cohere to signify under the rubric of *TRAUMA*, and what might be called the artist's 'in-yer-face' hyper-sexuality. When it is discussed, *The Art of Tracey Emin* follows the artist's lead to pattern her experience of abortion within an economy of corporeal and sexual excess. The astute analysis of 'We Love You, Tracey', written by the late Lorna Healy, however, identifies Emin's 'treatment' of termination as the point at which her 'potential radicalism is most apparent'. Emin's articulation of 'untheorised experience', Healy tells us, breaks the cultural agenda's 'code of silence' that represses the experience of abortion.[18] Writing from an awareness of the repression of abortion in Ireland, Healy, quite rightly, reads Emin's references to termination as an affirmation of a woman's right to exercise reproductive choice. Emin says 'yes to life'—that is, to her own life—rather than 'yes to abortion'.[19] A political analysis of the implications of Emin's practice is highly productive, for it counters the tide of interiorized psychic trauma that has characterized the myths constructed for this artist.

Such an analysis can only leave the viewer with a limited understanding of the experience Emin articulates, however. For the radicalism of Emin's 'homage' to her 'dead children' exceeds both the clear-cut and politicized representation of 'choice' in which it is framed. The political or sexual 'patterning' of that reality cannot sufficiently explain her desire to represent dimensions of termination again and again. Thus the means by which the affection, respect and sense of loss Emin has for them is transformed and re-made with-in the visible field remains 'untheorized'. As yet the reality of that event and its legacies cannot, therefore, be said to truly 'exist' within the narratives constructed for and by Emin. This artist's practice thus demands an analysis of its psychic motivations in and of the social. For, I want to suggest, Emin's repeated references to termination put forward an ethical vision that at once exceeds that present in popular culture, and testifies to the scission between this act/event and the prevalent perception of it.

How has abortion, or rather 'choice', been represented in popular culture? *Life is Sweet*, directed by Mike Leigh in 1990, provides a key example. Central to the film's narrative is the troubled mother-daughter relationship between the characters Wendy and Nicola, played by Alison Steadman and Jane Horrocks. Nicola's anti-capitalist and feminist 'politics' enable her to justify her inactivity to herself but not those around her. They see her apathy for what it really is: a mask for her eating disorders, low self-esteem and consequent lack of direction in life. In a cutting argument between mother and daughter, Wendy tells Nicola that she gave up on her education, the future and her life when she stopped eating at seventeen:

Wendy: *I could have given up, right? Sixteen I was doing my A-levels.*
Nicola: *What A-levels?*

Wendy: *English and Business Studies if you must know. Then I got pregnant with twins.*
Nicola: *Well, why didn't you have an abortion?*
Wendy: *Because I didn't want one. Because I had two little lives growing inside me! I don't believe in it. That's the easy way out ... and when the two of you were born we were thrilled to bits because we had two lovely little babies. We came through laughing.*

Without any warning or preamble Steadman's vehement reply is a slap in the face for the woman who has already terminated her pregnancy. Nice girls, like Emin's mother it might be suggested, bite the bullet and go through with it—so says popular culture. In *Life is Sweet* Wendy declares and defines her love for her daughters by her acts of maternal selflessness. She reveals the personal sacrifice she made once she discovered she was pregnant: abandoning the education that was the key to her own life. She was responsible for the lives inside her, and they came first.[20] Thus, in contrast to Leigh's later work *Vera Drake* (2004), *Life is Sweet* can be read as a product of a British society that has continued to be inherently 'pro-natalist'.[21] *Childless by Choice*, written by Jan Veevers in 1980, makes clear that for society in the UK, career and/or educational success do not testify to femininity, and remain only adjuncts to women's true raison d'être.[22] For women, normal mental health and the full development of the adult individual are still signified by the desire for, and passage into, motherhood. Narratives such as those present in *Life is Sweet* demonstrate the ways in which secular Britain still lives with the legacy of the figure of the self-sacrificing and non-sexual mother that underpins Christian, and particularly Catholic, doctrine. Those who reject the traditional female gender role are stigmatized as unnatural, socially immature, unfeminine and selfish.[23] Crucially, therefore, to the woman who has chosen to end her pregnancy, her 'choice' is represented to her as no choice at all.

That such critiques are necessary in 2006, 20 years since the publication of Germaine Greer's *Sex and Destiny*, written in 1985, is both absurd and testimony to the intransigence of the politics of reproduction. In that text Greer put forward a highly detailed and cogent argument that human reproduction is, on the whole, a 'wasteful business'.

A Catholic woman losing her blastocyst at menstruation has never been told of the possibility that a human life has just ended. It may seem very complicated to keep a jug of holy water beside the lavatory bowl to baptise sanitary napkins ... it would certainly dramatise the fact that Catholics take life before birth very seriously. The fact that they do not carry out rituals of this kind suggests that in fact they do not really believe what they maintain in polemic.[24]

'Abortion,' Greer tells us, 'is as natural, and possibly more prevalent, than birth.'[25] The statistical evidence that proves the frequency of ovum or sperm abnormality, the rate of embryo mortality and the fact that approximately 20 per cent of pregnancies fail to produce a 'live birth' are well documented. Natural wastage is thus the means Greer employs to assuage guilt on the part of the woman who aborts. The key to Greer's argument, based on medical procedures at the time of going to print in 1984, is the way in which the woman is shielded from the 'abortive material's' potential to be a child. It is the belief in this potential, most apparently in the Catholic notion of the presence of a human soul from the moment of conception, and its loss that Greer seeks to destabilize.

Recent advances in ultrasound imaging technology and in foetal and neo-natal care have wrongly held sway over Greer's argument to situate the child in potential more firmly in the popular imagination than ever before (15.5). As Anne Weyman, chief executive of the Family Planning Association (FPA), noted in 2004, representation has become increasingly crucial to the politics of reproduction.[26] Magnified, emotive representations of thumb-sucking 'children' in intra-uterine isolation appeal to viewers on the grounds of their proximity to our own *human-ness* and vulnerability. The vessels that contain these 'babies' are rendered inhuman in so far as they are not represented beyond their emptiness and role as that which sustains another life. The baby is presented as a being without context; denuded of the history, geography, and social and financial pressures that govern not only its mother's choice, but also the quality of life it would lead if carried to term. Thus it is representation that counters one of the basic premises of the Human Rights Act 1998, that the 'foetus is not a legal person, and its

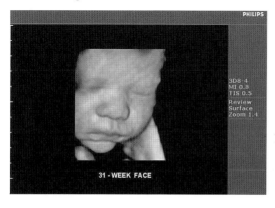

15.5 Foetal image, taken using a Philips Ultrasound HD11 XE, capable of 3D/4D colour imaging.

interests cannot trump those of the pregnant woman'.[27] The absence or trivialization of 'mitigating' circumstances enables society's clear-cut narratives of 'the easy way out' to form the prism through which the woman that aborts sees her own actions; they represent her to herself as someone who is selfish, unnatural, a murderer. The only emotion sanctioned in this scenario is guilt. The relation of the woman to the aborted 'foetus' is hardly ever perceived beyond the terms of her not wanting her 'child'.[28] In the case of Emin, therefore, her persistent references to termination often serve to exasperate her reviewers: why can't she just 'get over it'? People, after all, usually forget about the things they have lost but did not want.

What neither position recognizes, however, is the way in which, as Pattis Zoja tells us,

> An unwanted pregnancy places a woman in a wholly unreasonable and paradoxical situation that entraps her as though in a tragic destiny. Real choice has been done away with, and the woman concerned is unprepared for the possibilities that present themselves. Such a situation is best described by the Greek idea of *anànke*— necessary destiny—rather than by moral ideals or by notions that spring from the language of psychotherapy, which always bear suggestions of preventing or curing an affliction.[29]

The co-existence of entirely contradictory states of mind and feeling are crucial to the understanding of the aftermath of this procedure. Emin's work points directly to this paradox. It is her awareness of her and her twin's precarious viability that galvanized her identification with her 'dead children' to posit them at the centre of her representations of abortion. Works such as *Everyone I Have Ever Slept With 1963–1995,* (1995) or *Feeling Pregnant II* (1999–2002), within which were embroidered the names of two aborted foetuses among the names of Emin's family members, again position Emin as a mother-not-to-be.[30] Stood in room 30 in Tate Britain audiences in 2005 could weigh up the consequences of Emin's actions from both sides of the fence, from the representations of the kinds of choices that are acceptable to mainstream culture (her mother's) and those that are not (her own).

It is, therefore, not only the larger cultural silence cited by Healy that has inhibited the degree of significance that the act/event of termination has lent to the production of meaning for Emin's oeuvre. As Leigh's cinematic text makes clear, this silence can also be attributed to the kinds of representations of abortion that are presently acceptable to mainstream culture. To turn again to the writing of Shoshana Felman is to facilitate an understanding of Emin's art practice whose complexity transcends the notion of confession. Felman's text enables us to discern how the woman who has taken the decision to have a termination, perhaps more than any other person, is traumatized by the confrontation with such representations day after day in popular culture and the media. Such women are, in Felman's words, met at every turn by themselves 'positioned as the Other'. She goes on to say that, 'estranged to ourselves, we have a story that by definition cannot be self-present to us, a story that, in other words, is not a story, but *must become a story*.'[31] Emin's artworks thus negotiate the creative legacies of the late nineteenth and twentieth centuries within the context of contemporary popular culture. These are languages that cannot articulate her experience of grief and loss; they cannot confess to it. Emin's is a story in *becoming*.

It is from this non-place, of a story in becoming, that the means with which to read this dimension of Emin's practice must be constructed. The discourse of counselling psychology accords the first language with which sense can be made of Emin's engagement with termination. In the testimonies that shape its 'therapies', the need to mourn after abortion, a process dependent upon the loss of an object to which there was a libidinal attachment, a seeming oxymoron, is prevalent.[32] In *Abortion and Afterwards*, author Vanessa Davies recalls her own experience, as follows:

> I felt relieved after the abortion and remember walking away from the hospital thinking: 'well, that wasn't too bad.' For months afterward I did not feel the same person. I still don't—and isolating the feeling enabled me to label it as a sense of loss. Everything else I had experienced—anger, guilt, sadness—was attributable to that loss. I needed to grieve, not only for the life that could not be but also more on a symbolic level for the 'old me.' I would never be the same again.[33]

Healy's sensitive analysis locates *I Don't Think So*, a short black and white film from 2000, not only within the creative legacy of *Sleep* (1963) by Andy Warhol, but also within the tension of ambivalence identified by Davies in her account:

> Emin's bed here is similar to that featured in the installation *My Bed*, but it is not surrounded by any of the clutter that was an integral part of that work. The bedroom is spacious and dream-like, everything is white and curtains blow gently in the background … the silence is broken intermittently by the sound of a baby crying. The crying could be a haunting, dreamt reminder of her unborn

15.6 Tracey Emin, *The First Time I was Pregnant I Atarted to Crochet the Baby a Shawl*, 1999, yarn, needle, wood and Plexiglas and framed text, 141.5 × 40.5 × 40.5 cm. Copyright the artist. Courtesy Jay Jopling/White Cube (London).

babies which disturbs Emin even as she sleeps. However, as the title of the piece suggests, it could also be a confirmation of her decision not to have children. Emin could be reaffirming her refusal ever to have to jump to the attention of a crying infant instead of having a lie in.[34]

At this point I would like to return to *My Bed* and its clutter; the bed that, Emin said, was 'made for me'.[35] In *Bedtime*, Merck's contribution to her and Townsend's collection, Emin's now iconic use of blood-stained knickers and soiled sheets are read as indexical to a vocabulary of abject sexuality and trauma.[36] Among the debris that litters *My Bed*, however, are packets of the contraceptives Cilest and Persona, and Schering PC4, otherwise known as the morning-after pill. These artefacts, together with Emin's earlier oft-quoted statement about her 'emotional suicide', and initial installations at the Sagacho Exhibition Centre Tokyo and Lehman Maupin New York, underscore not only the installation's engagement with sex and contraception, but also with abortive technologies and experience. To consider *My Bed* within the context of the 1999 show *Every Part of Me is Bleeding*, in particular that included *The First Time I was Pregnant I Started to Crochet the Baby a Shawl* (15.6) is to supplement the meaning of blood in this work.

As the marker of gender specificity blood has been read, in 'Why is My Art Not As Good As Me?' by Rosemary Betterton, as part of Emin's continued engagement with feminist art practice of the 1970s. In her interview with Jean Wainwright Emin recounts the events behind the 1999 monoprint *Poor Love* (15.7):

There was … a drawing in the White Cube show called *Poor Love*, where you have the hospital drip—that comes from one of my

15.7 Tracey Emin, *Poor Love*, 1999, monoprint, 29.7 × 42 cm. Copyright the artist. Courtesy Jay Jopling/ White Cube (London). Photograph: Stephen White.

abortions. It went wrong, I had to have a scrape. I was in a ward with lots of old ladies for some bizarre reason, who had all had hysterectomies and when I got up to have breakfast I was still attached to a drip. I was walking past the long thin breakfast table and they were all eating boiled eggs, and they all went, 'Oh, poor love.' I thought they meant because I had the drip, but it was because the back of my gown was completely saturated with blood and I didn't know, I had no idea.[37]

When conceived within Greer's argument about the wasteful business of reproduction, the bodily fluids and foetal matter issued after termination could be assimilated within the model put forward in Kristeva's analysis of 'The Improper/Unclean' in *The Powers of Horror*. To live, the body extricates itself from the bodily fluids and filth that signify its proximity to death. The necessary loss of 'waste' is the means by which life is facilitated; 'such wastes drop so that I might live.'[38] In order for a woman to preserve her life as it is, the foetus must become waste; as Healy states, Emin said 'yes' to her own life, not 'yes' to abortion. In this paradigm, the repeated expulsion of blood and, by association, foetal tissue in the visible would be the means of moving on. Implicit within this Kristevan economy of expulsion is, I would argue, a violent forgetting; a forgetting that cannot account for the ambivalence of Davies's testimony or of Emin's making.

To track Freud's theorization of mourning from 'Mourning and Melancholia' to 'The Ego and the Id' is to elucidate the shifting significance that can be ascribed to the psychic implications of the body's expulsions after termination. In 'Mourning and Melancholia', he hypothesizes that, after the death of a loved one, the process of 'reality-testing' teaches the subject that:

The loved object no longer exists, and it proceeds to demand that all libido shall be withdrawn from its attachments to that object. This demand arouses understandable opposition—it is a matter of general observation that people never willingly abandon a libidinal position, not even, indeed, when a substitute is already beckoning to them. This opposition can be so intense that a turning away from reality takes place and a clinging to the object through the medium of a hallucinatory psychosis. Normally, respect for reality gains the day. Nevertheless its orders cannot be obeyed at once. They are carried out bit by bit, at great expense of time and cathectic energy, and *in the meantime the existence of the lost object is psychically prolonged*. Each single one of the memories and expectations in which the libido is bound to the object is brought up and hypercathected, and detachment of the libido is accomplished in respect of it. *Why this compromise by which the command of reality is carried out should be extraordinarily painful is not at all easy to explain in terms of economics*. It is remarkable that this painful unpleasure is taken as a matter of course by us. The fact is, however, that when the work of mourning is complete the ego becomes free and uninhibited again.[39]

First I wish to suggest that, for the woman who terminates her pregnancy, menstruation can perform the task of reality testing central to the 'work of mourning'. Blood is a signifier of what Emin and women like her are not: pregnant. As Davies makes clear in her testimony, the sight of blood during and after termination can be a source of relief and grief; it signals the desired end of the pregnancy but also the loss of what could not be. Like post-partum bleeding, a woman can lose blood continuously for weeks after the procedure. It can be argued, therefore, that after a period of latency this original loss is revived and revised by the return of the menses. The body thus acts as a mnemonic reservoir. Its significance is double and paradoxical, however, for it not only reminds the woman that she is no longer pregnant by evoking the bodily condition of that loss, but via the symptoms of menstruation it can revive the symptoms of early pregnancy. This corporeal mnemonic reservoir, whose markers are blood, swollen, tender breasts and cramps, thus at once attests to the 'killing off' of the lost object and yet 'psychically prolong' it. The experience of termination thus resists the woman's and Freud's act of forgetting until the onset of the menopause or a subsequent pregnancy, for it is continuously relived in the present.

The framework of reality testing and psychic prolonging made available by 'Mourning and Melancholia' thus presents an understanding of the embodied processes of mourning that follow termination. It is

Freud's *economic* analysis that underpins his belief in the substitution of love objects. For Freud's 1917 hypothesis cannot account, as he says, for the extraordinarily painful nature of the giving up of such a libidinal attachment. This hypothesis has, moreover, particular implications for women who terminate their pregnancies in pro-natalist societies that always already perceive the foetus as a 'child'. For the absence/impossibility of an appropriate substitute may thus augment and/or prolong mourning. The pressures of the loss of a 'child' within this context may lead, in total contradiction to those reasons that lead to the first termination, to the desire for a second pregnancy, and may even manifest in a desire for a 'replacement child'.[40] I would argue, however, that this 'economic' understanding, though elaborated by an understanding of the social context in which it takes place, may be compelling, but remains only partial.

The shift from Freud's concept of mourning in 'Mourning and Melancholia' to that in the 'Ego and the Id' is highlighted by *Precarious Life: The Powers of Mourning and Violence*, written by Judith Butler. Her powerful analysis seeks to question the politics of grief and retaliation post-9/11. In so doing she draws attention to Freud's theory of the 'interchangeability' of lost love objects, made possible by the notion of a celibate human subject, to that of a more relational social form of subjectivity. In the 'Ego and the Id', Butler argues, Freud

claimed that incorporation, originally associated with melancholia, was essential to the task of mourning. Freud's early hope that an attachment might be withdrawn and then given anew implied a certain interchangeability of objects as a sign of hopefulness, as if the prospect of entering life anew made use of a kind of promiscuity of libidinal aim. That might be true, but I do not think that successful grieving implies that one has forgotten another person or that something else has come to take its place, as if substitutability were something for which we might strive.

Perhaps, rather, one mourns when one accepts that by the loss one undergoes one will be changed, possibly for ever. Perhaps mourning has to do with agreeing to undergo a transformation (perhaps one should say *submitting* to a transformation) the full result of which one cannot know in advance. There is losing, as we know, but there is also the transformative effect of loss, and this latter cannot be charted or planned …

When we lose certain people, or when we are dispossessed from a place, or a community, we simply feel that we are undergoing something temporary, that mourning will be over and some restoration of prior order will be achieved. But maybe when we undergo what we do, something about who we are is revealed, that these ties constitute what we are, ties or bonds that compose us. It is not as if an 'I' exists independently over here and then simply loses a 'you' over there, especially if the attachment to 'you' is part of what composes who 'I' am. If I lose you, under these conditions, then I not only mourn the loss, but I become inscrutable to myself. Who 'am' I, without you? When we lose some of these ties by which we are constituted, we do not know who we are or what to do. On one level I think I have lost 'you' only to discover that 'I' have gone missing as well. At another level, perhaps what I have lost 'in' you, that for which I have no ready vocabulary, is a relationality that is composed neither exclusively of myself nor you, but is to be conceived as *the tie* by which those terms are differentiated and related.[41]

Butler's attention to the 'transformative effect of loss' draws an understanding of mourning closer to Davies's lament for the 'old me' that had existed prior to her termination. More specifically, however, the inter-subjective nature of loss highlighted in *Precarious Life* also brings this text back to Felman's analysis, and what could be argued as a double destabilization of the subject in the case of loss after abortion. First, this takes place via the ideologies that have shaped the politics of reproduction and that impact upon that missing 'I' that so estranges the woman's self. In addition however, I would wish to pursue Freud's desire for 'optimism'. A lost loved one, a person that has informed the continuous process of our becoming as a subject, is not simply remembered as a past object. The ability to grieve for those who have been precious to us and for whom there is no substitute is facilitated by our knowledge that they forever travel with us. A sense of self formed via a bricolage of constitutive encounters enables the subject-us to look to the future with those we have lost. For who they were remains fundamental to who we continue to be. We are, therefore, compelled by them to pick ourselves up as that newly differenced 'I'. In the case of a woman that aborts, however, I would argue that there is no such consolation. There is no memory or encounter beyond the corporeal experience of an unknown other. Thus the means by which abortion 'stays' with the women who have experienced it becomes clearer and is depathologized, for it remains their only signifier. In a culture in which the condition of abortion continues to be silence, Emin's art practice, I would argue, renders that loss and encounter visible at an intersection between creative protocols and a society that conceives the foetus as always already a 'child'.

For Emin, the continued physical act of making reaffirms the decision to be a maker and not a mother. The continued repetition of the subject of abortion may attest to a desire to work through and psychically bind the unpleasure that characterizes the Freudian concept of symbol formation theorized in 'Beyond the Pleasure Principle'. But the ambivalence of loss after termination and the function of these works, I would argue, transgress the expulsion and aggression that underpin the understanding of Freud's theorization.[42] The notion of creative production as a purgative construes its visual results as dead objects; what has been worked-through in the making no longer has any value for the artist. But, to state the obvious, to make is to bring into existence something where before there was nothing. This something exists beyond its making in the studio. The maker has a relationship with his/her artwork, via the memory of both the physicality of its production and what creatively, culturally and historically facilitated it. Thus an artwork cannot be considered with reference only to what is expelled via its making, but also as an object, to what it sustains for the artist. This is particularly pertinent in the case of *The first time I was pregnant I started to crochet the baby a shawl* (1990–2000), because it not only references loss but revives that moment before the loss; it is that point at which, to return to 'Mourning and Melancholia', the existence of the lost object is psychically prolonged.

To conclude with *My Bed*: not all women are traumatized by the experience of termination, but Emin was. Trauma is dependent on two events, the actual event and then, after a period of latency, its revival and revision by a concomitant experience. A detailed reading of the specific circumstances that surround the production of *My Bed* must be carried out before this reading can progress any further. Emin's creative engagement with her abortions transcends, and, I suspect, negotiates existing representations of this experience in popular culture. It sustains in the visible world the experience of loss and grief of which she cannot let go, because there is nothing else that connects her to it, nothing else to show for it.

# NOTES

### Editors' Introduction

1 Catherine Clément and Julia Kristeva, *The Feminine and the Sacred* [1998], trans. Jane Marie Todd (New York: Columbia University Press, 2001).
2 Clément and Kristeva: *The Feminine and the Sacred*, p. 27
3 Sigmund Freud, *Moses and Monotheism* [1939], The Penguin Freud Library, vol. 13 (London: Penguin, 1985), pp. 237–86.

### Chapter 1. Sacred Cows

1 Catherine Clément and Julia Kristeva, *The Feminine and the Sacred* [1998], trans. Jane Marie Todd (New York: Columbia University Press, 2001), p. 1.
2 Clément and Kristeva: *The Feminine and the Sacred*, p. 2.
3 Clément and Kristeva: *The Feminine and the Sacred*, p. 12.
4 Clément and Kristeva: *The Feminine and the Sacred*, p. 14.
5 Clément and Kristeva: *The Feminine and the Sacred*, p. 14.
6 For a fascinating and important collection of varying traditions of the sacred and women of Africa, see Ivan van Sertima (ed), *Black Women in Antiquity* (London: Transaction, 1992).
7 Clément and Kristeva: *The Feminine and the Sacred*, p. 28.
8 Julia Kristeva, 'The System and the Speaking Subject' [1973], in Toril Moi (ed), *The Kristeva Reader* (Oxford: Basil Blackwell, 1986), pp. 24–33. This is a basic summary of the argument of Kristeva's doctoral thesis published as *Revolution in Poetic Language* [1974], trans. Margaret Waller (New York: Columbia University Press, 1984).
9 Catherine Clément, *Opera, or, The Undoing of Women* [1979], trans. Betsy Wing (London: Virago, 1989) and Hélène Cixous and Cathérine Clément, *The Newly Born Woman* [1975], trans. Betsy Wing (Minneapolis: University of Minnesota Press, 1991).
10 'Dialogue with Julia Kristeva', in Griselda Pollock (ed) *Julia Kristeva: Aesthetics.Politics.Ethics*, *parallax* 8 (1998), p. 9, emphasis added.
11 Julia Kristeva, 'Signifying Practice and the Mode of Production', trans. Geoffrey Nowell-Smith, *Edinburgh Magazine* 1 (1976), p. 65. For an extended reading of this argument see Griselda Pollock, 'To inscribe in the feminine: A Kristevan Impossibility?' *parallax* 8 (1998), pp. 81–118.

12  Julia Kristeva, *Powers of Horror: An Essay on Abjection* [1980], trans. Leon Roudiez (New York: Columbia University Press, 1982).

13  Julia Kristeva: *Powers of Horror*, p. 133.

14  The term imaginary has two sources. Jean-Paul Sartre, *The Imaginary; Phenomenological Psychology of the Imagination* [1940] (London: Routledge, 2004). Lacan took this up by making the imaginary one of the three registers of the subject theorized by his psychoanalytical reworking of Freud's topographies: Real, Imaginary and Symbolic. The Imaginary, dominated by the imago and the mirror phase, is the register of fantasy and the image, as opposed to word, thought and the unconscious in the Symbolic. See Frederic Jameson, 'Imaginary and Symbolic in Lacan: Marxism, Psychoanalytical Criticism and the Problem of the Subject', *Yale French Studies* 55–56 (1977), pp. 338–95.

15  Claude Lévi-Strauss, *The Savage Mind* [1962] (London: Weidenfeld and Nicholson, 1988).

16  Jane Harrison, 'Introduction,' in *Themis: A Study of the Social Origins of Greek Religion* [1912] (London: Merlin, 1963), p. xi.

17  Aby Warburg, *Images from the Region of the Pueblo Indians in North America*, trans. Michael Steinberg (Ithaca: Cornell University Press, 1995), p. 53. Written in 1923, this was originally published as 'Lecture on the Serpent Ritual', *Journal of the Warburg and Courtauld Institutes* 2 (1938–9), pp. 277–92.

18  Karl Marx, *Grundrisse: Foundations of the Critique of Political Economy* [1857–78], trans. Martin Nicolaus (Harmondsworth: Penguin, 1973), p. 110.

19  Walter Benjamin, 'The Work of Art in the Age of Mechanical Reproducibility', in *Illuminations*, ed. Hannah Arendt, trans. Harry Zohn (London: Fontana, 1973), pp. 219–54.

20  Virginia Woolf, *Three Guineas* [1938] (Harmondsworth: Penguin, 1977), p. 55.

21  Virginia Woolf, *A Room of One's Own* [1928] (Harmondsworth: Penguin, 1974), p. 19, emphasis added.

22  Martha C. Carpentier, *Ritual, Myth and the Modernist Text: The Influence of Jane Harrison on Joyce, Eliot and Woolf* (Amsterdam: Gordon and Breach, 1998), p. 67.

23  Jane Harrison, *Ancient Art and Ritual* [1913] (Montana: Kessinger, n.d.).

24  In addition to Jane Harrison, the group included Gilbert Murray, A. B. Cook, and Francis Cornford. See Robert Ackerman, *The Myth and Ritual School* (London: Routledge, 2002).

25  A band of revelling worshippers such as the *Bacchae*. My thanks to Lois Williams for this definition. Jane Harrison's argument is that the original is the band of which one individual emerges to become its representative figure, thus producing the god as a late personalization and individuation of what was originally the group of communal activity of the ritual. See Harrison: *Themis, passim*.

26  Harrison: *Themis*, p. xiii. My thanks to Miranda Mason for finding this book for me. See also Sue Blundell and Margaret Williamson (eds), *The Sacred and the Feminine in Ancient Greece* (London: Routledge, 1998), which deals with Classical Greece.

27  See also Robert Graves, *The White Goddess* (London: Faber and Faber, 1948).

28  For a study of this figure and its role in Christianity's mythos, see Hyam Maccoby, *The Sacred Executioner: Human Sacrifice and the Legacy of Guilt* (London: Thames and Hudson, 1982).

29  Julia Kristeva, 'Experiencing the Phallus as Extraneous, or Women's Twofold Oedipus Complex', in Griselda Pollock (ed), *Julia Kristeva: Aesthetics.Politics.Ethics. parallax* 8 (1998), p. 40.

30  Kristeva: 'Experiencing the Phallus', p. 41.

31  Kristeva: 'Experiencing the Phallus', p. 41.

32  Gayatri Chakravorty Spivak, 'French Feminism in an International Frame' [1981], in *In Other Worlds: Essays in Cultural Politics* (New York and London: Methuen, 1987), p. 150.

33  On this point see Ellen Handler Spitz, 'Psychoanalysis and the Legacies of Antiquity', in Lynn Gamwell and Richard Wells (eds), *Sigmund Freud and Art: His Personal Collection of Antiquities* (New York: Harry Abrams, 1989), pp. 153–72. On Freud's missed relation to the Isis myth, see Joan Raphael-Leff, 'If Oedipus was an Egyptian: Freud and Egyptology', *International Review of Psychoanalysis* 17 (1990), pp. 309–35 and 'Freud's Dark Continent', *Aspects of Egypt, parallax* 43 (2007), pp. 41–55.

34  Ilse Grubrich-Simitis, *Early Freud and Late Freud* (London: Routledge, 1997).

35  Mary Douglas, *Purity and Danger: An Analysis of Concepts of Pollution and Taboo* (London: Routledge, 1969).

36  Hyam Maccoby, *Ritual and Morality: The Ritual Purity System and its Place in Judaism* (Cambridge: Cambridge University Press, 1999), p. vii. The relation between the ritual system and morality argued for by Maccoby parallels the work of Julia Kristeva who explains how concepts such as justice and mercy emerged out of the 'abomination' system of Judaic monotheism: see Kristeva: *Powers of Horror*, pp. 90–112.

37  Kristeva: *Powers of Horror*, p. 90–1.

38  Kristeva: *Powers of Horror*, p. 91.

39  This traumatic quality of the infant's encounter with the outside, sexuality, language and desire that are introduced into the child too premature to grasp their meaning is the basis of the seduction theory advanced by Jean Laplanche, *Life and Death in Psychoanalysis* [1970], trans. Jeffrey Mehlman (Baltimore: Johns Hopkins University Press, 1993) and *Essays on Otherness* (London: Routledge, 1999).

40  Sigmund Freud, *Totem and Taboo* [1913], in *The Origin of Religion*, Penguin Freud Library vol. 13 (London: Penguin, 1985), pp. 43–224. Citation is from Kristeva: *Powers of Horror*, p. 56.

41  There is a vast literature on this area. René Girard, *Violence and the Sacred* [1972], trans. Patrick Gregory (Baltimore: Johns Hopkins University Press, 1977). On Bataille, see Carolyn Bailey Gill (ed), *Bataille: Writing the Sacred* (London: Routledge, 1995).

42  Kristeva: *Powers of Horror*, p. 58.

43  Bracha Ettinger contrasts two infantile complexes mentioned by Freud in his essay 'The "Uncanny"', those of castration and those of fantasies of the mother's body *Muttersleibphantasien*; the former was frightening in the first place, the latter only as an effect of the 'return of the repressed', Bracha L. Ettinger, *The Matrixial Gaze* (Leeds: Feminist Arts and Histories Network, 1995), p. 8; reprinted in Bracha L. Ettinger, *The Matrixial Borderspace*, ed. Brian Massumi (Minneapolis: University of Minnesota Press, 2006).

44  Maccoby: *Ritual and Morality*, pp. 105, 109.

45  Maccoby: *Ritual and Morality*, p. 110.
46  Maccoby notes a connection with the ideas of Christian baptism which is declared to be a kind of rebirth in which the subject is washed in the blood of the lamb. Maccoby: *Ritual and Morality*, p. 113.
47  Bracha L. Ettinger, 'The Red Cow Effect: The Metramorphosis of Hallowing the Hollow and Hollowing the Hallow', *ACT 2 Beautiful Translations* (London: Pluto, 1996), pp. 82–119; reprinted in Mica Howe and Sarah Appleton (eds), *He Said, She Says* (London: Farleigh Dickinson, 2001).
48  See Ettinger: *Matrixial Borderspace*.
49  The phallic functions through figures of metaphor and metonym, substitution, displacement and contiguity. The matrixial figure is *metramorphosis*, deeply associated with the aesthetic processes of painting: 'an organisational mode, based on self-mutual-attunings of borderlinks, which creates and forms matrixial subjectivity. Through metramorphosis a continuous attuning goes on between co-emerging *I(s)* and *non-I(s)*. Metramorphosis regulates asymmetrical libidinal investments in the joint space without aspiring to homogeneity … Metramorphosis is the becoming-threshold of a borderline which allows for relations-without-relating between co-emerging *I(s)* and unknown Other(s). It is the transgression of a borderlink, its transmissability, its conductability … without ever freezing into a frontier.' Bracha L. Ettinger, 'Metramorphic Borderlinks and Matrixial Borderspace' in John Welchman (ed), *Rethinking Borders* (Basingstoke: Macmillan, 1996), p. 129.
50  Lacan developed this concept specifically in his revision of the specular and retheorization of the gaze in *The Four Fundamental Concepts of Psychoanalysis* [1973], trans. Alan Sheridan (Harmondsworth: Penguin, 1977). Ettinger: *The Matrixial Gaze*, is a commentary on this text, extending the field of the gaze into a matrixial stratum. Across her work, Ettinger explores the implications of Lacan's theories of *objet a* and the eternally lost and unsignifiable Thing /Woman. See especially Bracha L. Ettinger, 'Wit(h)nessing Trauma and the Matrixial Gaze: From Phantasm to Trauma, from Phallic Structure to Matrixial Sphere,' *parallax* 7 (2001), pp. 89–114. Here she writes: 'Indexing absence of contact with a psychic originary Thing, resulting from an incision from the Other (the Other as body, or as the body of the mother, or as the m/Other)—the *objet a* engenders the subject along few unconscious dimensions, and vision is a privileged one of them. A left-over of the activity of the scopic drive in the Real, the *objet a* is cleft from the subject as well as from the Other, and it has no direct representation by image. In the field of vision such a split *objet a* is the gaze,' p. 89, and 'The Other is here to be understood as archaic body/mother first amalgamated in symbiosis and then forever separated from me. The subject is founded "*only as a* [relation] of *lack* to this *(a)*",' p. 92.
51  Ettinger: 'The Red Cow Effect', p. 87.
52  Ettinger: 'The Red Cow Effect', p. 87.
53  Ettinger: 'The Red Cow Effect', p. 105.
54  Sigmund Freud, 'The "Uncanny"' [1919], in *Art and Literature*, Penguin Freud Library vol. 14 (London: Penguin, 1985), p. 371.
55  Ettinger: 'The Red Cow Effect', p. 106.
56  Ettinger: 'The Red Cow Effect', p. 107.

57  Ettinger: 'The Red Cow Effect', pp. 107, 108.
58  Ettinger: 'The Red Cow Effect', p. 108.
59  Ettinger: 'The Red Cow Effect', pp. 108–9.
60  Julia Kristeva, 'Women's Time', in Toril Moi (ed), *The Kristeva Reader* (Oxford: Basil Blackwell, 1987), 187–231.
61  Ettinger: 'The Red Cow Effect', p. 109. This will lead Ettinger onto Antigone and her sacrifice which she discusses in 'Transgressing With-in-to the Feminine' in Penny Florence and Nicola Foster (eds), *Differential Aesthetics* (London: Ashgate, 2000), pp. 185–210.
62  Bracha L. Ettinger, 'The Becoming Threshold of Matrixial Borderlines', in George Robertson, *et al.* (eds), *Travellers' Tales: Narratives of Home and Displacement* (London: Routledge, 1994), p. 40.
63  Bracha Lichtenberg Ettinger, *Matrix: a Shift Beyond the Phallus* (Paris: BLE Atelier, 1993), p. 3.
64  Kristeva: 'Women's Time,' pp. 188–93.
65  Emmanuel Levinas in conversation in Bracha Ettinger, *Que Dirait Eurydice?/What Would Eurydice Say?* (Paris: BLE Atelier, 1997), p. 29.

## Chapter 2. 'The Priestess of Athena Grows a Beard'

1  The material assembled here and much of the argumentation derives from my book *Citizen Bacchae: women's ritual practice in Ancient Greece* (Berkeley CA: University of California Press, 2004) and is published here by the kind permission of the University of California Press. Other recent works on ancient Greek women's religion include Matthew Dillon, *Girls and Women in Classical Greek Religion* (London: Routledge, 2002) and Susan Guettel Cole, *Landscapes, Gender and Ritual Space* (Berkeley CA: University of California Press, 2004).
2  A comprehensive introduction to Greek religion is offered in Walter Burkert, *Greek Religion*, trans. John Raffan (Cambridge, MA and London: Harvard University Press, 1985). More recent but more modest is Louise Bruit Zaidman and Pauline Schmitt Pantel, *Religion in the Greek City*, trans. Paul Cartledge (Cambridge: Cambridge University Press, 1995).
3  The number of good introductory books on women in the ancient world is large, and growing. Perhaps the best place to start is Elaine Fantham *et al.* (eds) *Women in the Classical World.: image and text* (New York: Oxford University Press, 1994). But see also Helene P. Foley (ed), *Reflections of Women in Antiquity* (New York, London and Paris: Gordon and Breach, 1981); Averil Cameron and Amelie Kuhrt (eds), *Images of Women in Antiquity* (London: Routledge, 1993); Richard Hawley and Barbara Levick (eds), *Women in Antiquity: new assessments* (London and New York: Routledge, 1995); Sue Blundell, *Women in Ancient Greece* (London: British Museum, 1995).
4  As well as the books mentioned in note 1, on the topic of ancient Greek women's ritual practice. see Pierre Brulé, *La Fille d'Athènes: la religion des filles à Athènes à l'époque classique* (Paris: Belles Lettres, 1987), Ross Kraemer, *Her Share of the Blessings* (New York: Oxford University Press, 1992) and Sue Blundell and Margaret Williamson (eds), *The Sacred and the Feminine in Ancient Greece* (London: Routledge, 1998).
5  See Roger Just, *Women in Athenian Law and Life* (London and New York: Rout-

ledge, 1989), p. 23.

6    On this myth see especially Helene P. Foley, *The Homeric Hymn to Demeter* (Princeton NJ: Princeton University Press, 1994). On the *Thesmophoria* see especially Froma I. Zeitlin, 'Cultic Models of the Female: Rites of Dionysus and Demeter', *Arethusa* 15 (1982), pp. 129–57.

7    The legal speech is Isaeus 8.19–20; the inscription is *Inscriptiones Graecae* ii²1184, a fourth-century inscription which concerns women in the Athenian neighbourhood of Cholargos providing the priestess of Demeter with supplies for the celebration.

8    This inscription is *Lois Sacrées de l'Asie Mineure* no. 61, 5. See also Marcel Detienne, 'The Violence of Well-born Ladies' in Marcel Detienne and J. P. Vernant (eds), *The Cuisine of Sacrifice among the Greeks*, trans. Paula Wissing (Chicago and London: University of Chicago Press, 1989).

9    See on this topic Susan Guettel Cole, 'Demeter in the Ancient Greek City and its Countryside', in Susan E. Alcock and Robin Osborne (eds), *Placing the Gods: sanctuaries and sacred space in Ancient Greece* (Oxford: Oxford University Press, 1994), pp. 199–216.

10   A well-known work on this aspect of initiation is Pierre Vidal-Naquet, *The Black Hunter: forms of thought and forms of society in the Greek World*, trans. Andrew Szegedy-Maszak (Baltimore and London: Johns Hopkins University Press, 1986).

11   The classic statement is Joan Bamberger, 'The myth of matriarchy: why men rule in primitive societies', in M. Z. Rosaldo and L. Lamphere (eds), *Woman, Culture and Society* (Stanford CA: Stanford University Press, 1974).

12   See also Detienne: 'The Violence of Well-born Ladies'.

13   On sacrificial distribution of meat between men and women see Robin Osborne, 'Women and sacrifice in Classical Greece', *Classical Quarterly* 43 (1993), pp. 392–405.

14   On this topic see Dennis D. Hughes, *Human Sacrifice in Ancient Greece* (London: Routledge, 1991).

15   Scholars have different explanations for the prevalence of young women as victims; see e.g. Brulé: *La Fille d'Athènes*, p. 206, and Walter Burkert, *Homo Necans*, trans. Peter Bing (Berkeley CA: University of California Press, 1983), pp. 64–6.

16   See e.g. Douglas Feaver, 'Historical developments in the priesthoods of Athens', *Yale Classical Studies* 15 (1957), pp. 123–58, and Robert Garland, *Introducing New Gods: the politics of Athenian religion* (London: Duckworth, 1992).

17   The best place to start reading about the *Oresteia* is Simon Goldhill, *Aeschylus: the Oresteia* (Cambridge: Cambridge University Press, 1992).

18   This is a fascinating topic that I cannot investigate here. Recent discussions include Gail Holst-Warhaft, *Dangerous Voices: women's laments and Greek literature* (London and New York: Routledge, 1992) and Karen Stears, 'Death Becomes Her: gender and Athenian death ritual', in Sue Blundell and Margaret Williamson (eds), *The Sacred and the Feminine in Ancient Greece* (London: Routledge, 1998).

19   The Greek text may not be completely preserved here and editions differ on exactly how they envisage this procession. For instance, the word I have translated 'girls' could be 'youths' or even 'children'. But it is definitely the case that in the present state of the Greek text there is a preponderance of females.

## Chapter 3. The Sacred, the Feminine and French Feminist Theory

1   G. W. F. Hegel, *Phenomenology of Spirit* [1807], trans. A.V. Miller (Oxford University Press, 1977), pp. 111–19.

2   Simone de Beauvoir, *The Second Sex* [1949], trans. H. M. Parshley (Harmondsworth: Penguin, 1983), p. 174.

3   Julia Kristeva, 'Stabat Mater' in *Tales of Love* [1983], trans. Leon Roudiez (New York: Columbia University Press, 1987), p. 235.

4   Comparing 'Hosea' with modern male pornographic literature, Drorah Setel shows in both cases the presence of such imagery: 'Prophets and Pornography: Female Sexual Imagery in Hosea' in L. Russell (ed), *Feminist Interpretations of the Bible* (Oxford: Blackwell, 1985).

5   Julia Kristeva, *About Chinese Women*, trans. Anita Barrows (New York: M. Boyars, 1974), pp. 19–22. This is given in a slightly different translation in Toril Moi (ed), *The Kristeva Reader* (Oxford: Blackwell, 1986), pp. 141–3.

6   Julia Kristeva, 'La femme, ce n'est jamais ça', an interview by 'psychoanalyse et politique' in *Tel quel*, Autumn 1974, English translation in Elaine Marks and Isabelle de Courtivron (eds), *New French Feminisms* (Brighton: Harvester, 1980), pp. 137–41.

7   Luce Irigaray, *Speculum of the Other Woman* [1974], trans. Gillian C. Gill (Ithaca: Cornell University Press, 1985).

8   Luce Irigaray, 'La Mystérique', in *Speculum of the Other Woman* [1974], trans. Gillian C. Gill (Ithaca: Cornell University Press, 1985), pp. 191–202.

9   Compare Nancy Chodorow, *The Reproduction of Mothering* (Berkeley and Los Angeles: University of California Press, 1978).

10  Luce Irigaray, 'Sexual Difference', trans. Séan Hand, in Toril Moi (ed), *French Feminist Thought: A Reader* (Oxford: Blackwell, 1987), p. 123.

11  Elisabeth Grosz, *Sexual Subversions* (Sydney: Allen & Unwin, 1989), p. 120.

12  Compare Kristeva's discussion in *New Maladies of the Soul* [1993], extract in M. Joy *et al.* (eds), *French Feminists on Religion: A Reader* (London: Routledge, 2002), p. 167.

13  Jean-Paul Sartre, 'Conclusion I'; 'In-Itself and For-Itself: Metaphysical Implications', in *Being and Nothingness* [1943] (London: Routledge, 1989), pp. 617–25.

14  See for example Rosemary Ruether's insightful comments here, *Sexism and God-Talk* (London: SCM, 1983), pp. 159–60.

15  Kristeva: 'Stabat Mater', pp. 234–63. There is further on this theme her 'Motherhood According to Giovanni Bellini', in Julia Kristeva, *Desire in Language* [1975], trans. Leon Roudiez (Oxford: Blackwell, 1982), pp. 237–70.

16  Luce Irigaray, 'Religious and Civil Myths', in *Je, tu, nous* [1990] (London: Routledge, 1993), p. 25.

17  Jacques Derrida, 'The Politics of Friendship', *The Journal of Philosophy* 85 (1998), p. 642.

18  Virginia Woolf, *A Room of One's Own* [1928] (Harmondsworth: Penguin, 1945), p. 81: 'Then I may tell you that the very next words I read were these—"Chloe liked Olivia … " Do not start. Do not blush. Let us admit in the privacy of our own society that these things sometimes happen. Sometimes women do like women. "Chloe liked Olivia," I read. And then it struck me how immense a change was there.'

19  Kristeva is aware of this. See 'Stabat Mater', pp. 236–7.

20 Cf. Rosemary Radford Ruether, *Mary—The Feminine Face of the Church* (London: SCM, 1979).
21 Kristeva: 'Stabat Mater', pp. 241–2.
22 Martin Luther, *Weimarer Ausgabe* (henceforth *WA*) 7.38.6–9 (German), 7.69.12–15 (Latin).
23 *WA* 39.I.521.5–522.3.
24 *WA* 31.II.405.2–5.
25 I remember the impression it made on me in France in 1959 (only ten years after de Beauvoir's famous book) that Madame and Monsieur in the family with whom I stayed, lived separate and gender-specific lives. When not at work Monsieur sat in the park, the home and family entirely the concern of the motherly woman who included me among her brood. It was a world away from that in which I had grown up.
26 Luce Irigaray, 'Towards a Divine in the Feminine', in G. Howie (ed), *Women and the Divine* (Basingstoke: Palgrave Macmillan, forthcoming 2007).
27 WA 45.356.17–19.
28 Elisabeth Schüssler Fiorenza, *In Memory of Her* (London: SCM, 1983).
29 Luce Irigaray, 'Equal to Whom?', trans. Robert L. Mazzola, *Differences* 1/2 (1989), pp. 59–76.
30 Daphne Hampson, 'On Not Remembering Her', *Feminist Theology* 19 (1998), pp. 63–83.
31 Ludwig Feuerbach, *The Essence of Christianity* [1841], trans. G. Eliot (New York: Harper Torchbooks, 1957), pp. 29–30.
32 Luce Irigaray: 'Sexual Difference', p.125.
33 Luce Irigaray: 'Sexual Difference', p. 124.
34 Luce Irigaray: 'Sexual Difference', p. 121.
35 Luce Irigaray: 'Sexual Difference', p. 127.
36 Nancy Fraser, 'The Uses and Abuses of French Discourse Theories for Feminist Politics', in Nancy Fraser and S. L. Bartky (eds), *Revaluing French Feminism* (Bloomington, IN: Indiana University Press, 1992), pp. 177–94.
37 The ideas present in this rather dense paragraph I consider in detail in Daphne Hampson, *After Christianity*, second edn. (London: SCM, 2002).

## Chapter 4. The Feminine, the Sacred and the Shared

1 Catherine Clément and Julia Kristeva, *The Feminine and the Sacred* [1998], trans. Jane Marie Todd (New York; Columbia University Press, 2001), p. 165.
2 Helene Basu and Pnina Werbner (eds), *Embodying Charisma: Modernity, Locality and the Performance of Emotion in Sufi Cults* (London: Routledge, 1998), pp. 3–4.
3 For these issues, see, for instance, Saiyid Athar Abbas Rizvi, *A History of Sufism in India*, 2 vols (New Delhi: Munshiram Manoharlal, 1978–83), and Riazul Islam, *Sufism and its Impact on Society in South Asia* (Oxford: Oxford University Press, 1999).
4 Clément and Kristeva: *The Feminine and the Sacred*, p. 167. For a recent investigation into South Asian Sufism that would suggest a very different picture, see S. B. Abbas, *Female Voice in Sufi Ritual: Devotional Practices of Pakistan and India* (Austin: University of Texas Press, 2003).
5 For orientation in this complex area, see the work of the classic scholars of Su-

fism, Annemarie Schimmel, Henry Corbin and Louis Massignon; see also I. R. Netton, *Muslim Neoplatonists* (Edinburgh: Edinburgh University Press, 1991).

6   See Helene Basu and Pnina Werbner, 'The Embodiment of Charisma', in Helene Basu and Pnina Werbner (eds), *Embodying Charisma: Modernity, Locality and the Performance of Emotion in Sufi Cults* (London: Routledge, 1998), p. 8.

7   Mark R. Woodward, 'Modernity and the Disenchantment of Life: A Muslim-Christian Contrast', and Lukas Werth, 'Pakistan: A Critique of the Concept of Modernity', both in Johan Meuleman (ed), *Islam in the Era of Globalization: Muslim Attitudes towards Modernity and Identity* (London: Routledge Curzon, 2002), pp. 111–42 and 143–70 respectively.

8   Basu and Werbner: 'The Embodiment of Charisma', p. 3. See also Katherine Pratt Ewing, *Arguing Sainthood: Islam, Modernity and Psychoanalysis* (Durham, NC: Duke University Press, 1997).

9   Sam Landell Mills, 'The Hardware of Sanctity: Anthropomorphic Objects in Bangladeshi Sufism' in Helene Basu and Pnina Werbner (eds), *Embodying Charisma: Modernity, Locality and the Performance of Emotion in Sufi Cults* (London: Routledge, 1998), pp. 31–55.

10  I refer here to the debate surrounding the exact nature of South Asian 'syncretism'. It is now acknowledged that the labelling of popular South Asian Islam as 'syncretic' participates within a complex discursive tradition of subordinating it to Hinduism while cloaking, too, the myriad Hinduisms that exist across South Asia. Rather than read the relationship between the two religions as syncretic, glossed as the indigenization of Islam, revisionist scholars are now calling for a model that re-reads that relationship as the Islamicization of the indigenous. The debate is usefully summarized by Basu and Werbner: 'Embodiment of Charisma', p. 19; see also Richard Eaton, *Essays on Islam and Indian History* (Oxford: Oxford University Press, 2000).

11  For *qawwali* see Regula Burckhardt Qureshi, *Sufi Music From India and Pakistan* (Cambridge: Cambridge University Press, 1986), Omar Khalidi, 'Qawwali and Mahfil-i-sama', in Christian W. Troll (ed), *Muslim Shrines in India: Their Character, History and Significance* (Delhi: Oxford University Press, 1992), pp. 257–61, and Abbas: *Female Voice*.

12  Some very useful websites, which replicate the oral traditional sphere for the circulation of hagiography, are <http://www.Dargahajmer.com>, <http://muslim-canada.org/sufi/chishti.htm>, <http://www.ajmerikhawaja.com/systmpl/thecityofajmersharif/>. The last website has excellent audio links to recordings of live *qawwali* performances. All websites last accessed 28 February 2005.

13  As declared by the driver of my taxi during my recent visit to Ajmer Sharif: 'Khwajaji is the hotline to Allah' (the English word was used).

14  For a critique of some of these narratives, see Romila Thapar, *Narratives and the Making of History* (Delhi: Oxford University Press, 2000).

15  Basu and Werbner: 'The Embodiment of Charisma', p. 8.

16  See Ananya Jahanara Kabir, 'Islam', in Prem Poddar and David Johnson (eds), *A Historical Companion to Postcolonial Thought in English* (New York: Columbia University Press, 2005); for Islam in the deserts of Western India and Pakistan, see Dominique Sila-Khan, *Conversions and Shifting Identities: Ramdev Pir and the Ismailis in Rajasthan* (Delhi: Manohar, 2003); for Sufi madmen, see Lukas Werth, 'The Saint

who Disappeared: Saints of the Wilderness in Pakistani Village Shrines', Jurgen Wasim Frembgen, 'The *Majzub* Mama Ji Sarkar; 'A Friend of God Moves from One House to Another', and Katherine P. Ewing, 'A *Majzub* and his Mother: The Place of Sainthood in a Family's Emotional Memory', all in Helene Basu and Pnina Werbner (eds), *Embodying Charisma: Modernity, Locality and the Performance of Emotion in Sufi Cults* (London: Routledge, 1998), pp. 77–94, 140–59 and 160–86 respectively.

17  As pointed out also by Basu and Werbner: 'Embodiment of Charisma'.

18  The *qawwali* in question is 'Chhati aaj hai mere khwaja piya ki/ karam hi karam ki ghata chha rahi hai' (It's the sixth day of the *urs* of my darling Khwaja/ monsoon clouds of blessing and grace are gathering). During my most recent visit to Ajmer Sharif in December 2004, I witnessed a performance of this particular *qawwali*, but have been unable to track down a recording. To make my own practice clear while bringing to this oral traditional primary material the requirements of Western academic convention: questions of authorship and performative ownership are, I suspect, epistemologically inappropriate. Nevertheless for the information especially of would-be listeners, I note details of discography wherever possible. For the ideological issues, see the illuminating discussions surrounding 'copyleft' at <http://www.sarai.net/journal/reader3.html> (accessed 28 February 2005), the online version of the *Sarai Reader 03: Shaping Technologies* (Delhi and Amsterdam: Sarai, CSDS, and the Waag Society for Old and New Technologies, 2003). Following tradition, I cite all *qawwalis* by first couplet or first line, except where they have come to be known by, or have entered discography via a 'title'; all translations from Urdu/ Hindi/ Hindustani are my own.

19  'Apni masti mein' (In my own ecstasy), in Hamsar Hayat and Friends, *Apni Masti: Qawwalis from Delhi* (New Delhi: Ektara Music, 2002).

20  For example, 'Bhar do jholi meri tajdar-e-madina' (Fill my sack, O Crowned One of Medina), Sabri Brothers, *Tajdar-e-Haram* (Birmingham: Oriental Star Agencies, 1996); this *qawwali* is, however, addressed to the Prophet.

21  For Meera, and her songs, see Parita Mukta, *Upholding the Common Life: The Community of Mirabai* (Oxford: Oxford University Press, 1997); for 'Meera' qawwalis, see 'Khwaja ki deewani' in Sabri Brothers, *Soofiana Qawwalian* (Hayes End: Shalimar Recordings, 1980); and 'Apni Masti Mein', in Hamsar Hayat and Friends, *Apni Masti: Qawwalis from Delhi* (New Delhi: Ektara Music, 2002).

22  Sabri Brothers: 'Khwaja ki deewani'.

23  Qawwali heard by author at Ajmer Sharif, January 2005.

24  For the Amir Khusrau tradition, including some excellent translations of Khusrauvian proto-qawwalis, see <http://www.alif-india.com/> (accessed 28 February 2005; the site has a link to Hayat: *Apni Masti*). These qawwalis are comparatively accessible: for different versions of 'Chhaap tilak', for instance, see Nusrat Fateh Ali Khan, 'Main jaagi piya ke sangh', in *Nusrat Fateh Ali Khan: Live at the Kufa Gallery, London, December 1989: Traditional Sufi Qawwalis* (London: Navras Records, 1993), and Jafar Husain Khan Badauni and Party, *Qawwali, Volume 1*, side B (Delhi: Music Today, 1992), only available on audio cassette.

25  'Bahut kathin hai dagar panghat ki' (the way to the water is fraught with difficulty), Badauni and Party: *Qawwali Volume 1*, side A.

26  Badauni and Party: *Qawwali Volume 1*, side A.

27 *Qawwali* heard by author at Ajmer Sharif, January 2005.
28 Hamsar Hayat, 'Sajdah', in Hamsar Hayat and Friends, *Apni Masti: Qawwalis from Delhi* (New Delhi: Ektara Music, 2002).
29 In DVD video, Qasim Riza Shaheen, *Anokha Ladla: Only the Moon to Play With* (Manchester: Anokha Ladla, 2004).
30 Qasim Riza Shaheen, *Only the Moon to Play With* (Manchester: Anokha Ladla, 2004), p. 14.
31 Qasim Riza Shaheen, personal communication, Manchester, 13 December 2004.
32 Basu and Werbner: 'Embodiment of Charisma', p. 8.
33 This paper is born out of a long affective investment in *qawwali* and Sufism. Those who appeared, often seemingly mysteriously, as shaping influences, include: Huma Dar, Nalini Delvoye, Mahmood Farooqui, Jay Prosser, Qasim Riza Shaheen, Montu Saxena, Samira Sheikh; thanks to them and the forces that enable such capricious yet benevolent connections; and eternal gratitude to my family for the space to express these thoughts.

## Chapter 5. The Sacred and the Feminine
1 Catherine Clément and Julia Kristeva, *The Feminine and the Sacred* [1998], trans. Jane Marie Todd (New York: Columbia University Press, 2001).
2 Mercy Amba Oduyoye, *The African Experience of God through the Eyes of an Akan Woman.* <http://www.aril.org/african.html> pp. 1–9. Mercy Amba Oduyoye is a widely known African woman theologian, author of several books and articles and the initiator of The Circle of Concerned African Women Theologians, <info@icwt.org> that was conceived to enable African women to contribute to the theological literature being developed by Africans. Since its inauguration in October 1989, The Circle has published pan-African books and regional African ones.
3 Simone de Beauvoir, *The Second Sex* [1949], trans. H.M. Parshley (London: Four Square, 1960), p. 9.
4 I first presented this theory at an AAWORD (Association of African Women for Research and Development) conference in 1981, proceedings of which were published as *Women and Rural Development in Africa* in 1986. A longer discussion of the concept appears in another paper, 'The Feminist Writer and Her Commitment', first published in the *Nigerian Guardian*, 21 December 1983 and later in Eldred Jones and Eustace Palmer (eds), *Women in African Literature Today* (London: Heinemann, 1986). Both essays can be found in my collection of essays, Molara Ogundipe-Leslie, *Recreating Ourselves: African Women and Critical Transformations* (Trenton, African World, 1994).
5 Clément and Kristeva: *The Feminine and the Sacred*, p. 13.
6 Clément and Kristeva: *The Feminine and the Sacred*, p. 14.
7 Clément and Kristeva: *The Feminine and the Sacred*, p. 21.
8 Clément and Kristeva: *The Feminine and the Sacred*, p. 22.
9 Clément and Kristeva: *The Feminine and the Sacred*, p. 6.
10 Babacar Mbow, Personal communication, 4 October 2005.
11 Mbow: Personal communication.
12 Clément and Kristeva: *The Feminine and the Sacred*, p.7.
13 Mbow: Personal communication.

14   Clément and Kristeva: *The Feminine and the Sacred*, p. 64.

15   Mbow: Personal communication.

16   Clément and Kristeva: *The Feminine and the Sacred*, p. 9.

17   Marieme Gueye, Personal communication, 1 November 2005. Babacar Mbow, Personal communication, 3 November 2005.

18   Omar Sougou, Personal communication, 30 December 2004. Aissatou Kane, Personal communication, 31 December 2004.

19   Mbow: Personal communication, November 2005.

20   Mbow: Personal communication, October 2005.

21   Gueye: Personal communication.

22   Gueye: Personal communication.

23   Mbow: Personal communication, October 2005.

24   Toni Morrison, *Beloved* (London: Chatto and Windus, 1987).

25   Oduyoye: *The African Experience of God through the Eyes of an Akan Woman*.

26   Clément and Kristeva: *The Feminine and the Sacred*, p. 14.

27   Marcel Griaule, *Conversations with Ogotommeli* (London, Oxford University Press, 1976). Ogotommeli, a sage of the Dogon of Mali, West Africa discusses at length the Dogon balance of gender and the body and the important place of menstruation in the creation of the world.

28   Ogundipe-Leslie: *Recreating Ourselves: African Women and Critical Transformations*, pp. 212–14.

29   Mbow: Personal communication, November 2005.

30   Chinua Achebe (b.1930) is the renowned Nigerian novelist.

31   Griselda Pollock, Personal communication, 12 October 2005. The film, *To Walk Naked* (Dirs. Meitjes, Maingard and Thompson), a short documentary about a 1990 incident in apartheid South Africa in which a group of black women stripped in front of white policemen intent on bulldozing their homes, was shown by Penny Siopis in the section *Myth*, of her installation, *Three Essays on Shame*, at the Freud Museum, London, in June 2005, curated by Jennifer Law.

32   I was told by a very reliable source who would wish to be anonymous that Mrs Funlayo Ransome-Kuti, the great fighter for women's rights in Nigeria and the mother of the legendary musician, Fela Anikulapo-Kuti, stripped in the palace at the king's throne, before the king at the time, the Alake of Abeokuta.

33   Stephen A. Akintoye, 'Yoruba History from Early Times to the 20th Century', in Nike S. Lawal, Matthew N. O. Sadiku, and P.Ade Dopamu (eds), *Understanding Yoruba Life and Culture* (Trenton, Asmara: Africa World, 2004), pp. 4–5.

34   See Wande Abimbola, *Ifa Divination Poetry* (New York, Nok, 1977).

35   Perhaps the habit of insisting on one lone female member in government cabinets and other administrative groups is an atavistic echo in modern Nigeria from the deep unconscious memory or the imaginary of the ethnic group!

36   Abimbola: *Ifa Divination Poetry*, p. v.

37   Wande Abimbola, 'The Bag of Wisdom: Osun and the Origins of Ifa Divination', in Joseph M. Murphy and Mei-Mei Sanford (eds), *Osun Across the Waters: A Yoruba Goddess in Africa and the Americas* (Bloomington: Indiana University Press, 2001), p. 141.

38   Wande Abimbola: 'The Bag of Wisdom', p. 149.

39   Wande Abimbola: 'The Bag of Wisdom', p. 144.

40  Wande Abimbola: 'The Bag of Wisdom', p. 144.

41  Wande Abimbola: 'The Bag of Wisdom', pp. 144–6.

42  See for instance a discussion of such modern day religious conflicts and compe-
    titions for the mind of the contemporary Nigerian in Jacob Olupona, 'Orisa
    Osun: Yoruba Sacred Kinship and Civil Religion in Osogbo, Nigeria, in Joseph
    M. Murphy and Mei-Mei Sanford (eds): *Osun Across the Waters: A Yoruba Goddess
    in Africa and the Americas* (Bloomington: Indiana University Press, 2001), pp. 46–
    67.

43  Rowland Abiodun, Personal communication, 2 January 2005. See also his 'Hidden
    Power: Osun, the Seventeenth Odu' in Joseph M. Murphy and Mei-Mei Sanford
    (eds), *Osun Across the Waters: A Yoruba Goddess in Africa and the Americas* (Bloom-
    ington: Indiana University Press, 2001), pp. 10–33.

44  Rowland Abiodun: Personal communication.

45  Diedre L. Bádéjò, 'The Goddess Osun as a Paradigm for African Feminist Crit-
    icism', *Sage* 6/1 (1989), pp. 27–32.

## Chapter 6. The Becoming-Woman of the East/West Conflict

1   Giorgio Agamben, *Homo Sacer: Sovereign Power and Bare Life,* trans. Daniel Heller-
    Roazen (Stanford, CA.: University of Stanford Press, 1998), p. 3.

2   Agamben: *Homo Sacer*, p. 9.

3   Agamben: *Homo Sacer*, p. 8.

4   Agamben: *Homo Sacer*, p. 8.

5   Agamben: *Homo Sacer*, pp. 100, 114.

6   As Joyce M. Davis writes, martyrdom is 'the biggest threat, according to some
    scholars, facing the United States and the Western world since the Soviet missiles
    of the cold war'. See Joyce M. Davis, *Martyrs: Innocence, Vengeance and Despair in the
    Middle East* (New York: Palgrave Macmillan, 2003), pp. 14–15.

7   Christoph Reuter, *My Life is a Weapon: A Modern History of Suicide-bombing,* trans.
    Helena Ragg-Kirkby (Princeton: Princeton University Press, 2004), p. 16.

8   Jean Baudrillard, *Screened Out*, trans. Chris Turner (London: Verso, 2002), p. 69.

9   Michel Foucault, *The History of Sexuality Volume 1: The Will to Knowledge* [1976],
    trans. Robert Hurley (Harmondsworth: Penguin, 1990), pp. 138, 139.

10  Foucault: *History of Sexuality*, p. 138.

11  Foucault: *History of Sexuality*, pp. 138, 139.

12  Foucault: *History of Sexuality*, p. 138.

13  Baudrillard: *Screened Out*, p. 68.

14  Baudrillard: *Screened Out*, p. 69.

15  Baudrillard: *Screened Out*, p. 48.

16  Baudrillard: *Screened Out*, p. 48.

17  Baudrillard: *Screened Out*, p. 67.

18  Baudrillard: *Screened Out*, p. 48.

19  Agamben writes: 'If today there is no longer any one clear figure of the sacred
    man, it is perhaps because we are all virtually *homines sacri*.' See Agamben: *Homo
    Sacer*, p. 115.

20  Agamben: *Homo Sacer*, p. 133.

21  Alain Badiou, *Ethics: An Essay on the Understanding of Evil,* trans. Peter Hallward
    (London: Verson, 2001), pp. xiii, 13.

22 Agamben: *Homo Sacer*, p. 176.

23 Foucault: *History of Sexuality*, p. 145.

24 Badiou: *Ethics*, p. xiii.

25 Emmanuel Levinas, *Otherwise than Being Or Beyond Essence,* trans. Alphonso Lingis (Pittsburgh: Duquesne University Press, 1998), p. 117.

26 Agamben: *Homo Sacer*, p. 171.

27 Levinas: *Otherwise than Being*, p. 112.

28 Davis: *Martyrs*, pp. 99, 110. See also the words of Munir al Makdah, quoted by Davis: 'As long as there is one occupier on Palestinian land, there should not be any security for this occupation and for the Israeli people in their houses, not even in their bedrooms. They shall be a target for all of our freedom fighters no matter where they are on Palestinian land. They are not allowed to walk in the streets in peace. They are not allowed to eat pizza …' Davis: *Martyrs*, p. 161.

29 See Jacques Derrida and Anne Dufourmantelle, *Of Hospitality. Anne Dufourmantelle invites Jacques Derrida to respond*, trans. Rachel Bowlby (Stanford: Stanford University Press, 2000), p. 4.

30 Shaykh Muhammad Husayn Fadlallah, 'Interview: 11 September, terrorism, Islam, and the Intifada', *Journal of Palestine Studies* 31/2 (2002), p. 80.

31 See Derrida and Dufourmantelle: *Of Hospitality*, pp. 93–109, especially Derrida's discussion of *Oedipus at Colonus*.

32 This literally means occupying the passenger's seat next to the driver. This is undoubtedly a position that exposes its occupier to a risk of death over which s/he has no control and with regard to which s/he carries no responsibility. See Baudrillard: *Screened Out*, p. 66.

33 Levinas: *Otherwise than Being*, p. 112.

34 Baudrillard: *Screened Out*, p. 66.

35 Baudrillard: *Screened Out*, p. 67.

36 Baudrillard: *Screened Out*, p. 68.

37 G. W. F. Hegel, *The Phenomenology of Mind* [1807], trans. J. B. Baillie (Mineola, NY: Dover Philosophical Classics, 2003), pp. 258–9.

38 Reuter: *My Life is a Weapon*, pp. 1–2.

39 Foucault: *History of Sexuality*, p. 139.

40 This love of death is emphasized repeatedly in interviews with suicide bombers or individuals supporting the practice. Reuter, for example, quotes a young Taliban fighter saying: 'The Americans love Pepsi-Cola. We love death!' In Reuter: *My Life is a Weapon*, p. 139. Often the suicide bomber's love of death is opposed to the West's preoccupation with life. For Israelis, a Palestinian fighter argues, 'life is the most precious of all treasures.' In Barbara Victor, *Army of Roses: Inside the World of Palestinian Suicide-bombers* (London: Constable and Robinson, 2003), p. 250. See also the words of another Palestinian quoted by Reuter: 'We love death just as much as the Jews fear it. For this is the only thing our enemies are afraid of!' Reuter: *My Life is a Weapon*, p. 87.

41 Foucault: *History of Sexuality*, p. 139.

42 Hegel: *Phenomenology of Mind*, pp. 259, 266.

43 Hegel: *Phenomenology of Mind*, p. 276.

44 See Victor's discussion of Ayat al-Akhras, a woman who blew herself up in Jerusalem on 29 March 2002. Victor: *Army of Roses*, pp. 202–11.

45  See Victor: *Army of Roses*, p. 170 and Davis: *Martyrs*, p. 121.
46  Hegel: *Phenomenology of Mind*, p. 266.
47  Hegel: *Phenomenology of Mind*, p. 259.
48  Hegel: *Phenomenology of Mind*, p. 266.
49  Hegel: *Phenomenology of Mind*, p. 266. Hence the custom in the Middle East to stage the burial of suicide bombers as a wedding feast.
50  Derrida and Dufourmantelle: *Of Hospitality*, p. 113.
51  Derrida and Dufourmantelle: *Of Hospitality*, p. 107.
52  Derrida and Dufourmantelle: *Of Hospitality*, p. 113. Israeli authorities do not release the bodies of suicide bombers to their families. The bodies are buried in unmarked graves in a large cemetery in the North of Israel. See Victor: *Army of Roses*, p. 53.
53  I am drawing on Derrida's discussion of *Oedipus at Colonus* here. See Derrida and Dufourmantelle: *Of Hospitality*, pp. 109–15.
54  I am quoting from a draft of the essay "'No woman's law will rot this state": The Israeli racial state and feminist resistance'. The essay was published in *Sociological Research Online* 9/3 (2004), available at <http://www.socresonline.org.uk/9/3/9/3/lentin.html>.
55  Jenny Edkins, *Trauma and the Memory of Politics* (Cambridge: Cambridge University Press, 2003), p. 213.
56  Victor's main question in her analysis of the contemporary phenomenon of female suicide bombing is 'how it can be that women, who are bearers of life, are turned into killing machines?', Victor: *Army of Roses*, p. viii. On p. 171 she writes: 'When religious or political leaders within the Palestinian culture expect their mothers to express joy and pride when their sons and daughters commit suicide attacks, they are inadvertently creating a breed of women who are different from other mothers in other parts of the world.' The woman who has repeatedly been represented as exemplifying this 'other' breed of mothers is Um Nidal. See Victor: *Army of Roses*, pp. 166–73, 176–83.
57  As Reuter tells us, for Khomeini 'weeping counted both as a prelude to martyrdom and … as a terrible weapon against oppression … It was something that should turn into anger and action'. Reuter: *My Life is a Weapon*, p. 49.
58  I am quoting Carol Jacobs' words here in her discussion of Sophocles' *Antigone*. In Carol Jacobs, 'Dusting Antigone', *MLN* 115/5 (1996), p. 908.
59  For Deleuze's understanding of 'minority' see Gilles Deleuze and Félix Guattari, *Kafka: Toward a Minor Literature* [1975], trans. Dana Polan (Minneapolis: University of Minnesota Press, 1986).
60  Agamben: *Homo Sacer*, p. 180.
61  Quoted by Davis: *Martyrs*, p. 185.
62  Reuter: *My Life is a Weapon*, p. 77.
63  Davis: *Martyrs*, p. 143.
64  Reuter: *My Life is a Weapon*, p. 86.
65  Reuter: *My Life is a Weapon*, pp. 83, 101. Reuter emphasizes this again in his discussion of the Iranian dilemma in the 1981 Iran-Iraq war: 'Only one item was in plentiful supply,' he writes, 'people.' *My Life is a Weapon*, p. 44.
66  Judith Butler, *Antigone's Claim: Kinship Between Life and Death* (New York: Columbia University Press, 2000), p. 82.

67  Jean Genet, *Prisoner of Love*, trans. Barbara Bray (New York: New York Review of Books, 2003), p. 429.

68  Agamben: *Homo Sacer*, p. 114.

69  See Thomas R. Flynn's 'Lyotard and history without witnesses', in *Lyotard: Philosophy, Politics, and the Sublime,* ed. Hugh J. Silverman (New York and London: Routledge, 2002), pp. 151–63.

70  Edkins: *Trauma*, p. 189.

71  Shoshana Felman and Dori Laub, *Testimony: Crises of Witnessing in Literature, Psychoanalysis, and History* (New York: Routledge, 1992), p. 82.

72  It might be interesting to compare the 'historical reality of the Holocaust', as Felman and Laub describe it, with the reality of contemporary biopolitics. In her letter to the US ambassador in London, *Guardian* journalist Naomi Klein provides detailed evidence demonstrating her claim in an earlier article (*Guardian*, 6 November 2004) that the US forces in Iraq are eliminating all witnesses. At the end of her letter she writes: 'Mr Ambassador, I believe that your government and its Iraqi surrogates are waging two wars in Iraq. One war is against the Iraqi people, and it has claimed an estimated 100,000 lives. The other is a war on witnesses.' Naomi Klein, 'You asked for my evidence, Mr Ambassador. Here it is', *Guardian*, 4 December 2004.

73  Agamben: *Homo Sacer*, pp. 114, 188.

74  Derrida and Dufourmantelle: *Of Hospitality*, p. 118.

75  Edkins: *Trauma*, p. 189.

76  Badiou: *Ethics*, p. 46.

77  Badiou: *Ethics*, p. 43.

78  Badiou: *Ethics*, p. 40.

79  I am quoting from John Beverley's unpublished essay 'Testimonio and the politics of empire'. The essay was sent to me by the author. It was later included in John R. Beverley, *Testimonio: On the Politics of Truth* (Minneapolis: University of Minnesota Press, 2004).

80  Hannah Arendt, *The Human Condition* [1958], second edn. (Chicago and London: University of Chicago Press, 1998), pp. 178–9.

81  Primo Levi, *The Drowned and the Saved*, trans. Raymond Rosenthal (New York: Vintage International, 1989), pp. 63–4.

82  Borrowing Ranajit Guha's phrase, Beverley calls testimonio 'the small voice of history'. Beverley: 'Testimonio'.

83  Jacques Derrida, *The Gift of Death*, trans. David Wills (Chicago and London: University of Chicago Press, 1995), p. 41.

84  Derrida: *Gift of Death*, p. 41.

85  Amy Wilentz, *Martyr's Crossing* (New York: Simon and Schuster, 2001), p. 261.

86  See Derrida and Dufourmantelle: *Of Hospitality*, pp. 144-54.

87  Beverley: 'Testimonio'.

88  See Gayatri Chakravorty Spivak, 'Can the subaltern speak?', in Patrick Williams and Laura Chrisman (eds), *Colonial Discourse and Post-Colonial Theory: A Reader* (New York: Columbia University Press, 1994), pp. 66–111.

### Chapter 7. Enunciating the Christian *Dieue* and Obscuring the Other

1   Katie Geneva Cannon, *Katie's Canon: Womanism and the Soul of the Black Community*

(New York: Continuum, 1997); Mary Shawn Copeland, 'La différence: Catégorie des théologies critiques pour la libération des femmes', *Concilium* 263 (1996), pp. 187–99; Monique Dumais, 'The Other Salvation: Women as Subjects in Search of Equality', in Don Schweitzer and Derek Simon (eds), *Intersecting Voices: Critical Theologies in a Land of Diversity* (Ottawa: Novalis, 2004), pp. 83–95; Louise Melançon, 'Je crois en Dieue … La théologie féministe et la question du pouvoir', *Théologiques* 2/8 (2000), pp. 77–97.

2   Copeland: 'La différence'; Elspeth Probyn, 'Technologizing the Self: A Future Anterior for Cultural Studies', in Lawrence Grossberg, Cary Nelson and Paula A. Treichler (eds), *Cultural Studies* (New York: Routledge, 1992), pp. 501–11.

3   Cannon: *Katie's Canon*; Mary McClintock Fulkerson, *Changing the Subject: Women's Discourses and Feminist Theology* (Minneapolis: University of Minnesota Press, 1994); Gayatri Chakravorty Spivak, 'Can the Subaltern Speak?' in Lawrence Grossberg and Cary Nelson (eds), *Marxism and the Interpretation of Culture* (Chicago: University of Illinois Press, 1988) pp. 271–313; Gayatri Chakravorty Spivak, 'Practical Politics of the Open End', in *The Post-Colonial Critic: Interviews, Strategies, Dialogues* (New York: Routledge, 1990), pp. 95–112.

4   Denise Couture and Marie-Andrée Roy, 'Dire *Dieue*', in C. Ménard and F. Villeneuve, (eds), *Dire Dieu aujourd'hui* (Montréal: Fides, 1994).

5   'Dieue au féminin', *L'autre Parole* 40 (1988), p. 34; Denise Couture, 'Désapprendre les habitudes inculquées par le "Prince Aspérité"', *L'autre Parole* 51 (1991), pp. 21–30.

6   Lise Baroni, 'Dieu, itinérance infinie', in R. Bergeron, G. Lapointe, and J.-C. Petit (eds), *Itinérances spirituelles* (Montréal: Mediapaul, 2002), pp. 137–51; Dumais: 'The other salvation'; Melançon : 'Je crois en Dieue'; Denise Veillette (ed), *Femmes et Religions* (Québec: Presses de l'Université Laval, 1995).

7   Marie-Éva De Villers, 'Les mots et les expressions propres au Devoir', *Le Devoir*, 5 January 2005.

8   De Villers: 'Les mots'.

9   Eleven per cent of the words and expressions of the lexical group do not belong to any of these three categories. These are 'non-specific, specialised terms from Québecois French, which French journalists have not used, for reasons relating to the subject matter being addressed'. De Villers: 'Les mots'.

10  De Villers: 'Les mots'.

11  Gayatri Chakravorty Spivak, *Outside in the Teaching Machine* (New York: Routledge, 1993), p. 6.

12  Claire Nouvet, 'Gayatri Spivak: Une éthique de la résistance aphone', *Études Littéraires* 31/3 (1999), p. 91.

13  Mary Heather MacKinnon, 'Experience of God' [1960], in Mary Heather MacKinnon and Marie McIntyre (eds), *Readings in Ecology and Feminist Theology* (Kansas City: Sheed and Ward, 1995), pp. 361–75

14  Rebecca Chopp, *The Power to Speak: Feminism, Language, God* (New York: Crossroad, 1989); Pamela Dickey Young, 'The resurrection of whose body? A feminist look at the question of transcendence', *Feminist Theology* 30 (2002), pp. 44–51; Marsha Aileen Hewitt, 'Do women really need a "God/ess" to save them? An Inquiry into Notions of the Divine Feminine', *Method & Theory in the Study of Religion* 10/2 (1998), pp. 149–56; Marilyn J. Legge, 'Colourful differences: "Otherness"

and the Image of God for Canadian Feminist Theologies', *Studies in Religion/Sciences Religieuses* 21/1 (1992), pp. 67–80; Elisabeth Schüssler Fiorenza, *But she said. Feminist Practices of Biblical Interpretation* (Boston: Beacon, 1992).

15  Anne Marie Dalton, 'Human rights and Liberation in Feminist Creation Theology', in Don Schweitzer and Derek Simon (eds), *Intersecting Voices: Critical Theologies in a Land of Diversity* (Ottawa: Novalis, 2004), pp. 121–34; Elizabeth A. Johnson, *She Who Is: The Mystery of God in Feminist Theological Discourse* (New York: Crossroad, 1992); Elizabeth A. Johnson, 'The Character of God' in *Friends of God and Prophets: A Feminist Theological Reading of the Communion of Saints* (New York: Continuum, 1998); Sallie McFague, *Models of God: Theology for an Ecological Nuclear Age* (Minneapolis: Augsburg Fortress 1992); Sallie McFague, *The Body of God* (Minneapolis: Augsburg Fortress, 1993); Sallie McFague, *Life Abundant: Rethinking Theology and Economy for a Planet in Peril* (Minneapolis: Augsburg Fortress, 2001); Anne Primavesi, 'Pantheism', in Letty M. Russell, and J. Shannon Clarkson (eds), *Dictionary of Feminist Theologies* (Louiseville: Westminster John Knox, 1996); Rosemary Radford Ruether, *Sexism and God-Talk: Toward a Feminist Theology* (Boston: SCM, 1983); Rosemary Radford Ruether, *Gaia and God: An Ecofeminist Theology of Earth Healing* (New York: HarperCollins, 1992); Rosemary Radford Ruether, 'Le Dieu des possibilités: transcendance et immanence repensées', *Théologiques* 8/2 (2000), pp. 35–48.

16  Denise Couture, 'La réception du divin féminin de Luce Irigaray en Amérique du Nord: Point de vue québécois', *Religiologiques* 21 (2000), pp. 83–99; Luce Irigaray, 'Femmes divines', in *Sexes et parentés* (Paris: Editions de Minuit, 1987); Luce Irigaray, 'Le divin entre nous', in *Le souffle des femmes: Luce Irigaray présente des crédos au féminin* (Paris: Action Catholique Générale Féminine, 1996), pp. 211–49.

17  Elizabeth A. Johnson, *Dieu au-delà du masculin et du féminin: Celui/Celle qui est* [1992], trans. Pierrot Lambert (Montréal: Paulines, 1999). [All translations of this volume are by the Editors.]

18  Johnson: *Dieu au-delà du masculin et du féminin*, pp. 72–3.

19  Johnson: *Dieu au-delà du masculin et du féminin*, p. 24.

20  Karl Rahner, 'Méditation sur le mot "Dieu"; La connaissance de Dieu', in *Traité fondamental de la foi: Introduction au concept du christianisme* (Paris: Centurion, 1976).

21  Johnson: *Dieu au-delà du masculin et du féminin*, p. 91.

22  Johnson: *Dieu au-delà du masculin et du féminin*, p. 90.

23  Johnson: *Dieu au-delà du masculin et du féminin*, p. 90.

24  Johnson: *Dieu au-delà du masculin et du féminin*, p. 94.

25  Johnson: *Dieu au-delà du masculin et du féminin*. The author also names the trinity 'mutual Love, Love born of Love and non-engendered Love' (p. 354). For the *auteure, She who is* is 'a flame that sets ablaze everything it touches' (p. 356); she is '*she* who is, by nature, pure vitality, *she* who constitutes the profoundly relational source of the being and the entire universe' (p. 376). The term enunciates 'the mystery of Sophia-God as pure vitality' (p. 377), 'an overabundance of actuality that transcends the imagination' (p. 372), or again 'as pure vitality, exuberant, relational in the midst of the vicissitudes of history, like an endless source of new life' (p. 377).

26  Ivone Gebara, 'Dieu pour les femmes', in *Le mal au féminin: Réflexions théologiques à partir du féminisme* (Montréal: L'Harmatton, 1999); Ivone Gebara, 'Dieu et la li-

berté', in *Les eaux de mon puits: Réflexions sur des expériences de liberté* (Bierges: Autres Regards, 2003), pp. 219–56; Dorothee Sölle, *The Silent Cry: Mysticism and Resistance* (Minneapolis: Augsburg Fortress, 2001).

27  Rosi Braidotti, *Patterns of Dissonance: A Study of Women in Contemporary Philosophy* (Cambridge: Polity, 1991); Olivette Genest, 'Langage religieux chrétien et différenciation sexuelle: De quelques évidences', *Recherches féministes* 3/2 (1990), pp. 11–30; Fulkerson: *Changing the Subject*; Luce Irigaray, *Ce sexe qui n'en est pas un* (Paris: Éditions de Minuit, 1977); Elspeth Probyn, *Sexing the Self: Gendered Positions in Cultural Studies* (New York: Routledge, 1992).

28  Rosi Braidotti, 'Sexual difference as a nomadic political project', in *Nomadic Subjects Embodiment and Sexual Difference in Contemporary Feminist Theory* (New York: Columbia University Press, 1994); Chopp: *The Power to Speak*; Spivak: 'Practical Politics'.

29  Rosi Braidotti, 'Towards Sustainable Subjectivity: A View from Feminist Philosophy', in Egon Becker and Thomas Janh (eds), *Sustainability and the Social Sciences: A Cross-disciplinary Approach to Integrating Environmental Considerations into Theoretical Reorientation* (London: Zed, 1999), p. 81. See also Laura Donaldson and Kwok Pui-Lan (eds), *Postcolonialism, Feminism and Religious Discourse* (New York: Routledge, 2002); Gayatri Chakravorty Spivak, *A Critique of Postcolonial Reason: Toward a History of the Vanishing Present* (Cambridge, MA: Harvard University Press, 1999).

30  Braidotti: 'Towards sustainable subjectivity', p. 83.

31  Hewitt: 'Do women really need a "God/ess"', p. 156.

32  Rosi Braidotti, 'Nomadic Subjects. Feminist Postmodernism as Antirelativism', in Ron Bontekoe and Marietta Stepaniants (eds), *Justice and Democracy: Cross-cultural Perspectives* (Honolulu: University of Hawaii Press, 1997), p. 351.

33  Courtney W. Howland, *Religious Fundamentalisms and the Human Rights of Women* (New York: Palgrave Macmillan, 1999).

34  Spivak: 'Can the Subaltern Speak?'; Spivak: *A Critique of Postcolonial Reason*.

## Chapter 8. Sringara Rasa

1  Three causal forces Creation, Preservation, and Destruction revolve in eternal repeating cycles, and the life we know is an infinitesimal part of these cycles. The human soul, a reflection of the Supreme, is born over and over again, until it reaches a level of consciousness which enables it to free itself from the cycle of rebirth, and becomes one with its source. Life as we know it is part of the illusory world, *Maya*. When the soul awakens from this illusion, the cycle of rebirth stops. The three causal factors are given names Brahma, Vishnu, and Siva. At the philosophical level the names serve to facilitate the discussion of phenomena. At the mythological level, they have spawned innumerable stories.

2  *Sivaling*: the term is variously translated as the body, or the symbol of Siva. It is one of the most popular and pervasive symbols of Hinduism. Visually it is a sexual symbol, consisting of an abstracted simplified domelike phallus, *lingam*, nestled in a shallow circular container representing a vagina, *yoni*. The *sivaling* is read on many different levels, one being the union of male and female; on another level, it represents the coming together of mind and body, and on another it is the dynamism of *purusha* and *prakriti* as principles of the manifest universe.

3  Manmohan Ghosh, *The Natyasastra: A Treatise on Hindu Dramaturgy and Histrionics*

*Ascribed to Bharata-Muni*, vol. 2 (Calcutta: Royal Asiatic Society of Bengal, 1950), chapter 6.

4   Scholars generally agree that the *Natya Sastra*, a written text dated between 100 BCE and 100 CE, is a recension of verses passed down orally for hundreds of years. There is some evidence of treatises on particular forms of the arts before and after the *Natya Sastra*, but it remains the sole philosophical and practical compendium of its kind in the ancient Indian world. It is firmly rooted in and makes references to the Vedas (see note 8, below). Commentaries on the *Natya Sastra* itself, critiquing and expanding on its theories, appear from the sixth century CE onwards. Seminal discourses on the *Natya Sastra* include the tenth-century work of Abhinavagupta who also discusses the earlier commentaries of Bhatta Lollata, Srisankuka, Bhatta Nayaka and Bhatta Tauta.

5   Kapila Vatsyayan, *Bharata—The Natya Sastra* (New Delhi: Sahitya Akademi, 1996), p. 19.

6   Theoretical and practical advice on all aspects of drama and dance given in The Natya Sastra includes: preferred building types for theatres, ceremonies for auspicious openings of theatres and for each performance, the making of props and costumes, and the theory of performance. Chapters six and seven focus particularly on the communication of emotion, dividing the process into categories of dominant and transitory 'states' which combine to create 'sentiments'. As well as suggesting appropriate bodily gestures and genres of movement required to express states and sentiments, Bharata expounds on character types ideally suited to convey the desired *rasa*.

7   V. P. Dhananjayan, *A Dancer on Dance: Bharata Kalanjali*, in <http://www.saigan.com/heritage/dance/dhanan.htm>.

8   The Rg Veda was composed between circa 1500 BCE and 1000 BCE. Considered the world's oldest religious text it is composed of 1028 hymns. It was followed by the *Sama, Yajur,* and *Atharva Vedas*. The *Upanishads* were composed c.600 BCE, expounding on ideas stemming from the *Vedas*, but differing in their less rigid emphasis on ritual. The idea of reincarnation and the individual *atman* (soul) is discussed, forming the basis of the later school of Vedanta.

9   The *Bhagavata Gita* recounts an episode of the epic *Mahabharata*, but is considered an important text in its own right. As a narrative it presents a discussion between Arjuna and Krishna on the brink of a decisive battle between warring kinsmen. While the story forms the backdrop, the book's real subject is the nature of life and death, and the role of duty, devotion, and renunciation in an ordinary person's life. Although in the *Gita* Arjuna is encouraged by Krishna to go into righteous battle, its allegorical meaning is well understood and it was one of the major inspirations for Mahatma Gandhi's non-violent resistance campaign.

10  The *Bhagavad Purana* c.300–500 CE, was expanded up to the twelfth century. These are the most recent of the major Hindu texts, and contain several books of mythological stories illustrating the philosophical ideas of the *Vedas* and *Upanishads*. The emphasis, however, is on moral guidance, and the stories reflect the changing mores of the societies and times in which they were recorded or created.

11  The twelfth-century *Gita Govinda* by Jayadeva is written in rhyme, while most Sanskrit poems use other forms of metre and rhythm. It is likely Jayadeva referred

to vernacular conventions in song and poetry, as the *Gita Govinda* was written as song. In turn, folk musicians and vernacular writers emulated Jayadeva's poetic style. Most manuscripts of the Gita Govinda are illustrated, and its scenes were favourite subjects as late as in the eighteenth- and nineteenth-century Pahari and Rajasthan schools of painting.

12  In the play by Kalidasa, King Dusyanta comes across a beautiful young woman living in a hermitage. He learns that the sage of the hermitage, Kanva, has brought her up and that she is in fact the daughter of a celestial nymph, Menaka, and another ascetic, Vishwamitra. He is told that behind this is the god Indra, who being jealous of the powers that Vishwamitra has been acquiring through his penances, has deliberately requested Menaka to seduce him and therefore disturb his spiritual progress. The product of the union is Sakuntala. Menaka, her job being done, abandons the baby in the woods, and returns to her heavenly abode. The baby is protected by woodland birds, and found by Kanva who takes her to his hermitage and brings her up as his daughter. King Dusyanta and Sakuntala fall passionately in love on first meeting, and Dusyanta persuades her to marry him in *Gandharva*—un-witnessed—fashion. Kanva is at this time away from the hermitage and they feel certain that he will give his blessings to the match as all who know of him consider Dusyanta an ideal catch. Soon afterwards, the king is called away on state business, and he reluctantly leaves, promising to send for Sakuntala. Sakuntala inadvertently offends another wandering ascetic, Durvasas, as she does not hear his request for water, being lost in thought about her husband. Durvasas curses Sakuntala, declaring that whoever she is thinking about will forget her, later softening the curse to say he will remember her when she produces a gift given by him. Eventually Kanva decides Sakuntala should go to her husband's home; Sakuntala's friends, aware of the curse, beseech her to take great care of the ring Dusyanta has left her. Unhappily, she loses the ring while bathing in a river, and Dusyanta fails to recognize her when she and the accompanying hermits arrive at his palace. It is decided that Sakuntala should remain near the palace until her baby is born. If the child is indeed King Dusyanta's, he will bear royal birthmarks. Distraught and infuriated at this humiliation, Sakuntala calls to the skies for help, and Menaka, in the form of a bright light, whisks her away to the heavens. Eventually the ring is found by a fisherman, and brought to the court where Dusyanta is devastated by regret as his memory of Sakuntala returns. Fate contrives to bring him to the celestial abode of Sakuntala where he is able to beg forgiveness and bring her back to his palace.

13  Barbara Stoller Miller, 'Sakuntala and the Ring of Recollection', in *The Plays of Kalidasa: Theatre of Memory* (Delhi: Motilal Banarsidass, 1999), pp. 85–176.

14  Among the finest examples of images of *apsaras* are paintings and sculptures of Ajanta and Ellora near Aurangabad, India. The caves were cut into the hillside, and carved and painted over a span of centuries as monsoon retreats for Buddhist monastic orders. The earliest caves date from the second and first centuries BCE and the later caves were completed during the Gupta period, fifth and sixth centuries CE. Cave Seventeen at Ajanta contains the often reproduced image of a dark skinned *apsara* in flight, whose meditative face seems to both accentuate and contradict the movement indicated by her swaying jewellery and head ornaments. Sculptures of *apsaras* are found in the Ellora caves of which there are 34 in total.

As an indication of the religious tolerance of ancient India, it is noteworthy that the Ellora caves contain the shrines and iconography of three faiths, Buddhism, Hinduism, and Jainism.

15  Romila Thapar, *Sakuntala: Texts, Readings, Histories* (New Delhi: Kali for Women, 1999), pp. 40–2.

16  See note 2, above.

17  The term Tantra refers to several traditions within Hinduism dating approximately to the tenth century CE. Much of the symbolism within *Tantra*, however, goes back further. The main thrust of *Tantra* as a particular interpretation of Hindu ideas is that action, not scriptural dependency, is the key to liberation or self-knowledge. Methods employed include breaking taboos of orthodox brahminical Hinduism such as meat-eating and intoxication. Hence the depiction of *Tantric* priests in many Sanskrit plays as drunken, happy-go-lucky, or frightening wanderers. Among many other *Tantric* meditative practices, sexual intercourse is suggested as a means of awakening internal powers within the body. In modern times *Tantric* practices have tended to be viewed with disdain and associated with black magic.

18  The 28 *agamas* associated with *Siva* worship are instructive manuals describing ritual and expounding on their purpose.

19  Excerpt from *The Madras Devadasis Act XXXI*, 27 January 1948. 'Dancing by a woman, with or without *kumbhaharathy* (pot-shaped temple *arati* lamp), in the precincts of a temple or other religious institution, or in any procession of a Hindu deity, idol or object of worship installed in any such temple or institution or at any festival or ceremony held in respect of such a deity, idol or object of worship, is hereby declared unlawful … Any person who performs, permits or abets [temple dancing] is punishable with imprisonment for … six months … A woman who takes part in any dancing or music performance … is regarded as having adopted the life of prostitution and becomes incapable of entering into a valid marriage and. the performance of any [marriage] ceremony … whether [held] before or after this Act is hereby declared unlawful and void.' Source: <http://www.hinduismtoday.com/archives/1993/9/1993-9-12.shtml>.

20  Excerpts of interviews by Frédérique Marglin in *Jagannath Temple: Puri 1975–1981*, published as *Wives of the God/King*, (Oxford: Oxford University Press, 1985): 'It is a custom for us to keep relations with a *brahmin* temple servant, but never with "outsiders." Why should I hide these things? When I had my puberty, I exchanged garlands with this priest (a widower) in whose brother's house I live and I have lived within the boundaries of that relationship always' (Radha of Puri). '[The "reformers"] say I was just a concubine of [my patron]. But he was also one of my gurus. Sometimes, he even worshipped me as a devotee, giving me sandal paste and flowers and doing *puja* to me. He was very religious and built a shrine and a hospital' (Amrapalli of Puri). Source: <http://www.hinduismtoday.com/archives/1993/9/1993-9-12.shtml>.

21  See note 1, above.

22  The root of the idea of the cycle of creation, preservation and destruction is in fact a monotheistic one. The ultimate cause or intelligence responsible for the creation of the universe is Brahman (not to be confused with Brahma). The term

Brahman comes from the word *brahat* that describes the largest thing conceivable by human beings.

23 A. Parthasarthy, 'Consorts of the Three Gods' in Swami Chinmayananda (ed), *Symbolism in Hinduism* (Bombay: Central Chinmaya Mission Trust, 1993), p. 157.

24 Durga and Kali are forms of Parvati, the consort of Siva. As Durga, she can appear benign and calm, or fierce and riding a tiger, ready to battle evil or ignorance. As Kali she becomes more ferocious, revelling in the slaughter of enemies. Kali is often depicted dark blue or black and garlanded with skulls, as is Siva in his destructive mode. Durga and Kali both contain the energizing *prakriti* element of Parvati, but their significance grew in the ninth and tenth centuries BCE. In mythology she was created from the combined energies of all the gods to come to the aid of the *devas* (saintly cosmic beings) in a battle with the *asuras* (cosmic demons).

25 David Frawley, *From the River of Heaven* (2001), at <http://www.hindubooks.org/david_frawley/riverheaven/sanskrit/spiritual_path_pg1.htm>.

26 In Kalidasa's *Sakuntala and the Ring of Recollection,* it is Vak who informs Kanva of Sakuntala's *Gandharva* marriage to King Dushyanta.

27 Samkhya philosophy: one of a number of classical schools of Hindu philosophy which sprang from the need to present ideas of the earlier Vedic and Upanishad ages in clearer form after the influences of Buddhism and Jainism.

28 The manifestations of *prakriti* as nature are an essential element in the visual repertoire of Indian aesthetics.

29 Interview of Kapila Vatsyayan by Uttara Asha Coorlawala, New Delhi, 12 January 2000, in Narthaki Online Interviews <http://www.narthaki.com/info/intervw/intrvw24.html>.

30 Vatsyayan: *Bharata; The Natya Sastra*, p. 19. In Ayurveda, the well-being of an individual is dependent on the balance of three energetic fields, *vata, pitta,* and *kapha,* each controlling distinct aspects of the body's functions.

31 *Sthayibhavas*: the expression of a *rasa* as the dominant state in a work of art or performance.

32 Vatsyayan: *Bharata; The Natya Sastra*, p. 139.

## Chapter 9. *Stabat Mater*—A Nameless Place

Nina Danino's films are distributed by Lux Distribution <http://www.lux.org.uk> and the BFI <http://www.bfi.org.uk>. Clips and stills of *Stabat Mater* can be viewed at <http: //www.luxonline.org.uk>. All images reproduced in this chapter are copyright Nina Danino.

1 Hélène Cixous and Catherine Clément, *La Jeune Née* (Paris: Union Generale d'Editions, 1975), quoted in Toril Moi, *Sexual/Textual Politics* (London: Methuen, 1985), p. 172.

2 Gilles Deleuze, *Cinema 1: The Movement Image* [1983], trans. Brian Massumi (London: Athlone, 1992), p. 73, quoted in De Witt: 'Transfiguration and Transmediation', p. 51.

3 Cixous and Clément: *La Jeune Née*, p. 172, in Moi: *Sexual/Textual Politics*, p. 114.

4 Marina Warner, *Alone Of All Her Sex* (London: Picador, 1976), p. 205.

5  Julia Kristeva, 'Stabat Mater', in *Tales of Love* [1983] (New York: Columbia University Press, 1987), p. 249.
6  Kristeva: 'Stabat Mater', p. 234.
7  Paul Schrader, *Transcendental Style in Film* (New York: Da Capo, 1988), p. 3.
8  S. Brent Plate, 'Ritualising Images: The Frames of Space, Time and Aesthetics', in Catherine Grant (ed), *Visionary Landscapes—The Films of Nina Danino* (London: Black Dog, 2005), p. 9.
9  Raymond Bellour's idea of this other cinema is that of 'a movement which was partial but essential and has never stopped haunting the great representational cinema as the reverse side of itself; abstract cinema or more or less abstract (it has also been called concrete, "integral", conceptual, structural)'. Raymond Bellour, 'The Double Helix', in *Passages de L'image* (Paris: Centre Georges Pompidou, 1990), p. 52.
10  Jacques Lacan, 'God and the *Jouissance* of The Woman', in Juliet Mitchell and Jacqueline Rose (eds), *Feminine Sexuality*, trans. Jacqueline Rose (London: Macmillan, 1982), p. 49.
11  Helen De Witt, 'Transfiguration and Transmediation', in Catherine Grant (ed), *Visionary Landscapes—The Films of Nina Danino* (London: Black Dog, 2005), p. 43.
12  Jean Matthee, 'On Wounds, Artificial Flowers, Orifices and the Infinite: A Response to the Films of Nina Danino', *Undercut* 19 (1990). Reprinted in Nina Danino and Michael Maziere (eds), *The Undercut Reader* (London: Wallflower, 2003), p. 88.
13  James Joyce, *Ulysses* (London: The Bodley Head, 1960).
14  Matthee: 'On Wounds', p. 88.
15  Cixous and Clément: *La Jeune Née*, p. 114.

### Chapter 10. Kathleen Raine

1  Kathleen Raine, *Le Monde vivant de l'imagination* (Paris: Édition du Rocher, 1998), p. 43. All translations in this paper are the author's own.
2  Mircea Eliade, *Le Sacré et le Profane* (Paris: Gallimard, 1956), p. 17.
3  Raine: *Le Monde vivant de l'imagination*, p. 104.
4  Kathleen Raine, *Blake and Antiquity* (London: Routledge, 2002), p. 59.
5  Raine: *Le Monde vivant de l'imagination*, p. 268.
6  Kathleen Raine, *Collected Poems* (Ipswich: Golgonooza Press, 2000), p. 63.
7  Raine: *Collected Poems*, p. 98.
8  Yves Bonnefoy, 'La question de la poésie', in *Entretiens sur la poésie* (Paris: Mercure de France, 1990), p. 305.
9  Raine: *Collected Poems*, p. 23.
10  Raine: *Collected Poems*, p. 94.
11  Raine: *Le Monde vivant de l'imagination*, p. 269.
12  René Lachaud, *Magie et initiation en Egypte pharaonique* (Paris: Dangles, 1999), p. 73.
13  Catherine Clément and Julia Kristeva, *Le Féminin et le sacré* (Paris: Agora, 1998).
14  Raine: *Collected Poems*, p. 129.
15  Christiane Singer, *Histoire d'âme* (Paris: Albin Michel, 2001), p. 148.
16  William Blake, 'Visions of the Daughters of Albion', in *The Complete Writings of William Blake*, ed. Geoffrey Keynes (New York: Random House, 1957), p. 289.

## Chapter 11. Paula Rego's (Her)ethical visions

1   Julia Kristeva, 'Stabat Mater', in *Tales of Love* [1983] (New York: Columbia University Press, 1987), p. 257.
2   Kristeva: 'Stabat Mater', pp. 257, 259.
3   Kristeva: 'Stabat Mater', p. 263.
4   As Kelly Oliver notes, 'insofar as this ethics of maternity would replace the Catholic image of the Virgin bearing her sorrow and her breast, it would be a heretical ethics, an ethics that does not reduce women to "milk and tears"'. Kelly Oliver (ed), *The Portable Kristeva* (New York: Columbia University Press, 1997), p. 297.
5   Rego's series of paintings on the life of the Virgin Mary enters a fruitful dialogue with sculptures of the Virgin from the sixteenth and seventeenth centuries, by artists from the Coimbra School, in the small, interior chapel.
6   Jacobus de Voragine, *Aurea Legenda* [1275], translated into English by William Caxton in 1483. As Rego explains: 'Há muito pouco sobre a Virgem na Bíblia. Li os poemas do Rilke sobre a Virgem. Mas não faço muita investigação das fontes nem nada disso. Baseio-me mais na minha própria experiência ou na minha identificação com o assunto.' See Kathleen Gomes, 'Paula Rego: A Virgem pintada por uma mulher' ('There is very little on the Virgin in the Bible. I read Rilke's poems on the Virgin. But I don't research sources very much. I draw mostly on my own experience or on my identification with the topic'; translation mine), *Público*, 8 February 2003, p. 38. Rego specifically mentions Rilke's poem 'Magnificat', see Rainer Maria Rilke, *New Poems: A Bilingual Edition*, trans. Stephen Cohn (Chicago: Northwestern University Press, 1998). See also Ana Marques Gastão, 'Quadros de Paula Rego atiram Belém para cima', in Ruth Rosengarten (ed), *Compreender Paula Rego: 25 Perspectivas* (Porto: Público e Fundação de Serralves, 2004), p. 141.
7   See also Maria Manuel Lisboa, *Paula Rego's Map of Memory: National and Sexual Politics* (Aldershot: Ashgate, 2003).
8   Quoted in Ruth Rosengarten, 'Nurturing the Adult Within: Drawings and Etchings by Paula Rego', in Memory Holloway (ed), *Open Secrets: Drawings and Etchings by Paula Rego* (Dartmouth: University of Massachusetts, 1999), p. 38.
9   *Communion*, 2000.
10  Jeanette Winterson, *Art & Lies: A Piece for Three Voices and a Bawd* (London: Vintage, 1995), p. 189.
11  See Timothy Verdon, *Maria nell'arte europea* (Milan: Electra, 2004).
12  Cardinal Virgilio Noé mentions several examples of medieval representations of pregnant Madonnas, such as Cavallini's images in the Church of Donna Regina in Naples, in the Reggio Emilia, in the Parmeggiani gallery, at the cathedral in Leon, in the Uffizi Gallery in Florence and in the church of S. Gennaro in Cappanori (Lucca). Virgilio Noè, *La Madonna nella Basilica Vaticana* (Rome, Libreria Editrice Vaticana, 1994), p. 67.
13  See John Pope-Hennessy and Aldous Huxley, *The Piero della Francesca Trail (with) the Best Pictures* (New York: The Little Bookroom, 1991), pp. 61–2.
14  Pope-Hennessy and Huxley: *The Piero della Francesca Trail*, pp. 194–5.
15  Michèle Roberts, *Food, Sex and God: On Inspiration and Writing* (London: Virago, 1998), p. 42.

16 Roberts: *Food, Sex and God*, p. 42.

17 For Mary Jacobus, reflecting on Raphael's Sistine Madonna and Piero della Francesca's *Madonna del Parto*, the 'Madonna's condition as depicted by Raphael images a maternity which is God's desire, not her own. The Christian dogma of the Immaculate Conception depends on the fantasy of the Madonna's unconsciousness … She must become a maternal body unawares in order to be sanctified as the mother of God.' Mary Jacobus, *Reading Woman: Essays in Feminist Criticism* (New York: Columbia University Press, 1986), p. 140.

18 Jacobus: *Reading Woman*, p. 145.

19 Jacobus: *Reading Woman*, p. 138.

20 Grünewald lived c.1455–1528.

21 Prominent instances of a discernibly expectant Virgin include Melchior Broederlam's *The Annunciation and the Visitation* (1393–9), John of Berry's *Petite Heures* (fourteenth century), *The Visitation* (c.1425), an illumination by the Limbourg Brothers, *Visitation* (1434–5) by Jacques Deret, a painter who worked at Robert Campin's workshop in Tournai at the same time as Rogier van der Weyden, the latter's own *Visitation* (c.1445), Albrecht Dürer's woodcut *The Visitation* (c.1503), *The Visitation* (1506) by Master S., a Hungarian painter, Marx Reichlich's *Meeting of Mary and Elizabeth* (c.1500) and Quellin, Artus II's *Visitation* in white marble (1678).

22 The statue, which was a present from Isabel de Aragão, Queen of Portugal, when she went on a pilgrimage to Santiago de Compostela (c.1325), represents a heavily pregnant Virgin Mary robed in a golden dress, with a blue covering on her head which descends around her shoulders and circles her protuberant belly, where she rests her hands. Her breasts are prominent and emphasized by her dress.

23 'Our lady of Ó' (ó means a sigh) is a Marian devotion, according to which pregnant women worshipped those figures of Our Lady, usually represented as pregnant, such as the fifteenth-century statues of *Nossa Senhora Ó* in the cathedral in Évora.

24 'A origem desta invocação está na recitação das 7 antífonas que começam por O, nas Vésperas do Ofício Divino, de 17 a 23 de Dezembro: O Sapientia …Venera-se em Tamengos, em Moita de Anadia e na Capela de S. Bartolomeu, Vera Cruz.' ('The origin of this invocation can be found in the recitation of the 7 antiphons which begin by O, in the Vespers of the Divine Office, from 17 to 23 December: O Sapientia … It is venerated in Tamengos, in Moita de Anadia and in the Chapel of S. Bartolomeu, Vera Cruz.' Translation mine). *Invocações Marianas na Diocese de Aveiro*. Museu de Aveiro. (Aveiro: Rocha/Artes Gráficas, 1988), p. 117.

25 Marina Warner, *Alone of All her Sex: The Myth and the Cult of the Virgin Mary* (London: Vintage, 1976), p. 47, referring to *Vierge Ouvrante*, Middle Rhine, c.1300.

26 Kathleen Gomes, 'As virgens de Paula Rego chegam a Belém', *Público*, 5 January 2003, pp. 30–1.

27 Other examples of pregnant Madonnas are at Our Lady of Guadalupe, in Mexico, where she is said to have miraculously appeared in 1531, as well as at the Sanctuary of the Pregnant Virgin Mary in Gdansk-Matemblewo, in Poland. In the central nave of the Church Nossa Senhora do Rosário dos Pretos (1725), in Recife, Brazil, there is also a painting of a pregnant Virgin Mary.

28 I was surprised that neither Julia Kristeva nor Marina Warner examined any

images of conspicuously pregnant Madonnas. Marina Warner does not even engage with this area at all, apart from the passing reference alluded to above.

29  Portuguese poet João Miguel Fernandes Jorge remarks on what he considers to be the links between Rego's *Natividade* and the images of Nossa Senhora do Ó: 'Aproximar-se-á das representações mais brutas da tradição das Senhoras da Expectação da Baixa Idade Média' ('it approaches the most down-to-earth representations from the tradition of Expectant Virgins of the early Middle Ages', translation mine), quoted in Gomes: 'As virgens de Paula Rego', pp. 30–1. Referring to contemporary religious art, João Miguel Fernandes Jorge comments: 'O sentido do religioso e do sagrado vai faltando às igrejas, sobretudo se pensarmos no mau gosto habitual do clero no que respeita a arte sacra actual' ('The sense of the religious and the sacred in churches is fading, particularly when we think of the clergy's usual bad taste as far as contemporary religious art is concerned'; the translation is mine). Gomes: 'As virgens de Paula Rego', p. 31. For him, Rego 'quebra, precisamente, essa beatice. O seu realismo, ao menos, anulará o delicodoce' ('breaks, precisely, with that overly sentimental tradition. Her realism, at least, cancels the sickly sweet'; translation mine). Gomes: 'As virgens de Paula Rego', p. 31.

30  See also Melissa R. Katz and Robert A. Orsi, *Divine Mirrors: The Virgin Mary in the Visual Arts* (Oxford: Oxford University Press, 2001).

31  See Catarina Fonseca, 'A Vida de Maria pintada por Paula Rego', *Activa* (Lisbon), September 2003, p. 39.

32  'Gabriel is an agent, but this one is her guardian' (translation mine). Richard Zimmler, 'Interview with Paula Rego: "Paula Rego: A Outra Face de Maria"', *Grande Reportagem* (Lisbon), April 2003, pp. 57–63.

33  Luce Irigaray, *Sexes and Genealogies* (New York: Columbia University Press, 1993), p. 35.

34  Gail M. Schwab, 'Mother's Body, Father's Tongue: Mediation and the Symbolic Order', in Carolyn Burke, Naomi Schor, and Margaret Whitford (eds), *Engaging with Irigaray: Feminist Philosophy and Modern European Thought* (New York: Columbia University Press, 1994), pp. 366, 369.

35  Irigaray: *Sexes and Genealogies*, p. 42.

36  Tina Chanter, *Ethics of Eros: Irigaray's Rewriting of the Philosophers* (New York and London: Routledge, 1995), p. 264.

37  Schwab: 'Mother's Body, Father's Tongue', p. 368.

38  Schwab: 'Mother's Body, Father's Tongue', p. 369.

39  Luce Irigaray, *Marine Lover of Friedrich Nietzsche* (New York: Columbia University Press, 1991), p. 164. As Irigaray further notes, referring to Jesus, 'were it not for the intervention of the angels and of dreams, he would not have received life, or would not long have survived'.

40  Irigaray: *Marine Lover*, p. 167.

41  Irigaray: *Marine Lover*, p. 167.

42  Luce Irigaray, *Between East and West: From Singularity to Community* (New York: Columbia University Press, 2002).

43  Irigaray: *Between East and West*, p. 53. Related to this, for Mary Jacobus, the 'Madonna's condition as depicted by Raphael images a maternity which is God's desire, not her own. The Christian dogma of the Immaculate Conception depends

on the fantasy of the Madonna's unconsciousness … She must become a maternal body unawares in order to be sanctified as the mother of God.' Jacobus: *Reading Woman*, p. 140.

44  Penelope Deutscher, *A Politics of Impossible Difference: The Later Work of Luce Irigaray* (Ithaca and London: Cornell University Press, 2002), p. 168.

45  Deutscher: *A Politics of Impossible Difference*, p. 168.

46  Catherine Clément and Julia Kristeva, *The Feminine and the Sacred* (New York: Columbia University Press, 2001), p. 64.

47  Michelle Boulous Walker, *Philosophy and the Maternal Body: Reading Silence* (London and New York: Routledge, 1998), p. 136.

48  Eça de Queirós, *O Crime do Padre Amaro*, Ilustrações de Paula Rego, Prefácio de Isabel Pires de Lima (Porto: Campo das Letras, 2001).

49  For a discussion of some of these themes, see Isabel Pires de Lima's Preface to Queirós: *O Crime do Padre Amaro*.

50  The model for the Virgin in the *Pietá* was Rego's own granddaughter, Lola, who was then 12 years old, while the model for Jesus was a friend of Lola's, Orlando, also 12 years of age.

51  'It was always men who painted the life of the Virgin and here we have a woman. It has a different point of view. Because we identify a lot more with her story. Indeed, this is a tribute to and a story of the Virgin' (translation mine). Gomes: 'Paula Rego: A Virgem pintada por uma mulher', p. 38.

52  See Jordi Vigué, *Great Women Masters of Art* (New York: Watson-Guptill, 2002). See also Kyra Belán, *Madonnas: From Medieval to Modern* (New York: Parkstone, 2001), p. 263.

53  'A woman telling a story—more specifically, Mary telling a story' (translation mine). Zimmler: 'Interview with Paula Rego', p. 59.

54  'The most important thing is that Jesus was a man and Mary was a woman who gave birth—he comes from inside her. They're people! They don't come from outer space. They are flesh and blood' (the translation is mine). Zimmler: 'Interview with Paula Rego', p. 59.

55  Warner: *Alone of All her Sex*.

56  According to Mary Jacobus, 'the first artificial family was the Holy family. The Virgin Mary herself constitutes the most famous (not to say miraculous) instance of the surrogacy arrangement, at least in the New Testament. Even Catholics would have to concede that God himself set a precedent for third-party intervention between husband and wife.' Mary Jacobus, *First Things: The Maternal Imaginary in Literature, Art, and Psychoanalysis* (New York and London: Routledge, 1995), p. 34.

57  Kristeva: 'Stabat Mater', p. 262.

58  Kristeva: 'Stabat Mater', p. 263. Dawn Ades states that the Virgin Mary 'gave birth to Christ parthenogenetically: the Son born without a father'. Dawn Ades, 'Surrealism, Male-Female', in Jennifer Mundy (ed), *Surrealism: Desire Unbound* (Princeton, NJ: Princeton University Press, 2001), p. 180. Ades' assertion can be read as offering an alternative, strongly iconoclastic and blasphemous vision of the birth of Jesus Christ. Although strictly speaking Jesus's birth could not have been parthenogenetic, since in that case he would have to have been a woman, Ades seems to be suggesting that the Virgin Mary became pregnant and gave birth without any divine intervention from God the Father. The implications of

this idea are far-reaching, for they offer a feminist vision of a (holy) woman pro-creating on her own, thus erasing God the Father from the Biblical picture. This amounts to a doubly transgressive concept, an unexpected subversive angle from which to consider the Virgin's pregnancy and the birth of Jesus, a novel perspective that affords a sudden dimension of strength and authority to the mostly silenced Virgin Mary.

59  Toril Moi (ed), *The Kristeva Reader* (New York: Columbia University Press, 1986), p. 161.
60  Warner: *Alone of All her Sex*, p. 339.
61  Henry James, *The Madonna of the Future: And other early stories* (New York: New American Library, 1962).
62  This is the word used by Arthur C. Danto in 'The Work of Art and the Historical Future', in *The Madonna of the Future: Essays in a Pluralistic World* (Berkeley: University of California Press, 2001), p. 422.
63  Jacobus: *First Things*, p. 24.
64  Introduction to Part IV, 'Spirituality and Religion', in Luce Irigaray (ed), *Luce Irigaray: Key Writings* (London and New York: Continuum, 2004), p. 145.

## Chapter 12. From Leda to Daphne

1  Ana Mendieta died by defenestration in 1985, in circumstances that remain obscure. Her husband, Carl Andre, was accused of homicide, then exculpated. See Robert Katz, *Naked by the Window: The Fatal Marriage of Carl Andre and Ana Mendieta* (New York: Atlantic Monthly, 1990).
2  Donald Kuspit also draws attention to the fact that Ana Mendieta is clothed in this performance, and that she assumes an active position in relation to the naked, animalized body of the woman, underlining through this the dual role played by her as woman and artist. Donald Kuspit, 'Ana Mendieta, Autonomous Body', in *Ana Mendieta* (Saint Jacques de Compostelle: Centro Galego de Arte Contemporanea, 1996), pp. 35–82.
3  Georges Bataille, *L'érotisme* (Paris: Editions de Minuit, 1957).
4  Georges Bataille: *L'érotisme*, p. 100.
5  Mendieta cites certain passages of Paz's text in her writing. Paz explicitly links the cult of life and the cult of death, and for him sacrifice constitutes, above all, a promise of continuity, a revelation. He establishes a clear link between sacrifice and redemption and, influenced by Bataille, conceives of sacrifice as expenditure. See Octavio Paz, 'Toussaint, jour des morts', in *Le labyrinthe de la solitude* (Paris: Gallimard, 1972), p. 58.
6  Donald Kuspit: 'Ana Mendieta, Autonomous Body', pp. 35–8.
7  Sigmund Freud, 'The Taboo of Virginity' [1918], in *On Sexuality: Three Essays on the Theory of Sexuality*. Penguin Freud Library, vol. 7 (Harmondsworth: Penguin, 1977), pp. 261–84.
8  In relation to this, she analyses Artemisia Gentileschi's painting 'Judith and Holophernes'. Julia Kristeva, 'Décollations', in *Visions capitales* (Paris: Réunion des Musées Nationaux, 1998), pp. 81–100.
9  Charles Merewether, 'From Inscription to Dissolution: An Essay on Expenditure in the Work of Ana Mendieta', in *Ana Mendieta* (Saint Jacques de Compostelle: Centro Galego de Arte Contemporanea, 1996), pp. 83–131.

10 Hannah Kruse points out that Ana Mendieta's identification with the victim amounts to a negation of her usual status as anonymous object. Hannah Kruse, 'A shift in Strategies: Depicting Rape in Feminist Art', in *The Subject of Rape* (New York: Whitney Museum of American Art, 1993).

11 Julia P. Hertzberg notes that Mendieta knew this group that Breder had introduced to the students in his class. Julia P. Hertzberg, 'Ana Mendieta's Iowa years', in *Ana Mendieta: Earth Body, Sculpture and Performance 1972–1985* (New York: Whitney Museum of American Art, 2004), pp. 150–2. Olga M. Viso also stresses the influence of Breder, a German artist and lecturer at the University Of Iowa, who was interested in the Viennese activities. Olga M. Viso, 'The Memory of History', in *Ana Mendieta: Earth Body, Sculpture and Performance 1972-1985* (New York: Whitney Museum of American Art, 2004), pp. 40–2.

12 Régis Michel, *Posséder et détruire* (Paris: Réunion des Musées Nationaux, 2000).

13 Elias Canetti, 'La métamorphose', in *Masse et puissance* (Paris: Gallimard, 1966), pp. 357–407.

14 As Olga M. Viso notes, Mendieta takes this quotation from the writings of Adorno. See Viso: 'The Memory of History', p. 40.

15 Charles Merewether: 'From Inscription to Dissolution', pp. 93–6.

16 Philippe Lacoue-Labarthe and Jean-Luc Nancy, *Le mythe nazi* (Paris: L'Aube, 1991).

17 Nicole Dubreuil-Blondin considers that the works of Alice Aycock, Mary Miss, Michelle Stuart, Nancy Holt and Suzanne Harris operate in relation to this conception of a double critical fold. According to her, Land Art, because it emphasizes context, constitutes a critique of modernism and of its transcendental character. Moreover, Land Art necessitates a confrontation, inciting the spectator to renew an experience had by the artist, connoted with the feminine when it is a question of women artists. 'The interest in women's Land Art resides in the fact that it does not replace the specificity of the medium with the specificity of the feminine. It prefers to change the rules of the game.' Nicole Dubreuil-Blondin, 'Les femmes dans la nature ou l'immanence du contenu', in *Art et féminisme* (Montréal: Museum of Contemporary Art, 1982), pp. 155–6.

18 See Olga M. Viso on the relations between Mendieta and Lippard. Viso: 'The Memory of History', pp. 46, 70–6. See also Hertzberg: 'Ana Mendieta's Iowa years', pp. 175–8.

19 Jean-Baptiste Pontalis, 'L'insaisissable entre-deux', in *Bisexualité et différence des sexes* (Paris: Gallimard, 1973), pp. 15–29.

20 On this topic see Mieke Bal, *Louise Bourgeois' Spider: the Architecture of Art-Writing* (Chicago: University of Chicago Press, 2001), pp. 87–105.

21 See Giulia Sissa on this subject and on the Greek world in general. Guilia Sissa, (ed), *Le corps virginal* (Paris: Librairie Philosophique Vrin, 1987); also see Nicole Loraux's preface to this book, 'Un secret bien gardé', in Sissa: *Le corps virginal*.

22 'Daphne Borghese', marble statue, Augustan (?), perhaps after a late Hellenistic model.

## Chapter 13. *Inside-out*

1 Teresa's account of her vision is quoted and translated by Suzanne Warma, 'Ecstasy and Vision: Two Concepts Connected with Bernini's Teresa', *The Art Bulletin*

66/3 (1984), pp. 508–11. 'Beside me, on the left hand, appeared an angel in bodily form … In his hands I saw a great golden spear, and at the iron tip there appeared to be a point of fire. This he plunged into my heart several times so that it penetrated into my entrails. When he pulled it out, I felt that he took them with it, and left me utterly consumed by the great love of God. The pain was so severe that it made me utter several moans. The sweetness caused by this intense pain is so extreme that one cannot possibly wish it to cease, nor is one's soul then content with anything but God. This is not a physical, but a spiritual pain, though the body has some share in it—even a considerable share. So gentle is this wooing which takes place between God and the soul that if anyone thinks I am lying, I pray God, in his goodness, to grant him some experience of it.'

2   'Bernini a construit, "au-dessus" du corps de Ludovica, un corps en représentation, composé d'un "corps réel" et d'un "corps imaginaire" en proie à la passion spirituelle.' Giovanni Careri, *Envols d'amour: La dévotion baroque dans le montage de la peinture, de l'architecture et de la sculpture du dernier Bernin* (Doctoral Thesis, Ecole des Hautes Etudes en Sciences Sociales, Paris, 1989), pp. 71, 234–5. Translations are my own except where otherwise indicated.

3   It is this oscillation between the spirit and body, purity and sexuality, which make the sculptures at once fascinating and difficult, and which demands a new approach to the sculptures in order to move away from more traditional analyses which would either sanctify or debase them, to instead further examine how this compelling tension operates.

4   Mieke Bal, *Louise Bourgeois' Spider: the Architecture of Art-Writing* (Chicago: University of Chicago Press, 2001), p. 94.

5   Bal: *Louise Bourgeois' Spider*, p. 94.

6   Bal: *Louise Bourgeois' Spider*, p. 100.

7   Bal: *Louise Bourgeois' Spider*, p. 94.

8   Laura Mulvey, *Fetishism and Curiosity* (Bloomington: Indiana University Press, 1996), p. 63.

9   St John Chrysostom (c.347–407), Doctor of the Church and Bishop of Constantinople, quoted in Marina Warner, *Alone of All Her Sex: The Myth and the Cult of the Virgin Mary* (London: Picador, 1976), p. 58.

10  Notably St. Clement of Alexandria (c.150–c.215), Tertullian (c.160–c.225), Origen (c.185–254), St Jerome (c.342–420), St Augustine (354–450), St John Chrysostom (c.347–407).

11  Mulvey: *Fetishism and Curiosity*, p. 59.

12  Georges Didi-Huberman, *Ouvrir Vénus* (Paris: Gallimard, 1999).

13  Kenneth Clark, *The Nude: A Study of Ideal Art* (London: Penguin, 1960).

14  A summary: 'When something unpleasant has happened to the subject, or when he himself has done something which has a significance for his neurosis, he interpolates an interval during which nothing further must happen…In endeavouring to prevent associations and connections of thought, the ego is obeying one of the oldest and most fundamental commands of obsessional neurosis, the taboo on touching. The avoidance of touching is of paramount importance in this illness because it is the immediate aim of the aggressive as well as the loving object cathexes.' Carrie Lee Rothgeb (ed), *Abstracts of the Standard Edition of the Psychological Works of Sigmund Freud*, 1926D 20/77: Inhibitions, symptoms and anxiety

(1926), available online at <http://www.nyfreudian.org/abstracts_24_20.html> (accessed 17 December 2006).

15  Didi-Huberman: *Ouvrir Vénus*, p. 28.

16  'les images organiques seraient donc … à double face'. Didi-Huberman: *Ouvrir Vénus*, p. 40.

17  'Ouvrir un corps, n'est-ce pas le défigurer, briser toute son harmonie?' Didi-Huberman: *Ouvrir Vénus*, p. 40.

18  'impossible de l'isoler, c'est à dire d'ignorer l'inquiétude mortelle que porte en soi toute nudité de la chair'. Didi-Huberman: *Ouvrir Vénus*, p. 63.

19  Lynda Nead, *The Female Nude: Art, Obscenity and Sexuality* (New York: Routledge, 1992), p. 6.

20  Nead: *The Female Nude*, p. 6.

21  Julia Kristeva, *Powers of Horror: An Essay on Abjection* [1980], trans. Leon Roudiez (New York: Columbia University Press 1982).

22  Nead: *The Female Nude*, p. 7.

23  Kristeva: *Powers of Horror*, p. 46.

24  St Teresa of Avila, *Interior Castle*, trans. Mirabai Starr (New York: Riverhead, 2004).

25  See Gilles Deleuze, *Le Pli: Leibniz et le Baroque* (Paris: Minuit, 1988), p. 39.

26  'La monade est l'autonomie de l'intérieur, un intérieur sans extérieur. Mais elle a pour corrélat l'indépendance de la façade, un extérieur sans intérieur.' Deleuze: *Le Pli*, p. 39.

27  Deleuze: *Le Pli*, p. 39.

28  'médiatisé, distendu, élargi'. Deleuze: *Le Pli*, p. 165.

29  Bal: *Louise Bourgeois' Spider*, p. 94.

30  Gen Doy, *Drapery: Classicism and Barbarism in Visual Culture* (London: I.B.Tauris, 2002); quotations taken from M. Perniola, 'Between Clothing and Nudity', in M. Feher , R. Nadaff and N. Tazzi (eds), *Zone 4: Fragments for a History of the Human Body* (New York: Zone, 1989).

31  Kristeva: *Powers of Horror*, p. 64.

32  Mieke Bal, *Quoting Caravaggio: Contemporary Art, Preposterous History* (Chicago: University of Chicago Press 1999), p. 27.

33  Anish Kapoor, *Turning the World Inside-Out* (1995), and *Turning the World Upside-Down #4* (1998), both at Barbara Gladstone Gallery, 515 West 24 Street, New York, 9 April–22 May 1998. Available online at <http://www.artnet.com/magazine_pre2000/features/kuspit/kuspit4-29-98.asp> (accessed 01 May 2007).

34  Anish Kapoor, *Cloud Gate* (2004-5, Chicago Millennium Park, Chicago). Available online at <http://www.millenniumpark.org/artandarchitecture/cloud_gate.html> (accessed 01 May 2007).

35  I do not propose to generalize about Kapoor's work as a whole. I refer to these isolated sculptures, as with the Klein bottle, in order to provide a visual metaphor or analogy for the problem articulated in the rest of the paper in relation to the female body, surface, interior and visuality, and to suggest that these particular artworks could be inscribed in a particular visual discourse.

36  See in particular Cindy Sherman's *Disasters* series, such as *Untitled #234* (1987–90), Museum of Fine Arts, Boston). Laura Mulvey deals with these photographs, in

particular in her essay, 'A Phantasmagoria of the Female Body: The World of Cindy Sherman', *New Left Review* 188 (1991). Mulvey argues against fetishism particularly persuasively in her landmark essay on 'Pandora's box', where a 'feminist curiosity' of looking into the box is posited against the masculinist and damaging fetishism mechanism. Laura Mulvey, 'Pandora's box: Topographies of curiosity', in *Fetishism and Curiosity* (Bloomington, Indiana: Indiana University Press, 1996).

37  Mulvey: 'Phantasmagoria', p. 148.

38  Konrad Polthier, 'Imaging maths—Inside the Klein bottle' (2003), <http://plus.maths.org/issue26/features/mathart/index-gifd. html> (accessed 01 May 2007), referring to F. Klein, *Über Riemann's Theorie der algebraischen Functionen und ihrer Integrale* (Leipzig: Teubner, 1882).

39  Polthier: 'Imaging maths'.

40  See Elizabeth Grosz, *Volatile Bodies: Towards a Corporeal Feminism* (Bloomington, Indiana: Indiana University Press, 1994) for a theorization of the female body based on the concept of the Möbius strip.

41  Cliff Stoll, 'Acme Klein Bottles', <http://www.kleinbottle.com/whats_a_klein_bottle.htm> (accessed 01 May 2007).

42  Kristeva: *Powers of Horror*, p. 64.

43  Georges Bataille, 'The Notion of Expenditure' [1933], in *Visions of Excess*, ed. and trans. Allan Stoekl (Minneapolis: University of Minnesota Press, 1985), pp. 116–29.

44  Rosalind Krauss and Yve-Alain Bois, *Formless: A User's Guide* (New York: Zone, 1997), p. 55.

45  Georges Bataille, 'The College of Sociology', in Denis Hollier (ed), *The College of Sociology (1937–39)*, trans. Elizabeth Wing (Minneapolis, MN: University of Minnesota Press, 1988), p. 337. Also cited in Krauss and Bois: *Formless*, pp. 205, 209.

46  See the chapter entitled 'Entropy' in Krauss and Bois: *Formless*, pp. 73–9.

47  Krauss and Bois: *Formless*, p. 78.

48  'Sa cuisse nue caressa mon oreille: il me sembla entendre un bruit de houle, on entend le même bruit en appliquant l'oreille à de grandes coquilles. Dans l'obscurité du bordel et dans la confusion qui m'entourait (il me semble avoir étouffé, j'étais rouge, je suais), je restai suspendu étrangement, comme si Edwarda et moi nous étions perdus dans une nuit de vent devant la mer.' Georges Bataille, 'Madame Edwarda', *Œuvres complètes*, ed. Denis Hollier (Paris: Gallimard, 1970), p. 21. See also Brian T. Fitch, *Monde à l'envers/Tête reversible—la fiction de Georges Bataille* (Paris: Gallimard, 1982), p. 14.

49  Krauss and Bois: *Formless*, p. 78.

50  Kristeva: *Powers of Horror*, p. 59, emphasis added.

51  Bal: *Louise Bourgeois' Spider*, p. 100.

52  Bal: *Louise Bourgeois' Spider*, p. 87.

53  Bal: *Louise Bourgeois' Spider*, p. 100.

## Chapter 14. The Word Made Flesh

Special thanks to the Leverhulme Trust for funding my research. I am also grateful to Professor Deborah Cherry and Professor David Mellor for their comments, to

Victoria Worsley at the Henry Moore Institute and to David Notarius and Zelda Cheatle of the Estate of Helen Chadwick.

1   Caresse was the daughter of artist Paula P. Orridge and her partner, artist and musician Genesis P. Orridge, neighbours of Chadwick in Hackney.
2   Helen Chadwick, annotations to her copy of Marina Warner, *Alone of All Her Sex: The Myth and the Cult of the Virgin Mary*, (London: Picador, 1976).
3   Rose Garrard's *Madonna Cascade*, for example, framed a self-portrait by the seventeenth-century Dutch painter Judith Leyster with three-dimensional figures of the Virgin Mary, which leave the frame and cascade down to the floor. See Rose Garrard, *Achieving My Own History: Documentation of Works 1969–1994* (Manchester and London: Cornerhouse and South London Gallery, 1994).
4   See, for example, Marjorie Allthorpe-Guyton, 'Helen Chadwick', *Art Monthly* 100 (1986), p. 18, and Hilary Robinson, 'Helen Chadwick', *Women Artists Slide Library* 31/32 (1989), p. 22. Allthorpe-Guyton and Robinson both suggest that representations of Chadwick's naked body may appeal to a dominating male gaze.
5   Later in her career, in one of her final works, *Unnatural Selection*—a series of three oversized pieces of jewellery studded with embryos in place of gemstones—Chadwick would go on to investigate the ways in which modern reproductive technologies have changed understanding of these issues.
6   Helen Chadwick, annotations to her copy of Warner: *Alone of All Her Sex*, p. 63.
7   Jacques Derrida criticized the notion that the *logos* (the word) could form a transcendental signifier which acts as the origin of all meaning. This critique of 'logocentrism' was at the heart of his thinking on deconstruction. See Jacques Derrida, *Of Grammatology* [1967], trans. Gayatri Chakravorty Spivak (Baltimore: Johns Hopkins University Press, 1977).
8   Helen Chadwick, annotations to her copy of Warner: *Alone of All Her Sex*.
9   Chadwick highlighted Warner's detailed examination of the development of the belief that Mary was *virgo intacta* both *post partum* and *in partu*. Helen Chadwick, annotations to her copy of Warner: *Alone of All Her Sex*, p. xxii.
10   Helen Chadwick, annotations to her copy of Warner: *Alone of All Her Sex*, p. 37.
11   See Warner: *Alone of All Her Sex*, p. 44.
12   Helen Chadwick, annotations to her copy of Warner: *Alone of All Her Sex*.
13   Helen Chadwick, working notes for *One Flesh*, (Papers of Helen Chadwick: Henry Moore Institute Archive, Leeds Museums and Galleries, c.1985).
14   See Warner: *Alone of All Her Sex*, pp. 50-67.
15   Helen Chadwick, annotations to her copy of Warner: *Alone of All Her Sex*.
16   See Mary Kelly, *Post Partum Document* (Berkeley and Vienna: University of California Press and Generali Foundation, 1983), pp. 72–3.
17   Helen Chadwick, *Enfleshings* (London: Aperture, 1989), p. 75.
18   Rosemary Betterton, 'Re-conceptions: Birth and Decay in Helen Chadwick's Art', lecture given at the Foundation for Women's Art, 8 July 2004. Luce Irigaray, 'Body against Body: In Relation to the Mother', in *Sexes and Genealogies*, trans. Gillian C. Gill (New York: Columbia University Press, 1993) pp. 7–21.
19   Irigaray: 'Body against Body', p. 16.
20   Highlighted by Helen Chadwick in her copy of Julia Kristeva, 'Motherhood Ac-

cording to Bellini', in *Desire in Language: A Semiotic Approach to Literature and Art*, (Oxford: Blackwell, 1981), p. 253.

21  Helen Chadwick: working notes for *One Flesh*.

22  Catherine Clément and Julia Kristeva, *The Feminine and the Sacred* (New York: Columbia University Press, 2001), p. 27.

23  Highlighted by Helen Chadwick in her copy of Kristeva: 'Motherhood According to Bellini', p. 247.

24  In her notes she made clear that she aimed to depict the body 'as a site of pleasure not power'. Helen Chadwick, working notes for *Of Mutability* (Papers of Helen Chadwick: Henry Moore Institute Archive, Leeds Museums and Galleries, c.1985–6).

25  Chadwick: *Enfleshings*, p. 69.

26  In *Le Toucher*, an exploration of the sense of touch, Jacques Derrida states that 'to touch so one believes is, touching what one touches, to let oneself be touched by the touched, by the touch of the thing, whether objective or not, by the flesh that one touches and that then becomes touching as well as touched.' Jacques Derrida, 'Le Toucher', *Paragraph* 6/3 (1993), p. 136.

27  Clément and Kristeva: *The Feminine and the Sacred*, p. 38.

28  In *This Sex Which is Not One*, Luce Irigaray describes women's sexuality as multiple because it involves this kind of contact of skin against skin—she argues that feminine sexuality cannot be unified because the double lips of women's mouths and labia are constantly making contact with themselves. Luce Irigaray, *This Sex Which is Not One* [1977], trans. Catherine Porter with Carolyn Burke (Ithaca: Cornell University Press, 1985).

29  Helen Chadwick: working notes for *One Flesh*.

30  Helen Chadwick: working notes for *One Flesh*.

31  Helen Chadwick: working notes for *One Flesh*.

32  Kelly: *Post Partum Document*, p. xxi. Speaking about these issues, Chadwick stated that 'the idea of a denial of one's body as a no-go area to explore themes of sexuality and desire seemed so tortuous that although I could sympathise with the theoretical position it just … didn't square with my own needs'. Helen Chadwick, interview with Mark Haworth-Booth for the *Oral History of British Photography*, National Sound Archive (London: British Library, 1984).

33  Chadwick: interview with Mark Haworth-Booth.

34  Jacques Lacan described the register of the Real, in which sensation is experienced directly, as existing prior to the entry into the Symbolic register, in which sensation must be mediated through language. He defined the Real as 'that which resists symbolisation absolutely'. Jacques Lacan, 'Some Reflections on the Ego', *International Journal of Psychoanalysis* 34 (1953), pp. 11–17.

35  Helen Chadwick: working notes for *One Flesh*.

36  Kristeva: 'Motherhood According to Bellini', p. 247.

37  Kelly: *Post Partum Document*, p. 108.

### Chapter 15. Something to Show for It?

I am indebted for their comments on this chapter to Dr Alison Rowley (University of Ulster) and Dr Sarah Handley, child psychologist.

1 This room was the second of only two devoted to artists that are women; the first displays the work of Vanessa Bell (1879–1961).

2 See Julian Stallabrass, *High Art Lite: British Art in the 1990s* (London: Verso, 1999) and Rosemary Betterton's intelligent and astute analysis in 'Why is My Art Not As Good As Me? Femininity, Feminism and "Life-Drawing" in Tracey Emin's Art', in Mandy Merck and Chris Townsend (eds), *The Art of Tracey Emin* (London: Thames and Hudson, 2002), pp. 23–38.

3 All references to the concept of the 'encounter' are directly derived from the writing of the artist and psychoanalyst Bracha Ettinger. See Bracha L. Ettinger, 'Matrix and Metramorphosis', *Differences: A Journal of Feminist Cultural Studies* 4/3 (1992), pp. 176–208.

4 Emmanuel Cooper, *People's Art: Working-Class Art from 1750 to the Present Day* (Edinburgh: Mainstream, 1994).

5 Shoshana Felman, *What Does a Woman Want? Reading and Sexual Difference* (Baltimore and London: Johns Hopkins University Press, 1993), p. 13.

6 Stallabrass: *High Art Lite*, p. 36.

7 Eva Pattis Zoja, *Abortion: Loss and Renewal in the Search for Identity* (London: Routledge, 1997), p. 6.

8 Pattis Zoja: *Abortion*, pp. 5–8.

9 The legacies of abortion explored in this paper must be distinguished from the belief in an automatic and inevitable Post Abortion Stress Syndrome (PASS) advocated by pro-life groups. See Ellie Lee, 'Reinventing Abortion as a Social Problem: "Postabortion Syndrome" in the United States and Britain', in Joel Best (ed), *How Claims Spread: Cross-National Diffusion of Social Problems* (New York: Aldine Transaction, 2001), Mary Boyle, *Re-thinking Abortion: Psychology, Gender, Power and the Law* (London: Routledge, 1997) and Vanessa Davies, *Abortion & Afterwards* (Bath: Ashgrove, 2003).

10 From the very beginning of the collection of essays entitled *The Art of Tracey Emin*, editors Merck and Townsend do much to debunk the mythic collapse of biography and art through unmediated expression that has surrounded what is a highly sophisticated and knowing art practice: 'drawing and writing are neither flesh nor emotion, and the apparent immediacy of Tracey Emin's work is both artful and ambiguous, the product of formal, technical and generic strategies that are anything but unmediated', p. 6.

11 Betterton: 'Why is My Art Not As Good As Me?', p. 23.

12 Tracey Emin, *Exploration of the Soul*, fourteenth panel.

13 Michael White and David Epston, *Narrative Means to Therapeutic Ends* (New York: W. W. Norton, 1990), p. 12. I wish to thank Dr Sarah Handley, who brought the writing of White and Epston to my attention in 2003.

14 Gregory Bateson, *Steps to an Ecology of Mind: Collected essays in Anthropology, Psychiatry, Evolution and Epistemology* (Aylesbury: Intertext, 1972).

15 White and Epston: *Narrative Means*, p. 2.

16 Tracey Emin, *The Interview*, on DVD, *The Eye: Tracey Emin* (n.p.: Illuminations, 2005).

17 Merck and Townsend: *The Art of Tracey Emin*, p. 10.

18 Lorna Healy: 'We Love You, Tracey', in *The Art of Tracey Emin*, p. 171. This silence can be ascribed to what Vanessa Davies, writing in *Abortion & Afterwards* in 1991,

perceived as the 'taboo' that inhibits the discussion of termination in contemporary British culture. Davies: *Abortion & Afterwards*, p. 123.

19  Healy: 'We Love You, Tracey', p. 170. Emin's decision to choose her own life echoes Pattis Zoja's argument for abortion as 'charged as an act of initiation'. Zoja: *Abortion*, p. xi.

20  From *Coronation Street* to *Coma* (1978) the same narratives run over and over again: true women give up their lives for their unborn children, unnatural ones do not. In those narratives where termination is handled more sensitively, such as in the film version of Nick Hornby's *High Fidelity* (2000), termination appears as an incident that further complicates the protagonist's relationship with his girlfriend Laura but is then forgotten for the rest of the film.

21  In 2004 Mike Leigh wrote and directed *Vera Drake*, his most sustained and sensitive consideration of abortion to date. As this film post-dates the artworks included, I have deferred analysis of this film to 'Cultures of Confinement' (working title), an essay forthcoming in Elisabeth Lamothe and Pascale Sardin (eds), *Mothers and Death: Ethical and Esthetic Issues Around the Lethal Mother-Child Relationship*. I am indebted to Dr Ika Willis, University of Bristol, for drawing this film to my attention.

22  Jean E. Veevers, *Childless by Choice* (Toronto: Butterworth, 1980), pp. 3–4.

23  In *Rethinking Abortion*, Mary Boyle has written extensively about the ways in which natural and unproblematic representation of pregnancy for women is the lynch pin of the pro-life/anti-abortionist's attack on women who reject motherhood. See Chapter Three, 'Motherhood, Morality and the Sanctity of Life', pp. 26-61.

24  Germaine Greer, *Sex and Destiny: The Politics of Human Fertility* (London: Secker and Warburg, 1984), p. 161. See in particular Chapter Seven, 'Abortion and Infanticide', pp. 159–96.

25  Greer: *Sex and Destiny*, pp. 159–62.

26  See Ann Weyman, 'Women are eclipsed when the foetus is larger than life', *Guardian*, 27 October 2004.

27  Pro-Choice Forum, 'Late Abortion: A Review of the Evidence—A briefing compiled by the Pro-Choice Forum' (2005). Brief presented to the House of Commons 27 January 2005. Available online at <http://www.prochoiceforum.org.uk/pdf/PCF_late_abortion08.pdf> (accessed 01 May 2007).

28  In *Sex and Destiny*, p. 195, Greer states that 'Foetuses are not presented to women as drawn teeth are and it is as well, for it is not the women's fault that what has been drawn from the uterus is so much more shocking than what is sloughed every month. A ten-week foetus is not pink jelly, but only the woman who looses her baby spontaneously is likely to know how human the tiny creature was and to grieve for it the rest of her life. Women presenting for abortion … are shielded from grief, which would be appropriate, and from guilt, which would not … so far it has been assumed that the only pregnancies which are aborted are accidental ones and the only fetuses destroyed those whose mothers could not bear the thought of their becoming children.'

29  Pattis Zoja: *Abortion*, p. 3. She continues by saying that the frame of mind of 'the ancients' restricted itself to recognizing certain events as charged with their own necessity, and to respecting the destinies they force us to follow, whereas modern humanity, after two thousand years of Christianity, attempts to distinguish good

from evil and to guide the course of events. Pattis Zoja's objection to the concept of 'therapy' can be further illuminated by reference to *Narrative Means to Therapeutic Ends*. In that text, White and Epston outline the problematic nature of the term 'therapy' that is particularly pertinent in the case of women who have terminated their pregnancies, saying 'the *Penguin Macquarie Dictionary* describes therapy as the "treatment of disease, disorder, defect, etc., as by some remedial curative process." In our work we do not construct problems in terms of disease and do not imagine that we do anything that relates to a "cure."' White and Epston: *Narrative Means*, p. 14.

30   A preliminary ultrasound scan is given to each woman awaiting termination to determine the stage of the pregnancy; in the NHS hospital waiting room she sits beside happily expectant mothers and their partners. The consent form that she must sign addresses, not the patient, but 'the pregnant woman'. For four weeks after the procedure the 'aborted material' is available to her for collection for burial or cremation. All these elements direct a woman's experience to the loss of a potential child. Post-abortion counselling encourages women to name their lost 'babies' as part of the grieving process as a means to resolve unfinished business, just as Emin did in *Everyone I Have Ever Slept With 1963–1995*. Lost in the Momart fire in 2004 were the names of the two aborted foetuses embroidered among those of Emin's family members.

31   Felman: *What Does A Woman Want?*, p. 14.

32   Sigmund Freud, 'Mourning and Melancholia' [1917], in *On Metapsychology: The Theory of Psychoanalysis*. The Penguin Freud Library, vol. 11 (Harmondsworth: Penguin, 1991), pp. 251–2.

33   Davies: *Abortion and Afterwards*, p. 147.

34   Healy: 'We Love You, Tracey', p. 170.

35   Emin: *The Interview*.

36   Though never stated explicitly, this focus recalls one of Emin's readings of *My Bed* in which she states that it 'looks like the scene of a crime as if someone has just died or been fucked to death'. Quoted in Deborah Cherry, 'Tracey Emin's My Bed 1998/1999', *SHARP Sussex History of Art Research Publication*, p. 6. Merck theoretically underpins her argument with the paradoxical relation expounded in Hal Foster's *The Return of the Real*, in which 'trauma discourse' is perceived as that in which 'the subject is evacuated and elevated at once'. Psychoanalysis, according to Foster and Merck, understands trauma as that which 'shatters subjectivity', whilst 'the more popular view [of trauma] grants the sufferer the authority of "witness, testifier, survivor"'. Merck continues: 'Tracey Emin's career might have been invented to illustrate this paradox. If, as Foster says of Cindy Sherman's disaster images, her "signifiers of menstrual blood and sexual discharge, vomit and shit … evoke the body turned inside out, the subject literally abjected", it is certainly possible to describe Emin's unmade bed, with its residue of bodily effluents and the gashed pillows emitting its pubic stuffing, in this idiom.' Merck and Townsend: *The Art of Tracey Emin*, p. 125.

37   Jean Wainwright, 'Interview with Tracey Emin', in Merck and Townsend: *The Art of Tracey Emin*, pp. 202–4.

38   Julia Kristeva, *Powers of Horror: An Essay on Abjection* [1980], trans. Leon Roudiez (Columbia: Columbia University Press, 1982), p. 3.

39  Freud: 'Mourning and Melancholia', p. 253.
40  See Alicia Etchegoyen, 'Inhibition of Mourning and the Replacement Child Syndrome', in Joan Raphael-Leff and Rosine Jozef-Perelberg (eds), *Female Experience: Three Generations of British Women Psychoanalysts on Work with Women* (London: Routledge, 1997), pp. 195–217.
41  Judith Butler, *Precarious Life: The Powers of Mourning and Violence* (London: Verso, 2004), pp. 20–2.
42  See Claire Pajaczkowska, 'Art: A Symptom of Not Dying', *New Formations* 26 (1995), pp. 74–89.

# SELECT BIBLIOGRAPHY

Abbas, S. B., *Female Voice in Sufi Ritual: Devotional Practices of Pakistan and India* (Austin: University of Texas Press, 2003).

Abimbola, Wande, 'The Bag of Wisdom: Osun and the Origins of Ifa Divination', in Joseph M. Murphy and Mei-Mei Sanford (eds), *Osun Across the Waters: A Yoruba Goddess in Africa and the Americas* (Bloomington: Indiana University Press, 2001).

—— *Ifa Divination Poetry* (New York: Nok, 1977).

Abiodun, Rowland, 'Hidden Power: Osun, the Seventeenth Odu' in Joseph M. Murphy and Mei-Mei Sanford (eds), *Osun Across the Waters: A Yoruba Goddess in Africa and the Americas* (Bloomington: Indiana University Press, 2001), pp. 10–33.

Ackerman, Robert, *The Myth and Ritual School* (London: Routledge, 2002).

Agamben, Giorgio, *Homo Sacer: Sovereign Power and Bare Life,* trans. Daniel Heller-Roazen (Stanford, CA.: University of Stanford Press, 1998).

Akintoye, Stephen A., 'Yoruba History from Early Times to the 20th Century', in Nike S. Lawal, Matthew N. O. Sadiku, and P. Ade Dopamu (eds), *Understanding Yoruba Life and Culture* (Trenton, Asmara: Africa World, 2004).

Allthorpe-Guyton, Marjorie, 'Helen Chadwick', *Art Monthly* 100 (1986).

Arendt, Hannah, *The Human Condition* [1958], second edn. (Chicago and London: University of Chicago Press, 1998).

Bádéjò, Diedre L., 'The Goddess Osun as a Paradigm for African Feminist Criticism', *Sage* 6/1 (1989), pp. 27–32.

Badiou, Alain, *Ethics: An Essay on the Understanding of Evil,* trans. Peter Hallward (London: Verson, 2001).

Bailey Gill, Carolyn (ed), *Bataille: Writing the Sacred* (London: Routledge, 1995).

Bal, Mieke, *Louise Bourgeois' Spider: the Architecture of Art-Writing* (Chicago: University of Chicago Press, 2001).

—— *Quoting Caravaggio: Contemporary Art, Preposterous History* (Chicago: University of Chicago Press 1999).

Bamberger, Joan 'The myth of matriarchy: why men rule in primitive societies', in M. Z. Rosaldo and L. Lamphere (eds), *Woman, Culture and Society* (Stanford CA: Stanford University Press, 1974).

Baroni, Lise, 'Dieu, itinérance infinie', in R. Bergeron, G. Lapointe, and J.-C. Petit (eds), *Itinérances spirituelles* (Montréal: Mediapaul, 2002), pp. 137–51.

Basu, Helene and Werbner, Pnina (eds), *Embodying Charisma: Modernity, Locality and the Performance of Emotion in Sufi Cults* (London: Routledge, 1998).

Bataille, Georges, *L'érotisme* (Paris: Editions de Minuit, 1957).

—— 'The Notion of Expenditure' [1933], in *Visions of Excess*, ed. and trans. Allan Stoekl (Minneapolis: University of Minnesota Press, 1985), pp. 116–29.

Bateson, Gregory, *Steps to an Ecology of Mind: Collected essays in Anthropology, Psychiatry, Evolution and Epistemology* (Aylesbury: Intertext, 1972).

Baudrillard, Jean, *Screened Out*, trans. Chris Turner (London: Verso, 2002).

Belán, Kyra, *Madonnas: From Medieval to Modern* (New York: Parkstone, 2001).

Benjamin, Walter, 'The Work of Art in the Age of Mechanical Reproducibility', in *Illuminations*, ed. Hannah Arendt, trans. Harry Zohn (London: Fontana, 1973), pp. 219–54.

Betterton, Rosemary, 'Why is My Art Not As Good As Me? Femininity, Feminism and "Life-Drawing" in Tracey Emin's Art', in Mandy Merck and Chris Townsend (eds), *The Art of Tracey Emin* (London: Thames and Hudson, 2002), pp. 23–38.

Beverley, John R., *Testimonio: On the Politics of Truth* (Minneapolis: University of Minnesota Press, 2004).

Blundell, Sue, *Women in Ancient Greece* (London: British Museum, 1995).

Blundell, Sue and Williamson, Margaret (eds), *The Sacred and the Feminine in Ancient Greece* (London: Routledge, 1998).

Bonnefoy, Yves, 'La question de la poésie', in *Entretiens sur la poésie* (Paris: Mercure de France, 1990).

Boulous Walker, Michelle, *Philosophy and the Maternal Body: Reading Silence* (London and New York: Routledge, 1998).

Boyle, Mary, *Re-thinking Abortion: Psychology, Gender, Power and the Law* (London: Routledge, 1997).

Braidotti, Rosi, 'Nomadic Subjects. Feminist Postmodernism as Antirelativism', in Ron Bontekoe and Marietta Stepaniants (eds), *Justice and Democracy: Cross-cultural Perspectives* (Honolulu: University of Hawaii Press, 1997).

—— *Patterns of Dissonance: A Study of Women in Contemporary Philosophy* (Cambridge: Polity, 1991).

—— 'Sexual difference as a nomadic political project', in *Nomadic Subjects Embodiment and Sexual Difference in Contemporary Feminist Theory* (New York: Columbia University Press, 1994).

—— 'Towards Sustainable Subjectivity: A View from Feminist Philosophy', in Egon Becker and Thomas Janh (eds), *Sustainability and the Social Sciences:*

*A Cross-disciplinary Approach to Integrating Environmental Considerations into Theoretical Reorientation* (London: Zed, 1999).

Bruit Zaidman, Louise and Schmitt Pantel, Pauline, *Religion in the Greek City*, trans. Paul Cartledge (Cambridge: Cambridge University Press, 1995).

Brulé, Pierre, *La Fille d'Athènes: la religion des filles à Athènes à l'époque classique* (Paris: Belles Lettres, 1987).

Burckhardt Qureshi, Regula, *Sufi Music From India and Pakistan* (Cambridge: Cambridge University Press, 1986).

Burkert, Walter, *Greek Religion*, trans. John Raffan (Cambridge MA and London: Harvard University Press, 1985).

—— *Homo Necans*, trans. Peter Bing (Berkeley CA: University of California Press, 1983).

Butler, Judith, *Antigone's Claim: Kinship Between Life and Death* (New York: Columbia University Press, 2000).

—— *Precarious Life: The Powers of Mourning and Violence* (London: Verso, 2004).

Cameron, Averil and Kuhrt, Amelie (eds), *Images of Women in Antiquity* (London: Routledge, 1993).

Canetti, Elias, 'La métamorphose', in *Masse et puissance* (Paris: Gallimard, 1966), pp. 357–407.

Cannon, Katie Geneva, *Katie's Canon: Womanism and the Soul of the Black Community* (New York: Continuum, 1997).

Careri, Giovanni, *Envols d'amour: La dévotion baroque dans le montage de la peinture, de l'architecture et de la sculpture du dernier Bernin* (doctoral thesis, Ecole des Hautes Etudes en Sciences Sociales, Paris, 1989).

Carpentier, Martha C., *Ritual, Myth and the Modernist Text: The Influence of Jane Harrison on Joyce, Eliot and Woolf* (Amsterdam: Gordon and Breach, 1998).

Chadwick, Helen, *Enfleshings* (London: Aperture, 1989).

Chanter, Tina, *Ethics of Eros: Irigaray's Rewriting of the Philosophers* (New York and London: Routledge, 1995).

Chodorow, Nancy, *The Reproduction of Mothering* (Berkeley and Los Angeles: University of California Press, 1978).

Chopp, Rebecca, *The Power to Speak: Feminism, Language, God* (New York: Crossroad, 1989).

Cixous, Hélène and Clément, Catherine, *La Jeune Née* (Paris: Union Generale d'Editions, 1975)

—— *The Newly Born Woman* [1975], trans. Betsy Wing (Minneapolis: University of Minnesota Press, 1991).

Clark, Kenneth, *The Nude: A Study of Ideal Art* (London: Penguin, 1960).

Clément, Catherine, *Opera, or, The Undoing of Women* [1979], trans. Betsy Wing (London: Virago, 1989).

Clément, Catherine and Kristeva, Julia, *Le Féminin et le sacré* (Paris: Agora, 1998).

Clément, Catherine and Kristeva, Julia, *The Feminine and the Sacred* [1998], trans. Jane Marie Todd (New York: Columbia University Press, 2001).

Cooper, Emmanuel, *People's Art: Working-Class Art from 1750 to the Present Day* (Edinburgh: Mainstream, 1994).

Couture, Denise, 'Désapprendre les habitudes inculquées par le "Prince Aspérité"', *L'autre Parole* 51 (1991), pp. 21–30.

——— 'Dieue au féminin', *L'autre Parole* 40 (1988).

——— 'La réception du divin féminin de Luce Irigaray en Amérique du Nord: Point de vue québécois', *Religiologiques* 21 (2000), pp. 83–99.

Couture, Denise and Roy, Marie-Andrée, 'Dire *Dieue*', in C. Ménard and F. Villeneuve, (eds), *Dire Dieu aujourd'hui* (Montréal: Fides, 1994).

Danino, Nina and Maziere, Michael (eds), *The Undercut Reader* (London: Wallflower, 2003).

Danto, Arthur C., 'The Work of Art and the Historical Future', in *The Madonna of the Future: Essays in a Pluralistic World* (Berkeley: University of California Press, 2001).

Davies, Vanessa, *Abortion & Afterwards* (Bath: Ashgrove, 2003).

Davis, Joyce M., *Martyrs: Innocence, Vengeance and Despair in the Middle East* (New York: Palgrave Macmillan, 2003).

De Beauvoir, Simone, *The Second Sex* [1949], trans. H. M. Parshley (Harmondsworth: Penguin, 1983).

De Queirós, Eça, *O Crime do Padre Amaro*, Ilustrações de Paula Rego, Prefácio de Isabel Pires de Lima (Porto: Campo das Letras, 2001).

De Witt, Helen, 'Transfiguration and Transmediation', in Catherine Grant (ed), *Visionary Landscapes—The Films of Nina Danino* (London: Black Dog, 2005).

Deleuze, Gilles, *Cinema 1: The Movement Image* [1983], trans. Brian Massumi (London: Athlone, l992).

——— *Le Pli: Leibniz et le Baroque* (Paris: Minuit, 1988).

Deleuze, Gilles and Guattari, Félix, *Kafka: Toward a Minor Literature* [1975], trans. Dana Polan (Minneapolis: University of Minnesota Press, 1986).

Derrida, Jacques, 'Le Toucher', *Paragraph* 6/3 (1993).

——— 'The Politics of Friendship', *The Journal of Philosophy* 85 (1998).

——— *The Gift of Death*, trans. David Wills (Chicago and London: University of Chicago Press, 1995).

——— *Of Grammatology* [1967], trans. Gayatri Chakravorty Spivak (Baltimore: Johns Hopkins University Press, 1977).

Derrida, Jacques and Dufourmantelle, Anne, *Of Hospitality. Anne Dufourmantelle invites Jacques Derrida to respond*, trans. Rachel Bowlby (Stanford: Stanford University Press, 2000).

Detienne, Marcel, 'The Violence of Well-born Ladies' in Marcel Detienne and J. P. Vernant (eds), *The Cuisine of Sacrifice among the Greeks*, trans. Paula Wissing (Chicago and London: University of Chicago Press, 1989).

Deutscher, Penelope, *A Politics of Impossible Difference: The Later Work of Luce Irigaray* (Ithaca and London: Cornell University Press, 2002).

Didi-Huberman, Georges, *Ouvrir Vénus* (Paris: Gallimard, 1999).

Dillon, Matthew, *Girls and Women in Classical Greek Religion* (London: Routledge, 2002).

Donaldson, Laura and Pui-Lan, Kwok (eds), *Postcolonialism, Feminism and Religious Discourse* (New York: Routledge, 2002).

Douglas, Mary, *Purity and Danger: An Analysis of Concepts of Pollution and Taboo* (London: Routledge, 1969).

Doy, Gen, *Drapery: Classicism and Barbarism in Visual Culture* (London: I.B.Tauris, 2002).

Dubreuil-Blondin, Nicole, 'Les femmes dans la nature ou l'immanence du contenu', in *Art et féminisme* (Montréal: Museum of Contemporary Art, 1982).

Dumais, Monique, 'The Other Salvation: Women as Subjects in Search of Equality', in Don Schweitzer and Derek Simon (eds), *Intersecting Voices: Critical Theologies in a Land of Diversity* (Ottawa: Novalis, 2004), pp. 83–95.

Eaton, Richard, *Essays on Islam and Indian History* (Oxford: Oxford University Press, 2000).

Eliade, Mircea, *Le Sacré et le Profane* (Paris: Gallimard, 1956).

Etchegoyen, Alicia, 'Inhibition of Mourning and the Replacement Child Syndrome', in Joan Raphael-Leff and Rosine Jozef-Perelberg (eds), *Female Experience: Three Generations of British Women Psychoanalysts on Work with Women* (London: Routledge, 1997), pp. 195–217.

Ettinger, Bracha L., 'Matrix and Metramorphosis', *Differences: A Journal of Feminist Cultural Studies* 4/3 (1992), pp. 176–208.

Ettinger, Bracha L., 'The Becoming Threshold of Matrixial Borderlines', in George Robertson, *et al.* (eds), *Travellers' Tales: Narratives of Home and Displacement* (London: Routledge, 1994).

—— *Matrix: a Shift Beyond the Phallus* (Paris: BLE Atelier, 1993).

—— *The Matrixial Borderspace*, ed. Brian Massumi (Minneapolis: University of Minnesota Press, 2006).

—— *The Matrixial Gaze* (Leeds: Feminist Arts and Histories Network, 1995).

—— 'Metramorphic Borderlinks and Matrixial Borderspace' in John Welchman (ed), *Rethinking Borders* (Basingstoke: Macmillan, 1996).

—— 'The Red Cow Effect: The Metramorphosis of Hallowing the Hollow and Hollowing the Hallow', *ACT 2 Beautiful Translations* (London: Pluto, 1996), pp. 82–119.

—— 'Transgressing With-in-to the Feminine' in Penny Florence and Nicola Foster (eds), *Differential Aesthetics* (London: Ashgate, 2000), pp. 185–210.

—— 'Wit(h)nessing Trauma and the Matrixial Gaze: From Phantasm to Trauma, from Phallic Structure to Matrixial Sphere', *parallax* 7 (2001), pp. 89–114.

Ewing, Katherine Pratt, *Arguing Sainthood: Islam, Modernity and Psychoanalysis* (Durham, NC: Duke University Press, 1997).

Fadlallah, Shaykh Muhammad Husayn, 'Interview: 11 September, terrorism, Islam, and the Intifada', *Journal of Palestine Studies* 31/2 (2002).

Fantham, Elaine, *et al.* (eds) *Women in the Classical World.: image and text* (New York: Oxford University Press, 1994).

Felman, Shoshana, *What Does a Woman Want? Reading and Sexual Difference* (Baltimore and London: Johns Hopkins University Press, 1993).

Felman, Shoshana and Laub, Dori, *Testimony: Crises of Witnessing in Literature, Psychoanalysis, and History* (New York: Routledge, 1992).

Feuerbach, Ludwig, *The Essence of Christianity* [1841], trans. G. Eliot (New York: Harper Torchbooks, 1957).

Fitch, Brian T., *Monde à l'envers/Tête reversible—la fiction de Georges Bataille* (Paris: Gallimard, 1982).

Flynn, Thomas R., 'Lyotard and history without witnesses', in *Lyotard: Philosophy, Politics, and the Sublime,* ed. Hugh J. Silverman (New York and London: Routledge, 2002), pp. 151–63.

Foley, Helene P., *The Homeric Hymn to Demeter* (Princeton NJ: Princeton University Press, 1994).

Foley, Helene P. (ed), *Reflections of Women in Antiquity* (New York, London and Paris: Gordon and Breach, 1981).

Foucault, Michel, *The History of Sexuality Volume 1: The Will to Knowledge* [1976], trans. Robert Hurley (Harmondsworth: Penguin, 1990).

Fraser, Nancy, 'The Uses and Abuses of French Discourse Theories for Feminist Politics', in Nancy

Freud, Sigmund, *Moses and Monotheism* [1939], The Penguin Freud Library, vol. 13 (London: Penguin, 1985), pp. 237–86.

—— 'Mourning and Melancholia' [1917], in *On Metapsychology: The Theory of Psychoanalysis.* The Penguin Freud Library, vol. 11 (Harmondsworth: Penguin, 1991).

—— 'The Taboo of Virginity' [1918], in *On Sexuality: Three Essays on the Theory of Sexuality.* Penguin Freud Library, vol. 7 (Harmondsworth: Penguin, 1977), pp. 261–84.

—— *Totem and Taboo* [1913], in *The Origin of Religion*, Penguin Freud Library vol. 13 (London: Penguin, 1985), pp. 43–224.

—— 'The "Uncanny"' [1919], in *Art and Literature*, Penguin Freud Library vol. 14 (London: Penguin, 1985).

Garland, Robert, *Introducing New Gods: the politics of Athenian religion* (London: Duckworth, 1992).

Garrard, Rose, *Achieving My Own History: Documentation of Works 1969–1994* (Manchester and London: Cornerhouse and South London Gallery, 1994).

Gebara, Ivone, 'Dieu et la liberté', in *Les eaux de mon puits: Réflexions sur des expériences de liberté* (Bierges: Autres Regards, 2003), pp. 219–56.

—— Ivone Gebara, 'Dieu pour les femmes', in *Le mal au féminin: Réflexions théo-logiques à partir du féminisme* (Montréal: L'Harmatton, 1999).

Genest, Olivette, 'Langage religieux chrétien et différenciation sexuelle: De quelques évidences', *Recherches féministes* 3/2 (1990), pp. 11–30.

Genet, Jean, *Prisoner of Love*, trans. Barbara Bray (New York: New York Review of Books, 2003).

Ghosh, Manmohan, *The Natyasastra: A Treatise on Hindu Dramaturgy and Histri-onics Ascribed to Bharata-Muni*, vol. 2 (Calcutta: Royal Asiatic Society of Bengal, 1950).

Girard, René, *Violence and the Sacred* [1972], trans. Patrick Gregory (Baltimore: Johns Hopkins University Press, 1977).

Goff, Barbara, *Citizen Bacchae: women's ritual practice in Ancient Greece* (Berkeley CA: University of California Press, 2004).

Goldhill, Simon, *Aeschylus: the Oresteia* (Cambridge: Cambridge University Press, 1992).

Graves, Robert, *The White Goddess* (London: Faber and Faber, 1948).

Greer, Germaine, *Sex and Destiny: The Politics of Human Fertility* (London: Secker and Warburg, 1984).

Griaule, Marcel, *Conversations with Ogotommeli* (London, Oxford University Press, 1976).

Grosz, Elisabeth, *Sexual Subversions* (Sydney: Allen & Unwin, 1989).

Grosz, Elizabeth, *Volatile Bodies: Towards a Corporeal Feminism* (Bloomington, Indiana: Indiana University Press, 1994).

Grubrich-Simitis, Ilse, *Early Freud and Late Freud* (London: Routledge, 1997).

Guettel Cole, Susan, 'Demeter in the Ancient Greek City and its Countryside', in Susan E. Alcock and Robin Osborne (eds), *Placing the Gods: sanctuaries and sacred space in Ancient Greece* (Oxford: Oxford University Press, 1994), pp. 199–216.

—— *Landscapes, Gender and Ritual Space* (Berkeley CA: University of California Press, 2004).

Hampson, Daphne, *After Christianity*, second edn. (London: SCM, 2002).

—— 'On Not Remembering Her', *Feminist Theology* 19 (1998), pp. 63–83.

Handler Spitz, Ellen, 'Psychoanalysis and the Legacies of Antiquity', in Lynn Gamwell and Richard Wells (eds), *Sigmund Freud and Art: His Personal Collection of Antiquities* (New York: Harry Abrams, 1989), pp. 153–72.

Harrison, Jane, *Ancient Art and Ritual* [1913] (Montana: Kessinger, n.d.).

—— *Themis: A Study of the Social Origins of Greek Religion* [1912] (London: Merlin, 1963).

Hawley, Richard and Levick, Barbara (eds), *Women in Antiquity: new assessments* (London and New York: Routledge, 1995).

Hayat, Hamsar *et al.*, *Apni Masti: Qawwalis from Delhi* (New Delhi: Ektara Music, 2002).

Hegel, G. W. F., *The Phenomenology of Mind* [1807], trans. J. B. Baillie (Mineola, NY: Dover Philosophical Classics, 2003).

—— *Phenomenology of Spirit* [1807], trans. A.V. Miller (Oxford University Press, 1977).

Hertzberg, Julia P., 'Ana Mendieta's Iowa years', in *Ana Mendieta: Earth Body, Sculpture and Performance 1972–1985* (New York: Whitney Museum of American Art, 2004), pp. 150–2.

Hewitt, Marsha Aileen, 'Do women really need a "God/ess" to save them? An Inquiry into Notions of the Divine Feminine', *Method & Theory in the Study of Religion* 10/2 (1998), pp. 149–56.

Holst-Warhaft, Gail, *Dangerous Voices: women's laments and Greek literature* (London and New York: Routledge, 1992).

Howland, Courtney W., *Religious Fundamentalisms and the Human Rights of Women* (New York: Palgrave Macmillan, 1999).

Hughes, Dennis D., *Human Sacrifice in Ancient Greece* (London: Routledge, 1991).

Irigaray, Luce, 'Equal to Whom?', trans. Robert L. Mazzola, *Differences* 1/2 (1989), pp. 59–76.

—— 'Femmes divines', in *Sexes et parentés* (Paris: Editions de Minuit, 1987).

—— 'Le divin entre nous', in *Le souffle des femmes: Luce Irigaray présente des crédos au féminin* (Paris: Action Catholique Générale Féminine, 1996), pp. 211–49.

—— 'Religious and Civil Myths', in *Je, tu, nous* [1990] (London: Routledge, 1993).

—— 'Sexual Difference', trans. Séan Hand, in Toril Moi (ed), *French Feminist Thought: A Reader* (Oxford: Blackwell, 1987).

—— 'Towards a Divine in the Feminine', in G. Howie (ed), *Women and the Divine* (Basingstoke: Palgrave Macmillan, forthcoming 2007).

—— *Between East and West: From Singularity to Community* (New York: Columbia University Press, 2002).

—— *Ce sexe qui n'en est pas un* (Paris: Éditions de Minuit, 1977).

—— *Marine Lover of Friedrich Nietzsche* (New York: Columbia University Press, 1991).

—— *Sexes and Genealogies* (New York: Columbia University Press, 1993).

—— *Speculum of the Other Woman* [1974], trans. Gillian C. Gill (Ithaca: Cornell University Press, 1985).

—— *This Sex Which is Not One* [1977], trans. Catherine Porter with Carolyn Burke (Ithaca: Cornell University Press, 1985).

Irigaray, Luce (ed), *Luce Irigaray: Key Writings* (London and New York: Continuum, 2004).

Islam, Riazul, *Sufism and its Impact on Society in South Asia* (Oxford: Oxford University Press, 1999).

Jacobs, Carol, 'Dusting Antigone', *MLN* 115/5 (1996), pp. 890–917.

Jacobus, Mary, *First Things: The Maternal Imaginary in Literature, Art, and Psycho-analysis* (New York and London: Routledge, 1995).

—— *Reading Woman: Essays in Feminist Criticism* (New York: Columbia University Press, 1986).

James, Henry, *The Madonna of the Future: And other early stories* (New York: New American Library, 1962).

Jameson, Frederic, 'Imaginary and Symbolic in Lacan: Marxism, Psychoanalytical Criticism and the Problem of the Subject', *Yale French Studies* 55–56 (1977), pp. 338–95.

Johnson, Elizabeth A., 'The Character of God' in *Friends of God and Prophets: A Feminist Theological Reading of the Communion of Saints* (New York: Continuum, 1998).

—— *She Who Is: The Mystery of God in Feminist Theological Discourse* (New York: Crossroad, 1992).

—— *Dieu au-delà du masculin et du féminin: Celui/Celle qui est* [1992], trans. Pierrot Lambert (Montréal: Paulines, 1999).

Joyce, James, *Ulysses* (London: The Bodley Head, 1960).

Just, Roger, *Women in Athenian Law and Life* (London and New York: Routledge, 1989).

Kabir, Ananya Jahanara, 'Islam', in Prem Poddar and David Johnson (eds), *A Historical Companion to Postcolonial Thought in English* (New York: Columbia University Press, 2005).

Katz, Melissa R. and Orsi, Robert A., *Divine Mirrors: The Virgin Mary in the Visual Arts* (Oxford: Oxford University Press, 2001).

Katz, Robert, *Naked by the Window* (New York: Atlantic Monthly, 1990).

Kelly, Mary, *Post Partum Document* (Berkeley and Vienna: University of California Press and Generali Foundation, 1983).

Khalidi, Omar, 'Qawwali and Mahfil-i-sama', in Christian W. Troll (ed), *Muslim Shrines in India: Their Character, History and Significance* (Delhi: Oxford University Press, 1992), pp. 257–61.

Kraemer, Ross, *Her Share of the Blessings* (New York: Oxford University Press, 1992).

Krauss, Rosalind and Bois, Yve-Alain, *Formless: A User's Guide* (New York: Zone, 1997).

Kristeva, Julia, *About Chinese Women*, trans. Anita Barrows (New York: M. Boyars, 1974).

—— 'Décollations', in *Visions capitales* (Paris: Réunion des Musées Nationaux, 1998), pp. 81–100.

—— 'Experiencing the Phallus as Extraneous, or Women's Twofold Oedipus Complex', in Griselda Pollock (ed), *Julia Kristeva: Aesthetics.Politics.Ethics. parallax* 8 (1998), pp. 29–44.

—— 'La femme, ce n'est jamais ça' [1974], in Elaine Marks and Isabelle de

Courtivron (eds), *New French Feminisms* (Brighton: Harvester, 1980), pp. 137–41.

—— 'Motherhood According to Giovanni Bellini', in *Desire in Language* [1975], trans. Leon Roudiez (Oxford: Blackwell, 1982), pp. 237–70.

—— *New Maladies of the Soul* [1993], trans. Ross Guberman (New York: Columbia University Press, 1995).

—— *Powers of Horror: An Essay on Abjection* [1980], trans. Leon Roudiez (New York: Columbia University Press, 1982).

—— 'Signifying Practice and the Mode of Production', trans. Geoffrey Nowell-Smith, *Edinburgh Magazine* 1 (1976), pp. 64–77.

—— 'Stabat Mater' in *Tales of Love* [1983], trans. Leon Roudiez (New York: Columbia University Press, 1987).

—— 'Stabat Mater', in *Tales of Love* (New York: Columbia University Press, 1987), pp. 234–65.

—— 'The System and the Speaking Subject' [1973], in Toril Moi (ed), *The Kristeva Reader* (Oxford: Basil Blackwell, 1986), pp. 24–33.

—— 'Women's Time', in Toril Moi (ed), *The Kristeva Reader* (Oxford: Basil Blackwell, 1987), 187–231.

Kruse, Hannah, 'A shift in Strategies: Depicting Rape in Feminist Art', in *The Subject of Rape* (New York: Whitney Museum of American Art, 1993).

Lacan, Jacques, *The Four Fundamental Concepts of Psychoanalysis* [1973], trans. Alan Sheridan (Harmondsworth: Penguin, 1977).

—— 'God and the *Jouissance* of The Woman', in Juliet Mitchell and Jacqueline Rose (eds), *Feminine Sexuality*, trans. Jacqueline Rose (London: Macmillan, 1982).

—— 'Some Reflections on the Ego', *International Journal of Psychoanalysis* 34 (1953), pp. 11–17.

Lachaud, René, *Magie et initiation en Egypte pharaonique* (Paris: Dangles, 1999).

Lacoue-Labarthe, Philippe and Nancy, Jean-Luc, *Le mythe nazi* (Paris: L'Aube, 1991).

Laplanche, Jean, *Essays on Otherness* (London: Routledge, 1999).

—— *Life and Death in Psychoanalysis* [1970], trans. Jeffrey Mehlman (Baltimore: Johns Hopkins University Press, 1993).

Lee, Ellie, 'Reinventing Abortion as a Social Problem: "Postabortion Syndrome" in the United States and Britain', in Joel Best (ed), *How Claims Spread: Cross-National Diffusion of Social Problems* (New York: Aldine Transaction, 2001).

Legge, Marilyn J., 'Colourful differences: "Otherness" and the Image of God for Canadian Feminist Theologies', *Studies in Religion/Sciences Religieuses* 21/1 (1992), pp. 67–80.

Levi, Primo, *The Drowned and the Saved*, trans. Raymond Rosenthal (New York: Vintage International, 1989).

Levinas, Emmanuel, *Otherwise than Being Or Beyond Essence,* trans. Alphonso Lingis (Pittsburgh: Duquesne University Press, 1998).

Levinas, Emmanuel, in conversation in Bracha L. Ettinger, *Que Dirait Eurydice?/What Would Eurydice Say?* (Paris: BLE Atelier, 1997).

Lévi-Strauss, Claude, *The Savage Mind* [1962] (London: Weidenfeld and Nicholson, 1988).

Lisboa, Maria Manuel, *Paula Rego's Map of Memory: National and Sexual Politics* (Aldershot: Ashgate, 2003).

Maccoby, Hyam, *Ritual and Morality: The Ritual Purity System and its Place in Judaism* (Cambridge: Cambridge University Press, 1999).

—— *The Sacred Executioner: Human Sacrifice and the Legacy of Guilt* (London: Thames and Hudson, 1982).

Marx, Karl, *Grundrisse: Foundations of the Critique of Political Economy* [1857–78], trans. Martin Nicolaus (Harmondsworth: Penguin, 1973).

Matthee, Jean, 'On Wounds, Artificial Flowers, Orifices and the Infinite: A Response to the Films of Nina Danino', *Undercut* 19 (1990).

McClintock Fulkerson, Mary, *Changing the Subject: Women's Discourses and Feminist Theology* (Minneapolis: University of Minnesota Press, 1994).

McFague, Sallie, *The Body of God* (Minneapolis: Augsburg Fortress, 1993).

—— *Life Abundant: Rethinking Theology and Economy for a Planet in Peril* (Minneapolis: Augsburg Fortress, 2001).

—— *Models of God: Theology for an Ecological Nuclear Age* (Minneapolis: Augsburg Fortress 1992).

Melançon, Louise, 'Je crois en Dieue … La théologie féministe et la question du pouvoir', *Théologiques* 2/8 (2000), pp. 77–97.

Merewether, Charles, 'From Inscription to Dissolution: An Essay on Expenditure in the Work of Ana Mendieta', in *Ana Mendieta* (Saint Jacques de Compostelle: Centro Galego de Arte Contemporanea, 1996), pp. 83–131.

Michel, Régis, *Posséder et détruire* (Paris: Réunion des Musées Nationaux, 2000).

Moi, Toril, *Sexual/Textual Politics* (London: Methuen, 1985).

Mulvey, Laura, *Fetishism and Curiosity* (Bloomington: Indiana University Press, 1996).

Nead, Lynda, *The Female Nude: Art, Obscenity and Sexuality* (New York: Routledge, 1992).

Netton, I. R., *Muslim Neoplatonists* (Edinburgh: Edinburgh University Press, 1991).

Oduyoye, Mercy Amba, *The African Experience of God through the Eyes of an Akan Woman*, <http://www.aril.org/african.html>, pp. 1–9.

Ogundipe-Leslie, Molara, *Recreating Ourselves: African Women and Critical Transformations* (Trenton, African World, 1994).

Oliver, Kelly (ed), *The Portable Kristeva* (New York: Columbia University Press, 1997).

Olupona, Jacob, 'Orisa Osun: Yoruba Sacred Kinship and Civil Religion in Osogbo, Nigeria, in Joseph M. Murphy and Mei-Mei Sanford (eds): *Osun Across the Waters: A Yoruba Goddess in Africa and the Americas* (Bloomington: Indiana University Press, 2001), pp. 46–67.

Osborne, Robin, 'Women and sacrifice in Classical Greece', *Classical Quarterly* 43 (1993), pp. 392–405.

Pajaczkowska, Claire, 'Art: A Symptom of Not Dying', *New Formations* 26 (1995), pp. 74–89.

Parthasarthy, A., 'Consorts of the Three Gods' in Swami Chinmayananda (ed), *Symbolism in Hinduism* (Bombay: Central Chinmaya Mission Trust, 1993).

Pattis Zoja, Eva, *Abortion: Loss and Renewal in the Search for Identity* (London: Routledge, 1997).

Paz, Octavio, 'Toussaint, jour des morts', in *Le labyrinthe de la solitude* (Paris: Gallimard, 1972).

Perniola, M. 'Between Clothing and Nudity', in M. Feher , R. Nadaff and N. Tazzi (eds), *Zone 4: Fragments for a History of the Human Body* (New York: Zone, 1989).

Plate, S. Brent, 'Ritualising Images: The Frames of Space, Time and Aesthetics', in Catherine Grant (ed), *Visionary Landscapes—The Films of Nina Danino* (London: Black Dog, 2005).

Pollock, Griselda, 'To inscribe in the feminine: A Kristevan Impossibility?' *parallax* 8 (1998), pp. 81–118.

Pontalis, Jean-Baptiste, 'L'insaisissable entre-deux', in *Bisexualité et différence des sexes* (Paris: Gallimard, 1973), pp. 15–29.

Pope-Hennessy, John and Huxley, Aldous, *The Piero della Francesca Trail (with) the Best Pictures* (New York: The Little Bookroom, 1991).

Probyn, Elspeth, *Sexing the Self: Gendered Positions in Cultural Studies* (New York: Routledge, 1992).

—— 'Technologizing the Self: A Future Anterior for Cultural Studies', in Lawrence Grossberg, Cary Nelson and Paula A. Treichler (eds), *Cultural Studies* (New York: Routledge, 1992), pp. 501–11.

Radford Ruether, Rosemary, 'Le Dieu des possibilités: transcendance et immanence repensées', *Théologiques* 8/2 (2000), pp. 35–48.

—— *Gaia and God: An Ecofeminist Theology of Earth Healing* (New York: HarperCollins,1992).

—— *Mary—The Feminine Face of the Church* (London: SCM, 1979).

—— *Sexism and God-Talk: Toward a Feminist Theology* (London: SCM, 1983).

Rahner, Karl, 'Méditation sur le mot "Dieu"; La connaissance de Dieu', in *Traité fondamental de la foi: Introduction au concept du christianisme* (Paris: Centurion, 1976).

Raine, Kathleen, *Collected Poems* (Ipswich: Golgonooza Press, 2000).

—— *Le Monde vivant de l'imagination* (Paris: Édition du Rocher, 1998).

Reuter, Christoph *My Life is a Weapon: A Modern History of Suicide-bombing*, trans. Helena Ragg-Kirkby (Princeton: Princeton University Press, 2004).

Rizvi, Saiyid Athar Abbas, *A History of Sufism in India*, 2 vols (New Delhi: Munshiram Manoharlal, 1978–83).

Roberts, Michèle, *Food, Sex and God: On Inspiration and Writing* (London: Virago, 1998).

Robinson, Hilary, 'Helen Chadwick', *Women Artists Slide Library* 31/32 (1989).

Rosengarten, Ruth, 'Nurturing the Adult Within: Drawings and Etchings by Paula Rego', in Memory Holloway (ed), *Open Secrets: Drawings and Etchings by Paula Rego* (Dartmouth: University of Massachusetts, 1999).

Sartre, Jean-Paul, *Being and Nothingness* [1943] (London: Routledge, 1989).

—— *The Imaginary; Phenomenological Psychology of the Imagination* [1940] (London: Routledge, 2004).

Schrader, Paul, *Transcendental Style in Film* (New York: Da Capo, 1988).

Schüssler Fiorenza, Elisabeth, *But she said. Feminist Practices of Biblical Interpretation* (Boston: Beacon, 1992).

—— *In Memory of Her* (London: SCM, 1983).

Schwab, Gail M., 'Mother's Body, Father's Tongue: Mediation and the Symbolic Order', in Carolyn Burke, Naomi Schor, and Margaret Whitford (eds), *Engaging with Irigaray: Feminist Philosophy and Modern European Thought* (New York: Columbia University Press, 1994).

Setel, Drorah, 'Prophets and Pornography: Female Sexual Imagery in Hosea', in L. Russell (ed), *Feminist Interpretations of the Bible* (Oxford: Blackwell, 1985).

Sila-Khan, Dominique, *Conversions and Shifting Identities: Ramdev Pir and the Ismailis in Rajasthan* (Delhi: Manohar, 2003).

Sissa, Guilia (ed), *Le corps virginal* (Paris: Librairie Philosophique Vrin, 1987).

Sölle, Dorothee, *The Silent Cry: Mysticism and Resistance* (Minneapolis: Augsburg Fortress, 2001).

Spivak, Gayatri Chakravorty, 'Can the subaltern speak?', in Patrick Williams and Laura Chrisman (eds), *Colonial Discourse and Post-Colonial Theory: A Reader* (New York: Columbia University Press, 1994), pp. 66–111.

—— *A Critique of Postcolonial Reason: Toward a History of the Vanishing Present* (Cambridge, MA: Harvard University Press, 1999).

—— 'French Feminism in an International Frame' [1981], in *In Other Worlds: Essays in Cultural Politics* (New York and London: Methuen, 1987).

—— *Outside in the Teaching Machine* (New York: Routledge, 1993).

—— 'Practical Politics of the Open End', in *The Post-Colonial Critic: Interviews, Strategies, Dialogues* (New York: Routledge, 1990), pp. 95–112.

Stallabrass, Julian, *High Art Lite: British Art in the 1990s* (London: Verso, 1999).

Stears, Karen, 'Death Becomes Her: gender and Athenian death ritual', in Sue Blundell and Margaret Williamson (eds), *The Sacred and the Feminine in Ancient Greece* (London: Routledge, 1998).

Stoller Miller, Barbara, 'Sakuntala and the Ring of Recollection', in *The Plays of Kalidasa: Theatre of Memory* (Delhi: Motilal Banarsidass, 1999), pp. 85–176.

Teresa of Avila, St, *Interior Castle* [1577], trans. Mirabai Starr (New York: Riverhead, 2004).

Thapar, Romila, *Narratives and the Making of History* (Delhi: Oxford University Press, 2000).

—— *Sakuntala: Texts, Readings, Histories* (New Delhi: Kali for Women, 1999).

Van Sertima, Ivan (ed), *Black Women in Antiquity* (London: Transaction, 1992).

Vatsyayan, Kapila, *Bharata—The Natya Sastra* (New Delhi: Sahitya Akademi, 1996).

Veevers, Jean E., *Childless by Choice* (Toronto: Butterworth, 1980).

Veillette, Denise (ed), *Femmes et Religions* (Québec: Presses de l'Université Laval, 1995).

Verdon, Timothy, *Maria nell'arte europea* (Milan: Electra, 2004).

Victor, Barbara, *Army of Roses: Inside the World of Palestinian Suicide-bombers* (London: Constable and Robinson, 2003).

Vidal-Naquet, Pierre, *The Black Hunter: forms of thought and forms of society in the Greek World*, trans. Andrew Szegedy-Maszak (Baltimore and London: Johns Hopkins University Press, 1986).

Vigué, Jordi, *Great Women Masters of Art* (New York: Watson-Guptill, 2002).

Viso, Olga M., 'The Memory of History', in *Ana Mendieta: Earth Body, Sculpture and Performance 1972-1985* (New York: Whitney Museum of American Art, 2004), pp. 40–2.

Warburg, Aby, *Images from the Region of the Pueblo Indians in North America*, trans. Michael Steinberg (Ithaca: Cornell University Press, 1995).

Warma, Suzanne, 'Ecstasy and Vision: Two Concepts Connected with Bernini's Teresa', *The Art Bulletin* 66/3 (1984), pp. 508–11.

Warner, Marina, *Alone of All Her Sex: The Myth and the Cult of the Virgin Mary* (London: Picador, 1976).

Werth, Lukas, 'Pakistan: A Critique of the Concept of Modernity', in Johan Meuleman (ed), *Islam in the Era of Globalization: Muslim Attitudes towards Modernity and Identity* (London: Routledge Curzon, 2002), pp. 143–70.

Weyman, Ann, 'Women are eclipsed when the foetus is larger than life', *Guardian*, 27 October 2004.

White, Michael and Epston, David, *Narrative Means to Therapeutic Ends* (New York: W. W. Norton, 1990).

Wilentz, Amy, *Martyr's Crossing* (New York: Simon and Schuster, 2001).

Winterson, Jeanette, *Art & Lies: A Piece for Three Voices and a Bawd* (London: Vintage, 1995).

Woodward, Mark R., 'Modernity and the Disenchantment of Life: A Muslim-Christian Contrast', in Johan Meuleman (ed), *Islam in the Era of Globaliza-*

*tion: Muslim Attitudes towards Modernity and Identity* (London: Routledge Curzon, 2002), pp. 111–42.

Woolf, Virginia, *A Room of One's Own* [1928] (Harmondsworth: Penguin, 1945).

—— *Three Guineas* [1938] (Harmondsworth: Penguin, 1977).

Zeitlin, Froma I., 'Cultic Models of the Female: Rites of Dionysus and Demeter', *Arethusa* 15 (1982), pp. 129–57.

Zimmler, Richard, 'Interview with Paula Rego: "Paula Rego: A Outra Face de Maria"', *Grande Reportagem* (Lisbon), April 2003, pp. 57–63.

# CONTRIBUTORS

**Céline Boyer** has recently completed a doctorate at the University of Bordeaux, France, entitled *Langue du Sacré et Langue du Secret: le mythe et le rite dans la poésie de Kathleen Raine et Ruth Fainlight*. She is a member of the research group ERCIF. Céline has taught English language, literature and culture at the University of Bordeaux for four years and is a holder of an *agrégation* in English.

Founded in the Joycean triadic concept of the 'monomyth', as separation-initiation-renaissance, her current work traces, through the poetry of Raine and Fainlight, the epiphanic revelation of a return to the sacred through myth, revealing cycles of life and death, paralysis and movement, fragmentation and unification. Céline has also worked on T. S. Eliot and Ted Hughes for her *Diplôme d'Etudes Approfondies*.

As well as the publication of several scholarly articles and participation in international conferences, Céline's own poetry has been published and she was awarded the ARDUA poetry prize in 2004 for her collection *Aile qui luit*. She is also an experienced dancer and will be launching her own dance company in 2008, a project of collaboration between dance, photography and poetry.

**Vanessa Corby** is a painter and art writer. Written from the position of a practising artist, her research focuses on the relationship between theory, history and practice. It examines the means by which particular social and psychic traumas can be creatively negotiated to transform the territories of cultural memory.

Her publications include *Encountering Eva Hesse* (Prestel, 2006), co-edited with Griselda Pollock, and the forthcoming monograph *Eva Hesse: Longing, Belonging and Displacement* (I.B.Tauris, 2008). She is currently working with Elsa Hsiang-Chun Chen on a collection of essays entitled *Makers and Making Between Trauma and Cultural Memory*. She currently lectures in Fine Art Practice and the History and Theory of Art at York St John University.

**Denise Couture** is Professor at the Faculté de théologie et de sciences des religions of the Université de Montréal. From 1997 to 2006, she was Secretary and Vice-Dean of this Faculty. Her research interests include feminist Christian theology, feminist interspirituality, contextual theological ethics, and the relation between the material and the spiritual in Christian theologies. She is co-founder of the Centre de théologie et d'éthique contextuelles québécoises at the Université de Montréal, director of the revue Théologiques, and member of the feminist collective L'autre Parole.

**Anne Creissels** is a holder of the Agrégation en Arts Plastiques and completed her doctoral studies in history of art, at the École des Hautes Études en Sciences Sociales (EHESS) in Paris, in June 2006. The subject of her thesis was 'Myth at work in contemporary art: sexual difference in question'.

In November 2006 she co-founded a research group, part of the EHESS research centre CEHTA (Centre d'Histoire et de Théorie des Arts). This research group, ACEGAMI (Analyse Culturelle et Études de Genre/Art, Mythes et Images), adopts the theoretical tools developed in British and American cultural studies and gender studies in order to examine questions of power relations and identity at the heart of cultural representation.

Anne Creissels has published 'Corps étranger: les métamorphoses du spectateur', *Les Cahiers du Mnam* 80 (2002), and 'L'ouvrage d'Arachné: la résistance en œuvre de Ghada Amer à Louise Bourgeois', in the first issue, 'Théories' (July 2005), of the online journal *Images revues*, <www.imagesre-vues.org>. Her current research, taking as a starting point the film *Der Eintänzer* by Rebecca Horn, deals with the gesture of dance as marker of identity.

**Nina Danino** is an internationally celebrated filmmaker. Her feature-length film *Temenos* (1998) has been screened at film festivals, galleries and cinemas and released on DVD by the BFI, and her collaborative film soundtracks are available on CD. Her other well known films are *Stabat Mater* (1990) and *Now I am yours* (1992). She has written and lectured extensively on artists' film and video. Nina is presently Lecturer in Fine Art at Goldsmiths' College, London.

**Maria Aline Seabra Ferreira** is an Associate Professor at the University of Aveiro, in Portugal, where she teaches English Literature. Her main interests include women's studies, feminine utopias and the intersections between literature and science as well as literature and the visual arts. Her book *I Am the Other: Literary Negotiations of Human Cloning* was published by Greenwood Press in 2005. Recent publications include articles on feminist utopias, eugenics, biotechnological dystopias and the Luso-British painter Paula Rego.

**Barbara Goff** was educated at King's College Cambridge and the University of California, Berkeley. She has taught in Cambridge and in Austin, Texas, and is currently Reader in Classics at the University of Reading. She is the author of *Citizen Bacchae: women's ritual practice in ancient Greece* (University of California Press, 2004). Her publications on Greek tragedy include *The Noose of Words: readings of desire, violence and language in Euripides'* Hippolytos (Cambridge University Press, 1990) and several articles. More recently her interests have expanded into the field of postcolonial studies, and she has begun to research the role of Classics in colonialist and postcolonial discourse. She edited the collection *Classics and Colonialism* (Duckworth, 2005) and with her husband, Michael Simpson, has recently completed *Crossroads in the Black Aegean: Oedipus, Antigone and Dramas of the African Diaspora*, which is due to be published by Oxford University Press (2007).

**Daphne Hampson** is Professor Emerita of Divinity at the University of St Andrews, Scotland, where she held a chair in Post-Christian Thought. She holds doctorates in Modern History (Oxford), in Systematic Theology (Harvard) and a master's in Continental Philosophy (Warwick). Long concerned with the implications of the equality of women for theology and with issues of truth in theology, she is the author of *Theology and Feminism* (Blackwells, 1990), *After Christianity* (SCM, 1997; second edn 2002), the editor of *Swallowing a Fishbone? Feminist Theologians Debate Christianity* (SPCK, 1997) and author of many articles on feminism and theology. Otherwise she is the author of *Christian Contradictions: The Structures of Lutheran and Catholic Thought* (Cambridge University Press, 2002) and is at present writing a volume on Kierkegaard. Daphne is well known for her post-Christian theological stance and has lectured and broadcast widely in the UK, in Europe and in North America. She was the founding president of the European Society of Women in Theological Research. In 2005 Daphne was a Visiting Fellow at Clare Hall, Cambridge. She now lives and works in Oxford where is an affiliate of the Faculty of Theology.

**Ananya Jahanara Kabir** is lecturer in Postcolonial Literature at The School of English, University of Leeds, UK. Her research focuses on the relationship between political conflict, collective trauma and cultural belonging, particularly in contemporary South Asia, and she is increasingly interested in exploring the political and affective possibilities of

Sufi Islam. She has recently completed a monograph on the discursive history of the Kashmir conflict, entitled *Territory of Desire: Representing the Valley of Kashmir* (forthcoming, University of Minnesota Press, 2008).

**Maria Margaroni** is Associate Professor in Literary and Cultural Theory at the University of Cyprus. She has held Visiting Fellowships at the Institute for Advanced Studies in the Humanities (University of Edinburgh) and the Centre for Cultural Analysis, Theory and History (University of Leeds). Her publications include: *Julia Kristeva: Live Theory* (with John Lechte, Continuum, 2004), *Metaphoricity and the Politics of Mobility* (with Effie Yiannopoulou, Rodopi, 2006) and *Intimate Transfers* (special issue of the *European Journal of English Studies*, 2005). Her essays (published in international journals and edited collections) cover different subjects in Continental Philosophy (the *chora* in Julia Kristeva and Jacques Derrida, the Gift, matricide, violence and mediation, Biopolitics) and Literary Theory (narcissism and the theoretical hubris, the crisis of *theorein* in the age of witnessing). She is currently working on a monograph on Julia Kristeva's Faith in the Political (forthcoming by Other Press) and an edited collection on The Politics of Waste (with Effie Yiannopoulou).

**Leila McKellar** is Leverhulme Junior Research Fellow in the department of Art History at the University of Sussex, where she teaches twentieth-century art and visual culture, cultural studies and gender studies. In 2006 she completed an AHRC-funded DPhil at the University of Sussex on the work of the artist Helen Chadwick. Her research interests are in contemporary art, critical theory and the sensory in art. She has contributed to a number of books and journals on the work of Helen Chadwick, on art and the senses and on hair as an artistic material. She is currently conducting further research into the Helen Chadwick archive, funded by the Leverhulme Trust.

**Molara Ogundipe** (also widely known and published as Molara Ogundipe-Leslie) is a distinguished critic, editor in various capacities, essayist, media columnist, interactive poet, cultural activist and distinguished scholar in literary theory, studies of Africa and her Diaspora, cultural and postcolonial studies. She is also one of the pioneering and leading African figures in feminist, women's and gender studies and activism. She was appointed a Leverhulme Professor in the School of English and Postcolonial Studies, Centre for Cultural Analysis, Theory, and History, and the Centre for African Studies at the University of Leeds, UK in 2006. A former Nigerian national director for cultural and political mobilization towards civilian rule, consultant and university professor with experience in three continents, she is also a much-anthologized and well-known poet. She is now a Professor of English and Africana Studies at a Ghanaian University in West Africa.

A winner of many academic awards in addition to her poetry and publicized interviews, Molara Ogundipe's scholarship has been cited in many articles, dissertations, encyclopedias, and internet sites. Her numerous publications include *Sew the Old Days* (1985), *Recreating Ourselves: African Women and Critical Transformations* (Africa World, 1994)—acclaimed as one of the best books from Africa and much cited and used internationally for teaching in colleges and universities—and *Moving Beyond Boundaries: Black Women's Diasporas* (New York University Press, 1995).

**Griselda Pollock** is Professor of Social and Critical Histories of Art and Director of the Centre for Cultural Analysis, Theory and History at the University of Leeds. Author of over twenty books and many articles on feminist cultural theory and aesthetics, as well as nineteenth- and twentieth-century art, she is currently working on a trilogy on trauma and representation in the wake of the Holocaust and has recently published on Eva Hesse, Agnes Martin, Amedeo Modigliani and Christine Taylor Patten. Recent edited publications include *Encountering Eva Hesse* (2006), *Psychoanalysis and the Image* (2006), and, with Joyce Zemans, *Museums after Modernism* (2007). New monographs include *Encounters in a Virtual Feminist Museum: Time, Space and the Archive* (2007), and a book on Charlotte Salomon's *Leben? Oder Theater?* is also forthcoming from Yale University Press (2008).

**Ranjana Thapalyal** was born in New Delhi, and attended schools in India, New York and Geneva. She studied at West Surrey College of Art and Design, University of London Institute of Education, and the University of Glasgow. Research interests include Yoruba and Hindu thought, intercultural and interdisciplinary education.

Recent exhibitions include sculpture and photography in *The Potter's Mirror* 2005 at *The Burrell Collection*, Glasgow. In 2002 *Talacchanda*, a collaboration with Delhi-based Bharata Natyam dancer Anjana Rajan was presented at *The Tramway*, Glasgow after premiering at the British Council Gallery, New Delhi, and travelling to Out of the Blue, Edinburgh.

Publications include reviews and critical pieces in India and the UK, a recent paper on inter-disciplinary approaches to anti-racist education in the *International Journal of Art and Design Education*. *Talacchanda* yielded a resource on ancient Indian art in the form of the catalogue publication, for which feminists, scholars and writers were commissioned to interpret ancient texts or examine the relevance of the past to contemporary artists and dancers.

Ranjana Thapalyal lectures at Glasgow School of Art in the department of Historical and Critical Studies and the School of Design; she has been honorary visiting research fellow at CentreCATH, University of Leeds.

**Victoria Turvey Sauron** is in the final stages of her PhD at the Centre for Cultural Analysis, Theory and History (CATH) at the University of Leeds, funded by the AHRC.

Victoria's research, entitled *Paradoxical bodies: femininity, subjectivity and identity in the visual discourse of ecstasy* focuses on representations of the female body in extreme states, the religious ecstasy of female saints in Baroque art, and in particular the way in which the reclining or convulsing body of the ecstatic saint operates as a multivalent, undecidable signifier of disparate states such as pleasure and pain, presence and absence. Victoria's research examines the impact such paradoxical encounters have on discourses of the body, subjectivity, sexuality and representation.

After completing her undergraduate studies at the University of Cambridge, in Anglo-Saxon, Norse and Celtic and History of Art, Victoria continued on to a *Diplôme d'Etudes Approfondies* in History of Art at the University of Toulouse in France, before arriving in Leeds. She has presented papers at seven international conferences with several publications forthcoming, and was a co-convenor (with Griselda Pollock) of the international symposium 'The Sacred and the Feminine: Image, Music, Text and Space' at the University of Leeds in 2005. Victoria has recently been awarded a grant from the Entente Cordiale scholarships scheme to pursue postdoctoral research at the University of Bordeaux in France.

# INDEX

Figures in italics indicate captions.